# Jack

## A Life with Writers

### The Story of
### Jack McClelland

James King

ALFRED A. KNOPF CANADA

Published by Alfred A. Knopf Canada

Copyright © 1999 by James King

All rights reserved under International and Pan American Copyright
Conventions. Published in Canada by Alfred A. Knopf Canada, Toronto,
in 1999. Distributed by Random House of Canada Ltd., Toronto.

Canadian Cataloguing in Publication Data

King, James, 1942–

Jack, a life with writers : the story of Jack McClelland

Includes index.

ISBN 0-676-97150-4

1. McClelland, Jack, 1922– . 2. Publishers and publishing—Canada—
Biography. 3. McClelland and Stewart Limited—Biography. I. Title.

Z483.M33K56 1999      070.5'092      C99-931137-9

First Edition
Printed and bound in the United States of America

10 9 8 7 6 5 4 3 2 1

*For Anna and Tony Luengo*

You were the real Prime Minister of Canada.
You still are. And even though it's all gone
down the tubes, the country that you govern
will never fall apart.

*— Leonard Cohen to Jack McClelland, 1996*

# CONTENTS

# LIST OF PHOTOS

*Except where noted, all photographs are from Jack McClelland's archive at Research Collections, Mills Memorial Library, McMaster University.*

# ACKNOWLEDGMENTS

ALTHOUGH THIS is not an authorized biography, I should like to express my heartfelt thanks to Jack McClelland for providing me with the opportunity to investigate his career as a publisher. I am under similar heavy obligations to Elizabeth McClelland, Jack's wife, and to their five children, Suzanne Drinkwater, Carol McCabe, Sarah McClelland, Anne McClelland and Rob McClelland. Jack's sisters, Betty Stark—and her husband, Henry—and Marg Barlow, have been generous in assisting me.

In interviews, the following have provided me with much needed and appreciated information: Margaret Atwood, Avie Bennett, David Berry, Pierre Berton, George Bowering, Phyllis Bruce, June Callwood, Matt Cohen, John Robert Colombo, Patrick Crean, Denis Deneau, Elsa Franklin, Sylvia Fraser, Trent Frayne, William French, Robert Fulford, Graeme Gibson, Peter Gzowski, Tony Hawke, Mel Hurtig, Janet Turnbull Irving, Sean Kane, Dennis Lee, James Lorimer, Linda McKnight, Louis Melzack, John Metcalf, Diane Mew, Lily Miller, Lorraine Monk, Claire and Farley Mowat, Ed Murphy, Frank Newfeld, John Newlove, Peter Newman, Iris Nowell, Alvin Potter, Anna Porter, Mordecai Richler, Peter Scaggs, David Shaw, Sam Solecki, Peter Taylor, Ruth Taylor, Jan Walter, Catherine Wilson and Bob Young. I have learned a great deal from the work of Ken Adachi, Donald Cameron, Elspeth Cameron, Roy MacSkimming, Sandra Martin, Marika Robert, Beverley Slopen and Judith Timson.

Funds for research on this book were supplied by the Social Sciences and Humanities Research Council of Canada. My colleague Carl Spadoni, the co-author of the McClelland & Stewart bibliography, has dispensed information and help in his usual generous way.

I wish to thank Alison Reid for copy-editing my typescript so thoroughly and sensitively. My publisher Louise Dennys made many useful suggestions. This book has benefited enormously from the friendly, helpful guidance supplied by Diane Martin, my editor at Knopf Canada. And I could not have written it without the steady, reliable, invaluable and often miraculous help of my research assistants, Sheila Turcon and Judy Donnelly.

# Jack

# PREFACE

JACK MCCLELLAND IS rightly regarded as the greatest Canadian publisher. Now seventy-seven, he retired from McClelland & Stewart in 1987. He divides his time between his cottage in Muskoka, his apartment in Toronto and his condominium in Florida. For about a decade, he has not taken an active part in the book world, but he still casts an enormous shadow on the publishing industry in his native land.

Promoter, nurturer, impresario, visionary, Jack is the stuff of legends both inside and outside the industry he irrevocably changed. Before him, there had been sporadic attempts to create a Canadian-centred publishing industry. These largely failed. His ability to give himself—heart and soul—to such a difficult enterprise ultimately led to a real renaissance in Canadian letters and to the establishment of a truly international marketplace for Canadian writers.

Jack McClelland was born into a publishing family, knew from childhood some of the great Canadian writers and dedicated himself to publishing from early manhood. His sister Marg once asked him what she should reveal to a journalist writing a piece about him. He facetiously instructed her as follows: "Well, basically I think you should just confirm what I have already told her—that I was the only one in the family with any brains, that we were deprived and poverty-stricken as children because our father was a publisher, that I was a star athlete, a naval hero—all those things that we have put into the standard publicity handout." She could add, he said, that "Stephen Leacock used to break us up at the dinner table, [and] I always thought Lucy Maud [Montgomery and her husband] were a bit on the strange side because they always liked to give me baths when I was very young. And, yes, I remember that Bliss Carman was the only person who was allowed to drink in our house until I had my sixteenth birthday."

Jack's recollections of his early life are extremely happy, centred on what he improbably claims was a very ordinary, somewhat economically reduced style of life. He scoffs at any intimation that he was born into a world of privilege. Yet his close friend Pierre Berton thinks that from Jack's heritage came a basic conflict—between being a member of an elite class and being a businessman who attempted to make money from books. "It was publishing that obsessed him, not profit. Yet profit was the acknowledged stamp of success in the old Toronto in which he was raised, and it hurt him to be called a bad businessman. He belonged to the upper-middle echelons of Toronto's WASP society. He knew all the right people. He had gone to the proper schools and had an illustrious war record in the navy behind him. . . . Jack moved between two levels. On one level was the raffish gang of artists, scribblers and poets with whom he hobnobbed. On the other were the old Torontonians, among whom his father's prominence as a publisher had placed him. He had the affection of the former; he craved the admiration of the latter."

Split down the middle between "raffish" and respectable, between art and commerce: Jack resists this interpretation of his life, claiming that it says more about Pierre Berton than about himself. Yet Jack—despite his assertion to the contrary—was born to a life of privilege. As an adult, he wanted to make money, but he attempted to do so in an extremely heterodox manner: transforming the literary culture of Canada.

Elizabeth, Jack's wife, who has lived with a publisher-husband for over fifty years, has had plenty of time to take stock of her husband's accomplishments. "He [was] like an old-fashioned doctor, always on call. Certainly, people used to phone him in the middle of the night. Some people took advantage of him. But authors work alone and need someone to talk to when they get frustrated . . . and he has a real flair for understanding." She also feels her husband is "a genius. He comes up with absolutely incredible ideas; they're just *wild!* He's basically shy and he hates parties, but he'd do almost anything to sell a book."

Jack's five children remember their busy father as a loving force in their lives. He made himself available to them and was always sympathetic. In matters of publishing, Jack was a maverick, but as paterfamilias he was an outspoken advocate of tradition.

Anyone encountering Jack at a public event, such as a reception at the Canadian Booksellers Association convention in June 1997, at which point Jack was still recuperating from a stroke, is immediately taken by his considerable charm. He is friendly, courtly in his manner, but his language—especially among close friends—is frequently colourful. If asked his real opinion on a recent publishing deal or a particular hardhearted politician, the four-letter words are unleashed. If Jack is left alone for a moment or two, a certain weariness flashes across his face as he prepares himself for his next encounter. As soon as he recognizes an old friend or even a mere acquaintance, a hearty smile reanimates him. He becomes once again Jack McClelland, the public figure—an intriguing mix of the sensitive and insensitive, a man who did many things extremely well, some things badly.

Jack's service in the navy during the Second World War helped him assume this public demeanour. In many ways a born leader, he used stratagems learned in battle to manage his publishing house. Since he was never comfortable delegating authority, he almost always followed his own inclinations.

Some other aspects of Jack McClelland the publisher are well known, but they have often been misunderstood. Certainly his charm and drive are deservedly legendary. With equal measure of love and hate, one competitor exclaimed: "He's got colour and panache and a kind of style about him. . . . But thank God there are no more of him!" Robert Fulford—speaking of Jack's seemingly hell-bent instinct for publicity—claimed he had the "instincts of a Barnum." Quite often Jack felt he was the ringmaster of a demented three-ring circus.

Still other aspects of his career and character have to be emphasized in order for a balanced and accurate portrait to emerge. Not always taken into account is his sensitive and discerning intelligence, his remarkable ability to identify talented writers and then to help them to realize their full potential creatively and commercially. Although Jack deliberately avoided the role of editor, he had an uncanny ability to nudge writers in the right direction. He once said, "I can usually tell if a manuscript is good, but I can't tell *why.*" He responds to books intuitively, which has made him an unusually receptive reader.

Jack is often called impatient, but the opposite is really true: he built his list of authors slowly and steadily. He is also regarded as something of a yahoo, a perception he did nothing to discourage. In fact, he gulled many into believing it. One part of the legend surrounding Jack is indisputable, however: his wry and playful sense of humour.

From early on in his publishing career, which lasted from 1946 to 1987, Jack McClelland wanted his company to respond to and interest Canadians specifically. The idea of acting as an importer of foreign books did not attract him; publishing Canadian writers did.

Telling the story of a major publisher and the publishing house he built is necessarily, in large part, about the development of writers. Since Jack published more than 2,500 books in his forty-one-year career, I have chosen to focus on the most celebrated M&S writers (Margaret Atwood, Pierre Berton, Earle Birney, Marie-Claire Blais, Leonard Cohen, Margaret Laurence, Irving Layton, Farley Mowat, Peter Newman, Al Purdy, Mordecai Richler and Gabrielle Roy); on many other authors (Roloff Beny, Patricia Blondal, Max Braithwaite, Ernest Buckler, Austin Clarke, Matt Cohen, Marian Engel, Sylvia Fraser, Hugh Garner, Phyllis Gotlieb, Sondra Gotlieb, Ralph Gustafson, Peter Gzowski, Simma Holt, Hugh Hood, William Kilbourn, Judy LaMarsh, Isabel LeBourdais, Norman Levine, Alistair MacLeod, Lorraine Monk, Claire Mowat, Terence Robertson, Sinclair Ross, Scott Symons, Charles Templeton, Harold Town, Margaret Trudeau, Aritha van Herk, Sheila Watson, Rudy Wiebe and Adele Wiseman) whose books presented him with interesting opportunities or difficult problems; on his sometimes comic, sometimes acrimonious interactions with his staff at M&S (particularly Hugh Kane, Anna Porter, Peter Taylor and Linda McKnight); and on a wide assortment of the miscellaneous dilemmas, traumas, obstacles and—as Jack would put it—"fuck-ups" that confronted him at every turn.

What is a publisher? He or she acquires manuscripts, produces and manufactures books, promotes and sells them—and supposedly makes a reasonable profit. Although it published educational, scholarly and verse titles, Jack McClelland's M&S was essentially a trade house, one whose books were intended for the general public. Such a publisher usually has a specific idea what kind of material is to bear his imprint (because the subject of this biography is male, I am using the male pronoun); he must then develop his list of books accordingly, with writers whose work fits his concept. Some authors will appear with suitable manuscripts or ideas; others must be found to be matched with certain projects; still others must be encouraged as they begin their careers. This is the acquisition process, an exciting, often exhilarating part of publishing.

Once an outline or a completed manuscript has been accepted, an author receives a payment, an advance. Occasionally, the publisher deals directly with the author, but increasingly, he deals with the author's agent. The advance is given against future royalty earnings and should realistically be based on what the book is expected to earn. The publisher must first estimate how many copies are likely to sell (a figure that is sometimes confused with how many copies *should* sell in the best of all possible worlds) and at what retail price. He must then determine the unit cost for manufacturing, as well as for promotion, publicity, selling, fulfilment and distribution, and overhead. The higher the print run, the lower the unit cost, but if he prints too many copies, he will have to meet the costs of keeping the book in inventory. And although his costs are based on the retail price, he will actually sell the books at discounts of 40 to 45 per cent to booksellers. While expectations vary according to title, he hopes to see a final pretax profit of between 6 and 10 per cent.

A publisher may be active in the marketing and promotion of a book, may have input into the design of the dust jacket which directly influences sales. Even after a book has reached the stores, a publisher may still be involved—for instance, if it is wildly successful, the print run will be rapidly exhausted and a decision whether to reprint will be necessary. Sometimes he will have to soothe an angry author who does not feel his or her book has been designed, marketed and promoted correctly or one who has received a negative review. These are just a few highlights of a publisher's intense participation in a high-risk industry and, of course, each book on a list must be evaluated along these lines.

My interest in Jack McClelland was piqued when I was researching my biography of Margaret Laurence—as her publisher he played a key role in her artistic life. When I asked him for permission to write about him (an absolute prerequisite as the huge McClelland & Stewart archive at McMaster University where his papers are deposited can be opened only with his permission), he agreed to give me his full co-operation, but with one caveat. I could say anything I wanted about Jack McClelland the publisher, but he asked me to tread carefully through his private life.

In her 1983 article in *Saturday Night*, Elspeth Cameron made a lot of Jack's reputation as a ladies' man. One of his associates at M&S once observed that Jack "woos constantly, but wins seldom, if ever. I've only seen him flaunt women if he thought it would do *them* some good." The literary agent and newspaper columnist Beverley Slopen put it this way: "He appreciates women in a natural way, automatically watching them walk past." A vibrant, vital charmer like Jack inevitably attracts many women and the rumour mill takes it from there. As Mordecai Richler puts it, "He's definitely not the Playboy of the Western World. He's as much a family man as I am." Indeed, while it is Jack's life as a publisher that is the focus of this biography, it is worth noting at the outset that because M&S was a family business—Jack taking the helm from his father—his private life and his public life as a publisher were inextricably meshed, the latter often spilling into the former. In any event, the latter is the focus of this biography.

Jack McClelland put his enthusiasm and his energy into his work as a publisher. The result was a tremendous contribution to the cultural life of Canada. This book attempts to be a candid assessment of that legacy.

Canada's position as less populous neighbour of the culturally dominant United States has meant that the domestic marketplace is inundated with American books, so Canadian publishing, a small industry by comparison, has needed public subsidies to survive. Like many other publishers, McClelland asked for and received government assistance. Despite such help, he had a difficult time surviving. He certainly did not set up in business to lose money, but lose money he did. This raises an obvious question: was Jack McClelland a good publisher but a lousy businessman? It is unlikely anyone could have made money undertaking the first-ever creation of an exclusively Canadian list on a large scale. The best response might well be that McClelland did the best possible job, given the situation he faced. Publishing has always been a precarious industry whose lessons of the past never provide sufficient guidance to cope with the future.

The story of Jack McClelland the publisher is an account of one man's forceful effort to provide an essential means for Canadian culture and identity to find vigorous and enduring expression. His role at M&S was very much like an orchestra conductor's. He oversaw most aspects of the business, but the author—the soloist—was central. It can be argued that this conviction ultimately led to his undoing. At the end of his career, McClelland saw his version of publishing as a recipe for financial disaster. Nevertheless, in spite of the relentless problems, he used his intelligence, savvy and gut instincts to transform M&S from an agency publisher, importing and distributing titles from the U.S. and Britain, into one of the great cultural institutions in Canada.

# I

## TO THE MANOR BORN

(1922-45)

"OH, I REMEMBER this city long ago. Why, they used to go ice-boating and skating on Toronto harbour. There was a toll gate on Bloor Street then for wagons coming in from the country. What excitement there was when the first electric light came to town! And I can recall when the men went off to fight in the Northwest rebellion."[1] These were the words of John McClelland, a Glasgow-born Irishman who had come to Toronto in 1882 as a boy of five. As his son Jack recalled, John was an Orangeman and a Mason: "When one of my cousins decided to marry a Catholic girl, I was the only member of the family who attended the wedding."[2]

If John McClelland was rigid in some of his beliefs, he was extremely resolute in his determination to make a success of himself. As a boy, he became involved in a get-rich-quick scheme: rowing across to Centre Island to sell newspapers. His mother put a stop to this because he did not know how to swim.[3] John was also renowned for the long time he considered his options; if a friend grew annoyed waiting for a decision, that was too bad for him. This tenacity also marked his adulthood.

Because of his family's financial difficulties, at the end of Grade 7, John had to go to work: his father, Robert, a checker and clerk for one of the railway firms, was a heavy drinker who was frequently unemployed. This situation forced John's mother, Elizabeth, to open a small store on Gerrard Street in order to support her five children.

So, at the age of fourteen, John, in order to assist his mother, went to work at the Methodist Book and Publishing House, established in 1829 by Egerton Ryerson (the name of the firm was changed to Ryerson Press in 1919). Despite its name, this firm had already been transformed in the 1890s, under the leadership of William Briggs, from a denominational publisher into a true Canadian publishing house, specializing in history and popular fiction; it also acted as Canadian agent for a number of important American and English publishing houses, such as Thomas Nelson & Sons and Blackie & Sons. Under two forceful editors, Briggs and later Lorne Pierce, the company set the early standard in the publishing of home-grown authors—the poet Charles G. D. Roberts, the novelist and poet William Kirby, the poet Isabella Valancy Crawford.

From humble beginnings, John rose to the position of manager of the library department; he also read and evaluated manuscripts. He was instrumental in having Robert Service's *Songs of a Sourdough* published, a book that his firm had initially rejected. After fifteen years working for Briggs, on April 6, 1906, at the age of twenty-nine, John McClelland opened his own publishing house in partnership with twenty-three-year-old Frederick D. Goodchild, also a Briggs employee.

McClelland & Goodchild, originally located at 42 Adelaide Street West in Toronto, was founded to act as a library supply house, advisers, distributors, wholesalers and booksellers to Ontario libraries. Both partners travelled extensively to sell books they imported. In order to increase their income, the two men would try to persuade town councils to establish libraries with funds provided by the Carnegie Foundation. They did have their own imprint, and the first book published under it was John D. Rockefeller's *Random Reminiscences of Men and Friends*, in association with Doubleday Page of New York in 1909.

In 1916, M&G brought out Lucy Maud Montgomery's book of verse, *The Watchman and Other Poems.*

The firm was incorporated in 1911; two years after that, expansion necessitated the move to 264 King West. George Stewart, who had the reputation of being the best Bible salesman in Canada, left Oxford University Press to join forces with the two original partners to create McClelland, Goodchild & Stewart. His slogan was "The Devil weeps when he sees Bibles sold as cheap as these."[4] In 1918, Goodchild left to form his own firm, although a rumour persists that John McClelland parted company with him after discovering him cavorting with nude women.

In 1919, the firm became McClelland & Stewart (M&S). A year later, they relocated to larger quarters on Victoria Street, in the heart of Toronto's smartest shopping district. During the next decade, M&S published Bliss Carman's *Later Poems* (1921), engaged prominent Canadian artists such as J. E. H. MacDonald and his son Thoreau

*Early M & S titles*

MacDonald as illustrators and published the popular A. A. Milne books and the romance adventures of the Italian-born Rafael Sabatini. But John's particular interest in fostering Canadian writing was evident on his office walls, which were covered with photographs of Canadian authors he had published (among others, the novelists H. A. Cody, Ralph Connor, Arthur Stringer, Marshall Saunders and Marian Keith). In 1929, expansion plans went awry, leading the company into serious financial straits. The expansion, intended to increase opportunities for the sale and promotion of Canadian titles, had been dependent on half the firm being sold to Cassell's in London. The infusion of money did not have the desired effect. As his son recalled, John McClelland took a terrible financial loss, but he bought back the stock, with considerable difficulty, over a period of about ten years.

In 1936 and 1937, the company's fortunes hit rock bottom: sales in 1936 totalled $196,000, whereas the figure for 1919 had been $431,000. During the Depression, many of the older, well-established Canadian writers such as L. M. Montgomery and Ralph Connor were past their prime in the marketplace (first printings of these two writers had been between twenty-five and fifty thousand; by 1947–48, they were thirty-five hundred to eight thousand); young writers like Morley Callaghan did not yet sell well.

In a more and more perilous marketplace, John McClelland and George Stewart became increasingly reluctant to assume responsibility for the original publication of books by Canadian writers, particularly poetry or "experimental" works. During all his years in publishing, John—not surprisingly, given the difficulties he had in marketing Canadian writers—was most proud of acquiring the rights to Winston Churchill's *History of the English-Speaking Peoples* (1956, 1957, 1958). However, one new Canadian initiative of John McClelland and George Stewart was the opening of an educational department under the direction of John Myers.

John McClelland did not marry until the age of thirty-seven, in 1914 (his bride, Ethel, was thirty-one). He seemed to cultivate eccentricity.

His son recalled, "Dad was a gourmet and an early health nut. He loved exotic foods, which he got down on King Street at an import place called Michie's. Every damn fad was tested in our home: strange honeys, rye crackers, special jams—you name it."[5] John was also renowned for his belief in the extraordinary healing powers of dulse, which he pressed on almost everyone he met. One person recalled his "urging me to eat some of the crunchy, horrid-tasting stuff he dredged up from his pockets."[6]

*John McClelland*

Lovat Dickson, a rival publisher at Macmillan of Canada, recalled another side of the senior McClelland—his imposing, cultivated appearance: "Though his generation of Canadian publishers made their living on imported books, he didn't buy many on his annual visits to England. I think he went for the pleasure of going to the international meetings. He always looked grand. If you were anywhere near him, you could feel the vibrations."[7]

He was an ardent teetotaller and opposed to smoking. On numerous occasions, he strode up to women he had never seen before and ordered them to put out their cigarettes. "Not that he was averse to a cigar with his cronies over bridge," his son said with a chuckle. In fact, John even allowed members of his men's bridge club to drink in his home.

His determination extended to his driving. In 1932, having purchased an elegant blue McLaughlin-Buick sedan, he took the family for an outing. As they approached Davenport and Dupont streets, a horse-drawn milk wagon was slowly making its way across their path. His passengers uttered hysterical screams, but he blasted the horn and proceeded ahead, shouting, "I'm going through!"

John, who considered himself a righteous man, was superintendent of the large Bonar Presbyterian Sunday school (once, he proudly recalled, they had more than a thousand in attendance). When Jack was born, his father was chairman of the Toronto Board of Education. His election to this position in January 1921 prompted one friend to tell *The Toronto Daily Star*: "I would not be surprised if John McClelland became mayor of Toronto one day."⁸ After the merger of the Presbyterian, Congregational and Methodist churches in 1925, John and his family became members of the newly formed United Church of Canada.

John McClelland's business motto was one his son readily identified with: "Late to bed, and late to rise/ Hustle all day and advertise."⁹ By definition, a successful publisher was a huckster. Jack would also have agreed with this credo of his father's: "The publisher must play his part in getting things done. He must come up with many of the ideas and he should go out searching for new talent."¹⁰ From his father the son derived another precious gift: tenacity.

Ethel McClelland, née Bunting, was a farm girl from just outside St. Catharines, the eldest of nine children. Her mother, Elissa, and father, William, owned the Carlton fruit farms in the township of Louth in the Niagara Peninsula near the Welland Canal; her father went as far as England to peddle his Macintosh apples. In 1912, the federal Department of Agriculture commissioned and published his *Inquiry into the Fruit Growing Conditions in Canada*. William was also one of the founders of the Royal Winter Fair in Toronto. In her late twenties, before her marriage, Ethel, who had studied agriculture at Macdonald College in Guelph, became the manager of her parents' farms. Following her marriage, those businesses eventually failed and her parents moved to Toronto.

Ethel loved holidays and festivals; the celebrations at her home were huge, jolly and spontaneous. One of her daughters recalls, "She could adapt to *anything*. No matter how many extra guests showed up, she could always make room for them and make them feel at home."¹¹ Years after her death, Jack had similar memories of her remarkable generosity and liveliness: "In fact, when she died of a stroke three or four days before Christmas, I was absolutely appalled to hear of her pre-Christmas schedule on the very day that she died. It all came to me in bits and pieces during and after her funeral. She had, among other things, been shopping, then she joined her church group to wrap parcels for the needy, she attended a school Christmas concert where one of her grand-children was performing, and she found time during that same day to drive my father to the office, pick him up and drive him home and still visit several long-standing friends who were shut-ins."[12] Temperamen-tally, Jack is Ethel's son, his charm and vivacity her legacy. Indepen-dence of mind was cultivated by both Ethel and John. "The wife and I very early made up our minds that if we had children they would be trained in their early period to make their own decisions."[13]

Both parents also provided their only son with the assurance from early childhood that he was very special, that he could overcome what-ever obstacles life placed in his path. That faith was enabling, endowing him with an enormous reserve of self-confidence. The family's three-storey home in Forest Hill, at 322 Russell Hill Road, had a large veranda and an extensive tree-shaded garden. It was a splendid place for a child to grow up.

Favourites—and Jack clearly was the favoured child of three—can run into obstacles, especially with their siblings. "He was the son and heir, Mother's little darling," one sister, Marg (Margaret b. 1921), the middle child, recalled. The other, Betty (Elizabeth, b. 1918), the eldest, added in neutral fashion, "We had a very happy home. Though Dad had strict moral standards and was a pillar of the Church, we were always doing fun things as a family."[14] John Gordon—called Jack, sometimes Jake, to distinguish him from his father—was born on July 30, 1922. He was not only the youngest child but also a frail one. Both sisters have vivid memories of the special attention their brother required. "He was quite sick as an infant," Betty remembered. "That's why we went up north to find cottages: the doctor recommended fresh air." Marg's feel-ings are a bit more candid: "Bet and I had to give our cats away because of Jack's allergies. I would rather have given *Jack* away."

Sibling rivalry and Jack's physical vulnerability notwithstanding, family photos—first from Centre Island, then Georgian Bay, and finally at Lake Joseph in Muskoka—give glimpses of what looks like a happy

*Marg, Ethel, John, Jack and Betty McClelland, circa 1924*

domestic life. One cottage photograph shows a dapper John reclining in a wicker chair, his austerely beautiful wife looking vaguely into the distance and two perky little girls. Jack, a serene, assured, almost white-haired toddler with a pudding-bowl haircut and clad in immaculate rompers, positioned between his parents, has an assortment of toys in front of him. In one of the photographs taken that day, Ethel holds a book on her lap; in another, Jack, seated on his mother's lap, holds the same book. According to family lore, the book was Jack's idea. "Just a minute!" he yelled just as the photographer was about to take the first snap. "We should have a book. It's Dad's business." He ran into the cottage and fetched the first volume he came across. His penchant for publicity was with him from the beginning.

Jack's career as a "bookman" also began early, at about the time he was afflicted with asthma at the age of three. His pediatrician, Dr. Alan Brown, was one of the best known of the day and had the distinction of being an M&S author. "His visits and his methods were like clockwork. He would put a thermometer in my mouth, a greased finger up my behind, and after roaming over my chest with a stethoscope, he would inevitably tell my mother that all she could do was to continue to burn camphor in my room which he considered the only cure for asthma."[15]

While following Dr. Brown's instruction, Ethel read her son various childhood classics: A. A. Milne, Beatrix Potter and Thornton Burgess. Occasionally Jack's father or one of his sisters took her place. "We moved on to [Marshall Saunders'] *Beautiful Joe*, and then to L. M. Montgomery, but I already knew that [her] books were considered to be for girls, so the switch to *Chum's Annual* and other annuals for boys soon took place."[16] At his mother's direction, his bedroom was moved to the family library, where he had free access to all the books. As a result, Jack enjoyed reading more than school, which was just as well because he was not really strong enough to attend school regularly until the age of ten. He had also become something of a pretender. Asthma, he recalled, was very easy to fake: "Mother would come to wake me in the morning and find a child wheezing, coughing and literally choking with asthma. She would quickly write a note to the teacher to be delivered by one of my sisters."[17] By the age of eight, he had decided that Jane Austen was his favourite writer. "How many children are exposed to such a great author at an early age?" the grateful son later reflected. "It is ironic to think that asthma should have been the chief cause of my love of books and reading. In truth, it must relate more to the fact that my father was a distinguished book publisher and that my [mother had an] appreciation of literature."[18]

Another early memory concerns Centre Island, where a ferry captain carved a model of his vessel for Jack, then age four or five. Jack sailed it for hours on the lagoons near his summer home. The cherished toy came to a premature end when he left it tied to the dock one day. He never saw it again but remained fascinated by boats of all kinds.

Jack may have been bookish, but he could also be extremely mischievous. On several occasions he and his friends tested the efficiency of the Forest Hill Village Volunteer Fire Department by setting field fires. They rationalized their behaviour by telling themselves they were keeping the volunteers on their toes. Occasionally Jack and a friend would go out on the roof of the house on Russell Hill Road to sit in the sun and gaze, supposedly, into the trees. "I remember one incident very clearly. It just so happened that the window that we came into on the third

*Jack McClelland, circa 1927*

floor was a bathroom window. In those days, most families living in that area had maids. Our maid of the day was having a bath when John and I climbed in through the bathroom window. She leaped out of the bath and ran downstairs" and the friend was sent home at once. While his mother was averse to corporal punishment, Jack received a "serious spanking"[19] from his father. Ethel once remarked to one of her daughters, "The thing about your brother is that we tell him not to do something again, and he doesn't; but he goes and does something just as bad that's *different!*"[20]

At the age of eight, Jack took his father's secretary out on a boating expedition at Muskoka and did not tie the boat up properly. "The boat started to move away. The more I tried to help her [get out of the boat], the farther the boat moved from the dock. As her legs spread wider and wider, Miss Gilmore inexorably and inevitably ended up in the water (not a dangerous situation, as it was less than three feet deep). Regrettably, I just lay down on the dock and howled with laughter."[21] One Christmas when he was ten or so, he presented each of his sisters with a cheque for $2,500, signed by Santa Claus.

His first school was Brown, on Avenue Road, where the children were separated into two groups: male only and mixed. He was delighted—

even at that early age—to have been given a spot in the mixed class. At the age of thirteen, in the fall of 1935, Jack entered University of Toronto Schools (UTS), to which he walked or biked. His sisters both attended Bishop Strachan, near their home.

"Whitey," as the pale blond teenager was called, was soon involved with school traditions reminiscent of those at Harrow and Rugby in Britain, and a very Canadian one—hockey. One friend, the former Ontario lieutenant-governor John Aird, remembered what an outstanding opponent Jack was: "He was a stand-up goaltender like Terry Sawchuk who would move out and challenge the shooter. He manoeuvred beautifully, had very fast hands, and was extremely competitive."[22]

After three years at UTS, Jack—because of his continued problem with asthma—was moved by his father to St. Andrew's College, north of Toronto. "The doctor thought the air up in Aurora would resemble the Swiss Alps or something," Jack, in a dubious mood, remembered. "I was reluctant to leave UTS partly because of the many friends I had made but primarily because our hockey team, for which I was the goalkeeper, had won two Metro Toronto hockey championships in a row. You can imagine my chagrin when the team won a third championship without their star goalkeeper. I have never forgiven them!"[23]

In the years at St. Andrew's, Jack was, according to his classmate and roommate Bob Hamilton, "one of the most nervous guys getting up in front of people. But he didn't have to work for his eighties, whereas I'd have to study all night to pull off seventies."[24]

Although Jack was not a particularly distinguished student in English, he did become president of the Literary Society. His attention remained fixed on hockey. He also became proud of his physical prowess, having all of a sudden become a hulking teenager. Bob Hamilton remembered that "he was terribly proud of his physique. He was always flexing his muscles in front of the mirror in our room and saying how lucky the girls were. He thought he was God's greatest gift to women. He talked a great game, as if he were a lady-killer, but there was no action. In those days, a girl who let you kiss her on the first date was considered fast. He and I both lusted after one of the maids at St. Andrew's who wasn't much older than us, but nothing happened."[25]

Deryck Thomson, a classmate of Jack's who was also a member of the Second String Football Team, recalled his teammate's "broken field running, for which he employed a kind of crouched canter, much resembling vintage Groucho, but in higher gear." The same friend described a more elegant Jack: "With his sandy hair and bared knees, young Jack cut a dashing figure in his red tunic, swinging sporran and swirling kilt, dress uniform of the College Cadet Corps." Jack could also be lazy: "He wasn't the type of young lad to suffer the almost daily imposition of sweaty struggle and strain imposed on the rest of us; but would frequently suborn some other hapless youth to run around the practice field on his behalf, in return for a book token and a couple of cigarettes."[26]

In the 1939 *Saint Andrew's College Review*, Jack's "ambition" was to "slay the fair sex."[27] When he turned seventeen that summer, he worked on a construction crew and purchased his first car, a 1934 Ford Roadster. A photograph of him taken a year later shows a very dapper young man (white slacks, dark sports jacket, striped tie) at a meeting of his school's Literary Society. Although his physical appearance has been said to be a combination of dimpled Kirk Douglas and sprightly Danny Kaye, a hockey team photo from about 1940 makes him look a bit like another film star, James Dean, the legendary rebel.

In a subtle way his time at St. Andrew's kindled Jack's ambition. According to his sister Marg, the whole environment there "was so much more restrictive than what he'd been used to.... And, like Dad, he wanted the best for himself. At

*Jack McClelland, circa 1940*

St. Andrew's there were boys who had more than he did. He was *in* it, but not *of* it."[28] The McClellands were well-to-do, but they never considered themselves wealthy. In part this explains Jack's reluctance to see himself as having a privileged childhood and adolescence.

In October 1939, John wrote to congratulate his son on his appointment as a prefect and to offer a little advice: ". . . take a little time to think out quietly and carefully what your responsibilities involve, what your duties will be, what problems are likely to arise in dealing with your fellow students."[29] In spite of wide divergences in their characters, Jack was a dutiful son who revered his patient, loving father and his father accepted Jack for himself. The bond between them buoyed Jack up during his darkest days in publishing—even at those times when Jack flatly disagreed with John. If the connection between father and son is strong, Jack learnt, it can provide sustenance for the remainder of the son's life.

Jack was also an emotional child, and John and Ethel were the kind of people—very much of their generation—who did not feel it appropriate to display feelings publicly. As children, Jack and Marg—very close in age—quarrelled, sometimes bitterly. Betty remained the remote older sister, who could provide her youngest sibling with much-needed advice. As her brother matured, she noticed he possessed their father's love of argument and his unwillingness to lose a dispute. She thought her mother continued to spoil Jack, to the consternation of John, who wanted his son to be more disciplined. Jack was respectful of their father and desired his companionship, yet he was much more at ease with his mother, whom he sometimes teased mercilessly—he could, as Betty put it, "twist her around his little finger."[30] John was perfectly aware that teenage Jack was a smoker, but the unspoken agreement was that the son never smoked in front of his father; the subject of Jack's smoking was never voiced. Betty, a sensitive observer of her sibling, was certain that the sixteen-year-old, despite his craving for independence, would follow their father into the family business.

In the very traditional McClelland household, more was expected of the only son than of the two daughters: he was well aware of this, and a part of him did not want to accept the responsibility of being the single male heir. During the summer of 1940, Jack, having finished at St. Andrew's, had reached "a crossroad." He was confident that his future would not include publishing. He decided to see if he could become a writer:

> Here I was from a home where I'd been surrounded by books, where authors were it. [My sister] Bet and I had been a couple of nighthawks, always reading later than we were supposed to. I guess I was "imprinted." Anyway, that summer I decided to write. I thought I'd first take a run through the philosophical options, decide what the hell I believed in. In God? No. Jesus? Not bloody likely. The Ten Commandments? No way. So I began trying out different positions. I started five or six realistic novels set around Ontario—up north, the Niagara Peninsula, in Toronto—and I never got further than a few chapters each time. It was bullshit. I could tell I didn't have anything to write that was relevant to anyone but me. I learned a few things by doing this: one was that there was nothing goddamned wrong with curiosity.[31]

Ethel, who read one of her son's novels, diplomatically told him that writing was not his calling. A career as a writer having been struck off the list (and a reverence for writers having been instilled in him), Jack, in consultation with his father, decided to take applied science and engineering at the University of Toronto. "I picked it because it was supposed to be the most difficult course around," almost as if he had chosen the discipline least like literature. "I thought an engineering physics course would be useful in business. I planned to go on to Osgoode, become a corporate lawyer, and clean up financially. Problem was, I just couldn't get interested."[32]

Although he made light of it, Jack reached a serious intellectual turning point at university. "I studied philosophy at university, and once I got as far as Immanuel Kant, I concluded that he was the final word, and everything that came after him was unnecessary garbage. . . . Up to that point, Mother and Father had insisted on a strict spiritual or religious upbringing—like church and Sunday school and church again every Sunday. Kant again solved all that for me and except for weddings, funerals, etc., I haven't been in a church since."[33]

Like many young men of his generation, he was attracted to the action and the glamour of the war in Europe, so he enlisted in the navy in 1941, at the age of nineteen. As an older man, he offered a more sardonic explanation of his motivation:

[I went] to the University of Toronto to study engineering, in the fall of 1940. In the early fall of 1941, several of the brothers [from his fraternity, Alpha Delta Phi] decided to join the army because it was perfectly clear that they had no hope of passing their second year. Because misery loves company, they became jealous of those of us who were still civilians and [they] acquired a supply of white feathers—a mark of cowardice in those days—with which they supplied most of the girls on campus. These particular brothers knew a lot of girls, because up until then they had spent most of their time drinking and chasing girls—broads, as we called them in those days—so it became difficult to go out with a girl without being handed a white feather. Have you ever tried to make a pass at a girl who has given you a white feather? Forget it. I decided to join the navy.[34]

Jack was even more cynical in describing his introduction to the navy: "To be accepted as a naval officer in training, you had to pass an interview conducted by senior naval officers. To give you the picture of how that interview went, let me select only one question and one answer. 'McClelland, it says in your application that you have sailing experience. Could it be said that you have been sailing all your life?' 'No sir,' I said, 'just since I was about six years old.' Intelligence has never been a highly rated commodity in the navy."[35]

His high-spirited account does not acknowledge his very serious side—it was more likely that his early fascination with and love of boats and ships led him to choose the navy. He became a probationary sub-lieutenant in Toronto in the fall of 1941 and trained at Royal Roads military college in British Columbia in the spring of 1942. From there he went directly to Sydney, Nova Scotia, where he joined the crew of a mine sweeper, the *Chedabucto*. At the end of 1942, he became the executive officer on a Fairmile—a type of mine sweeper—out of St. John's, Newfoundland. Six months later he obtained his own command, on another Fairmile, also working out of St. John's. "This was perhaps the high spot of my naval career," he says. "At night on patrol in Conception Bay, we encountered a large German submarine. We opened fire, and they immediately submerged. We reported the incident by radio to St. John's and it was perfectly clear they didn't believe us. They did the very next morning. The submarine had laid a mine field in the entrance to St. John's harbour."[36]

Later, in 1944, he volunteered for service in the U.K. in the Motor Torpedo Boat (MTB) service and ended up in one of the Canadian Flotillas, again as executive officer. Jack's impetuous, do-or-die side had found the perfect application.

The ever-present danger in manoeuvring MTBs in and out of dangerous situations invigorated him. The Coastal Forces—of which the all-Canadian MTB flotilla in the Royal Navy was a significant part—were known as the "Costly Farces" because of their only-sporadic success in battle. Their radar capacity was negligible, and eyesight was rendered almost useless in the usually foggy English Channel. The German equivalent of MTBs,

*Jack McClelland, circa 1944, at controls of an MTB*

E-boats, were far speedier. Sometimes it was impossible to know if a vessel was friend or foe. Occasionally the automatic six-pounder guns fired on their own ships.

When an MTB was reasonably sure it had spotted a German minesweeper, the crew immediately let their torpedoes fly, accompanied by exploding yellow-green star shells, searchlights and low-flying red or green tracer bullets. Having made a hit, the MTB quickly fled.

Jack's steadiness under fire quickly became celebrated. Even in such dire circumstances, his pep talks to his crew were capricious: "Now's our chance to shake hands over the port bow with Korvettenkapitän Götz von Mirbach. If we catch him with his pants down, we'll make it through to sing "God Save the King." But we'll probably get blown to bits in a couple of hours. That way we'll live forever and ever amen as glorious heroes. Better than feeling like this, that's for goddamned sure. Let's go! We don't need help from God or the Royal Navy to fix up a few E-boats on our own."[37]

Daniel Lang, who was twenty-four when he joined the 65th Flotilla, had vivid memories of those days: "We were all kids. The ratings [noncommissioned sailors] were eighteen or nineteen; the oldest man around was twenty-eight." All the men had nicknames: Jack's became Jake. Practical jokes were the norm: Jake would supposedly pull hairs out of food served up by "Cesspool" the cook in order to see a particularly fastidious officer turn green. Officers and men considered themselves a unified group, fighting a common enemy. Jake "shone," never panicking even when "there were some terrible boo-boos."

An air of nonchalance was certainly cultivated by Jack, who enjoyed living close to the edge. He could also be deeply frightened. In a National Film Board film clip of the 65th Flotilla, a shaken, exhausted-looking McClelland salutes flag-covered corpses as they pass off his boat. One colleague recalled, "Jake and I saw three of our crew killed and a dozen wounded seriously. It was traumatic for kids our age." Jack agreed. He knew that the survival odds for MTBs were fifty-fifty; of the sixteen Canadian-manned torpedo boats, eight were blown up. Twenty years later, he reminisced, "I guess you never forget [slain comrades].

I had a lot of our people being killed all around. When you're a small boat and crew, you don't forget that in a hurry."

There were many good times. "In a normal week," Jack remembered, "we had three nights off—in bad weather, more. One officer had to stay on board with a third of the crew; the rest could do what they damn well pleased." Off duty, there were trips into London. "We really lived it up, like gentlemen," said a colleague. "Blow all our money on exotic meals and shows, relish the clean sheets in some posh hotel or other, have our laundry done. You know what they say about sailors having a girl in every port? All I can say is, we didn't *get* to every port."[38]

There were more reflective moments. Once Jack visited a friend at an RCAF Spitfire unit based near London. The two got sloshed, but Jack insisted on being wakened to see the squadron take off for a sweep over German airfields. "I can see him now, standing at the end of the runway, his eyes bright red, shaking his head in disbelief that after a night's drinking those twelve buggers could actually make it."

One of Jack's best war stories comes from early 1945 when he had taken command of a new motor torpedo boat constructed in Scotland. He and his crew picked up the vessel—completely equipped except for ammunition and torpedoes—in Tarbert on Loch Fine. They were to sail south to Greenock, the harbour of Glasgow, take on ammunition and supplies, head for Wales for several weeks of intensive training and sail south to the English Channel for combat. Getting into that narrow harbour was not easy, but this was managed in spite of a lot of early-morning fog. When they reached the inner harbour, the sky was clear, the sun bright. Coming in their direction was a huge ship that resembled a mobile Empire State Building. Not one to miss an opportunity to train his apprentice crew, the twenty-two-year-old commander—supposedly wearing only a cap and a jock strap—ordered his crew to make a dummy torpedo attack. He assumed the captain of H.M.S. *Queen Mary* knew his boat was unarmed and harmless. He called the crew to action stations, running the boat up to full speed. "As we got closer I noticed about three lights signalling from the bridge, and all their guns—they had very few because they depended on speed to evade the enemy—were pointing at us. 'What are the lights saying, signalman?' I asked. He said, 'Sir, they are telling us to fuck off.' Not one to mess around, I slowed down and changed course and passed down the side of this giant ship. We waved fondly to the passengers— mainly children, war brides and other evacuees." As it turned out the harbour command had thought Jack's ship was a German boat that had somehow sneaked past the defences and was about to sink the ocean liner. Jack had a lot of fast talking to do, was upbraided publicly by the Commander-in-Chief, North West Approaches, but the young man was so earnest and charming that in private the senior officer confided in him: "It must have been an irresistible target. To tell you the truth, I doubt I could have resisted the target myself."[39] At the end of the war, the young man was commended in a dispatch: "Lieutenant John Gordon McClelland exhibited a high degree of seamanship and courage in command of a motor launch engaged in dangerous duties while assisting in the recovery of enemy mines."

Somewhat shamefacedly Jack now recalls the war with a great deal of affection: "It's terrible, but I loved the war. It was the best period of my life. The scary parts were few and far between, and even so it was exhilarating operating at night. MTBs had small crews, and I made very close friends. I learned how to survive fighting at incredibly close range. I was free from normal responsibilities, and from the heavy discipline you got in other parts of the navy. When you weren't at sea, you were a young naval officer—and there were women everywhere. I lived every day as if it was the last. I had fun all the bloody time. I never had a better time."[40] "The only problem with the goddamn thing was that you could get killed,"[41] he remarked some time later. So nerve-racking were some of the nights at sea that Jack—like many other men—drank heavily to forget the dangers he had undergone.

His military machinations exclude the side of Jack that is gentle and courtly, the young man who had fallen head over heels in love with Elizabeth ("Buttons") Matchett. They met early in 1943, through his sister Marg, while Jack was on leave before going overseas. "Though my family lived in Moore Park," Elizabeth, whose father was a dentist who later worked in real estate, recalls, "we'd known the McClellands for years. I was called 'Babe' then, because I was the youngest in my family; I'd always been a sort of kid sister to Jack. One time Marg brought him along for dinner when my date didn't show up. He was on a two-week leave just before going off to begin his stint on the MTB. We went out that night and for the rest of his leave. . . . We had a lot of things in common: my family on my mother's side was from County Antrim, the same part of Ireland as his father's family." Mostly she was attracted to his sense of humour—they had a lot of fun together.

Elizabeth excited the chivalrous side of Jack, a part of his character he sometimes pretends does not exist. It can be seen in a letter he wrote to his sister Marg in March 1944: "I have my own ship now. . . . It is a grand ship, though, bigger, faster and far better armed than my last one. We can really do a job in these babies. . . . Have been leading a very good life since coming over. Am not drinking too much and have ignored the girls pretty well. Buttons has changed me more than somewhat. She is my tonic. What a grand kid! I consider us engaged now, although she doesn't and the world can't know—but that's hardly the point."[42] When he met up with his brother-in-law Henry Stark, Betty's husband, at a naval base on the river Clyde in Scotland, Jack told him, "If you get home before me, tell my mother and father I'm going to marry Elizabeth Matchett." When he wrote to Elizabeth requesting a nude photograph, she amusedly told him this was not possible.

Jack's more serious side, manifested in old-fashioned good manners, can also be glimpsed in his letters to his parents. "Glad to hear you like Buttons so much. She is quite a marvellous character. I intend making her your daughter-in-law as soon as she will have me. . . . She is the type that everyone dreams about—the ideal that you never expect to meet. God knows how I could be so lucky."[43]

Jack's overseas service finished on July 13, 1945. He was discharged almost three months later, on October 10.[44] The couple married at Grace Church-on-the-Hill on December 15, not waiting to complete the bachelor degrees they were taking at the University of Toronto. Their reception was a supper-dance at the Royal York, their honeymoon a trip to Quebec. Apartments were scarce after the war, so the young couple took the third floor of the McClelland house, where, Elizabeth recalled, "We had to sneak our bottle of booze upstairs past Jack's father."[45] Jack—who liked to tease his mother and was now much more self-assured around his father—quipped in his parents' presence to his new wife when they returned from their honeymoon: "I hope you're pregnant because I don't want to go through all that again!" Ethel blushed; John pretended he had not heard the remark.

*Jack and Elizabeth McClelland, wedding photo, 1945*

Jack and Elizabeth's first child, Suzanne, was born in 1948; after her came Carol in 1950, Sarah in 1955, Anne in 1957 and Robert (Robbie) in 1961. After Suzanne's birth, the family moved to an apartment on Lonsdale Road. At the time Carol was born, they bought a house on Dundurn Road in the Lawrence Park area of Toronto; eight years later, they went to live at Inglewood Drive in Moore Park; and in 1966, the family moved to a large, comfortable—some visitors called it "tony"— home on Dunvegan Road in the Forest Hill section of Toronto.

Speaking of his university education, Jack self-deprecatingly explains, "I got a cheap B.A. [at Trinity College, University of Toronto]. I combined some correspondence courses in the summer with the regular winter session, taking just enough to scrape through." One of his teachers, Malcolm Ross, has a different recollection (Jack took Ross's summer course because he had failed one in engineering before he enlisted in the navy): "Though he was a bashful fellow, he sought me out in the breaks between classes. He explained that he was going into business and didn't

know what to read. . . . I encouraged him to look to Canadian writers."[46] In fact Jack had
read a great deal of Canadian
literature, but he did not yet see
it—as Ross did—in nationalist
terms, something to be pre-
served and nurtured. He was
also well aware that his father
had been badly burned in his
attempt to publish indigenous
writers.

Only gradually did Jack become aware of his own special
calling, although he downplays
his idealistic side. During the
war, like many other men who
served their country, he came
into touch with deeply patri-

*Elizabeth McClelland with daugh-
ters Suzanne and Carol, circa 1951*

otic sentiments at the very same time that he witnessed the brutality of
war. Jack McClelland himself is best understood as a person of often
widely divergent and conflicting feelings. Sometimes he speaks crudely,
almost obliterating all other sides of his personality; even in such moments, his gentlemanly, refined side is there, betraying the tough impression he is trying so hard to make. At times Jack's insensitivity rises
dramatically to the surface; at other times he is warm and gracious. As a
publisher he sometimes tried to access his ruthless streak, but quite often
his generosity and friendliness simply got in the way.

## 2

# THE BOSS'S SON

# (1946-51)

TOWARD THE END of his career, Jack suggested that he became a publisher by default, almost accidentally. This is not so. During the war, he developed strong, positive feelings about entering the family business. He broached the matter tentatively to his father in May 1944: "I don't know what to think of the future (I and millions of others). Still I am sure I can make a go of it and I honestly believe I could do a better job of it with Elizabeth with me than alone. Something about inspiration." (Another message given to Henry Stark on the Clyde: "Tell my parents I am going into publishing.") Having skirted what he really meant by "making a go of it," he finally told his father directly what he had in mind:

> I am sure of one thing which no doubt you will take a dim view of, and that is that I would not return to university. I have no future in engineering—I am sure of that—there was always a spark lacking. . . .
>
> One thing which has always confused me and which I find hard to understand is your seeming desire for me to avoid the publishing

business at all costs. Although I have never had an opportunity to delve into the mysteries behind it, it has always seemed to me most intriguing. Is there any other business which offers opportunities in so many varied fields? What I am trying to say is that what with buying, selling, travelling, advertising, risk, financial, personnel and I suppose many other ends, what other business could touch it? But I am not trying to sell you the business, am I? I do wonder why you always declaim [against] it to me. Don't you think I would make a publisher?[1]

Certain that his father would not heed his plea, he half-heartedly mentioned other possibilities: "Anyway, I am sure I will fit into an office somewhere. I should like a go at the advertising game. Time will tell. I hope someday to enter the political field in the Dominion."[2] If John McClelland responded to this overture, the letter does not survive. Until 1944 there had been an agreement—initiated when J. Wilfred Ford and George E. Nelson joined the company in 1936—that no partner's child could take charge of the company. By 1945, when this arrangement was dissolved, John was "very anxious" for his son to enter the firm, George Stewart's only child, a daughter, having no interest in doing so.

Business was booming in the wake of the war, and the future looked extremely promising. John now became enthusiastic about Jack's potential involvement. Knowing first-hand a publisher's travails (the long hours and the considerable risks), Ethel McClelland was "adamantly opposed" to the idea of Jack at M&S. Perhaps she also felt that he should undertake employment that would make him wealthy rather than comfortable like herself and her husband. She knew intimately the claims publishing had made on John; she did not want her son to be subject to the same pressures.

Jack was caught between opposing camps. He sided with his father, whom he found charismatic, and to whom he felt he owed a debt from childhood: "Although I had great respect and admiration for my father . . . he usually overwhelmed me, and I followed most of his requests implicitly. I loved my mother deeply, but he was the one who gave me hope during some bleak childhood years."[3] Jack's reference to an obligation to his father is cryptic, but he is likely alluding to his father's ongoing support. He also admired John's "terrifying honesty and integrity." When time and again Jack later faced financial ruin, he was sure he should have listened to his mother.

Yet by instinct and birth, Jack was a publisher. He shared his father's innate conviction that publishing was a belief in and commitment to his Canadian culture. Even when the younger man took M&S in directions his father could not appreciate or support, Jack knew he was displaying the spirit of adventure and enterprise that he had inherited.

In 1946, McClelland & Stewart occupied the basement and the first, second and third floors of 215–219 Victoria Street, a five-storey factory building. Jack's first day on the job in November did not begin well. George Stewart, in his typically cheerful manner, called Jack into his office. "Welcome, Sonny Boy ...let's have a chat." Jack disliked the nickname and was tempted to kick Stewart in the pants. In direct contrast to his partner, George Stewart was affable, outgoing and fun-loving. As Jack recalled, he was the "public relations type. The booksellers and the librarians were his friends, particularly the females. I fondly remember him putting his arms around a visiting lady, saying, 'Welcome, dear lady. It is great to see you again.' Not infrequently, as he clasped her warmly, he would whisper over his shoulder to me, 'Sonny Boy, find out who she is.'"[4]

John introduced his son to all the other employees in the office. Christina Gilmore, the rotund Scotswoman with grey hair, glasses and an eager smile whom Jack had dunked in the lake many years before, was the head bookkeeper. Tom Hunter, another exceedingly efficient person, was the warehouse boss. Before becoming editor-in-chief, the late Donald French, an early champion of Canadian literature, had held that job. Sybil Hutchinson followed him in that position; she was, Jack found, remote, almost always looking in the other direction when anyone spoke to her. Bob Nelson, the general manager, was the person most apprehensive about Jack's joining the company: "He saw competition ahead and made no great effort to hide his concern."[5]

It was into a somewhat old-fashioned world that the former midshipman was thrown. In those days, a publishing house was a formal place, employee comportment slightly starchy. John McClelland always arrived at the office immaculately dressed, usually in suits he had purchased during stays in London. George Stewart was a bit more foppish, but his overall look was elegant. One measure of the severity of the publishing world of the time was the tomato juice and tea served by Irene Clarke at all the book launches given by M&S's rival publisher, Clarke, Irwin—no alcoholic beverages were permitted.

McClelland & Stewart's chief competition remained the Methodist Book and Publishing House, but Macmillan Company of Canada Ltd. and Thomas Allen were also contenders. Most Canadian publishers acted as the "agents" for American and British enterprises. Canada's small population, in comparison to the United States and England, made it difficult to produce commercially viable books by Canadians for Canadians. An Ottawa-based firm, Graphic Publishers, made a heroic effort to this end, but expired after only seven years in business, 1925 to 1932. Books with its imprint included *A Search for America* (1927) by Frederick Philip Grove.

The physical vastness of Canada, the existence of few bookstores, the domination of foreign publishers, the lack of good indigenous writers, high production costs and the lure of educational publishing all conspired against the formation of a made-in-Canada literary book trade.

In the summer of 1946, a colophon—to give M&S's wares a new, distinctive look—was commissioned from E. W. Reynolds & Co., Ltd. Within an oval, Apollo stands on a chariot, taking aim with a bow and arrow. These lines from Blake's *Milton* inspired the design:

Bring me my Bow of burning gold:
Bring me my Arrows of desire:

Bring me my Spear: O clouds unfold!
Bring me my Chariot of Fire!

I will not cease from Mental Fight,
Nor shall my Sword sleep in my hand
Till we have built Jerusalem
In England's green and pleasant Land.

One wag pointed to the horse's behind and noted, "That's George Stewart. The driver is John McClelland."[6]

Originally, John McClelland, who remained at the helm until 1952, wanted his son to spend six months in each of the five major departments—orders, packing and shipping, accounting, sales and editorial—of the company known as "The Home of Good Books." (From the outset, Jack evaluated manuscripts in addition to his other duties.) Within five months, he had worked his way through all the divisions. He was never exactly sure why this happened: "I preferred to think that this was because I was unusually bright and ideally suited to the trade. It is much more likely, however, that the managers did not want a potential spy hovering in their area."[7] Jack's first year or so at M&S was decidedly "awkward and traumatic" for him and, he suspected, "for the rest of the staff. Here was the boss's son . . . joining the company in a position that would lead him to become the boss at some later date."[8] (In order to provide a sound financial basis for Jack's entrance into the family firm, John gave his son in September 1946 by deed of gift each year five of the two hundred shares of common stock he owned in M&S. Nine years later, in 1955, he sold Jack the remaining 150 shares at $217 each.)[9]

Father and son shared some comic moments. Soon after Jack joined the firm, John showed him a "model" rejection letter sent out by an American publisher. "Its salutation was 'Esteemed Author' or some such. The message was that the manuscript was so good that it would set an entirely new standard by which all other manuscripts would have to be judged in the future. For that reason, the publisher could not afford to publish."[10]

When Louis Melzack, who had been selling books in Montreal since 1927, came in to buy remainders (unsold copies of books no longer in demand that were being sold off cheaply by the publisher), John told him Jack would handle the order. The somewhat confused and ill-at-ease young man offered a huge mass of books at a "buck" each. The courtly Melzack informed Jack he could only sell such items at 49 cents each. "Oh, I guess a quarter will do," Jack assured him.[11]

Very shortly, in 1947, Jack became aware of the perils of the book world when M&S lost approximately half of its sales and more than half of its income as a result of one of its major U.S. clients, Doubleday, setting up its own Canadian subsidiary. Years later, Jack commented on an influential insight he had gained at the outset of his career: "I decided that if I were to stay in book publishing, I didn't want to be dependent on foreign agencies. I saw that a logical decision in London or New York could cut our volume in half. A Canadian nationalist was born overnight."[12]

Jack would claim he had informed both his father and George Stewart that he would not join M&S unless they ceased their concentration on agency publishing; 1947 seems the likely date for the emergence of these strong sentiments.[13] In 1956, when Jack severed his firm's close ties with the English publishing house Dent, he knew his decision might backfire: "While I am certain that both your Canadian company and our firm will prosper tremendously in their separate operations in the years to come, I have not yet come to the point where I believe that the separation at this particular juncture is to our mutual benefit. . . . I do recognize that I may well change my mind on this point in the years to come, for I realize that my current thinking is influenced by the necessity of undertaking a complete reorganization."[14]

What is certain is that Jack read *Social Planning for Canada* (1935) at about this time. F. R. Scott, Frank Underhill, Eugene Forsey, Leonard Marshall and Harry Cassidy were among the contributors to this seminal volume that defines the ideals of democratic socialism in a variety of ways. Jack was never a proponent of their political philosophy, but he was deeply influenced by the notion of ideas and products that

*Jack, circa 1950*

originated in Canada. The entire direction he was to take with M&S was in line with the tenets of this book (his early appreciation of it explains in part his later commitment to the Committee for an Independent Canada).[15]

Until about 1950, Lorne Pierce at Macmillan of Canada had been the dominant Canadian publisher. In many ways, Jack McClelland, who succeeded Pierce in his role as *the* self-appointed Canadian publisher, appeared on the scene at exactly the right time to take up a mantle that John McClelland and others were in the process of dropping.

Quick study in the world of publishing or not, Jack was in the sales department by January 1947. His first territory extended from Hamilton to Niagara Falls, with all the towns and villages in between. Two years after he joined the firm, on July 24, 1947, he was appointed a director—just before the executive and editorial staff moved to 228 Bloor Street West, leaving the other departments on Victoria Street. At the same time, his father arranged a cross-Canada tour in the guise of a second honeymoon trip for Jack and Elizabeth.

When John McClelland sent his son and daughter-in-law on their journey across Canada, he obviously meant a lot of business to be mixed with pleasure: Jack was to introduce himself to authors, booksellers and librarians. Having obtained a grounding in the fundamentals of the book trade, he was now ready to face its world. Through a naval connection, husband and wife obtained the first Ford convertible to come off the assembly line after the war. They and their brand-new car made their first major stop in Winnipeg, where they stayed at the Fort Garry Hotel.

Jack could hardly contain his enthusiasm for his new job, as can be readily seen in his "Dear Boss" letter to his father of June 15, 1947. Jack had come across some promising leads: ". . . learned that A. J. M. Smith in Vancouver has almost finished an anthology of Canadiana for an American publisher but has retained Canadian rights."[16] Malcolm Ross, Jack's former teacher, provided "a great deal of help and information."[17] The young publisher was becoming rapacious in his acquisitive bent, detailing all kinds of possibilities to his father.

Elizabeth realized that her husband had really come into his own, as she told her in-laws: "Jack has worked very hard to make contacts with people all across the country. . . . My opinion is that part of Jack's field of work lies in this type of job. He seems very happy and he certainly seems to use good judgment in handling all kinds of situations. Of course, I think he is wonderful and is doing a very good job. I just hope 'the bosses' will feel the same way."[18] Among the writers she enjoyed meeting on the western tour were W. O. Mitchell, the naturalist Roderick Haig-Brown, and Gabrielle Roy.

Without doubt the most riveting person Jack encountered on this trip was the francophone Roy, a native of Manitoba. Jack had phoned to arrange a meeting with Roy, who lived in Montreal but happened to be back in Manitoba visiting relatives, because M&S was the Canadian agent for the American edition of *The Tin Flute* (published in French as

*Bonheur d'occasion* in 1945 and a year later in the United States), a book that he had responded rhapsodically to. Yet it was really Gabrielle herself who deeply attracted him. "Drove out to St. Vital and picked up a most charming and engaging young woman by the name of Gabrielle Roy. Her appearance at first is disappointing—she is tiny, of sallow complexion, terrifying dark rings under the eyes—appears to be in the last stages of TB—but what a charmer!! She is the most interesting person I have ever met or ever will meet."[19] Years later, Jack would remember the encounter in a much different way: "I picked her up [in my car] on a beautiful sunny Manitoba day and, in truth, although it in no way related to my wife or my marriage, I would have to say I fell instantly in love. She had an ethereal beauty that never showed up in photographs. She was small, dainty, beautifully groomed and extremely bright and perceptive."[20]

If Jack's remembrance of Roy's physical appearance was romanticized over the course of time, his devotion to her was steadfast: "On that first day we made a deal that . . . we stuck to throughout her lifetime: I would publish and promote her books, and she would concentrate solely on writing."[21] Roy was the first great writer Jack acquired for his list. Seeing her commitment to all the difficulties of writing, he was deeply moved. He wanted to assist her in any way he could. In that sense, she was the first "great love" of his publishing life.

During their first encounter, Jack was dazzled by Roy's powers of observation. On their drive, they lost their way and stopped to ask for directions at a farmhouse near an unpaved road. It had a beautiful hedge at the roadside with a long walk to the front. They got out of the car, made their way to the house and received directions from the owner. Just as they were taking their leave, Roy turned to this woman and complimented her on her cat. "I looked around. I hadn't seen a cat. On the way out, [Gabrielle] showed me the creature virtually hidden as it nestled in the hedge."[22]

One of Roy's great gifts as a writer was the careful attention she gave to ordinary things not noticed by others. As a publisher, Jack was immediately struck by this trait. He also met a strong, perhaps inordinately self-reliant person. His first impression of Roy—"sallow complexion, terrifying dark rings"—as some sort of exotic creature hints at his instinctive understanding of the gulf between his world and hers. For the very first time perhaps, he recognized the significant variations in Canadian culture and identified his determination to become *the* publisher for *all* of Canada.

Roy had a tendency to live on nerves—the experience of writing was harrowing for her. Thirteen years older than Jack, she might not have been conventionally beautiful, but her inner complexity was evident in those sunken, penetrating eyes. Overall, her face had a driven look, as if she feared time might run out before she could fulfill all the demands life placed on her.

Roy was the last of eleven children. Her parents, Mélina and Léon, were respectively forty-two and fifty-nine when she was born in March 1909. Only seven of her siblings survived adolescence, the deaths of three young children leaving marked sadness in the family. But there were other, equally tragic, forces at work. Léon, born in Quebec, left Canada to travel in the United States before settling in Manitoba, where he worked as a colonizing officer, a person charged with the responsibility of helping immigrant groups settle on the western plains. He was also an ardent supporter of Wilfrid Laurier's Liberals. Four years after his youngest child's birth, he lost his job when Robert Borden's Conservative government came to power in 1911. Léon's dismissal left him an embittered and broken man.

From early on, however, Gabrielle was struck by his stories of the "outsiders" he had helped to settle; at the same time, she and the other members of her family became outsiders to any kind of economic stability. Years later she would claim, "Even today, if I hear a person living only a few miles away described as a 'stranger,' I cannot help feeling an inner tremor as if I myself had been the victim of an insult to humanity. Either there are no more foreigners in this world, or we are foreigners all."[23] This highly sensitive woman explored her empathy for tormented spirits like her father's and expressed a richness of feeling that had deeply touched her through him.

Just before her twentieth birthday, Roy's father had died. She felt compelled to support her mother and a mentally ill sister by teaching. For seven long years, she did this, her only creative outlet was acting in amateur companies. In the autumn of 1937, she decided to seize her own destiny: "I had no definite ideas in mind. I only know that I felt a strong need to travel, to see the world that existed outside of Canada."[24]

Her travels took her first to Paris, a city with energy and beauty that overwhelmed her. She retreated to her room. Unable to respond to any of the enticements of the City of Lights, she fled to London, where she enrolled at the Guildhall School of Music and Drama. Soon thereafter, she became involved in an unsatisfactory affair with a man named Stephen, a spy for a group of Ukrainian militants. In the course of her life, Roy never allowed any other man to mean as much to her, so humiliated and despondent was she when her lover chose his country over her.

Seeking sanctuary from the world, she entered fully the realm of her imagination and abandoned acting for writing. Back in France, she requested a day pass that allowed her into the area where refugees from the Spanish Civil War were streaming through the Pyrenees. On that day, she saw men and women who looked like living corpses, grieving children who could not deal with the deaths of their parents, dogs with festering sores that were slaughtered for food, and infants whose mothers had nothing to feed them. Not surprisingly, those images persisted in her mind.

Five months before the onset of the Second World War, Roy arrived back in Canada. She did not return to St. Boniface, deciding instead to pursue a career in journalism in Montreal. Over the next seven years, she published more than one hundred newspaper articles, travelled extensively across Canada and began to write short stories. In the same year as her return, *La revue moderne* selected "La Conversion des O'Connor" as best story of the year. Six years later, *Bonheur d'occasion*, her first novel, was published by Éditions Pascal.

The Montreal cityscape of *Bonheur d'occasion* is one of grim privation ultimately made worse by the promise of economic renewal following the development of wartime industries. The paradox that war creates prosperity is not only cruel but also false. In addition to exploiting this sad irony, Roy creates in Florentine a heroine who struggles valiantly to impose meaning in a world where chaos reigns. She is defeated, but her valour is transcendent. Although Gabrielle the reporter witnessed Montreal slum life, her own sense of the burden of poverty came first-hand from her childhood; her outrage at the injustices of war that she witnessed in France also assisted her in creating a vivid portrait of society's outcasts.

Roy's innate compassion for the impoverished, her painstaking re-creation of their lives and her graphic evocation of their heroic struggles in universal terms touched Jack McClelland, a man unfamiliar with the world she wrote about. In some ways, the bond between Jack and Gabrielle was one forged between opposites. She was reclusive, he expansive; she was an escapee from poverty, he was born to privilege.

*Gabrielle Roy*

Jack was temperamentally a shy person, although he did his best to conceal this side of himself. Essentially, Jack and Gabrielle were very much alike in their stubborn determination, in being loners who were going to impose their visions—damn the consequences—on others. She deeply influenced his commitment to other French-Canadian authors like Roger Lemelin (*Plouffe Family*) and André Langevin (*Dust Over the City*). More than any other writer, she steered Jack in the direction of Canadian literary writing.

Jack, who would later cajole and even force writers into all kinds of attention-getting stunts, always considered the deal he had made with Roy—that she would write; he would publish and promote—sacrosanct. And yet, a bit ironically, by refusing to take part in the selling of her books, she forced him to be aware of the crucial role of publicity in the successful marketing of writers. Roy's austere beauty, her compassion for the poor, her relentless dedication to her craft and above all her single-mindedness in achieving her goals—these aspects of her physical and spiritual presence deeply moved the young Jack McClelland. In making writers like her known to his fellow Canadians, he would discover real satisfaction.

During the next two years, Jack learned publishing well, paying particularly close attention to editorial matters, especially the reading, acceptance or rejection of manuscripts. Sybil Hutchinson felt he interfered too much, and Bob Nelson was still skeptical.

One of the first sightings of Jack McClelland publisher-editor can be glimpsed in a letter of July 1, 1949 to Earle Birney concerning his novel *Turvey*. The author had suggested that a preface by Malcolm Lowry, Vancouver's best-known writer, might be a good thing. Jack replied, "Just some offhand thoughts about Malcolm Lowry's suggested preface. Do not quote me on this as yet because we will want to think it over. But my immediate reaction would be this. Personally I think it would sell very few extra copies of the book. Secondly, I do not think you need the prestige. And thirdly, we do not want to lengthen the book any more than is absolutely necessary."

Jack's letter is polite but firm, an approach that did not always work with the outlandishly talented but difficult Birney, who had become an M&S author not only because of his friendship with Sybil Hutchinson, a former student, but also, and more importantly, because of his dissatisfaction with Ryerson Press's promotion of his work. Later he would bitterly remind Jack that the prestigious Indian File poetry series (so called because the designer used motifs from West Coast and Plains Indians) from 1948 to 1958—which included volumes by Roy Daniells, Robert Finch, P. K. Page, Phyllis Webb and John Glassco—had been Sybil's brainchild.[25]

By 1949, Birney was one of Canada's most celebrated literary figures, having won the Governor General's Award for poetry twice. A true

Renaissance man, he was an academic specializing in medieval literature, had acted as supervisor of the international service of the CBC, edited *The Canadian Forum* and served as a personnel officer during the Second World War. His war experiences provided the basis for *Turvey*, a scatological, picaresque adventure about an army private named Thomas Leadbeater Turvey, sometimes called "Topsy." Birney claimed the book was "partly an attempt to picture the Canadian character, partly a vehicle for mild satire against army red tape . . . partly just a humble descendant of Tom Jones, Sancho Panza and the Good Soldier Schweik." This novel provided Birney with the assurance that he was a master of prose as well as poetry. Yet the raw anger of the book goes against the public image he so carefully planned of himself as a cultivated intellectual. In fact, he was a man whose strong sexual drives took him in all kinds of dizzying directions; he was by temperament solitary, perpetually restless, never fully satisfied professionally or personally.

Alfred Earle Birney was born to destitute parents in a shack on the south bank of the Bow River near Calgary's Old Langevin Bridge on Friday, May 13, 1904. "Earle" was supposedly a mistranscription of "Errol," an error due to a government clerk's overcompensating for his mother's florid Scots accent as she supplied information for his birth certificate. Since Martha Birney could read and so could have corrected the error, she may well have been pleased by the aristocratic overtone. If Martha was strong and domineering, her husband, Will, aptly named, was a true will-o'-the-wisp.

The boy had a shadowy memory of his father: "My father moved around my consciousness as the definition of a man. . . . He was something accepted and uncompared, a being enormously high, scarcely ever still, but with the trick of making anything he did seem, at the moment, as important as a ritual."[26] In contrast, Martha, the only genuine companion of her son's formative years, was a very definite presence. She had enormous ambition on his behalf, instilling in him from the outset the desire for worldly success.

For Earle, no success ever seemed enough. Before enrolling in chemistry at the University of British Columbia in 1922, he worked as a bank clerk, a farm labourer and an employee of the nearby national parks. During his second year at university, he became interested in English literature and was appointed associate editor of the campus newspaper, *The Ubyssey*. He rose to become editor-in-chief, graduating in English in 1926. After graduate work at the University of Toronto, he attended the University of California at Berkeley, subsequently accepting a teaching post at the University of Utah in 1930. Later he completed his doctorate at the University of Toronto and became a party organizer for the Trotskyite branch of the Communist Party. He finished his doctoral dissertation ("Chaucer's Irony") while living in England, where he worked for the Independent Labour Party.

*Turvey*, a strong work by any standard, was a particularly strange book to be written by an academic. The central character's ambivalent nature is anticipated in a "PERSONAL, CONFIDENTIAL, and HIGHLY UNIMPORTANT" letter of 1943, wherein he wrote of a young, well-rounded young man, excellent officer material. In reality, this Turvey-like character was

suspected of playing only on his own organ;
athletically inclined only in respect to (1) nose-picking;
about as sociable and well-spoken as a spinster librarian with the curse;
possessed of abilities not worth a shit.[27]

Birney, well aware of the disparity between his appearance as the academic-military man of letters and the reality of his private self, found a way in his first novel of dramatizing his split-in-two sense of himself.

Jack McClelland, who knew first-hand the insanities and inanities of military life, responded warmly to *Turvey*, although he had to make some strategic changes to words deemed obscene. In July 1949, Birney agreed to his suggestions, although, he pointed out, "It's hard to change 'balls'. . . . The only other word I know commonly used was 'nuts,' which seems to be rougher and tougher."[28] In his reply, Jack, gratified that Earle was so amenable to enlightened censorship, told the writer, "Although some here think that 'smelling like a hoo-er' is too offensive, I can't agree and am glad to let it pass."[29]

A measure of the closeness between author and publisher can be seen in Jack's willingness to share with Birney his disgust at one of his first attempts to publicize a book:

> I tried to arrange a party at one of the two big department stores here for a book on hockey we have just published. I suggested [some NHL players] Max Bentley, Milt Schmidt, Syl Apps and a few others who would make a good drawing card not only for the book department but also for the sports department. Offered to do a radio broadcast from the store during the party at our expense. Offered to get advance radio publicity for the thing at our expense. Their reply? We want written guarantees from all the players that they will attend—the guarantees to be in our hands within 48 hours (This being six weeks before the date planned). You are to pay all expenses of bringing players here (some were from out of town), pay all expenses while they are here and split advertising costs with us. That may seem hard to believe but it is all true. I told them to stick the whole scheme up their kilt.

He lamented, "One doesn't have a chance to be a publisher in the real sense in this country."[30]

Even within M&S itself, Jack expected with pleasure that *Turvey* would cause an uneasy sensation. "If certain parties here ever read the finished book (they read it in ms only), I will be out on my behind for sure."[31] Birney was tickled: "I should really nip out and rape a debutante to get newspaper coverage. It's an

*Earle Birney*

idea. Will get in touch with you for bail money."[32] Neither the established poet nor the fledgling publisher had much to worry about: within three weeks of its publication on October 29, the first printing of five thousand copies was exhausted; in the next six months, two thousand more were sold.

Jack's first two major writers—Roy and Birney—were antithetical, reflecting the two strands in the publisher's personality: the reflective and the hyper-manic. No writer ever exerted as much control over Jack's imagination and dedication to his calling as did Gabrielle Roy; no writer was ever to exasperate Jack quite as much as Birney. Roy, except for her aversion to publicity, was the ideal author. Birney was the writer from hell. Yet in these two vastly different persons can be glimpsed the extent of Jack's commitment to publish literature that expressed the width, breadth and potential greatness of the Canadian imagination in whatever form it took.

In many ways, Jack the publisher was an enabler, someone whose creativity was directed to helping others realize their full potential. One editor remembered an observation—once made to an author—that displays just how instinctive a feeling Jack had for the rigours of the writing life: "You've got to be a little crazy to be a writer. Face it. It's not normal to sit by yourself in a room for hours thinking, writing, typing. That is not normal behaviour." During his entire career, Jack's empathy for authors' "not-normal" habits was shown in his solicitous generosity toward them. According to Mordecai Richler, "He's one of the few people I know I could telephone with a problem and he wouldn't respond by telling me his." Richler frequently had no patience with editors telling him how to write, but he would listen to Jack.

At a very personal level, Jack's great and abiding love for his parents also found expression in his support of his writers. He became the devoted father to his authors, offering them his unconditional approbation. He had the compassion of the old sinner, but he was also the father confessor. "Even books by men need fathers," Sylvia Fraser proclaimed, "and Jack developed into a marvellous patriarch."[33]

*Turvey's* success notwithstanding, Jack was learning by bitter experience how difficult it was to sell books, no matter how good they were. He continued to feel squeezed by both Sybil Hutchinson and Bob Nelson. Sure that she had nowhere to go in opposition to the young upstart, Hutchinson left M&S in 1950. When Bob Nelson became ill in the autumn of 1951 and Jack's father was away in England on business, Jack felt something radical needed to be done in the face of a projected loss of $33,000.

At the start of a long policy document, he wrote, "There are three things we can do. We can give up, we can pray, or we can do something about it." Bob Nelson, he lamented, "has been labouring under a severe handicap. Although we don't know it, it is conceivable that his condition has hampered him for a number of years. It is perhaps in poor taste to discuss his contribution while he is absent, but it is nevertheless necessary. While he has done parts of his job well, the fact that we are in the position we now face indicates that he has not been too successful as managing director. The responsibility belongs to the position, not to the man, and no matter what the extenuating circumstances, management has not done its job."[34] If he was willing to severely criticize Nelson—who resigned in 1953 to form his own firm with George Foster and John Scott—Jack did not remove blame from himself: "On many occasions, socially and in the trade, I have been asked what I do at M&S. This is a very good question, and one that I am not able to answer too satisfactorily. I can safely say, though, that I keep busier and work harder at doing nothing than anyone else I know. In the productive sense, I have contributed very little, if anything, to the firm. I have learned a good deal about the business. As the boss's son, I have been a liability over the past few years but for some time I have been ready to make a constructive contribution. I am prepared to do so now."[35] This take-charge document by a young Turk offers many suggestions how M&S could be made more profitable: the company had to move to more economical premises by the end of 1952; M&S was too top-heavy with management ("I am going to be very frank in this matter and undoubtedly feelings are going to be hurt. If anyone is sensitive they might as well get out right now because we are not going to have time for quibbling or hurt feelings"); unprofitable lines had to be discontinued; worthless inventory had to be cleared; some reductions in personnel were essential; budgets for editorial and promotion were to be left alone.

In the years ahead, Jack would write many such memoranda, often with similar sentiments. The general message: things are getting out of control. In 1951, having challenged Nelson's authority, he also signalled a possible conflict between himself and his father: "If we are to continue as Canadian publishers, I think [the editorial] department is one of our most important goodwill features and must be maintained. If [any] survey indicates that we are to get out of the original publishing field, the situation will be radically changed. If that proves to be the case, then the editorial department will have to go and I have little hesitation in saying that I would go with it because I see little other hope for the future."[36]

Jack's new style of leadership can be discerned—comically—in a letter of complaint from M. H. Lipton, a real-estate broker who managed the Victoria Street building where most of M&S was housed. Jack, who was determined to vacate those premises, offended Lipton, who wrote to George Stewart: "It would appear that Mr. McClelland Junior is very inexperienced in business and perhaps a little too cocky. . . . I do take exception to [his] actions. . . . I would suggest that you take this up with young Mr. McClelland and perhaps he will not feel so resolute [nor] take the position of a little dictator in the building."[37]

The new headquarters, including warehouse, at 25 Hollinger Road—the move was made between Christmas and New Year's 1952—was in what was Toronto's newest industrial and residential suburb: East York. Huge windows let large amounts of light into the outer part of the one-storey building, the decor was in subtle shades of grey, mushroom beige and light leaf green, and the 5,200 square feet of office space and 20,800 square feet of shipping space were organized in a state-of-the-art manner. Barbara Calder, the switchboard operator, presided in the reception hall, George Stewart could look across his desk at a handsome portrait of King George VI, Mark Savage, a director and the sales manager for medical, technical and educational books, had the office beside his, and Hugh Kane, who would become Jack's cautious lieutenant in the running of the firm, was next to Savage. The large corner office was the domain of John McClelland, who now allowed—and expected— his son to make all the important editorial and business decisions. Ross Yates, the newly appointed trade manager, and Millicent Rothwell, his assistant, had offices near Jack's. An early visitor to the new home of M&S was enthusiastic: all the elements were "keying and dovetailing into one another in one smooth logical operational flow, without waste of time or overlapping of effort."[38] Authors who made their way to East York were warmly welcomed.

Within six years, Jack, had acquired a very good idea of how his job description should be worded. The publisher was "almost like a wardrobe mistress. He should be behind the scenes—never in public. His equipment, ideally, should preclude his appearing in public, for it is my view that he should not be an authority on anything. He should be able to deal with authorities and concepts but should have an open mind and no prejudices. . . . I am ideally equipped for publishing because I know a little bit—very little, almost nothing in fact—about almost everything."[39]

# 3

## JACK OF ALL TRADES

(1951-59)

BY 1951, it was clear the publishing business had not been reinvigorated by the post-war boom. If Jack was worried that spring about the future of M&S as a Canadian publishing house, he put a good face on his anxieties in public appearances and pronouncements. It was well understood, he said, that upswings in population numbers, education opportunities, leisure time and improved communications boded well for books. Moreover, his recent tour of Western Canadian bookstores was a "practical demonstration that these factors are combining to produce a broader and more intelligent audience for good books." Privately Jack was often apprehensive, worried whether he was going to be able to develop his company as he envisioned.

He was filled with an enthusiasm "only very slightly dimmed by the volume of books returned unsold since the first of January." He went on to praise the vitality of owner-manager booksellers, a new breed that was more inclined to offer a good range of paperbacks and gift and reference titles than to fall back on best-sellers and non-book merchandise. But once again a hint of irritation emerged: M&S, he noted, had ranked high in a Canadian Booksellers' Association service survey, "although we were somewhat surprised to find that our policy of 100 per cent returns at any time of the year disappoints some booksellers. What next! Should we retrieve our own unsold books from their shelves?"[1]

At the end of 1952, the year the entire company moved to the new building in East York, Jack became general manager and executive vice-president. In practical terms he was de facto head of the company. The firm he was now running seemed poised for something new, partially in response to transformations in the Canadian cultural scene.

In general, Canada—Toronto in particular—seemed ripe for change, although that change was slow in arriving: "The notorious Toronto Sunday was on its way out, too—but not yet. There was, literally, nothing to do except to go to church. Sporting events, movies, and all forms of popular entertainment were banned. You couldn't even window-shop at Eaton's; in tribute to its Methodist founder, the curtains were tightly drawn. There were no newspapers."[2] So Pierre Berton remembered Toronto in the late forties and early fifties. No matter how much the lily was gilded, the city was still Hogtown. The unappetizingly named Diet Kitchen on Bloor was the most inventive restaurant and the then tawdry old Royal Alexandra was the only theatre, running third-rate road shows when it was not dark.

In spite of its parochialism, Toronto had gradually become the media centre of English-speaking Canada. The cultural future certainly seemed bright. The arts in post-war Canada were developing in wonderful ways. By 1955, 96 per cent of Canadian homes had radios, 63 per cent televisions. After the war, the National Film Board in Montreal had established itself worldwide as a maker of documentary shorts. The cumbersomely named Opera Festival Association of Toronto, which became the Canadian Opera Company, was formed in 1946. The Royal Winnipeg Ballet and in Toronto the younger National Ballet had started to attract significant audiences. The painters Jack Shadbolt, Paul-Émile Borduas, Alfred Pellan and Alex Colville produced major canvases and were attracting critical attention. Northrop Frye's study of Blake, *Fearful Symmetry* (1947), established him as one of the premier critical theorists in the English-speaking world. The composer Healey

Willan's *Veni Sponsa Christi* for unaccompanied chorus was first performed in 1953. E. J. Pratt's nationalist poem *Towards the Last Spike* appeared in 1952. Some notable works of Canadian fiction were published—Morley Callaghan's *The Loved and the Lost* (Macmillan, 1951), Robertson Davies's *Leaven of Malice* (Clarke, Irwin, 1954) and Ethel Wilson's *Swamp Angel* (Macmillan, 1954).

M&S now had two serious rivals in the acquisition and marketing of Canadian books—Macmillan of Canada and Clarke, Irwin. Macmillan's headquarters was downtown, at 70 Bond Street, and its energetic and cagey managing director, Hugh Eayrs, had achieved an astounding success with the publication in 1921 of W. H. Blake's translation of Louis Hémon's *Maria Chapdelaine*, which became an overnight success in the United States and England as well as Canada. Eayrs further secured the company's financial future by acquiring the agency for the Cambridge Bibles and prayer books. He died in 1940 and was succeeded after the war by John Gray, who built a strong Canadian list including Mazo de la Roche, Morley Callaghan and Hugh MacLennan. Clarke, Irwin, established in 1930, became the dominant educational publisher; its literary output included Robertson Davies's early plays and comic novels.

Jack was trying to increase his competitive edge. He was actively involved in accepting or rejecting manuscripts; trying to find a way of obtaining government subsidies from Quebec for the translation into English of authors like Gabrielle Roy and Roger Lemelin; pleading with librarians to purchase M&S titles directly rather than from English or American suppliers; and attempting to formulate a plan to make Canadian classics available in paperback format. He even had to fight a new enemy, the television set. He asserted that people were apologetic about watching television, whereas the "book has an aura of culture attached to it. The value of a good book can truly never be measured, but there is no value in a book simply because it is a book. Poor books will be replaced by television, much as the horse and buggy was replaced by the car. Television will never replace a good book."[3]

In retrospect, there were some comic moments, such as Jack's worry about the solvency of a young Edmontonian who would become one of

Canada's best-known independent booksellers and publishers: "On Saturday morning, I met with Mel Hurtig, the young chap who is opening the bookstore. His location does not seem too bad, although it is off the main street and he may yet learn, to his discouragement, the truth of the retail axiom that traffic is more important than rent. In any case, he seems very enthusiastic, if perhaps a bit impractical. I think we shall have to watch his account fairly carefully."[4] On trips west, Jack relied on the advice of Bill Duthie, a former M&S sales rep, who, to the amazement of many, had opened a bookshop in 1957 next to a library. Like many of the new breed of booksellers, Duthie embraced the still disreputable paperback, devoting his basement store shelves to them from 1959. Three years earlier, Louis Melzack had started his all-paperback Classic's Little Books across the street from his flagship Montreal store. (Well before publishers like Jack McClelland fully recognized their central importance in the book world, Duthie and Melzack knew paperback publishing was an important key to the future.)

Jack, who was trying to stay abreast of all changes in the marketplace, became legendary for being constantly on the lookout for new material, asking, as one journalist recalled, almost everyone he met, "'Have you got a book?' The question comes straight from the hip, almost before the first hello. The answer is often no, but this fair-haired handsome Torontonian is not shattered, because it's his job to ask the question . . . the problem [he claimed] is not selling books, but in finding enough books to publish."[5] Of course Jack's quest for books could lead to fool's gold. There was the case of the fellow who had a "fantastic book" that he stored in a bank vault. After many protracted discussions with this person, Jack learned the man lived in a mental home and was allowed out only once a week.[6]

In Toronto, the merchandising moxie of the Cole brothers, Jack and Carl, was producing results. They had opened their second Coles bookstore at 726 Yonge in 1941, the one that became a shrine because the rock musician Neil Young worked there. Soon the brothers introduced their "supermarket" approach to merchandising: books sold sometimes by the pound, sometimes by the penny. Down Yonge at 224, W. H.

Smith's established its own beachhead in 1949. During the next ten years, Coles and Smith's expanded rapidly, forever changing the face of book selling in Canada with the establishment of their chains of stores. On the surface it seemed that there was a growing demand for books and thus a huge new market for publishers.

Behind the scenes, things were not so bright, as can be seen in snippets from Jack's memos to Hugh Kane, his right-hand man, from 1954 and 1957:

> Let's face it that in view of last year we are running into trouble—serious trouble—with increased costs & investment.[7]

> Suffice to say I have arranged for an additional $25,000 from the bank—we already have borrowed $65,000 (our normal limit)—and there is no real reason to believe this will be enough. I don't know whether we can get more or not. If we can't—who knows? Anyway, it couldn't be more tight than it is.
>
> It is temporary in the sense that we will pull back to, say, $50,000 at some point with luck, but the real problem is (a) how to get thru the summer and (b) where to get long-term capital which the bank will not provide. There is no reason to be alarmed—it's enough that I am having continual strokes every hour. . . . I don't really think we are going bankrupt, but it will be close.[8]

Jack did have a tendency to exaggerate, but he faced many crises in his career. The financial problems at M&S were brutally simple. Under Jack's direction, the company was attempting to find and publish Canadian titles while at the same time maintaining a decent profit. An assortment of variables was at work: some books, despite high expectations on the part of the publisher, did not sell well; sometimes the advance paid for a book was too high to make the book profitable, even though it might seem to do well enough in sales. Among the literati were strong advocates of Canadian literature, but to the ordinary Canadian those poems and novels were perceived as drab. In general the public did not have sufficient appreciation of the political and cultural importance of buying made-in-Canada books. On this score, Jack nevertheless had no doubts: "If we want to continue to be Canadian for very long, we can't follow a course of passive acceptance of everything American and everything that seems easy."[9]

Amazingly, Jack, at the very same time he was facing financial difficulty, defended and maintained the publishing of a real money-loser: poetry. He explained "house policy" on this touchy matter to an editor who had asked for guidance:

> I promised to give you some sort of note on why we publish
> Canadian Poetry [as a] general policy. I would say that we pub-
> lish Canadian poetry first and foremost because we are Canadian
> publishers and we still consider poetry one of the most important
> forms through which the creative writer may express himself. We
> don't do very much publishing in the field because although we feel
> that there is a lot of outstanding poetry being written in Canada, we
> don't feel that there are too many individual poets to build up a
> sufficient body of outstanding work to justify publication in book
> form. We also limit our publications in the field for economic rea-
> sons. We inevitably lose money even on a relatively successful
> volume because the market is at best a confined one.[10]

What is even more remarkable is that Jack wanted to publish "experi-mental" as opposed to "traditional" poetry. Earlier, in 1948, John, still very much on the scene, had stormed into his son's office, aggrieved to learn Jack was publishing the poems of the unknown James Reaney in preference to a collection of verse by the late Duncan Campbell Scott. John told Jack, "I have to question the publishing judgment of anyone who would make this decision."[11] This was one of the few times John second-guessed his son.

In 1961, Jack informed the West Coast poet Phyllis Webb, who was distressed by contradictory readers' reports on a volume of verse she had submitted to M&S, that "poetry is not a personal interest of mine and therefore I don't care too greatly what we publish in the field. We publish it because we consider it an essential part of our function that we do so."[12] But Jack's actions belied his expressed lack of interest: he paid a great deal of attention to the Indian File books, which brought prestige to M&S in the form of three Governor General's Awards, and, later, in 1960, for example, he published the sumptuous *Rivers among Rocks* by Ralph Gustafson with elaborate illustrations and typeface designs by Frank Newfeld. To do this book and several other volumes of verse that followed, Jack appealed to the patriotic instincts of his paper suppliers and printers in exchange for reduced production costs: he undertook to give them further monies from any profits realized by these publications, but he told them how important it was to establish a poetic tradition in Canada that found expression in beautiful books.

The businessman, the publisher and the Canadian nationalist—all real sides of Jack—were never quite in sync. There was certainly considerable scope for disagreement between Jack and Hugh Kane. Born in the north of Ireland in 1910, Hugh Pyper Kane came to Canada in 1921, joining members of a literary family who had already established themselves in North America. From a youth spent in acting circles in New York City's Greenwich Village, Hugh Kane became steeped in American letters and theatre and in the glory years of publishing associated with Grove Press, Alfred A. Knopf, Lippincott and Atlantic Little, Brown— firms of which he later became a director and represented in Canada through M&S. His first real job was in the bookstore of Eaton's in Montreal. Later, he sat outside the office of S. J. Reginald Saunders until the Toronto publisher gave him a job.

Hugh, who was twelve years older than Jack and had joined M&S eleven years before him, had worked as a sales rep as well as in marketing and promotion. Jack and Hugh's friendship dated from their times at the Bloor Street office, from which the two conspirators worked together to dislodge Bob Nelson and two other directors, George M. Foster and John R. Scott.

Hugh was oriented toward the book trade and networks he fostered among booksellers, librarians and other publishers; Jack was more taken with the glamour and fun of Canadian authors and their promotion. Hugh's style of publishing was international in scope, Jack's nationalist. Hugh looked for the enduring book, Jack the celebrity author. Hugh's trusted management of the day-to-day affairs of the firm allowed Jack to be daring. Although their relationship had its troubled moments, the two men depended upon each other and were effectively complementary in their roles. Hugh tended to steer a cautious path whereas Jack was volatile. Like Jack, Hugh did not mind venting his anger.

One disagreement between the two can be seen in their varying responses to the distribution of the unexpurgated version of *Lady Chatterley's Lover*. In order to head off a possible backlash from members of the media and the reading public who might be offended by the book, "Dear Reviewer" and "Dear Customer" letters were sent out to explain why the book was in stock but not in the M&S catalogue: "The controversial aspect of the publication of this book is no secret. However . . . it is our view that it should be made available in Canada so that the reading public here can judge it on its merits. While we are making this work available in Canada, we do not seek undue publicity for it. It is for this reason that we are sending you [the reviewer] this complimentary copy for information rather than for review." This subterfuge angered Kane, who fired off a memo to Jack: "This is the most demoralizing document to come my way in a long, long time. We are ashamed to see our imprint on a major work of art but we sign our name to a piece of pussyfooting piffle like this without a blush. Excuse me while I vomit." As his rejoinder makes clear, Jack was not amused: "Your comment—particularly when you are not in possession of the facts concerning the sending of this notice—strikes me as both ill-considered and unnecessary. I think you can occupy your time better than by sending me memorandums of this character."[13]

Kane was also quite willing to tell McClelland off when he was too interfering, or when he felt his young boss was not doing his job effectively: "I am not being hypersensitive about this or in any way wound up. Neither am I foolish enough to question your right to inquire into or interfere in any part of our operation. As the chief executive officer of the firm, you obviously are free to do as you like. I'm just trying to get across (and probably not succeeding too well) the point I mentioned to you a few weeks ago. I think it is time you disentangled yourself from this sort of detail and concerned yourself with larger and more vital issues. You are now [executive vice-]president of McClelland & Stewart and, as such, you should be free to behave like a president. If you lack confidence in the people you have around you, then they should be replaced. This is all offered with more respect than perhaps is apparent." Jack did not like to delegate—he tried to run an increasingly large company all by himself. Hugh, the shrewd, older mentor, was reminding Jack to manage things better, to govern effectively by thinking ahead. There was much justifiable substance in the subordinate's complaint. If someone wished to speak to Hugh, he or she made an appointment, whereas Jack's door was open to all and sundry.

When a publisher decides to embark on the creation of a new and distinctive list, it can take blood, sweat, and tears as well as time, as Jack McClelland was finding out. When Alfred Knopf, the distinguished, successful and widely respected American publisher, visited Canada in 1955, he said he came to "see if I can uncover some Canadian writing talent—which I don't expect to do. The country seems to be peopled with involuted and convoluted Englishmen who don't have much to say."[15] The remark did not cause much of a stir, and it was precisely this complacency that Jack was battling.

In a speech the following year, he spelled out the problems of the publishing industry in Canada, starting with the observation that there was a relatively small English-language population and too few stores that sold books (only five years earlier, he had thought there might be enough). As well, he said, "Overhead costs for sales and distribution are fantastically high. And, paradoxically enough, nowhere else are so many different book titles offered for sale. . . . As a consequence, the publisher interested in publishing Canadian books has had first to involve himself in the importation of foreign works. As more foreign works are imported, more Canadian books can be published, but because of the increased competition, relatively fewer Canadian books will be read." A year earlier, John Gray, the Macmillan publisher, went on record saying, "I doubt that any Canadian publisher derives any important part of his revenue (or any net profit) from Canadian general publishing. . . . Similarly, those Canadian writers who derive any important part of their income from their books (apart of course from textbooks) do not earn it in Canada and are not dependent on a Canadian publisher."[16]

Booksellers and publishers were deeply suspicious of each other. Canadian publishers were well aware that many booksellers sold English and American imprints of certain titles, even though there might be an "exclusive" Canadian edition. Roy Britnell, whose distinguished Toronto bookstore was founded in 1893, was outspoken in his accusation that publishers *tried* to sell many books themselves (direct mail campaigns, for example) before giving stock to booksellers. Waggishly, I. M. Owen, the Oxford University Press publisher in Canada, made this claim in 1956: "Any librarian or professor will gladly address any luncheon we care to organize on the subject of publishers' cultural indispensability—if he is not already engaged that day in addressing his colleagues on 'How to Buy Books More Cheaply and Quickly Abroad.'"[17]

In 1959, Jack, in the midst of the various book wars, averted financial disaster by having supplementary letters patent issued and by augmenting substantially the original capital and stock of the company through a loan from the Royal Bank. He was holding on—but barely. His luck seemed to take a turn for the better when he acquired two emerging Canadian authors whose first books had originated in the United States.

Part of Jack's strong bond with Pierre Berton and Farley Mowat derives from their common memories of fighting in the Second World War for Canada, as though that event created an invisible link between them. All three men knew first-hand the sordidness and destructiveness of war. Between Berton and Mowat there was a constant tension, in large part activated because they were the son-authors vying for the approval of the same father-publisher. Jack, who is fascinated by other strong egos, often competed with Berton and Mowat. He also did not mind pitting Berton and Mowat against each other.

"'What a lovely child, Mrs. Berton! And what are your plans for him? What do you intend him to become when he grows up?' For that, Laura Beatrice Thompson Berton had a ready answer. 'Why,' says she, cheeks glowing, eyes alight with pride, 'we're intending that he should become a Personality.' She adds: 'A Well-Known Personality.'"[18] This exchange took place in Whitehorse in the Yukon in 1920, the year of Pierre Francis de Marigny Berton's birth. As a child, the celebrity resented being named after an eighteenth-century ancestor who, as soon as he arrived in Rhode Island from France, had the good sense to change his name to Peter Berton.

A year after Pierre's birth, the Berton family moved to Dawson City, a junkyard of history that had seen glory during the Gold Rush. History confronted the Bertons at every turn. Robert Service's cabin was nearby, although Pierre and his sister Lucy did not consider it of any significance in their young lives. Their own property, boasting all kinds of unusual and wonderful horticulture, was also a landmark for tourists. Permafrost invaded everything: "My father," Berton recalls, "was forever jacking up or propping up our house as the ground melted around the foundations. The derelict buildings were ignored, so that the town looked warped, each structure adopting its own cockeyed position, like dying trees tottering in a swamp."[19]

Frank Berton had more or less drifted to the Klondike after he completed his education as a civil engineer at the University of New Brunswick. Encouraged by gold fever, he travelled to the Chilkoot Pass, climbed it, built a raft and floated down the river to Dawson. He intended to stay for two years; he remained for forty. Compelled by curiosity of all kinds, he read *Beowulf* in Old English, Homer in Greek. He was a chess player, a collector of wildflowers, a weaver, an astronomer and an amateur dentist. He made his living as a mining recorder.

*Pierre Berton and Jack at launch party for* The Last Spike

As her son describes it, Laura Thompson's friends thought she was mad to head from genteel Oakville to the wilderness. The explanation is simple enough: "she was crowding thirty and had no prospects. She may not have admitted to herself that she was looking for a husband . . . but surely it was in her subconscious."[20] The couple married in 1912.

The connection of two remarkable and unusual people helps explain in part their famous son. Frank was arch-conservative in his leanings; Laura was the daughter of the journalist Thomas Phillips Thompson, the Canadian socialist and labour leader, who sometimes wrote under the name Jimmy Briggs. Frank pressed all manner of scientific instruments on his young son—a microscope, a miniature catapult, a toy steam engine; Laura imposed on him his destiny as a writer—she herself worked on a novel (never published) for years. The son combines his father's insatiable curiosity with his mother's love of words.

Pierre's childhood in the Yukon—with only occasional visits to the outside world—and his gruelling summer job in the mud flats north of Dawson impressed on him that his was an unusual heritage, located as he was in one of the most remote parts of the wilds of Canada. A "self-made man" may seem an easy way to describe Pierre Berton, but in his case the term is highly appropriate.

The Bertons abandoned the Yukon when Frank retired. Pierre was eleven, eager for a change. For the next seven years, he lived in Victoria, attended college there and transferred to the University of British Columbia for his junior and senior years. Pierre developed a strong affinity for journalism while he was living in Vancouver; gradually he switched from working for the campus *Ubyssey* to the Vancouver *News-Herald*. A year after graduating, he became that newspaper's city editor. He served in the army, rising to the rank of captain, although the war was largely over by the time he reached Europe. Back home, he became a feature writer for *The Vancouver Sun*. A man always in pursuit of "more"—whatever that happened to mean at a particular time—he accepted an offer to work for *Maclean's* in Toronto, figuring that city would be a stepping stone to a lucrative job in the United States with *Life* or *The Saturday Evening Post*. He never counted on his new job making a nationalist out of him. From 1952 to 1958 he was managing editor of *Maclean's*.

As a young man, Berton modestly thought he was simply a reporter. "Like most newspapermen I was a prisoner of the cult of objectivity and conformity. Since you assumed that most readers would never get past the first paragraph, you told everything at the outset. Just the bald facts ... You kept your own personality, your own feelings ... out of the story."[21] Calculation and detachment: these were essential ingredients in a journalist's life.

Skepticism—also vital—led Berton just after the war to investigate a series of mysterious deaths in the Headless Valley, the watershed of the South Nahanni River in British Columbia. The "facts" about the valley were ultimately more interesting than the "legends": "I tracked down the stories of each of the thirteen missing men, most of whom had drowned or been attacked by wild animals, and had no difficulty writing a lively but factual article about the South Nahanni and its history."[22] In that observation can be seen the genesis of all Berton's future work.

In 1953, having worked on a series of articles on the monarchy in the wake of post-coronation fervour, he decided to turn them into a book, *The Royal Family*. His agent in New York sold the book to Alfred Knopf, who informed Pierre that he wrote like an angel. The book turned out to be a flop commercially, but as Pierre recalls, "I was drawn into Jack McClelland's stable [when M&S bought Canadian rights to *The Royal Family*]. I would have preferred to publish with Macmillan . . . but McClelland & Stewart was Knopf's Canadian outlet [for distribution], and I had signed a North American contract [allowing Knopf to sell Canadian rights to his book]."²³ At their first meeting, Jack summarily told Pierre that the elegant, sedate Knopf dust jacket—designed by the Bauhaus' Herbert Bayer—was useless. A book jacket, he informed Pierre, had to be a poster proclaiming the wares within. For the austere royal coat of arms, Jack substituted photographs for a striking, popular look that attracted much attention.

Pierre, more aware than most authors at that time of the central role of publicity in marketing a book, suggested a cocktail-party launch. Jack was not particularly impressed with such a tepid proposal. "I am inclined to think it would be too costly, but it should not be discarded altogether if we can think of a special gimmick. . . . I personally think our angle . . . should be to face squarely the problem that the book presents instead of trying to ignore it. That is to say, that this book presents the Royal Family as real people, as humans. This has not been done many times before, and for this reason most of the letters received by *Maclean's* [where the book was serialized] were antagonistic." What about producing a poster, he asked in a memo to Hugh Kane, of various vituperative comments? "It may be a lousy idea, but it may be novel enough to make it interesting. It should at least get some attention in the press and if we were having a press conference it would be an interesting talking angle. . . . Even if it doesn't sell, it should be a lot of fun, and it may sell very well. I think it is particularly important that we do a good job on this one, promotion-wise, if we want to keep Berton as an M&S author. I am not absolutely sure that we do, but a lot of people . . . think that he has a tremendous future ahead of him.

All I am asking for is a couple of million dollars worth of publicity for an expenditure of about ten bucks."[24]

Even books by a writer as well regarded as Berton were not necessarily financially profitable. In February 1956, Hugh Kane tried to boost his boss's confidence in *The Mysterious North*, the author's second book with M&S, which had received an enthusiastic press: "There is not a single instance of a bad review. Sales, however, are rather disappointing. The bite has not been felt yet. Keep talking this one up. It is a wonderful book and will find a good market."[25] The book went on to win the Governor General's Award for non-fiction that year.

Another writer with a "tremendous future" was Farley Mowat, who became an M&S author in 1955—a year after Berton—with his second book, *The Regiment*. Whereas Pierre, who is only a year older than Farley, cultivates the appearance and manner of a man of the world, the younger man's persona is a kindly court jester, a genial buffoon. Berton rarely appears in public without his signature bow tie, whereas Farley's attire is deliberately dishevelled, homespun, as if to say Love me the way I am.

Farley's early boyhood was spent in Trenton, near Belleville, Ontario. He was named in memory of his mother's beloved younger brother who had been killed in a fall from a cliff. His real first name, bestowed on him by his father, was Bunje (from a character in a novel by H. G. Wells). When Farley's mother, Helen, remonstrated with her husband, Angus, for giving their son such a hideous name, he informed her that Bunje was a "working title" until their son decided what he wanted to be called.

Angus, the son of Robert McGill Mowat, himself a son of a professor at Queen's University in Kingston and the nephew of Sir Oliver Mowat, a premier of Ontario and one of the Fathers of Confederation, was a librarian by profession, although he was trying to make a living as a beekeeper when Farley was born. Helen was the youngest daughter of Henry Thomson, who had been manager of the Molson's Bank branch in Trenton before he made some injudicious loans. The couple, who lived in a derelict house they called the Fortress, were what would later be termed counterculture.

From his earliest days, Farley has mixed fact with fiction, with incredibly successful results: "One night during our final winter [in that home], my bedroom was visited by an enormous bear. I woke to find him standing upright by the window. He was wearing a checked tweed cap with matching visor and staring about him as if in surprise and even confusion. He did not seem inimical but I was nevertheless too startled to move a muscle."[26] Eventually Farley cried out, his parents rushed to his room and he was assured it had only been a dream. Mowat was never completely convinced of this explanation: "My parents were partially correct. It was a dream all right, *but it was the bear's dream.*"[27] In this instance—and many others—Mowat proudly admits that he is a non-fiction writer who never allows a fact to get in the way of a good story.

The Mowats left Ontario when Angus obtained a library job in Saskatchewan, where Farley spent the rest of his boyhood. During the Second World War, he served in the Hastings and Prince Edward Regiment, which his father had been a member of. In *The Regiment* and later in *And No Birds Sang* (1979), *My Father's Son* (1992) and *Born Naked* (1993), he has returned to those formative, decisive years. The innocence of young Farley Mowat was irrevocably destroyed when he witnessed the deaths of some close friends:

> Alex had sent what was left of Five Platoon—my old platoon—to launch the attack, and Five had been caught by enfilading fire from three machine guns. Seizing a tommy-gun Alex levered his great bulk to its full height, gave an inarticulate bellow, and charged straight at the enemy. He could have gone no more than three or four paces before he was riddled by scores of bullets. The blanket that screened the shattered cellar door was thrust aside and a party of stretcher-bearers pushed in amongst us. My closest friend, Al Park, lay on one of the stretchers. He was alive, though barely so . . . unconscious, with a bullet in his head.
>
> As I looked down at his faded, empty face under its crown of crimson bandages, I began to weep.

I wonder now . . . were my tears for Alex and Al and all the others who had gone and who were yet to go?

Or was I weeping for myself?[28]

A more detached—but nevertheless profound—sorrow can be seen in the young soldier's indecision about what to do with his life after the war. To his parents he was able to confide his anguish:

Don't pay much attention to this letter. I'm just damn tired at the moment and my carefully nourished spark of ebullience burns low. I still wonder if I am right to let you in on my low spells. But the business of writing cheery notes whether you are in the depths or not is just silly. It doesn't fool anyone. I am becoming more than ever determined to do the hermit stunt *après la guerre*. . . .

Have overcome my fear that a corrosive bitterness might be my heritage from *la guerre*. I know my point of view has changed dramatically from the dewy-eyed visions of earlier years, but I don't think the way I see things now is necessarily all bad. Caution, suspicion and selective intolerance are not evil of themselves, as long as they are not directed at the true beliefs and honest actions of others.[29]

All Mowat's writings are suffused with an elegiac quality. Whether he is writing of his own childhood, the Second World War, the Arctic and its inhabitants or endangered species, his work, though sprightly and often comic, is filled with a deep sense of both sadness and nostalgia—sadness at how things are destroyed or misused or misappropriated, nostalgia for what once existed in a paradisical state. In the process he, more than any other writer, has made his fellow Canadians aware of vital ecolog-ical issues.

After the war, Mowat attended the University of Toronto but was drawn almost at once to the Far North. His first book, *People of the Deer* (1952), published in Boston by Little, Brown, was severely criticized for its condemnation of the government officials and missionaries who had

disrupted the existence of the cari-
bou-hunting Ihalmiut Inuit.[30]

M&S "inherited"[31] Farley's second book, *The Regiment*, from Little,
Brown, a firm McClelland & Stewart
represented in Canada; however,
this book was published in Canada
under the M&S imprint. Farley was,
as Jack later recalled, "not easy to get
to know in the early days. Scarred by
his role in World War II, he was brash
and abrasive. . . . The so-called northern experts claimed there were many

*Farley Mowat*

fallacies in the book. Farley was not intimidated. He responded with
fervour and brilliance."[32] He was pleased to receive Jack's en-dorsement
of his second book, even though it was qualified: "I think the book is
slightly terrific, that it is one of the most interesting reading experiences
I have had in a long time and that its publication will undoubtedly
enhance the not inconsiderable reputation that you have already
achieved."[33] Mowat was relieved: "That's the first professional opinion
I've had, and despite my heavy armoury, my body-armour is light and
subject to rust holes. I feel much happier about the book."[34]

That the two men quickly became personal as well as professional
friends did not hinder Jack from being brutally honest when he felt
it necessary. In 1958, he did not like the foreword Mowat supplied to
*The Coppermine Journey*, a selection he had made from the journals of
Samuel Hearne (1745–1792):

> I don't know why you gave it to me. I don't want to be a bloody
> editor. However, since you have done so, you will reap the reward. In
> general outline and in scope I like it. I think it is entirely suitable for
> the book and probably just what is needed. There are two things
> I would like to see you do to it. Firstly, I think it's a little too long.
> And secondly, I think it is badly overwritten. Some of the phrases and

some of the pictures that are conveyed are extremely good, but it's a bit too contrived and a bit too purple for my liking, and I think you should tone it down so that it will read more smoothly. To return to your own immortal words: "I don't think, Mr. Mowat, that this is up to your best standard." It's far better than I would expect to see from another author. It's terrific, fabulous and fantastic, but it isn't your best work and needs further effort. In short, it's none too good.[35]

One of Jack's most idiosyncratic tendencies as a publisher-editor was to make seemingly contradictory statements in the same breath, so Mowat's writing could be simultaneously "a bit too purple" and "fantastic." The truth for Jack was often located somewhere in the middle.

One bond shared by Jack and Farley was a love of pranks. In late November 1956, publisher asked author to make an impromptu appearance at a staff Christmas dinner at a Toronto restaurant, Fantasy Farm. Farley was to announce himself as a delegate of the authors, who had been excluded from the event. He was to begin in a laudatory manner and then refer to "the beautifully designed [dust] jacket" with his name misspelled; he was to mention the autograph party at which nobody turned up. In short, he was to recite a litany of complaints. Farley was game: "All right, you bastard … I shall be guided by that invidious document you sent me, and will embellish upon it as the mood strikes me."[36] The ploy succeeded admirably, given that the mischievous Farley loves star turns.

Two years later, Jack learned that Farley had spoken out against his supposed overzealousness in publicizing books: "I was only sorry that I learned far too late that you had been saying all sorts of shocking things about me on the television show. I say far too late because I lost the opportunity to beat you over the head."[37] When he felt it necessary, Jack could tap in to Farley's insecurities, assuring him that his book *The Grey Seas Under*, a year after publication in 1958, was "selling but setting no record. It's still slightly ahead of the Berton [*Klondike*], if that makes you feel better."[38] Jack was deliberately fuelling the competition between Pierre and Farley, obviously feeling that M&S would obtain better books in the process. In turn, Farley told Jack, "You're such a depressing son of a bitch. There are times when I darkly suspect that you are too interested in making money."[39]

The truth was that few of Jack's writers ever became as successful in the marketplace as Berton or Mowat. In 1958, Jack took a considerable financial risk when he decided to publish Sheila Watson's highly experimental work *The Double Hook*, an elliptical, highly poetic narrative set in a small village, considered by many to be the first truly modern Canadian novel. Jack did this even in the face of a very dismissive letter from Earle Birney: "I think it is a stylistic *tour de force*, monotonous, self-conscious, artificial and lacking in real fictional interest. . . . I just don't know what the damn novel is about. . . . No, I would not publish this novel."[40]

Twenty years later, when Sylvia Fraser met Sheila Watson, Sylvia reported to Jack, "She said her book had been turned down heartbreakingly, and even insultingly, over seven years. You read it, said instantly that you would publish it and did so, with great sensitivity and style, and without changing a word."[40] In 1960, Jack commented on this particular decision: "We didn't expect to sell enough copies to break even on it, but we did, and the majority of the critics received the book enthusiastically. Miss Watson has a unique style, poetic and polished, and she is not writing for the average reader."[42] In general he was persuaded that "Canadian books . . . have to be better than they used to be to find acceptance.

*Pierre Berton, Jack McClelland and Farley Mowat at a picnic*

It isn't enough for a book to be Canadian to appeal to today's reader; it must be good enough to compare favourably with those coming from New York or London."[43]

Earlier, in 1953, Jack had wanted to become Ralph Gustafson's publisher. Born in the Eastern Townships of Quebec in 1909, Gustafson, who was educated at Bishop's University and Oxford, published his first volume of verse in 1935. Although he published further collections in 1941, 1942 and 1944, there was a huge interval before he published another in 1960, *Rivers among Rocks*, his first book with M&S and the first to be published in Canada.

At Earle Birney's instigation, Jack approached the poet in 1953, when he was teaching at Bishop's, to ask if he could see the novel Gustafson was working on. The poet explained that he had a contractual obligation to Viking in the States but was certain a separate Canadian contract could be arranged. Jack replied by outlining the best procedure for publication of the novel—the tentative title of which was *No Music in the Nightingale*—explaining that American and English publishers wanted Canadian rights, but when an author was Canadian it was better to be published in one's own country.

In August 1955, Gustafson thanked Jack for his interest, but the manuscript did not arrive until August 1956. Conway Turton, the fiction editor at M&S, sent a lengthy, enthusiastic letter in November to the author with detailed comments. Meanwhile, nothing more was heard from the writer about revising his novel, although he signed a contract in 1959 with M&S for *Rivers among Rocks*. That volume of verse was published to stunning reviews. In 1962, Gustafson asked Jack to take another look at his novel. A very pleased Jack replied, "We shall read the novel as quickly as possible—our Triple A VIP treatment—but why you should insist that I read it myself I don't know. You must be living in the past. The days of the great individual publishers are gone. I read nothing but comic books. You would probably be miles further ahead if I didn't look at the script."[44]

When Jack read the book, he was puzzled, obviously having hoped he was about to receive a work comparable in quality to *The Double*

*Hook*: "This is a baffling novel. Beautifully written in part but obscure as hell. Not unlike Sheila Watson in technique but not as carefully worked out, I think. I can't help feeling that this is close to being a superior novel—if only because I don't understand it."[45] Nevertheless, Turton now had more mixed feelings about the book, and another reader thought the book might be "imaginative and compelling" but lacked focus.

Jack told Gustafson the book could only be published in Canada if an American or English co-publisher could be found. Jack offered to assist in this matter. First, he wrote to Alan D. Williams at Little, Brown in Boston: "We have read it here and are reserving judgment. It's either very, very good or very, very bad. I'm damned if I know which. It certainly doesn't get anywhere between those two points, and it's certainly not going to be a raging best-seller. It's original, maybe to the point of being unique, and could, in fact, be very, very good. After you read it you will understand why I am so uncertain—or maybe you won't."[46] The American publisher was very dubious: "Your note . . . sounds like a blurb for the Theater of the Absurd or a Sarraute novel. I shall be looking forward apprehensively to receiving [the manuscript]."[47] Jack also tried unsuccessfully to place the novel at Atheneum with Pat Knopf, Alfred's son. No one took the book.

The matter rested again for three more years, at which time Gustafson sent yet another version of the book to Jack. The reader's report was very definite: "unpublishable, and M&S will not be losing a poet by turning back this novel, which I can't imagine any other publisher taking. . . . As a poet he is a consummate craftsman—but as a novelist: ugh!"[48] Gustafson was remarkably good-natured and philosophical when Jack broke the bad news to him: "You have been more than kind and helpful toward my novel. . . . I was deflated by the readers' reports and haven't got up enough courage to read through the novel again—I know I should, in fairness to you, and I know that it needs one revision. I suppose, on the whole, after that reader's 'ugh,' you better ship the thing home to me, alas."[49] The novel has never been published. Gustafson continued to publish poetry with M&S, but

Jack never obtained from him another book of the prestige value of *Double Hook*.

Another poetic novelist whom Jack published was Marie-Claire Blais, whose surrealistic writing did not impress him. She had been reviewed enthusiastically in Quebec, become something of a literary curiosity in France and been given a very mixed reception in English-speaking Canada and in the United States. In November 1960, he told Ned Bradford of Little, Brown, "I have to admit that I found *Mad Shadows* [*La belle bête*] almost as difficult as Pogo [the comic strip character]. What are we going to do with this gal? I guess we would be boneheads not to go along with at least one more book."[50] In the instance of the Quebec author, he resolved to follow the enthusiasm of two editors, Claire Pratt and Conway Turton. He also decided to take the advice in this instance of a publisher he greatly admired:

> We had better give the young Miss Blais more time to prove herself one way or the other [he told G. Wren Howard at Jonathan Cape in London]. I was speaking to Alfred Knopf the other day about this type of problem, and he expressed the view that book publishers would probably be miles ahead in the long run if they were required by law to sign a contract for five novels whenever they take on a bright new author. It's probably a sensible point of view. When you give up on the third book, the fourth one usually turns out to be the best seller on somebody else's list, etc. In any case, our evaluation here is that the new book is a slight improvement over the first one but that it's not likely to be a publishing success.[51]

In all, Jack published six books by Blais either in hardback or, later, in the New Canadian Library and one book about her. In the seventies, when Blais's work sold poorly, he continued his support: "She *is* someone we should continue to publish."[52]

As Jack soon discovered, authors could be demanding and overly critical of all aspects of book publication. A year after the appearance of

*Turvey*, Birney complained bitterly about M&S's inability to sell the book outside Canada—and took on the task himself. On November 14, 1950, Jack, who had learned the poet-novelist had had no luck placing his book with a foreign publisher, wrote him a told-you-so letter: "You have since found out that you have not been able to do much better."[53] Three years later there was a different kind of problem: Birney's new novel (*Down the Long Table*) had serious flaws. "[T]he danger that I see is at the level of the superficial reader—the reader who buys the most books . . . I can visualize the reader being curious about [the protagonist's] position at the end of the book but not really giving a damn. Could you not warm him up so that the reader feels an identification with him?. . . Now write and tell me I have missed the whole point."[54] According to Birney, Jack had indeed missed the point.

In 1955, further commissioned reports on the book were decidedly unfavourable, placing Jack in a ticklish position: "Our best readers feel that the book is not right and that its publication might seriously damage your reputation. . . . [There are various options.] (1) We could publish as it stands. We are opposed to this but would do so if you feel sure enough. (2) The script could be set aside for a period with a view to your re-examining it some months from now. (3) You could give the manuscript a major overhaul. . . . (4) Substantial but not fundamental changes could be made. . . . We are aware, Earle, of the time, thought and serious effort that you have put into the writing of this novel. It is a thoughtful piece of work, tremendously complex in every aspect."[55]

Birney was not inclined to make major changes. The typescript was eventually improved to their mutual satisfaction, although no one at M&S expected it to sell as well as *Turvey*, and indeed it did not. A year later, Birney was thinking of another novel, "an educated nymphomaniacal *Turvey*—the comedies of screwing."[56] His publisher wanted a more conservative book: a *Turvey*-like satirical look at the life of an undergraduate. Neither book was written.

In October 1956, Jack had become outraged at being accused of unfair business practices by Birney: "It may be that I am a particularly touchy individual, but if I added up all the times in the past that you have suggested or implied that we are dishonest, it would come to quite a few. Perhaps you have a peculiar sense of humour that doesn't always get through to me, or perhaps you fancy yourself as a sharp business-man who has to be on constant guard against the possibility of being shortchanged by an Eastern publisher, but whatever the motivation, I can tell you frankly that a little of it goes a long way, as far as I am con-cerned."[57] When Birney replied, with some justification, that Jack was overreacting to mild jibes, Jack admitted he had written the letter in a foul mood.

Two years later, in the autumn of 1958, Jack was flummoxed by an interview the poet-novelist gave to an English trade journal in which he excoriated Canadian publishers, who were accused of taking excessively high "rake-offs" for their products as opposed to a supposedly more beneficent system in England. He wrote to Birney, "You son of a bitch, I would be far more inclined to agree to give books away on your behalf if you wouldn't involve yourself in such vicious and incredibly stupid interviews as the one that appeared in *Smith's Trade Journal.* I would like to think that you were misquoted, but I am sure that you weren't, and I think you must have taken leave of your senses. What the hell have you got against Canadian publishers? I presume you realize that when you make statements like this, most people construe it as an attack on your own publisher as well as the rest of the people who are trying to do a job in this country. . . . As usual, however, I forgive you." The for-giveness was real, but so was the tension.

Throughout, Hugh Kane constantly had to nudge Jack in the direction of financial caution, making their relationship strained at times. As a publisher, Jack was forced to pursue a numbers game, something as scientific as "backing horses at Woodbine [racetrack] on a sunny after-noon. One can study all the form charts and records, one can consult all sorts of experts, one can acquire years of experience, but in the final analysis it boils down to a question of chance. If you guess correctly more often than not, you are a successful publisher. If you don't, the books that pile up in your warehouse will be as much use to you as the torn parimutuel tickets that litter the racetracks."[59]

Over the years, Jack wrote many memorable letters. An early glimpse of his ability at a comic turn can be seen in a missive he wrote to his mother in June 1954 about his journey to England on the *Queen Elizabeth*. On a previous crossing, he had admitted to being a publisher and had been subjected to four excruciating manuscripts from his fellow passengers. He learned his lesson, or so he thought. On his next voyage, since his new shoes were painfully tight, they were on his mind. Accordingly, when he was asked what he did for a living, he said he was in the shoe business. His table companions were delighted, one of them being a shoe manufacturer. He was asked what his firm was called, and Bata was the only name that came to mind. The industrialist seated with Jack was a close friend of the Canadian shoe magnate, so Jack soon owned up to his lie.

A bit later on this trip, Jack became friends with Mrs. Hague, a gangster's wife, and her daughter, who both insisted on calling him "Baby Doll." One evening, Mrs. Hague gave a "broad hint" that she would like to dance with him.

> I dutifully led her ponderous bulk out on to the floor. The purser, a too cheerful SOB, chose this moment to announce a balloon dance. Migawd! They lowered balloons from the ceiling and we danced, balancing balloons between our foreheads. The next step was to do the same thing without our hands. Finally, the deal was to put the balloon between your backs and when the music stopped the first couple to burst their balloon won a bottle of champagne. We were the only couple that couldn't burst our balloon. My companion had such a magnificent behind that the balloon fitted into the small of her back and I couldn't exert pressure on it. Fortunately, we were travelling east, and as they kept putting the clocks forward the evening soon ended.[60]

Jack claimed his original account, on the Dictaphone he had installed in his cabin, of his tale of life aboard the ocean liner had been ruined. In that version, "I became a P. G. Wodehouse, A. P. Herbert and S. J. Perelman rolled into one.... Perhaps it was sabotage, perhaps it was the proximity of the engine room or possibly it was merely fate, but the transcription [of my own words] could not be deciphered. It sounds rather like someone with a high falsetto reading James Joyce and tap dancing at the same time."[61]

Three years later, in 1957, Jack had one of the most satisfying but terrifying encounters of his life. As the Canadian publisher of Winston Churchill's *History of the English-Speaking Peoples*, he was invited to lunch at Sir Winston's London home. Jack was so nervous about arriving exactly on time that he had his taxi circle the block several times so he could arrive on the dot. The former prime minister, looking "absolutely beautiful, like someone who'd just been embalmed," greeted him with great cordiality and Jack, who remained on his "best behaviour," was, after sherry, the meal and a good cigar, dropped off at his hotel by Churchill on his way to Parliament. When the Rolls-Royce pulled up in front of his hotel, Jack felt more important than he ever had in his life.[62]

Jack also attempted to perpetrate a sly scam on his world-famous author, as he confessed years afterward to the novelist Ernest Buckler: "He used to reply to all my letters in a very brief, cordial and punctilious fashion. We published his *History of the English-Speaking Peoples*, and once I found he would reply every time his Canadian publisher wrote, I used to invent all sorts of inane excuses to write him (having calculated that his signatures would be worth a vast sum of money one day). I sent him all sorts of useless reports on the progress of his book. He inevitably replied. Through a sense of duty perhaps, but more because I think he was fascinated by publishing. I compiled a vast file of his letters, but nothing turned out properly in the end because the file was either lost or stolen, which is the way it should have been."[63]

There were more mundane but more personally satisfying encounters and journeys. From the mid-fifties, the McClelland family vacationed every summer in northern Ontario on an island near Temagami owned by Marian Matchett, Elizabeth's mother. Elizabeth and her four daughters, Suzanne, Carol, Sarah and Anne would be there for weeks at a time, and Jack would make the long drive most Friday evenings after work. Once or twice he even arrived by seaplane. A young teenager, Tony Hawke, who later worked at M&S, was employed by Mrs. Matchett for three or four summers to look after her cottage, the various cabins and the boathouse on the island. He remembers Jack's arriving in the middle of the night or descending from the plane. In those days, Jack's hair was "flaming" blond and he used a cigarette holder. To the young man, Jack was a miraculous figure, the epitome of male glamour. He played bridge, charmed his mother-in-law, who was very much "old school," and was extremely attentive to his wife and daughters. There was, Tony recalls, an old-fashioned gentlemanliness about Jack, a quality not always seen by his colleagues in the publishing world.

The professional conflict for Jack McClelland was always between his intuitive understanding of writers and his desire to make a business out of that very same understanding. He became too close to his authors, too apt to make decisions not in his best financial interests. His closest friends were writers; he voiced enthusiasm about the books he was publishing at social events; he would talk about politics at dinner, but he was happiest talking shop about his new finds, his publicity gestures and his desire to publish truly Canadian books. This side of him is obvious in one pronouncement in a speech: "As a book publisher, I speak to you from a position of prejudice. I could urge you to read books simply to try to enlarge the market for my own publications. This I would never do. I urge you to read books because I know what a book can do for people. I can say to you with all the sincerity and conviction at my command that almost always where I have found a truly successful man or woman, I have found a reader of books."[64]

But by 1956 when he had been a publisher for a decade, Jack had become intimately aware of all the hazards of his job. Almost by definition, a publisher was for him a jack-of-all-trades, but in the eyes of many perhaps a master of none: "To the man-in-the-street you are a profiteer because your mark-ups are too high; to the bookseller and librarian you are inefficient because you never have stock of the particular titles that they want; you have been underbuying occasionally as some of your agency connections are shaky; you have been overbuying occasionally to offset this and your bank relations have deteriorated; to your staff you are a Simon Legree for you demand much and pay little; to your wife you are an idiot for you work long hours and don't make much money."[65]

# 4

## THE BOY PUBLISHER

## (1959-60)

AT THE RIPE OLD AGE of thirty-seven in 1959, Jack was very young-looking for his age, his light blond hair adding to this impression. Some days, he would be clad in loud, closely tapered, tweed sports coats accompanied by equally brightly coloured cravats, as if he had just stepped out of a Jaguar commercial. He resembled an English aristocrat who just happened to have dropped into the office for an hour or two. But the days at the office were long, sometimes tedious, always demanding. He pushed himself constantly, attending to authors, reading manuscripts, worrying about sales figures, firing off memos and directives. The combination of appearance, vitality and drive led to the nickname "boy publisher." He might still have looked like a tyro, but he was an experienced and driven man. Jack assumed the title of president of M&S only in 1960.

Shortly after George Stewart's death in 1955, Jack acquired from Stewart's widow the founding partner's 49 per cent of the M&S shares for $65,000. He did this in an unorthodox way: Hugh Kane and Mark Savage agreed to take less than normal salaries in future years against their future minority ownership of the company through the Stewart shares, in the proportions of 24 per cent to Kane and 19 percent to Savage, these being purchased on their behalf by Jack.[1]

William Arthur Deacon, the literary editor of *The Globe and Mail*, confided to a friend, "Offhand, I'd guess Young Jack is shrewder than his father, better equipped to be a publisher, and I shouldn't wonder that he will pull things together nicely. . . . There is at least this—right or wrong, he's trying to be a publisher. He is, further, a believer in Canadian books."[2]

Jack's role models included two Americans, Bennett Cerf at Random House and Alfred Knopf. Cerf had enormous charm, but he was assiduous in maintaining the bottom line of profitability. He would pay a large advance for a book only if he was certain he was going to get every penny back. He was also one of the first publishers to insist that publicity was the key to successful sales. A brilliant huckster, he discarded the image of the publisher as the reclusive resident of an ivory tower. Once he interviewed Gertrude Stein on NBC radio, a coast-to-coast broadcast: "This is going to be your chance to explain to the American public what you mean by those writings of yours," he began. "I'm very proud to be your publisher, Miss Stein, but as I've always told you, I don't understand very much of what you're saying." She replied promptly: "Well, I've always told you, Bennett, you're a very nice boy but you're rather stupid."[3] Cerf may have been taken aback, but he was delighted to have such interesting sparks flying. Although Jack was not fond of Cerf the man, he admired him. "I didn't like his attitudes, but I certainly have to respect his promotional genius, and picked up a lot of tricks from him."[4]

Jack's adoration of Knopf was boundless. After all, he was a man who did what many thought was impossible: he made a fortune publishing. He was someone to emulate. Jack never really got over his amazement at Knopf's "style": his chauffeur-driven Rolls-Royce, his estate at Purchase, New York. Later Jack would say, "Why he was so nice to me I've never really understood."[5] The bond is not that difficult to explain: Knopf understood that Jack was attempting to import his style of publishing into the Canadian marketplace: high-end books, high-end profits. He once told Jack that a secret to a book's success could often be found in the letter that accompanied a manuscript: "If they can't write a good letter, how can they write a good book?"[6]

Bennett Cerf commented on the differences between himself and Knopf when he recalled, "The books that Alfred is most ashamed of [having published] are the ones that have made him the most money! At one time he had on his list both Irving Wallace and Harold Robbins, two of the great sellers of today. He says in all sincerity, 'Two of the things that I'm happiest about is that I'm rid of those two hacks. The stuff they're writing now I wouldn't publish.'"[7]

Another Manhattan figure with whom Jack shared a similar approach to his profession was William Shawn, the editor of *The New Yorker*. Shawn believed steadfastly that he published writers, not articles and stories. Once, the renowned broadcaster Peter Gzowski, in hopes of being the famous magazine's Canadian correspondent, prepared a lengthy piece, which he sent to Shawn, who rejected the piece but sent the startled young journalist a cheque for one thousand dollars. Another figure in Jack's pantheon of publishers was James Laughlin of New Directions. Laughlin, a fierce promoter of serious, experimental American poets like Ezra Pound and William Carlos Williams, relished the challenge of marketing such writers. When Laughlin visited Toronto, Jack took him around the city and to the Toronto Islands. In a remarkably similar way to the American, Jack wanted to present serious poets and prose writers to the Canadian reading public.

Like Knopf, Jack had decided ideas about quality; like Shawn, the author came first; like Cerf, Jack had a knack for publicity; like Laughlin, he welcomed the opportunity of taking on writers whose work was difficult to sell. One early promotional effort on behalf of Canadian literature almost backfired. In April 1959 Jack orchestrated the Meet the Authors Dinner in the grand ballroom of Toronto's Royal York Hotel. Sixty-nine authors were the main attraction. They included not only Morley Callaghan, Hugh MacLennan, E. J. Pratt and Pierre Berton but also Kate Aitken, a leading woman broadcaster (*Making a Living Is Fun*) and the sports broadcaster Ron McAllister. Max Ferguson did a skit and John Drainie his legendary imitation of Stephen Leacock, who had died in 1944.

The purpose of this grand assembly was to raise money to repair the porch at Leacock's house in Orillia, which was being turned into a museum. The audience was a good one: 650 people at $10 a ticket. Everything would have turned out satisfactorily but for the authors, who were to be introduced by Drainie one by one under a spotlight as they entered the ballroom. Unfortunately some of the writers had imbibed far too much, grew impatient as they waited for their moments of glory and stumbled in randomly. According to one source, a trucu-lent Hugh Garner took matters into his own hands and marched into the room, the others falling in behind him in the wrong order. Drainie did not realize what was happening, so chaos reigned—for example, Mazo de la Roche was introduced as Pierre Berton. Sometimes, as Jack was to find to his considerable cost, Canadian authors simply did not appreciate what was being done to promote them. William Arthur Deacon nonetheless judged the event a great success: "No such demon-stration of literary strength has ever happened" before.[8]

*The Telegram*, one of the event's sponsors, noted that most Canadi-ans were scared of "getting mixed up with a bunch of intellectuals who sit on the floor and discuss Freud." They should "smarten up." Ten years earlier, the Massey–Lévesque Commission on National Development in the Arts, Letters and Sciences had begun its work; on June 1, 1951, this Royal Commission, the most exhaustive examination of the state of cul-ture and the mass media ever undertaken in Canada, made its report public. Although the document in part mourned a rural, somewhat am-ateur, distinctly community-oriented culture that was passing away, it also looked forward to what Canada was becoming: urban, professional and multinational. The challenges of the future had to be met.

In the short term, the work of the commission led to the establish-ment of the National Library (1953) and the Canada Council (1957). Before the Second World War, the Canadian Broadcasting Corporation had been founded in 1936. In some ways the report's recommendations helped fit two significant pieces into the puzzle, even though the com-missioners warned that American newspapers, books and magazines threatened the existence of their Canadian counterparts. In 1957, the

Royal Commission on Broadcasting reemphasized the role of the CBC in maintaining Canadian identity, as did the 1961 Commission on Publications, centred on the magazine industry. For Jack McClelland, all these reports *seemed* to be harbingers of a future he was attempting to help engineer in the book industry. Meanwhile, he was acquiring authors at a rapid pace.

Some authors proved outlandishly difficult to deal with, although Jack was quite willing to push them in the direction of outlandishness in their writings. Irving Layton was famous for being crude well before he came to Jack's attention. In 1943, the broadcaster and critic Patrick Waddington wrote this fierce denunciation of the Montreal-based poet: "The extension of emotion which is permissible in the third person is not in the first; it is too close to us. It is like a man pushing his face into yours when he talks to you. Involuntarily you turn your face aside. But Mr. Layton gives us no relief. Alas, like an old farceur, an unnatural exposer of himself, he has not learned the dignity of privacy, the strength of restraint. He neither laughs at nor condemns himself, nor is impartial, but loves, pities, caresses and admires that person whom he shows us."[9]

Waddington's attack was a familiar refrain to Layton, even in his early thirties. Born in Romania in 1912, he had immigrated to Canada, settling in Montreal with his parents, Moishe and Keine, when he was one year old. The family's flight from their homeland was prompted by the increasingly anti-Semitic violence in their native land. In Canada the family was often on the edge of destitution. Whether he wanted to admit it or not, poverty left a dark mark

*Leonard Cohen and Irving Layton*

on the soul of Irving Layton, whose first home in Canada was the four-room downstairs flat of a little unpainted shack on the east side of Montreal's St. Elizabeth Street.

His real name was Israel Lazarovitch; Irving Layton, loosely based on the original name, was, like so much about the man, a reinvention of the self or—perhaps more accurately—an exploitation of the self in pursuit of fame, literary and otherwise. Like Byron, another great romantic poet, Layton was a skilled boxer. A relentless self-promoter, he eventually found in Jack McClelland a publisher very much after his own heart.

After Baron Byng High School, Layton attended Macdonald College, where he earned a B.Sc. in agriculture. His real interest, however, was in debating politics from a Communist perspective, which made him realize just how different he was from most of his fellow students: "There they all were, all healthy-looking English philistines, red cheeked, blue eyed, with not a thought in their heads, and here was myself, eager, enthusiastic, concerned about the affairs of the world, the rise of Nazism, the unemployment situation, and in no time I got myself involved in an argument. . . . I was met with incomprehensible stares. After a while I could see that they regarded me as some sort of queer animal who had somehow or other been let in by some grotesque mistake."[10] Layton was also an outsider in his own family, Keine having absolutely no comprehension of or sympathy with her son's desire to get an education and, later, to become a writer.

As child and man, Layton—sensual, magnetically handsome, out-spoken—did his best to live up to his reputation as a firebrand. A deeply learned man with enormous curiosity, he is also relentlessly self-centred, writing about himself—his emotions, his obsessions, his adventures, his penis—in an aggressive yet profoundly moving way, as no other Canadian has ever done. In 1951, Earle Birney, who should have been able to identify with many aspects of Layton's excesses, attacked him: "He's rough and tough with language, spits audibly in the sink, slaps buttocks with a sombre zest, and retires early to the delights of the bedroom. He can unfortunately be bad-tempered, egotistic, childishly crude and sentimental."[11]

In "Whom I Write For" (1963), Layton proclaimed his purpose in writing poetry:

> When reading me, I want you to feel
> as if I had ripped your skin off;
> Or gouged out your eyes with my fingers;
> Or scalped you.[12]

Layton has created his own myth as the energetic virile lover, but at the same time he often shows his antipathy to women, almost as if he is angry at them for his dependence on them for sexual gratification. The link between sex and death forcefully proclaimed in Layton's poetry also sets him apart from most of his contemporaries. He remains the most unpredictable and vigorous of Canadian poets.

Layton was decidedly not, like Birney, an academic poet. In fact his verse is in many ways un-Canadian, having much more in common with the American tradition, especially as espoused by Walt Whitman in the "Song of Myself" section of *Leaves of Grass*. Well into the 1940s, English poetry in Canada was, according to one of Layton's supporters, "colonial because it is the product of a cultured English group who are out of touch with people who long ago began adjusting themselves to life on this continent."[13] The enthusiasm for Layton's writing by American poets such as Robert Creeley propelled the Canadian to prominence in his own country.

Layton was published by a variety of presses, including the poet Raymond Souster's Contact Press, until the mid-fifties. Irving came to Jack's attention when the Ryerson Press (by then affiliated with the United Church) agreed to order from the originating U.S. publisher, and publish under their own imprint, two hundred copies of the poet's collection *The Improved Binoculars*. Unfortunately, Lorne Pierce decided that the texts of two of the poems would give his publication committee problems—"De Bullion Street" described churches as "haemorrhoids upon the city's anus" and "The Poetic Process" spoke of the blood and "balls" of Christ. Pierce was pleasant but firm: "Erotic poetry forms an important part of the great tradition, but I dislike this focus on the genitals, say, moist with dancing, and such. You achieve the artistic expression of such experience quite splendidly very often by implication and suggestion and veiled metaphor, and are best when you avoid this latrine cartoon business."[14] Layton offered to make changes, but the die was cast. Ryerson did not publish this collection. Jack McClelland, who wanted to find a way to promote poetry, became intrigued by the radical new direction Layton was taking, one very much in opposition to M&S's now staid Indian File series.

McClelland and Layton had no illusions about each other. In January 1957, the interested publisher told the poet, "We are guilty of all sorts of sins around this place [M&S]; to the best of my knowledge one of them isn't censorship." If Layton was interested in avoiding that, Jack advised him to get in touch: *The Improved Binoculars* "sounds . . . like a book that we would have enjoyed publishing. I am sorry that we didn't have a look at it." That volume was not published in Canada. Soon afterward, Jack became Irving's publisher.

Of course, Layton was a serious writer whose wares could be promoted. In August 1959, at the time M&S published *A Red Carpet for the Sun*—which sold eight thousand copies, an unprecedented record for a book of Canadian poetry—McClelland was in the midst of stage-managing a "gimmick": "We are publishing a novel [Katherine Roy's *Gentle Fraud*] by a Montreal gal on the 26th, and we're going to make it a joint party for the two of you. Unfortunately there is a bit of a clash with quality . . . in that her book is not a literary masterpiece and indeed is not as good as her last novel [*Lise*, 1954]. She is, however, a beautiful gal—fantastically so. As a result, unless you complain too bitterly, our gimmick is that we are calling it 'Beauty and the Beast' (you're the Beauty, of course). I'm sending out invitations with pictures of the two of you."[15] The resulting event—a mix of Katherine Roy's socialite circle and Layton's beatnik gang of beards and black stockings—was an outstanding success.

It was the publisher who encouraged what many felt was the outrageous side of the flamboyant poet when he was selecting poems for an anthology of erotic verse: "I would like to see a little more emphasis on the erotic. I don't think we are justified in including a poem simply because it is erotic, but if there are any good poems that you happen to come across that are basically good but also more erotic than some in the present collection, I for one would welcome them. . . . We're not going to sell the book as a book of sex poems. We're going to sell it as a book of love poems, but the more sex the better."[16]

When Layton did not respond enthusiastically, Jack became even more insistent: "Harold Town and other male readers who have looked at the collection agree with me that we still need a stronger injection of sex if you can find it. . . . There must be some more sexy poetry around."[17] Not to be outdone, Layton baited Jack: "Here's your title! *Love Where the Nights Are Long*. . . . I think it's an even more provocative title than *Love in a Cold Climate*. In heaven's name, use it. If you use your own trashy title, *But Darling, It's Cold Outside*, I'll land with a helicopter on your head and pull out all your teeth one by one. We've got a good book; don't foul it up with gimmicks and with flash, mash and trash. All for the sake of cash!"[18]

Jack's insistence on more eroticism from Layton incensed the poet, who wrote in 1962, "Now you turn around and bleat, 'Layton, I want young love; Layton, think of all the cocks, cunts, campuses and coffee houses of this country; Layton, think of your reputation; think of ours. Go out and drink the reddest wine you can find and regurgitate all the virile, violent and unvirtuous poems you can find'. . . . And so on, and so on, all the raving of a panic-stricken publisher."[19] The apostle of erotic freedom, whose gimmick was obviously sex, was not going to perform on demand. Jack maintained a cautious but sometimes distant friendship with Layton: "I'd rather have my daughters learn the beauties of the English language from Irving than from anyone, but I'm not sure I'd ever leave him in the same room alone with them."[20]

One Canadian writer whose "gimmick" Jack did not want anything to do with was Norman Levine, in his mid-thirties, whose *Canada Made Me* (1958) offended Jack and many others in its examination of the underside of Canadian life. A publisher wishing to promote his country may not be eager to distribute a book that highlights its complacency and mediocrity. (Three years earlier, Jack told Levine, who lived in England, that he had a very imperfect idea of Canadian literature: in an article in *The Times Literary Supplement*, Jack felt that Levine had vastly inflated the talents of Mordecai Richler and Brian Moore; he was also upset that Ethel Wilson was given pride of place over Gabrielle Roy.)

In the spring of 1959 a columnist in the *Victoria Daily Times* accused Jack of "indirect censorship" because, according to the journalist, M&S was not doing an adequate job in promoting Levine's book and making it available on behalf of the American publisher, Putnam. Publicly, Jack had asserted he did not like the book. In his reply to the columnist, he pointed the finger at booksellers, saying if they did not reorder a book when it was sold out, M&S could not do anything about it (after all, M&S had stock of the book on hand). He continued: "There is only one aspect of the situation that could in any way be construed as 'indirect censorship.' I am not enthusiastic about the book personally, nor are any of our editors or any of my associates. The book has some merit because Levine has considerable literary skill, but we did not and do not think that this book warranted publication, at least under our imprint. If this is censorship, we believe in it. [Moreover,] when enthusiasm is lacking, it's bound to have a dampening effect on sales. Again, if this is indirect censorship, I am guilty of it, because I refuse to recommend a book that I don't believe in."[21] Jack was willing to change his mind about an author. Two years later, in 1961, he eagerly acquired the Canadian publishing rights to Levine's collection of short stories, *One-Way Ticket*.

Sometimes there were considerable difficulties in rejecting a manuscript. Once when Jack had refused a volume of poetry, the author—a very beautiful young woman—insisted on an appointment with him to discuss the matter.

> I would probably have agreed to publish her on the spot had it not
> been for the fact that most of our editorial staff of the day had read
> the script and they were uniform in their view that we should not
> publish. In any case, she stormed into my office and proceeded to
> point out to me that her poetry was much better than much of the

poetry we had published in recent years. She was prepared to document this. She had with her a great file of letters from admirers and, in fact, from some reasonably established critic who attested to this view. She was quite forceful about the whole matter. And to say the least I was on the defensive but I pointed out to her what was true at that time—that poetry was inevitably a money-losing proposition for a publisher and that there were frequently considerations beyond the quality of the work that affected the publishing decision. At this point she leaned across the front of my desk with the most tempting display of cleavage and announced that this was no great problem and that she could be at least as cooperative as most. As it happened, this wasn't the sort of consideration I had in mind. A wealthier publisher might have been more receptive.[22]

At about this time, Jack was introduced in an unorthodox way to a writer in whom he would come to have a strong, unqualified belief. In March 1959, an acquaintance wrote him concerning a Vancouver homemaker whose writing might possibly be of some interest.

> I have been hearing a good deal about an unpublished novel [*This Side Jordan*] which is being passed around here in certain circles. The novel concerns the independence issue in Ghana and was written by a Mrs. Margaret Laurence, a Canadian, who was with her husband in Africa for six or eight years.
>
> I have not read the novel myself but others I know have and report that it is good. She has not as yet attempted to have it published, I understand, but I thought that you might be interested.
>
> I write this letter only to keep something reported to be good out of American hands because I have been told that some of her friends are trying to persuade her to send the manuscript to the States or to England first.[23]

Gordon Elliott, a close friend of Margaret's, who had read the book and knew of Jack's search for Canadian writers, was baiting McClelland, whose response was immediate: "I very much appreciate the tip re Mrs. Laurence and I have written to her asking her to let us have a look at the manuscript."

By May 15, Peggy Laurence had at his invitation submitted the manuscript to McClelland, although she was certain he would not take the book. Four months later, he told her he would publish it if he could find an American or English publisher to bring it out simultaneously (and thus make the project financially viable). By the end of November, Macmillan in England had accepted the book. Although Jack was not thrilled by the African subject matter of her first novel, he saw enormous potential.

*Margaret Laurence*

As a first step in helping Margaret Laurence to become a professional writer, he undertook the task of obtaining an agent to act for her. On October 18, 1960, he approached Willis Wing, a New York agent who represented, among others, Brian Moore and Pierre Berton. "I presume you do handle women (don't we all?) even though yours seems to be a predominantly male list." Having insinuated that Wing might be a bit of a chauvinist, Jack told him

I suspect that she could turn into the bread-and-butter type of client. I will give you a brief account of our association with her.... Her name is Margaret Laurence. She is a housewife. I would guess she is in her late thirties. . . . I heard about her through a mutual acquaintance and received a copy of her script hot off the typewriter. We thought it extremely good. She has a somewhat unique style, powerful, virile, vigorous—when I read it I found it hard to believe that the novel had been written by a woman. I'm not suggesting that she is the greatest literary discovery of the last ten years, but she is a serious writer, a writer of quality, and she tells a very good story. . . . She is, Willis, a gal who is serious about her writing and intends to continue.[24]

Wing promptly accepted Peggy as a client. McClelland's acumen always worked overtime. He knew full well that eventually he would have to pay higher advances to an agented author, but he also realized Wing could help him to promote Margaret Laurence and thus provide the kind of broad base necessary to gain her recognition internationally.

McClelland was unaware at first just how ambitious Peggy Laurence was. Having lost both birth parents by the age of nine, she carried within herself the stigma of the orphan. Seeing life from the vantage point of the outcast or outsider gave her considerable power as a writer, and during her five years in Vancouver from 1957 to 1962, she determined to devote her life to writing. Unaware as yet of the high personal cost that she would be forced to pay for her craft, she was nevertheless desperately eager to make her mark.

In November 1960, she met Jack McClelland at a launch party held in Vancouver to celebrate the publication of her first novel. As he told a fellow publisher, Jack was more impressed than he had anticipated: "I have just returned from a trip to Western Canada, during which I had the opportunity to meet Margaret Laurence for the first time. I thought you might like to know that I found her to be a thoroughly charming woman, much younger and much less severe than her pictures make her out to be. She is determined to have a full writing career, will have another novel under way shortly, and I think we can both be confident that we have on our hands a writer who will produce many good books for us in the years to come."[25] Jack's hunch was not simply lucky—it came about from his instinct for talent, a prescience that led him to writers of potential greatness. This was what publishing was all about for Jack: the thrill of the chase, the joy of discovery.

McClelland's enlightened self-interest had extended in another direction, when he sent Peggy in July 1960 the novel *A Candle to Light the Sun*, set on the prairies, by the recently deceased Patricia Blondal. Blondal, Peggy's former classmate at Winnipeg's United College, had

died of breast cancer in 1959. Sending
the novel to Peggy was probably not
felicitous. In all likelihood, Jack was
nudging her toward Canadian subject
matter; however, he may not have realized she had never really liked the
glamorous Blondal when they were
students together. Peggy had in fact
been jealous of her classmate's magnetic sex appeal. Nevertheless, Mc-
Clelland's ploy was to pay enormous
dividends, as can be gleaned in Peggy's
letter to the writer Adele Wiseman,
her close friend, in July 1960:

*Patricia Blondal*

> Jack McC (obviously totally unaware that I had known Pat) asked me
> to read it and said he would like my opinion of it. . . . It would have
> been better to have been cut in places, but even as it stands, it is quite
> an achievement. She attempts such a lot—an overall picture of a small
> prairie town and all its people; an historical picture of the late thirties
> and the war and the post-war years and our generation, a wonderfully
> complex analysis and picture of a man's search for his own identity
> and meaning. . . . Am I being influenced too much by her death?. . .
> I think her novel is really one of the best things on a prairie town that
> I've ever read, and it is much more as well. . . . If she had lived to work
> more on it, it would have been truly excellent, but even as it stands it
> is a remarkable job. I wish I could have told her so.[26]

Three months later, Peggy was working up the courage to begin a
new novel. In her mind's eye, it was "planned in rough, but what I fear
more than anything else is that the theme will be too explicit and will
overshadow the characters."[27] Three months after that, she was able to
focus in a much more precise way on her new project, the book that
became *The Stone Angel*:

Right now I think I'd like to come back home [in terms of subject matter]. This, of course, coincides with my own state of mind. I feel I'm here to stay, for better or worse, and that I don't need to go away any more, in fact can't go away. It's here, and in me, and I can't run forever to countries (real or imaginary) which I like because they didn't know me when I was young. If that makes any sense to you. I hated being here, for several years, you know. But now, for the first time, I feel the urge to write about the only people I can possibly know about from the inside.

I don't want to write a "Canadian novel." It's just that I feel I might at last be able to look at people here without blinking. Having hated my own country most of my life, I am now beginning to see why. It's the mirror in which one's own face appears, and like Queen Elizabeth I, you smash the mirrors but that doesn't change yourself after all. Very strange. I am glad I did not write anything out in this country before, because it would have been done untruthfully, with bitterness, but perhaps not any more.

Realizing she was contemplating a completely new step, she relinquished her African writings and expectantly looked forward to what the future might bring: the past was "over, and I have a strange sense of release and relief."[28]

She felt transformed, led towards a new, heightened sense of identity, one that can be clearly seen in the postscript of her letter to Adele of January 22, 1961: "I've changed my name to Margaret . . . it was Peggy I hated, so I have killed her off." In parentheses, she added wistfully, "I hope."[29] Jack McClelland had been the catalyst pushing her in the direction of Canadian subject matter. Intuition hardly ever gets better than this. In large part, Jack nudged because he had lost Patricia Blondal, the woman writer whom he felt at that time had even greater potential than Laurence.

Patricia Blondal had been decidedly peremptory when she approached Jack.

Sometime in [1959] I received a phone call from Winnipeg.[30] The caller was a woman by the name of Patricia Blondal. The message was clear: "I sent a manuscript to your company almost a month ago and I have heard nothing. I'm arriving in Toronto tomorrow morning and if you don't want to publish it and have not made a decision by then, I'll withdraw it and submit it to Macmillan. . . ."[31] It was after-hours, and I decided to look around and see if I could find the manuscript. I finally located it in a pile of [mainly] unread material. At about eight o'clock my wife called and asked why I wasn't home for dinner. "I'm really sorry, dear," I apologized, "but I'm reading a manuscript. I have to finish it, and I won't be home for dinner." I arrived home about three in the morning. I found Patricia Blondal's novel, *A Candle to Light the Sun*, powerful and gripping. It was the first gutsy, tough Canadian novel I had read.

Pat Blondal called from the airport, and we arranged to meet at noon for lunch at the Royal York Hotel. We were still in the Imperial Room at five-thirty that afternoon. She was articulate, intelligent and strikingly beautiful, and I was stunned by the woman. Later I learned that she had been the campus beauty queen, envied by many of her classmates. She also happened to be the top student. I decided to publish *A Candle to Light the Sun* at the earliest possible date. I offered to marry her too, if that was a requirement, but I pointed out that I would have to get permission from my wife.[32]

Jack's unilateral decision did not sit well with Hugh Kane, who reminded his boss of some decisions reached with Claire Pratt, the senior editor:

Claire tells me we have accepted this manuscript for publication, which surprised me since we had agreed one night not too long ago that such decisions would be made only after discussion. I suppose circumstances made an immediate decision necessary, although I can't imagine what they might be. I honestly don't know what we're going to do with this now that we're committed. The gal can write, there's no question of that—and she has an interesting future—but this novel, *in my opinion*, needs about eighteen months of [extensive editing] and a complete capitulation on the part of the author, if we're not to lose our shirts. There is a certain amount of excellent writing in it and a great deal of very bad writing. It is careless and incoherent and far too long [discusses problems with plot] . . . Did you notice some almost inexplicable blank spots in her background? Like the complete inability to sort out her personal pronouns. This sort of weakness is really remarkable when you consider her other gifts.[33]

Realizing that Hugh had raised some excellent points, Jack was contrite:

You are correct in assuming that circumstances forced me to make a decision without consultation. You—and in fact Claire (who had read and liked the ms although I didn't know this)—were away. I am by no means sure I won't live to regret the decision, but I had to move one way or the other. We haven't bought the book—we have made a contingent offer for it that has not been accepted. A rather complicated situation exists, but I expect we will get it. My view is that she is easily the best novelist that has come to my attention in Canada in years. She has the vigour, the power and the flow and the eye for significant detail that has been one of the prime lacks in Canadian writing to date. I also think her appeal is a commercial one, although that's only a guess. As to this novel, I would agree at once that it could be improved markedly. . . . Our chances of inducing her to substantial revision are, I regret to say, nil. She is a very dedicated, serious, knowledgeable gal who is convinced that she has written a good book. She will probably revise herself when she reads it again. Amazing though it may seem, she wrote and typed this herself in three months, despite having several [two] children and a few complexes.[34]

Hugh Kane was well aware that the reader's report, completed before the author's phone call to Jack, was lukewarm: "It is much too long. It is doubtful that it would be popular. In spite of this, there is something interesting about it, and is an effort worth consideration."[35] What McClelland did not know when Patricia Blondal phoned him was that this woman, who seemed so alive, had written *A Candle* at top speed within three months because she knew her life was soon to end. She wanted to be sure her book was placed. When he subsequently saw Blondal in Montreal, Jack noticed how obsessed she was with a desire to write, a desire so intense that she seemed out of control. He had been puzzled by a remark she had made at a party: "I'll be dead within a year."

There were, indeed, special "circumstances" and "complexes" of a very poignant kind. On November 6, 1959, Jack received a telegram from Hollywood: JERRY WALD TWENTIETH CENTURY FOX WANTS TO READ A CANDLE TO LIGHT THE SUN. This telegram crossed with another from Montreal: PATRICIA BLONDAL DIED TODAY IN ROSS MEMORIAL HOSPITAL.

Jack was haunted by that death. At a dinner in honour of Irving Layton, Blondal had felt "compelled to talk about the re-emergence of her cancer. 'For God's sake, Pat,' I pleaded, 'we're here tonight to honour Irving Layton. I really don't want to hear about cancer.' She survived for less than two months after that party. I'll carry the mark of that insensitivity to the grave."[36] As Hugh had observed, *A Candle* required a great deal of revision, which was undertaken by the Toronto writer and translator Joyce Marshall, who became so "absorbed in the thing that I actually dreamed one night that I met Patricia Blondal."[37]

In addition to adding new writers to his ever-increasing stable, Jack had to worry about the existing ones. Publicity remained a bugaboo, especially with major writers who did not appreciate or cultivate it. Farley Mowat was a special case in point when *The Grey Seas Under* appeared in 1958; Jack told the publicist responsible for Farley,

The party can be much less ambitious than the one for Pierre. I think we can justify this on the grounds that we will get more mileage out of Farley because of his nature, at a small, less formal group. . . . [P]erhaps so that there can be no possibility of misunderstanding, I'd better spell out this business of economy again. I don't want to be misunderstood on this. Mowat is at least as important to us as Berton and has to be treated as such. We know, however, that he doesn't react well to the same sort of things as Pierre. He's much less formal and he despises expensive, showy places, etc. For this reason we don't want to waste money unnecessarily. . . . Keep Mowat as busy as possible. If he's allowed to sit around he'll drink and get depressed.[38]

Although Jack did not publish *The Boat Who Wouldn't Float* until 1969, the friendship between Farley and Jack had grown to such an extent that by the summer of 1960 they had purchased *Happy Adventure*, a schooner, with the ambition of refitting it and putting out to sea. In part *The Boat*, the story of *Happy Adventure*, is a tribute to Jack, a man temperamentally very different from Farley.

There is, however, a marked discrepancy between Farley's account of their ensuing travails and Jack's. The publisher's first appearance in a small, remote fishing village in Newfoundland has been comically told by Farley in a tribute to Jack:

Jack McClelland's magnificent elan even in dire adversity is legendary. How well do I remember his arrival . . . to join me and the little schooner we had bought to make a voyage around the world.

True to form Jack arrived at Muddy Hole in a huge, red Buick convertible, the like of which had never before been seen in Newfoundland. The fish plant had just let out and scores of workers were pouring out of the building. They were transfixed by the raucous blare of the Buick's horn. Looking up in astonishment, they beheld a mass of gleaming chrome posed on the lip of the steep, rocky slope behind the plant. A hundred arms began to wave, and as many voices were raised in a great shout.

Jack, serene behind the wheel, was delighted. He thought the admiring villagers were welcoming him. He did not realize there was no road beyond the point that he had reached; and that the fisher-folk were frantically trying to warn him of that salient fact.

Jack started down; realized that all was not well and tramped on the brakes. Too late. The red behemoth lunged down the slope leaping and bounding like an insane hippopotamus. The trunk flew open and Jack's modest assortment of sea going clothing, contained in five pigskin cases, was flung high into the air.

Then it was over. The car stood still, its shiny face buried in a sheep shed. Before anyone could run to the rescue Jack emerged in a pungent dust cloud. He had lost nothing of his fabled cool. With a casual wave at the stunned onlookers he strode blithely down the remainder of the slope toward our tattered little vessel—as noncha-lantly as if about to board the Royal Yacht at Cowes.

That's Jack McClelland as I knew him.

The legend lives![39]

Jack's more prosaic account in a letter to Elizabeth is perhaps a trifle more accurate as to details:

I left about 3 p.m. for where the boat is located, still with the rented car which by now was packed full of gear of every description. The drive is about sixty miles over very rocky, hilly dirt road. You pass through some of the most majestic scenery one would find anywhere. . . . It was a beautiful drive on a lovely sunny day. The dust was incredible and I wouldn't have wanted to drive my own car here. . . . I followed direc-tions and found myself driving up the face of a precipitous cliff on one of the worst roads I have ever seen in my life. When I got to the top I found the road led to a sheep pasture of sorts. Obviously, I had taken the wrong fork, so I turned around and went back down. All this was a good start for me here—I found out later the road had been con-demned. However, I got down safely—losing, I think, the bottom out of the car and could see our little vessel. . . . I parked the car and got to the ship by walking about two hundred yards through dead codfish, sheep dung, tin cans, flotsam and jetsam of every description.[40]

In 1961, Farley jokingly threatened he would write *The Boat Who Wouldn't Float*: "You're a stupid old bastard at best, but thank the Old Gods for you." That book would be "part repayment for your forbearance, understanding and damned practical aid."[41] Farley's portrait of Jack is a splendid one, especially the bossy side of his personality. Not realizing that it is not possible to organize the insurmountably chaotic, the publisher tries to give orders to Obie, Enos and a host of would-be "helpers": "Jack proceeded to take charge. He concluded that our major problem was our lack of organization and the first thing he did was hold a conference in Enos's kitchen. . . . In his best boardroom manner Jack explained that we had been wasting too much time. The almost daily trips to St. John's were not necessary, he said. Instead, we would make up a detailed list of every item of gear and equipment needed to complete the boat, then he and I would go to the city and in one day of intensive shopping would obtain everything we required.

"Upon our return, the four of us, working to a carefully scheduled list of priorities, would pitch in and complete the vessel in a hurry."[42] Of course everything goes wrong. Later a very disillusioned Jack abandons the project. When *The Boat* came out, the publisher, although delighted by the book's spectacular success, was sure he had been made into a fool by his friend. Years later, when he reread the book, some of the "scenes from *The Boat* [still strike] me as hilarious even though I had forgotten what a complete ass he made me out to be."[43] Leaving aside the book's wonderful, comic exaggerations, Jack's involvement with the boat can be seen as a metaphor for his life at M&S. He thought the book world could be brought to order, organized in a logical fashion, and that financial success would follow. He could not have been more wrong— like *Happy Adventure*, M&S was always springing leaks.

Another of Jack's closest friends in the fifties was an artist, not a writer, although Harold Town would illustrate various M&S books and help write *Tom Thomson: The Silence and the Storm* (1977). The two, who shared a similar off-the-wall sense of humour, would carouse in Toronto together. One friend, Beverley Slopen, recalled that the closest she ever saw Jack come to a lovers' quarrel was with Town: "There was a time when they weren't speaking to each other, and Jack would say things like, 'It's Christmas Eve, and I'm going to collect all his bloody paintings, hire a truck, and have them delivered on his doorstep.'"[44]

*Harold Town*

Despite the bickering, the relationship worked exceedingly well—very much like Jack's with Farley, probably because their very different temperaments were similar in their acute, high-strung responses to the world, sensitivities that they often did their level best to conceal. They both had very salty mouths; for them, swearing was not only a fine art but also a form of competition.

The often overwound Harold Town did not suffer any kind of intervention lightly; when one editor attempted to make some slight adjustments, a concerned Jack offered to take the brunt of the artist's fiery temper. Once Jack, who admired Harold's writing, informed him, "If you didn't spend all your time drawing those funny pictures, you would almost certainly [have] become one of the great literary figures of contemporary times."[45]

In 1957, Jack had been fortunate to secure the many talents of (Mildred) Claire Pratt, the only child of the famous poet E. J. Pratt. Educated at Victoria College in the University of Toronto, Columbia University and the Boston Museum of Fine Arts School (she had many one-woman shows of her woodcuts), she owned and managed the Claire Pratt Book Service from 1946 to 1950. Before joining M&S, she had been an editor at Harvard University Press in Cambridge, Massachusetts, from 1950 to 1957. A charming, quiet and laid-back woman, she suffered from osteomyelitis and had to husband her energy carefully. At home she and her mother looked after her father, the frail poet, who died at the age of eighty-two in 1964, the year she left M&S.

At the office, Pratt was a dedicated and meticulous editor, but she refused to take work home with her, leaving M&S every day at four o'clock, the official closing time. In hiring her, Jack acquired an exceptional editor with contacts in the book world. "Hard work and happy times" was how she characterized her job, although she "worked like a slave." Once she jokingly offered her post to a friend who was fed up with her own job; the offer was promptly refused: "No, thank you, I'd rather languish in prison than die on the battle front."[46] Pratt's days at M&S were hectic: "press conferences, editorial discussion, meetings with authors, indexing . . . daily the manuscripts were piled high."[47] In her refined and understated way, she once observed, "Life at the office was like labouring in a whirlwind."[48]

A masterful, genteel politician and the embodiment of elegance, Ruth Taylor, who first came to M&S in 1960 as Claire's assistant, became Jack's executive assistant from 1961 until she left in 1964. One of her tasks was to look after the "slush pile" of unsolicited manuscripts, where she came across Marie Martin's *Samoan Interlude* (1961), her big "find." When she worked for Jack, Taylor had to be ready at a moment's notice to represent him. She also worked long hours. One year, just before Good Friday, he seriously inquired, "Well, do you have all your reading ready for the weekend?"

Jack appointed Taylor his assistant because she wrote excellent, extremely tactful but firm rejection letters. She quickly learned to accept praise and blame as a regular part of her duties. Soon after joining the firm, Jack asked her to write jacket copy for Laura Berton's *I Married the Klondike* (1961); he was overjoyed—at long last, he had found someone adept at this difficult job. Soon thereafter, when she wrote—she thought just as effectively—copy for a Mowat book, Jack pronounced it incredibly bad. No offence was intended and none was taken: everyone at

M&S worked as a team—Jack being the notable exception—under their young publisher's magnetic, dazzling leadership. Work was fun; there was never time for hurt feelings. Once Taylor spent her entire working time for three weeks attending to the author (and later, the politician) Simma Holt, who was put up at the Four Seasons Hotel by Jack in order to get *Terror in the Name of God: The Story of the Sons of Freedom Doukhobors* (1964) into publishable shape.

In 1961, Diane Mew, who was at M&S until 1968, became a member of the editorial division; she had immigrated to Canada from England, where she had previously worked at Methuen. In the mid-sixties, Pratt and Mew nominally worked for Jim Totton, the editor-in-chief. A sometimes difficult and pernickety former schoolteacher who had joined M&S in 1951, he did not get along with Jack. Gradually he was given less and less responsibility for trade books and was shunted off into educational publishing.

Although Jack had been at M&S for fourteen years in 1960, that year was really the first when his impact on the firm—and that of editors hired by him—can be seen in the creation of lists that bear his special mark. In 1946, the year he joined the firm, M&S books by Canadian authors included Roderick L. Haig-Brown's *Return to the River*, Marion Keith's *As a Watered Garden* and Thomas Raddall's *Pride's Fancy*. Other titles had been British classics and American best-sellers such as Ayn Rand's *The Fountainhead* and Napoleon Hill's *Think and Grow Rich*. In 1960 appeared Pierre Berton's *Adventures of a Columnist*, Marie-Claire Blais's *Mad Shadows*, Patricia Blondal's *A Candle to Light the Sun*, Robertson Davies's *A Voice from the Attic*, Margaret Laurence's *This Side Jordan* and Farley Mowat's *Ordeal by Ice*.

By 1960, Jack was publishing more books (twenty-nine that year; fifteen in 1946), all of which were by Canadian authors. For every Berton, Mowat or Laurence, Jack took a chance on perhaps four or five writers whose books were either artistic or financial flops. A person who bets on potential is often going to make some bad decisions at the very same time he uncovers gold. In the early sixties, Jack was keenly aware of one other difficult problem: his fiction list had to be bolstered in order to make it the equal of his non-fiction titles. In this regard, Margaret Laurence was his first major acquisition.

Ultimately another project, the New Canadian Library, would prove a solid business gamble, but it was exceedingly risky. When Malcolm Ross approached John Gray at Macmillan about a paper-back reprint series of Canadian titles, the reluctant publisher predicted his firm would "lose their shirts" if they embarked on such a venture. Then, in early December 1952, Ross asked Jack, his former student, "Do you have any plans for college or school texts? What about a series of low-priced paper-cover Canadian classics? Would do wonders for the teaching of Canadian literature."[49] This hint was followed three weeks later by a much more detailed proposal:

> Glad to know of your interest in the Canadian paperbacks idea. We have from seventy to one hundred students in the Canadian literature course and at least one title could be used in the course I give to the medical students—fifty-four students. I think more use would be made of Canadian titles everywhere once they became available at low cost. You might check this—certainly that is the impression I get from talking to colleagues from other universities. The same holds true of the high schools, I am told. Offhand I would suggest titles like *Roughing It in the Bush*, a *single* volume *selection* of Roberts, Carman, Lampman, Scott, a novel each by Grove, Callaghan, MacLennan, Raddall, W. O. Mitchell, a volume of short stories, etc. (a volume of Leacock). I'd like to think the thing through in consultation with teachers in the field. But I believe the project *has* to be done by someone. Perhaps the Canadian publishers would agree to pool their rights. We should talk this over carefully someday.[50]

In a reply of January 27, 1955, just over two years later, Jack told his former teacher that after a "long struggle with costs, we are finally able to turn on the green light . . . sink or swim." He could offer little in the way of remuneration, but he hoped the "prestige value" would entice

Malcolm to persevere with the series.[51] In 1958 the NCL was finally born when the first four titles appeared: Grove's *Over Prairie Trails*, Callaghan's *Such Is My Beloved*, Sinclair Ross's *As for Me and My House* and Leacock's *Literary Lapses*.

The economics of the series was extremely worrying at the start. Ross had made his inquiry of Gray and then McClelland because Canadian libraries and universities had been complaining for years that no paperbacks of Canadian texts—particularly fiction—were readily available (although some titles existed in this format from Clarke, Irwin). The teaching of Canadian literature in high schools and universities had been stymied. Hardbacks were too expensive and therefore unusable.

The selection of Grove, Callaghan and Leacock is self-explanatory: they were well-recognized writers whose works were already seen as classics; Sinclair Ross's *As for Me and My House* was largely unknown to the Canadian public. It had been published in the States in 1941 and was a text known to only a few cognoscenti. By including it in the first four titles in the NCL, Ross and McClelland obtained for it the attention it deserved. The two men "created" a classic in Canadian literature.[52]

The first four NCLs were printed in England because book production there for soft-covered books was markedly cheaper. In 1958, Jack was very candid about the whole process: "We began planning these paperbacked books two years ago. Our first sales campaign through Canadian bookstores brought a total order for 300 copies of each of the four titles. This was disappointing. We sent our salesmen out again the next year, backed with a promotion campaign, and came up with 1,200 copies of each book. This was still not enough to make the venture break even. Last fall our sales campaign netted us a total of 1,800 copies for each title, and we decided to make the long gamble. We must sell 5,000 copies of each title to show even the slightest profit."[53] Each of the four volumes was priced at $1: the retailer made 45 cents, the author 7 cents and production and distribution costs ate up about 35 cents. The profit margin was so small that M&S could not in this instance advertise extensively. For once Jack simply had to hope that market forces would work in his favour. Years later, in 1962, Jack complained on television about the NCL, but when John Gray phoned to offer him $10,000 to take over the series, Jack refused: "If it's worth ten thousand to Gray, it must be a good idea."

The trade journal *Quill & Quire* was ecstatic in its reaction to the venture:

> Our warmest wishes accompany the first four titles in McClelland & Stewart's paperbound New Canadian Library as they begin to travel the cold Canadian scene. . . . [I]t is well-designed and well-produced and will contain only titles of considerable merit. The fact that it will contain only reprints of *Canadian* classics is, as far as it goes, admirable too, but is not necessarily its greatest claim to praise. The number of Canadian classics is limited and it would be sad to see the series die eventually for lack of further materials to reprint, or decline into reprinting Canadian books which could be viewed as "classics" only through the fumes of the most ardent nationalism.[54]

By 1960, the "boy publisher"'s optimism was muted, but it was very much intact. His determination to publish Canadian writers for the Canadian public was on target, although he was well aware of the financial obstacles confronting him. He was, at the age of thirty-eight, about to undergo a troubled "adolescence."

# 5

## THE JUGGLER

## (1961–63)

A PERENNIAL DIFFICULTY for Jack was the re-
cruiting and retaining of good editors. After an annoyingly long search
in 1960, he finally found Jack Rackliffe, an American in his mid-fifties
with considerable experience, who was "terrific"; he would be an excellent person to help Claire Pratt. The arrangement backfired. As McClelland reminded Farley, for some months he and others had congratulated
him on finally locating an exceptionally good worker: "And guess where
he is?" Jack wrote. "That's right, 999 Queen Street West [mental hospi-
tal] . . . people have said they would be driven around the bend if they
had to work for me. Now it's finally happened."[1]

Rackliffe was a manic depressive. He got on very well with authors
but could fly off the handle unexpectedly with his fellow workers. When
Jack visited the incapacitated editor, Rackliffe—who was at M&S for
about a year—had the manuscript of J. W. Pickersgill's *Liberal Party*
(1962) with him. Rackliffe desperately wanted to work on it but was
not allowed the use of a pencil. If Jack could smuggle one in, he could
get down to business. Jack thought to himself, "Migod, this guy is still
sane enough to do the editing, but if the Conservatives ever found out

that the history of the Liberal Party in Canada was edited at 999 Queen Street, that's all we need."[2] The pencil was not provided. Rackliffe never returned to M&S after his hospitalization on Queen Street.

Jack, who had a propensity to think incorrectly that he was a difficult, overly demanding employer, had to face an even more overwhelming sense of despair when his mother had a severe coronary in December 1961, leading to her death a few days later. He told Farley: "Peculiarly enough, it's the first major personal grief that I have experienced, and it's been a rather shattering emotional upheaval. Although I have maintained, to a reasonable degree, the outward appearance that society expects, I have found it damn difficult and have privately gone through a considerable siege of tears. It really makes you feel pretty lousy as a human being to contemplate how much your mother has done for you and how much she has meant to you and how little you have done in return.... If it has done nothing else for me, it has at least made me more sensitive to the grief of others."[3] As a publisher, Jack always maintained the "outward appearance" of calm, sometimes exuberant, friendliness that his employees had come to expect. He was also a man who attempted to keep his personal discontents out of his working environment. For the most part, he was able to do so, but at this point his drinking and smoking began to pick up, perhaps in reaction to stress; having from youth been trained to mask emotions, he was uneasy with their direct expression. Many of his feelings about not being sufficiently grateful to his parents were, as an adult, rechannelled into the attention he gave to his writers. Nevertheless, he remained a man who did not like to wear his heart on his sleeve. Jack *wanted* to experience strong feelings for others but often he was not able to do so. In many ways he sublimated those emotions in his work as a publisher.

One measure of the closeness between Jack and Farley is that the publisher could confide in him; he also allowed the writer to inform him directly how limited he was in his understanding and appreciation of passion: "You big, blond, bifurcated bastard! . . . you have no more goddamn romance in your soul than a rorqual [a whale]."[4]

Although Jack tended to take his minor ailments too seriously, he did have the ability to mock himself. In August 1962, he wrote to Farley that he'd had "something of a collapse":

> The doctor has not yet given me any precise diagnosis, but the closest I can come is that my problem comes under the category of nervous exhaustion, tension, etc. The symptoms are magnificent in their ramifications—at least for a hypochondriac like myself—minor stroke, dizziness, fainting spells, etc., probably caused, according to the doctor, by too little sleep, too much drinking, too much emotional stress, etc. . . . . It sounds ludicrous, but it's true. I have been in conditions similar to the present one on many different occasions over the past ten years, but I've always been able to pull out of it with a good night's sleep. I've done little but sleep for the last four days now, and I've made damn little progress. The doctor had a rather cheering comment on this. He asked if it had not occurred to me that I was getting older and that one has to slow down and adjust to this, and also that one can't expect to recuperate so quickly.[5]

The simple truth was that quite often Jack felt overwhelmed by everything he had to deal with—publishing problems, difficult authors, finding sufficient time for his family. However, he was fortunate to be a working man at a time when many wives still stayed home to look after the children and household. So while he may have missed the children, he knew they were in Elizabeth's loving and capable hands. And, of course, he had the necessary support of his wife in many dark times.

Pierre Berton was intractable. In 1961, he was fighting for his first book for children, *The Secret World of Og*. He had deliberately written "about real children with whom [other children] can identify, and who do real things, such as reading comics or watching TV." The book was turned down by Knopf, whereupon Jack suggested Doris Patee, another children's editor in New York. She also disliked the book, finding it too unorthodox. Meanwhile, Berton was rightly convinced that he had uncovered a new direction in children's literature and that librarians and editors were "engaged in a vast conspiracy to take the guts out of juveniles."[6] Despite the poor opinion of two experts, Berton expected Jack's support. Jack expressed strong reservations at the very same time he made it clear he would back Pierre completely.

> I think in a way, Pierre, the problem is a simple one. You have been right far more often than you have been wrong. The success of your career has depended on your being right. Here is a case where you are being judged wrong by the majority in advance. Who's to say who is right? You alone can make that decision. My own guess is that you are, in fact, making a mistake in that you are not concentrating entirely on the problem at hand, that problem being that of writing a good book for children. That should be your target. The weakness of the book is, in my view, that you grind a lot of private axes and prejudices. . . . If you revise, and we don't like the revision we will certainly be frank enough to tell you so. However, as I have said right from the start, having done that we would be quite prepared to publish . . . because we feel you have earned that right.[7]

To Hugh Kane and the senior editorial and production staff at M&S, Jack was blunt about the risk he was taking on a potentially disastrous title: "There are two general points that I would want to make at the outset. The first is that, as usual, Pierre has some very definite ideas as to the sort of book that he wants. I think we should indulge him as much as possible. He thinks the book will sell and maybe it will. But if it doesn't, I don't want it to be attributable to the fact that we didn't come close to what his concept of the book was. Secondly, I think this must be treated as a priority item. . . . Whether this juvenile succeeds or not, we're all going to have to give it our best thought and our best effort. . . . He wants the book published in Canada this fall."[8] Once Jack made his decision, the unrevised *Secret World of Og* was picked up by Little, Brown in the States. It has sold more than 200,000 copies worldwide.

Sometimes, as he realized full well, Jack made exactly the wrong decision, such as rejecting the first novel by Sheila Burnford, a writer who was born in Scotland. Two hundred thousand copies of *The Incredible Journey* (1961) were sold in the States. Hodder & Stoughton bought Canadian rights and it topped the best-seller list for weeks. Jack missed out on the windfall that would have come his way had he accepted her tale of the trek of two dogs and a cat across the wilds of northern Ontario. Her second book, *The Fields of Noon* (1964), which in Jack's opinion was far better and which he did publish, had a struggle to sell seven thousand copies.

Some writers made it difficult for him to do his best for them. Even in the face of a great deal of pressure, Gabrielle Roy held firm to her decision not to be actively engaged in publicizing her books. His tender feelings for this sometimes off-putting and manipulative woman are evident in the careful way he tried to persuade her that she might consider a change of heart. Although he was himself very much in need of rest, he was aware of vital political issues of concern to both of them: "I think it would be a useful thing and in the public interest if you were to make such an appearance on the subject of Quebec and separation. . . . However, I don't want to put myself in the position of seeming to try to talk you into doing something that you may not want to do at all. If you would be willing, I should be delighted to make the arrangements. If you would really rather not, then let's forget it."[9] In her terse reply, Roy reaffirmed her long-standing opposition to taking part in the marketing of her books but expressed her concern about Jack's health: "I do hope that you will find the calm and leisure you need to set yourself right. That is what I too need precisely, by the way. Therefore, I'm afraid I have to decline all invitations for interviews, and so forth. Besides I'm really too tired for this sort of thing."[10]

Trouble—not unexpected—of another kind was served up by Irving Layton, who had become enamoured of Jacqueline Kennedy and her fame. Although he was a great admirer of her husband's, he wrote a poem commiserating with her on the lonely existence endured by the wife of a world statesman: "My lovely, unlucky Jacqueline!/ Still, when a husband/ is so harassed,/ shall I add to his burdens/ by running off with his attractive wife?" Hugh Kane did not wish to allow this already-published poem into the poet's new collection, *The Swinging Flesh*; he thought the poem self-indulgent and silly. Jack urged caution: "Layton is far from reasonable but . . . I made an agreement with Irving sometime back whereby I express no editorial opinions on his work."[11] Years later, he said that he was delighted to publish Irving as long as he did not have to read anything by him.

The poet, who had become intrigued by Fawzia, a belly dancer who performed at a nightclub in Montreal, then suggested a promotion scheme even Jack found a bit tasteless: "I think I'll try to persuade Jack McClelland to hire her to go up and down the country, selling my book. All she has to do is paste a copy of *The Swinging Flesh* on her navel or between her ample breasts. Neon lights would flash on and off between her thighs, and then you'd see the sales mount and mount. And not only the sales."[12]

A year later, Jack was not amused to hear that Layton, without informing him, was publishing a poetry anthology with a rival firm:

Believe me, the bloom is really off the rose. What you need is a god-damn wet nurse. Some weeks ago a mutual friend suggested to me that you were editing the *Ryerson Anthology*. I replied that even though you had no contractual obligation to us, I presumed that you were neither that hard up nor that thick skulled. So I was wrong! . . . You've been selected to edit a volume of poetry by the United Church Publishing House . . . But let me make it clear that my criticism is directed at you, not the Ryerson Press. I have only the greatest respect for them. I was raised in the United Church. My father was employed by the Ryerson Press (then the Methodist Book and Publishing House) before he started his own firm. I think they have done more for Canadian literature than any other single publishing house through the years. But if you don't understand why—at this stage in your career—that I would prefer to have you arrested for relieving yourself at the corner of Peel and St. Catherine than being exposed as the editor of an anthology of new poetry published by the United Church Publishing House, then you are a goddamn blockhead, and it ain't kosher.[13]

Things reached such an impasse between McClelland and Layton that Aviva, his new wife, acted as intermediary when the poet did not like the photograph of himself chosen for a dust jacket. She was certain Jack would tell her to go to hell, something he assured her he would never think of doing. Irving wanted his newly bearded self to be presented to the public; Jack was appalled by the idea. "The first time I saw him with his beard I told him to shave it off. I think the goatee is even more revolting. I think he's out of his mind to go in for this sort of adornment. But if this is what he wants, this is his business. . . . If Irving is in agreement with you and you have got a better picture of him that we like, we'll even substitute that. But apart from that, dear heart, we ain't goin' to do nuttin'"[14]

Poets and their poetry proved not only unprofitable but also on occasion unpleasant, as can be glimpsed in Jack's letter to Birney of April 3, 1962, when Jack told him how sorry he was to learn of yet further dissatisfactions the poet had with M&S:

I have no doubt that we deserve a good deal of your criticism, but there is not much more that I can say other than that we are sorry. . . . There is no author on our list who is held in greater esteem or affection than you, and if you have suffered you can be bloody sure that others have done less well. . . . Through circumstances beyond our control (simply because you can't replace key personnel in this country on short notice), [the editorial division has] been without adequate staff; we have been operating under difficult physical circumstances because of an addition that was put on our building; and it's a wonder that we have made any progress at all. The situation has not been improved by the fact that I have been under personal and business pressures of such a nature for the last three months that I have been virtually inaccessible to anyone.

The pressures that Jack alluded to were both comprehensive and, as he hints, overwhelming.

Throughout 1962, Jack tried to find various ways to make M&S realize a modest profit of $50,000. In March, he decided to add four American publishers to the firms whose books he distributed in Canada, wanting sales to increase from $1,400,000 to $2 million, and hoping inventory would expand by 100,000 units. He had, however, an immediate cash-flow problem: he needed $50,000 plus $76,000 for the addition to the building. He raised the money through mortgages.[15]

Beyond the financial, there was the whole question of the direction M&S was taking. "We have grown from a small house to a large one—we need a new approach to decision making—the decisions can't be made by one person, but they must be made within clearly defined policy limits." In order to be certain where M&S was going, a review of basic principles was necessary: "The most obvious statement about book publishing is that the only thing that distinguishes it from any other line of business is the publishing of books. It is the raison d'être, the single most important thing we do. Assuming for the present that the company has strong corporate management with appropriate financial controls, strong operational controls, sensible service, sales and promotional direction (similar to those that exist in any industry), what is suggested is that all our business policies should relate to publishing policies or principles, not the reverse."

But in trying to merge financial/organizational concerns with publishing policies, Jack was attempting something inherently difficult: he was in effect blending what should be the cut-and-dried (non-personal) aspects of merchandising with the producers of his product, writers (very personal). This led to two corollaries, which appear to be contradictory: "1. *The single most important figure in the publishing structure is the author. 2. A publishing house must not be totally dependent on the author for its product.*"

The first of these two statements, seemingly innocuous enough, is, of course, the most important of the two. Its ramifications are enormous. It means in effect that the real purpose of a publishing house is that of fulfilling a service function—of middleman between the creative artist and the reading public. Too many publishing houses have forgotten that function; the great ones have not.

A number of the greatest retail merchandising organizations in the world have been built on one simple principle: the customer is always right. The corollary in sound book publishing is that the author is always right. It is suggested that such a policy should be just as literal as the application of the customer-is-always-right principle.

Jack cautioned that such an approach could only be meaningful in an environment where there also existed sound financial structure and control. He was also aware that his concern for the author went beyond the notion of service to creative persons.

1. Most of the great books, those that live, have been totally initiated by authors. This has always been the case; it will always be the case. Great works of art are created by great creative artists— not by publishers or committees. Great creative artists are few and far between. A publishing house should hold on to any that come its way. Individual authors are the greatest source of product available to a publisher.

2. Great authors attract other great authors. . . . A satisfied author is the greatest continuing advertisement a publishing house can have. An unhappy author, conversely, can do more damage to a publishing house than anything else.

From these two principles, policies emerged: contracts should—as much as possible—favour the authors' interests; books should not be taken on unless they could be handled properly; for the purpose of establishing priorities, writers had to be divided into (1) major house authors; (2) authors with the potential to become major; (3) occasional authors; (4) one-time and specialized authors. In addition, experimental writing should be encouraged.[16]

In another document from 1962 labelled "Publishing Policy at M&S," Jack expanded on some of his concerns: "Perhaps, for example, M&S could make more profit by producing cassettes. Should it do so? I don't think so. It might also make more profit in oil or animal exploration in the Arctic. Should it switch? No! The objective of the company is not profit, but profit from a particular field of endeavour. . . . In my view, it is to promote a service for Canadian authors. It is that simple!" But the problems were far from "simple." Jack was trying to find a way to run a profitable firm that was also a service company and (to a degree) a philanthropic endeavour. He also had many more mouths to feed: M&S in the early sixties had just over ninety employees, up from about seventy in 1953.

His ruminations took him in many directions. Fiction, though not necessarily the most profitable line, was the kingpin of the M&S program, with many subdivisions (serious creative, mainstream, commercial, light, entertaining, mystery, western, experimental). "For the moment, it is my theory that we should publish only in the first two categories and that we should do eight to twelve books a year evenly divided between seasons." M&S could not "escape" its obligation, which now had the force of custom, to publish eight books a year of poetry, even though profits remained negligible. Non-fiction, in all its various manifestations, was "the most important for us commercially."

If the publishing program was rationalized, a reasonable growth pattern of a 10 per cent increase in sales per annum was possible. He also wanted to achieve a 5 per cent profit on the resulting sales, which in effect meant 10 per cent before tax. Inventory control was vital.

At the end of 1962, Jack took a stab at a "Policy Book" into which many of his earlier reflections could be subsumed. This document, very different from previous ones, looks at how the company was malfunctioning as a business unit. "We are not making sufficient profit; we continue to make errors; we work hard but don't accomplish the targets set. Why?

"There are many answers: overlap of duties and responsibilities; confusion as to responsibility; carelessness; inadequate supervision; time wasted on unessentials; lack of belief in targets; lack of statistical control; lack of realistic analysis; and possibly even in some cases a sheer lack of willingness to do what is necessary to accomplish our goals. The business has been running us. We have not been running the business."[17] In what was essentially a *volte-face* from his resolves earlier that year, he had now reached some inescapable conclusions:

We have not been a profit-orientated company.

That sounds deceptively simple. By it, I do not mean that we have not been making a profit. I mean specifically that as a corporation we have put the cart before the horse. We have tried to make a profit by running a good publishing house. It has not worked. I now propose that we try to run a good publishing house by first making a profit.

There is a corporate truth here that I for one (and in my function I am completely and solely responsible) have been slow to recognize. It means a fundamental change in policy for me. There is nothing new in the concept and, as I have said, it is a simple point.

I believe it to be of the greatest significance. I now believe that it is a rule of commerce that successful companies are made successful by the profits they earn. If they do not earn satisfactory profits, they cannot be good or successful corporations by any yardstick that can be logically applied to a commercial operation.

Thus, until further notice, or until this theory is proven wrong in practice, the keystone of our company policy will be profit. If it will earn a profit, do it; if it won't, don't. It's that simple. I don't propose that we debate the issue.[18]

Jack really did not wish to change his philosophy of publishing established earlier in the year, but he was obviously tormented by the mediocre performance of M&S sales. There were two additional factors he did not take into account in a realistic way: the possibility that he did not, despite intentions to the contrary, delegate responsibility effectively;

and the reality that the method of engaging staff at M&S was often of the friend-of-a-friend-needs-a-job kind.

Jack certainly tried to find novel ways of marketing books. In the autumn of 1962, he experimented with a new advertising scheme with Duncan's bookstore in Hamilton. Anyone who brought in an old copy of *The Joy of Cooking* would be given $2 off the new, revised edition of this classic. "McClelland feels," said the amused reporter from *The Hamilton Spectator*, "that people in 1962 like to drive a new car so why shouldn't they want to use a new cookbook? However (and this is the razzle-dazzle) when they turn in their old car they are allowed a trade-in. 'Ergo' thought McClelland, 'why not a trade-in on a cookbook?' This kind of promotion appeals to me as does anything that takes the long-haired solemnity away from the book world."[19]

Certain difficulties, no matter what editorial policy or financial procedures were in place, defied solution. One problem was that of the fifty titles published in 1962, 60 per cent of M&S's "dollar-volume" would be produced by only eight titles, including Roy's *The Hidden Mountain*, Terence Robertson's *The Shame and the Glory* and Berton's *Fast Fast Fast Relief.* Somewhat facetiously, Jack joked with Hugh Kane: "Perhaps we should have a sweepstake and sell tickets to recoup our losses."[20] The list was already too large, too unmanageable and too unprofitable.

Even a risky, though profitable, book could cause problems. One that Jack was deeply proud to have published was *The Canadian Dictionary, French-English, English-French: Concise Edition* (1962). In that instance, there had been a major sticking point: bad reviews. Rather sourly Jack pointed out, "Despite the supposedly humorous and largely irresponsible attack on the book by Barbara Moon in *Maclean's* magazine, we managed to sell close to 50,000 copies."[21]

Another of Jack's schemes at this time to invigorate publishing was the formation of the Bookman's Lunch Club. The first meeting took place in Toronto at Les Cavaliers restaurant on Tuesday, January 16, 1962. The original members were the bookseller Roy Britnell; Macmillan's John Gray; George Renison, the president of W. H. Smith; the CBC broadcaster and anthologist Bob Weaver; *The Star*'s Robert Fulford; Ivon Owen, the president of Oxford University Press; William French, the book columnist for *The Globe and Mail* who had replaced William Arthur Deacon; Hugh Kane; Harry Campbell, the chief librarian of the Toronto Public Libraries; *Saturday Night*'s Kildare Dobbs; and, of course, the Founder himself. (The first women members were not elected until the late sixties: the editor Shirley Gibson, the bookseller Beth Appeldoorn and the M&S publicist, Catherine Wilson.) More conflicted are the surviving accounts of the Sordsmen's Club, another group Jack had a hand in establishing. According to some, these were literary lunches that some women in the media (Doris Anderson, Adrienne Clarkson) were invited to; according to others, there were occasions when prostitutes were present. No clear account of the proceedings survives.

In 1961, when twenty-five-year-old John Robert Colombo, destined to be another mainstay of the Toronto literary scene, met Jack, he was mesmerized. He saw the publisher across the room at a cocktail party and beheld a compact, golden Adonis who moved confidently, exchanging greetings with everyone. When he wanted to, he could work a room more effortlessly than anyone. Colombo, who after university worked at University of Toronto Press and then Ryerson, had known and respected Lorne Pierce, then in poor health. Colombo knew instinctively that Jack was Pierce's replacement in the world of letters.

Colombo also beheld the "riverboat gambler" side of Jack, the man who wanted to exploit the Canadian publishing scene in his own, and his country's, best interests. Since he decided to operate as a freelancer, Colombo was never on the M&S payroll as an employee, although he edited many books for them. In his own words, Colombo became the firm's SOS man. When Walter Gordon was deeply offended because he regarded the editor assigned to him as both foolish and high-handed, Jack took John Robert to the lawyer/politician's office and offered him as the best editor in Canada. Colombo subsequently edited four books by Gordon.

In May 1961, Jack moderated a panel titled "What We Book Reviewers See Wrong with Canadian Publishing" at the Canadian Booksellers'

Association convention. The panelists included Robert Weaver, Robert Fulford and William French. Ahead of time, Jack wrote an irreverent letter to the three, asking them to meet with him in the McClelland & Stewart suite beforehand. He wanted them to reflect on a number of questions, which included these: "Since you get all your books free and have probably never been in a bookstore, do you consider yourself qualified to discuss Canadian bookstores? . . . Do you dispose of all your review copies to one store or do you spread your trade around? . . . Why does your particular paper . . . do such a totally inadequate job of reviewing? (Or have you stopped beating your wife?)."

> Since most of those in attendance at this convention will have had thirty-six solid hours of drinking time at this point, I don't expect that the questions from the floor will be exceptionally lively. . . .
> Questions from the floor will take the form:
> Why do you review books that are not in stock in my store? . . .
> Why do you select books for review that nobody is interested in? . . .
> Why don't you drop dead?[22]

At the very same time Jack himself felt like dropping dead from a combination of exhaustion and frustration, there were new authors' mouths to feed. In 1961, M&S published Leonard Cohen's second volume of poetry, *The Spice-Box of Earth*. Two years earlier, the twenty-five-year-old, elegantly clad Montrealer had arrived at Jack's office with the manuscript, which the publisher scanned. To his own amazement and that of the young poet, he accepted the book on the spot. "I think it's the only time I ever—without reading a manuscript or without having it read—made the publishing commitment. . . . I said OK, we're going to publish this guy; I don't give a shit whether the poetry's good, although I did look at a couple of the poems and thought they were pretty good."[23] John McClelland told his son flatly that he had made a big mistake in taking on such licentious material. On such occasions Jack listened patiently to his father, but, aware that publishing had changed dramatically since his father's heyday, ignored his advice.

Given that Cohen was very much a disciple of the troublesome Irving Layton, the quick and favourable decision is a bit startling. Jack must have immediately intuited, however, that Leonard—very much a rebel—was an altogether quieter, more reflective and certainly much more charming person than his mentor. Unlike Layton, Cohen—though Jewish too—was from a wealthy Westmount family, whose money had been made in clothing. Like Layton, Cohen, from the time he began writing, was preoccupied with the sexual. Cohen's eroticism, however, is far more connected to the mystical than the older poet's.

After his degree from McGill, Cohen tried graduate work at Columbia University. He was then employed in the family business while working on the unpublished novel "A Ballet of Lepers." From the age of fifteen, he was fascinated with both the guitar and the Spanish poet Federico García Lorca. A line from García Lorca's verse anticipates much of Cohen's work as a poet and musician: "Am I to blame for being a Romantic and a dreamer in a life that is all materialism and stupidity?" One friend added another ingredient: "Leonard always had an image of himself as a rabbi."[24] One way of seeing Cohen is as a Jewish poet who celebrates the mystical and the exotic. His robust sexuality also contributed to his development as a poet, since he used writing to advertise himself as a would-be lover: "I wanted [women] and couldn't have them. That's really how I started writing poetry. I wrote notes to women so as to have them. They began to show them around and soon people started calling it poetry. When it didn't work with women, I appealed to God."[25]

Jack McClelland and Claire Pratt soon learned that they were dealing with an extraordinarily pleasant but headstrong man. On July 21, 1959, Cohen thanked Claire profusely for her letter confirming Jack's earlier verbal agreement: "I have bought several people several rounds of drinks since your generous and historic letter arrived. One of my uncles smiled, one disturbed relative had an instant of lucidity."

Yet in the very same missive, Cohen told his editor that he did not wish to be part of the elegantly designed Indian File series: "May I say something about the format? I would prefer not to parade in the Indian File because it is not a parade at all but a depressingly well camouflaged retreat. . . . I think the expensive, hardbound poetry book is obsolete. Even ardent poem lovers rarely buy one. . . . I would love to work with your designer on a cheap, beautiful cover and format which would appeal to . . . all that holy following of my Art. Please let me know if I can break from the File."[26] After this was agreed to, Jack and Claire learned that Leonard did not approve of contracts. In fact, after *The Spice-Box of Earth*, he refused to sign any, one break with tradition that worried Jack enormously.

Within six months of his first meeting with his new publisher, Leonard quit his family job, briefly worked for the CBC, wrote reviews and continued to experiment with drugs. By the end of 1959, he left for England and the Continent.

In September 1963, a year after Jack had tried to rethink the company's extensive problems, M&S was hovering on the brink of insolvency. Much of the blame, Jack was certain, rested on his shoulders: "In the past we have been guilty—and I am largely responsible—for sacrificing short-term facts to the long-term objectives. It's a weakness of mine. Now, as a result of this type of thinking, we are faced with a short-term crisis. We *must* favour the short term over the long term. We must do things that may seem pound foolish and pennywise."

In the first six months, $87,000 in losses had been recorded; the loss should have been no greater than $35,000 to maintain the projected year-end budget position. Inventory growth continued to be massive ($570,000 rather than the hoped for $450,000). Gross profit was low: 25.5 per cent as compared with a normal 32 per cent.

On the surface the company's achievements might not have looked bad: "Now, if someone stopped me on the street and said, 'I have a business which has a gross profit of half a million in dollars. Will you run it for me?' I would automatically say yes. My salary will be $50,000, profit will be $50,000; we will spend $400,000 in operating expenses." But expenses were eating into the gross profit to such an extent that the balance sheet was alarming. There was the slight possibility of taking increased margins on the cost of books, of insisting on larger discounts from suppliers and of reducing editorial and production costs. These options were not really viable—reductions in operating expenses and the elimination of subsidiary income from the representation of foreign publishers were the only really negotiable openings.

In the midst of these difficulties, there was the strong possibility of changing the direction of the firm drastically, cutting down on Canadian titles, for instance. Jack could envisage reducing the company's size to the extent of publishing only authors like Berton and Mowat along with key backlist writers like Leacock. However, this was self-defeating as far as he was concerned because the firm's uniqueness and marketing advantage would be crushed: it would no longer be fostering new talent or promoting serious fiction. In any event Jack was certain that this was not the root cause of the problem; for him, the danger was the inventory "becoming clogged with bad publishing decisions [and] we certainly have made our share of bad publishing decisions and bad book purchases."

Hugh Kane was convinced that the elimination of unprofitable foreign lines would appropriately streamline the infrastructure of the company. In November 1963, the company announced that fifteen foreign houses (five thousand active titles) would be dropped (only Little, Brown, Dodd, Mead, Van Nostrand, Lippincott, Atheneum and New York Graphic Society were retained).

Jack was uncertain that Kane was correct but remained committed to finding workable solutions. At about this time, an employee walked into Jack's office one day to find Jack hyperventilating on the floor, claiming he had suffered a "stroke." Although Jack always exaggerated such events, employees were concerned about their boss's stress level On more than one occasion, several of them gathered at Hugh Kane's home at 14 Summerhill Gardens asking him to intervene. Kane would calm them down, assuring them he would do his best to make things better.

Very much in his best naval manner, Jack was fighting a war he was determined to win. He maintained that M&S would not go bankrupt, although "in my total experience in the book business things have never—and I think I can say never—worked out better than I had hoped."[27] He also jokingly but rigorously maintained that his firm had a special talent for doing everything badly.

6

# A SEAT-OF-THE-PANTS
# PROFESSION

## (1963-66)

JACK HAD GOOD FRIENDS who could commiserate with him about the increasing amount of energy it took to keep his company afloat. The heavy personal burdens of publishing were shared by many, as recalled by Mel Hurtig, the young Edmonton bookseller whose solvency Jack had worried about some eight years earlier. Since then, he had gotten to know Jack well.

> While I was a bookseller we spent quite a bit of time together. I remember one night that began with Nathan Cohen [the theatre critic and broadcaster], Farley Mowat, Hugh Kane, [bookseller] Bill Duthie, Jack, and I downing Scotches at the King Edward Hotel in Toronto. By mid-evening Nathan, cape and all, had departed into the night, and Farley, Hugh, and Bill had all become quite incapacitated. Jack and I left for more drinking and partying. We ended up at ten the next morning, sitting on counter stools in some dive on Spadina, eating corned beef sandwiches.
> For reasons I cannot explain, drinking and the book trade went hand in hand. Publishers, booksellers, authors, and sales reps were

frequently heavy drinkers. In Toronto the standard was two martinis before lunch. One Toronto printer was known to order a carafe of gin martinis at lunch. One well-known bookseller opened the shop with a full bottle of rye underneath the counter and, without fail, when the shop closed at five-thirty, the bottle was empty. A Bible salesman for a staid Toronto publishing house was the champion boozer and womanizer on the road. Call it what you will—conviviality, entertainment, hospitality, relaxation—drinking was an accepted fact of life.[1]

Part of the challenge of the book trade was uncertainty, the fact that even successful books were gambles. What if a book was selling, but not as well as expected and not well enough to earn off the advance paid to the writer? What if a title proved extremely and unexpectedly successful but the print run had been small, so stock became unavailable?

Some days were particularly distressing, given that publishing decisions seemed to be made "strictly on a seat-of-the-pants basis." On such days, "the truth [for Jack is] that we don't know what the hell we are doing."[2] He developed a deep and abiding dissatisfaction and sense of frustration, feeling he did not have the "professional qualifications to be a great individual book publisher." A master at the art of putting himself down, he was most decidedly, he claimed, not an intellectual. "I read for business purposes only. I remember almost nothing, and as a consequence derive little benefit from it. I think I might have been just as successful as a lumber dealer, car dealer or what have you."[3]

Very much down in the dumps in March 1963, he told William Arthur Deacon he was totally disenchanted with the Canadian publishing scene: "I have become increasingly discouraged by Canadian authors. So few of them produce anything that's really worth publishing. I've become discouraged by Canadian book pages. I think it's fair to say that the three Toronto newspapers have reached their lowest level in twenty years, as far as their book pages are concerned. I've become discouraged by the Canadian booksellers and their apathetic promotion effort. I've become discouraged by our own activities." In spite of these reservations, he then reveals that he has decided only in the past three weeks "against selling the firm and seeking greener fields."[4]

Almost from the time he started at M&S, Jack's secretary had been Verna Camplin, who often said about her boss's use of four-letter words, "I wish he would have some regard for my maiden state." (If Jack dictated "God damn" in a letter, she would type it as "goddam.")[5] In 1963, she died suddenly while vacationing in England. Jack was distraught, convinced that he had by overworking her contributed to her death (she was in her early sixties). Marge Hodgeman, who was working as a temp on a two-month assignment, was asked in July to remain on as his secretary. She later recalled, "I said no. I didn't like the job. But I did agree to stay on until he found someone else. It soon got to be December; he wasn't even looking for someone else, and I was still being paid by the employment agency. Finally, I said, 'I'm here already. I guess I'll stay.'"[6]

Marge also had to look after John McClelland, who was brought at least twice a week by limousine to the office. If he was interfering with the work of others, Marge had to return him to his own office. He could be troublesome in a mild sort of way. "He used to hide the ashtray from the boardroom because he didn't like anyone to smoke." Sometimes, a bit confused, John would claim Hugh Kane's office was his own and order him out. The senior McClelland would eventually wander off to the cafeteria, where he would converse with the two Scots ladies who ran the place. At this time, he discarded large sections of the M&S archives: correspondence with the likes of Lucy Maud Montgomery and Bliss Carman were lost forever.

One of Marge's responsibilities was to untangle Jack from commitments: he made promises to lunch, drink and party with far too many people. About this aspect of her job, she reminisced, "Lying is another way of putting it. I became a master at it." She also became skilful at transcribing Jack's late-night (11 p.m. to 2:30 a.m.) dictation into beautifully written letters.

Jack's candid manner led to a corresponding frankness on Marge's part. In 1966, she told a reporter that her boss was not at all "punctual, often looks as if he's slept in his clothes and is in constant need of a hair-cut." Nevertheless, he was "the best boss a secretary ever had."[7] He always, she fondly recalled, thanked her at the end of each day. A woman of exquisite tact, considerable acumen and a lively sense of humour, she would occasionally explode. One day she caught—in the nick of time—a parcel of proofs being sent out to "Mr. Pierre Burton." The air was blue as she remonstrated with the culprit.

Jack's life remained chaotic in spite of Marge's much-appreciated as-sistance. "Sometimes my day is like the story of the drunk who's charged for setting fire to his hotel bed with a lighted cigarette. He pleads not guilty, 'Oh no, your honor, the bed was on fire when I got into it.'"[8] This was Jack's capsule description of his existence, which began every morn-ing between seven forty-five and nine, after only five hours' sleep. He dressed quickly, usually in whatever was back from the dry cleaner's. For breakfast he would have cereal and the first of the twenty cups of instant black coffee he drank every day. At the office, he would, in addition to

*Jack with Marge Hodgeman,* Quill & Quire

chairing meetings and speaking with colleagues, on average take or make thirty phone calls (authors, agents, other publishers) every day. He arrived home between seven-thirty and eight most nights, accompanied by two briefcases, ate dinner, watched television for an hour and then went to his den, which was full of "skeletons" (unfinished work, manuscripts and correspondence). He would speak into the Dictaphone for hours. Jack's "day" often ended at four in the morning, and in addition to coffee, he often consumed a large amount of vodka (martinis but sometimes straight up). He smoked two packs of Rothmans cigarettes a day. On a "long" day, that would increase to three packs.

McClelland & Stewart's marketing schemes produced some stressful though comic moments. In November 1965, in an effort to promote Earnest Weir's *The Struggle for National Broadcasting in Canada*, M&S sent letters to the media addressed "To the Wife or Mistress Of" [the addressee]. Some recipients wrote to gripe about the bad taste, including the manager at a Niagara Falls radio station: "My wife and my mistress are my business and I fail to see anything to be achieved by addressing mail to them." Half-heartedly Jack apologized to complainants: "Certainly it was not our intention to offend anyone. Although I am by no means certain that the world isn't losing its sense of humour." He was, after all, simply trying to draw attention to the book by a marketing ploy that "perhaps got carried away."[9]

In September 1962, another gimmick had worked brilliantly—at first. Jack informed Terence Robertson, who was in Nassau, that he was holding a press party in the author's honour in Montreal to celebrate *The Shame and the Glory*, Robertson's book on Dieppe (the idea for the book was Jack's, suggested to the young author when he applied unsuccessfully for a job at M&S). Jack told the same story to Farley Mowat, who was living in Newfoundland, to Pierre Berton, who was in the midst of a hectic TV schedule in Toronto, to Irving Layton and to the prize-winning Quebec novelist Diane Giguère. After all the authors, overwhelmed by the attention supposedly being bestowed individually on them, had accepted, he phoned the Montreal media to announce his first authors' soirée. Only when photographers arrived at the event did the puzzled authors realize that a hoax had been perpetrated on them. They were good-natured about it, but the event inspired only one short news report and a column in *The Montreal Star* attacking the whole idea of literary cocktail parties.

At about the same time there were some memorable disasters, such as the book on drug addiction. At the time of publication the writer, who knew the drug scene from considerable first-hand experience, landed in jail on bad cheque charges. One forged cheque, payable to the Windsor Arms hotel, was signed Jack McClelland. Another book, the lavish *Art Treasures in the Royal Ontario Museum*, arrived from its European printers with all the illustrations glued in the wrong way.

In the early sixties, everyone at M&S was deeply absorbed in work. Since M&S was in the industrial area of East York, there was nowhere to go for lunch except the cafeteria, an extension of the warehouse. The result was a strong sense of community. However, the once-elegant building was becoming decrepit, and the work areas were crowded.

A major disintegration in the editorial staff took place in 1964 when Claire Pratt left after her father's death: her health was not good, but she and her mother were now free to travel. The editors who replaced her were not always well suited to their jobs. One—hired by Jack—was a good-looking, charming American aristocrat without any idea how to edit a book or deal with authors.

The economics of the book trade also remained difficult, as Jack recalled in 1965: "A basic rule is that two-thirds of a first printing, whether it be 1,000 copies or 10,000, must be sold for us to break even.... We try to keep the cost of a book down to a fifth of the retail price. More often it is a quarter. When it reaches a third we lose money."[10] While sales were beginning to increase markedly—25 per cent from 1964 to 1965—the cost of running M&S was accelerating at a higher rate. In general, sales projections were far from accurate, production costs were not adequately monitored and promotion was sometimes unsuccessful. Lack of co-ordination among the editorial, sales, production and promotion divisions was one of the firm's principal problems, the end result being that, as Jack said, "We are publishing badly—truly badly."[11] The Policy Book was not really being consulted: ". . . None of our departments are running on a smooth operational basis. We are still just getting by. We are not improving, we are not working on a planned schedule of advancement."[12]

One of the reasons the Policy Book was not being followed must be attributed to Jack himself: "At M&S we had publishing committees which were composed of senior people from the editorial, accounting, sales and promotion departments. But the publishing decisions were usually made in my office and by me alone. A friend once gave me an interesting gizmo—a small circular plate alternating with yes and no around the base. I frequently spun this gadget in the quiet of my office in order to solve a tough publishing decision. So much for level-headed management."[13]

Another source of aggravation was the system of data processing introduced in 1963—punch cards, statistical control of ordering and shipping and lots of new equipment. The only trouble was that none of it worked. "There was a period from June 1963 to September 1964 when it was almost impossible to get books from us," Jack wearily told *The Toronto Daily Star* journalist Robert Fulford.[14] (In 1965, M&S was the first publishing house in Canada to acquire a computer, but this acquisition merely led to a further series of crises.)

In such circumstances, Hugh and Jack clashed. In 1963, Hugh told his boss, "The corsage [for an otherwise unidentified person and event] has been ordered. I suggested at the beginning that *either* you or I organize the affair so that we would not both have to worry about details of this sort. If you have doubts about my ability to do it properly and would like to take it on, you're very welcome." Jack replied, "God, you're a sensitive bastard. G.F. Y."[15]

On the question of censorship, Kane was once again much more reluctant than his boss to bow to authority. In 1963, the police in Toronto seized the stock of William Burroughs's *Naked Lunch*, which M&S was distributing on behalf of Grove Press. Jack's press release was diplomatic, making it extremely clear he did not approve of the actions of the police but also indicating he was not going to get involved in costly litigation to protect a book he was merely distributing. Hugh not only threatened to resign but also offered to put up $5,000 of his own money to defend the right to free expression. On this thorny issue, Jack's stand was clear: he was opposed to censorship, but "I am a businessman, though. I am not a crusader. I will not knowingly jeopardize our business in a censorship battle."[16]

The difference in publishing styles between Jack and Hugh reached new heights over the breakthrough success of Pierre Berton's *Comfortable Pew*. On April 7, 1965, Jack said Berton's wishes regarding advertising had to be obeyed: "Pierre has no right to insist on this, of course, but he is being a little difficult and I think that we must do it." Hugh Kane was furious. Although he would place the ad, he knew it was "an unjustified waste of money. . . . I contend that we have no obligation to any author to spend money foolishly." He quoted from the M&S Policy Book, which backed up his opinion. Further, he asserted that Berton's book "has been far more widely and successfully promoted than any other in history. The only thing such an advertisement will do is to further inflate an already overinflated ego." Although Jack defended the decision, adding, "I don't think his ego is any concern of yours, overinflated or not," his actual views on newspaper advertising can be glimpsed in a letter of December 20, 1963. Print and other media in Canada were too small to make advertising worthwhile: "the only reason we take any space advertising ever is for one of three reasons (a) as a means of thanking newspapers for their reviews (b) for special events (appearances . . . etc.) or (c) to make an author feel good. But I can assure you, and I can even prove to you, that it's a very effective way of pouring money down the drain."[17]

Of course Kane was telling Jack that money was being misused because it was being diverted from the infrastructure of the company, particularly the hiring of more greatly needed employees. Berton's book, published simultaneously in hardback and paper, sold 7,600 and 130,000 copies respectively. There was a particularly embarrassing moment when several hundred copies were sent to Coles bookstores a few days before any other store received a shipment. Coles put them on sale at a discount price and scooped their rivals. Some retailers suggested a plot, but Jack put it this way: "It's difficult to publish the most successful book in the history of the country and still alienate the book trade, but we did it."[18]

M&S perennially achieved tremendous sales results on a few titles, but the issue of concern for Kane was the fact that many others never got close to market expectations. As a result, money had to be managed prudently. Kane felt that a great deal—perhaps too much—had been done over the years to promote Berton. Three hundred elk-skin and moosehide bags of black sand, with instructions on how to pan for gold (every fifth bag actually contained tiny gold nuggets worth a dollar or two), had been given away to promote the Klondike book. A cooking contest between Berton and other columnists had been held to call attention to his *Just Add Water and Stir*. (Copies of *The Luck of Ginger Coffey* by Brian Moore were sent to bookstores accompanied by small boxes containing coffee and candied ginger.)

In addition to Berton, many other authors were certain that not enough was being done for them. The Barbadian-born writer Austin Clarke was such a one. Clarke's *Survivors of the Crossing* originated with William Heinemann in London, but the writer lived in Toronto when M&S published it. (Sometimes M&S bought the printed pages in the form of sheets from foreign houses but published under its own imprint. In such co-publishing arrangements, one publisher would assume the responsibility for the production of the book, which would benefit both houses by reducing costs.) Clarke complained loudly to M&S staff about the promotion of his book, and Jack was not amused. He was quite willing to cancel all agreements to publish further books by the writer, who, he felt, lacked civility:

> I am truly sorry to have this publishing association end. We have never questioned your writing talent or the possibility that you might eventually become an author who could be published on a sensible economic basis in this country. Eventually this may come

to pass, but in the meantime it appears to me that you may be doing yourself a disservice by being too eager. The writing of several novels does not make one front-page news automatically. Judging from the number of television and radio shows that have been approached and don't wish to have a return visit from you, and the nature of your letter in contrast with the reports that I have from those who have been working on your book and its promotion, I think that your main problem is personal, not one of being associated with a reluctant publishing house.

Because I happen to believe in publicity, and also happen to believe in the rights of authors, it has always been my personal policy to take the part of the author in most disputes that have occurred with McClelland and Stewart personnel.

[In your case,] I am convinced that what you need more than anything else is a good swift kick in the ass. Someday I hope that it will be delivered, and when it has been delivered, I think there will be some chance that you will receive the respect and recognition that your writing talent seems to indicate that you deserve.[19]

Even more fascinating, and a glimpse into the "hidden" Jack McClelland, a man habitually unable to carry a grudge, is the letter he wrote to John Gray on November 8, just two weeks after berating Clarke. Jack had heard a rumour that Macmillan was about to reject a book by Clarke and decided to say something, in the event the decision might have been based on the fact that Clarke was difficult. "Clarke expected a great deal of us. Far too much, I guess, but the fact is that we did not deliver nearly enough in terms of promotion of sales exposure. Why our people couldn't have done a better job, I don't know. . . . Our break with Clarke was the culmination of increasingly abusive phone calls and letters. I had the choice of either continuing to defend our position (without too much heart) or apologizing for our efforts. Neither stance is one that I admire or have the time to pursue."[20] He goes on to suggest that the establishment of firm "ground rules" might overcome the difficulties M&S had encountered with Clarke.

Another writer who had serious reservations about Jack and M&S was Hugh Garner, whose novel *The Silence on the Shore* came out in 1962: "[Jack] held up my book for a year before he published it. When it finally came out, it was too late for the Christmas business and he sent uncut copies to the reviewers. And he didn't arrange a single interview for me."[21] In Jack's view, Garner was an old-fashioned writer whose working-class Cabbagetown books were passé. Since Garner's work did not speak to him, he was not particularly upset by the angry author's grievances.

Hugh Hood was rightly upset when the manuscript of his short-story collection, *Flying a Red Kite*, was returned to him without any explanation in July 1961. He questioned not so much the decision not to publish as the sloppy way it was rendered. He was also more than a trifle arrogant: "Who is there as good in Canada, at thirty? Nobody." He concluded, "I won't forget this. And naturally I have no intention of risking another such slap in the face. I won't submit to McClelland & Stewart again, and the loss is yours."[22] In his reply of August 2, 1961, Jack tried to pour oil on the troubled waters. Artistic considerations— the collection was judged uneven—had governed the decision, but the publisher made a point that was to remain a cardinal rule with him: such collections were a tremendous commercial risk and best avoided. He invited Hood to visit him in Toronto but could not refrain from offering some candid advice: "Unless you plan to open your own publishing house, you [should] refrain from writing too many letters to publishers of the sort that you have sent to me."[23] *Flying a Red Kite* was published by the Ryerson Press the following year; Hood did not publish with M&S until *The Camera Always Lies* appeared in the NCL in 1982.

There were many other kinds of complaints. One competitor noted snidely, "There aren't fifty-two publishable books *in* Canada." Robert Weaver, the book critic for *The Toronto Daily Star* in 1962, reinforced this assertion when he added, "McClelland publishes without any policy. He'll put out anything—first novels, religious books, sex books, political tracts, anything." The broadcaster Gordon Sinclair, one of Jack's authors, made a similar criticism: "I have come to the conclusion that M&S

publish altogether too much, and much of what they publish is of such limited interest that Jack's wasting his money and sometimes my time." The author had a suspicion about the real reason behind such "waste": "I think it's that he doesn't like to say no to a hopeful author or direct them toward vanity publishers who will bleed them for their money. Figuring that he might break even, he'll take on people through a sense of national responsibility."[24]

The uneven quality of the growing list seemed to indicate a scatter-shot approach to publishing. But it was also true that Jack was trying to manage a company that was becoming increasingly large and more expensive to run. Fifty books were published by M&S in 1962, fifty-six a year later, although Jack had planned on seventy-six.[25] He also had to deal with the one thousand unsolicited manuscripts that arrived each year: only an average of ten ever saw their way into print. Publicly, he put on a brave face: "The more Canadian books we publish, the better books we can publish. The better books we publish, the more money we make."[26]

Jack's optimism for "the numbers game" remained undiminished: "In the 1960s, the mere fact that we announced we were printing 10,000 copies of a book created a stir in the retail trade. It had a profound effect on the public. It helped get exposure for the author and sold books. If you put that many copies in the market-place, you'd get 3,000 or so back, but you've sold 7,000. If you put out 2,000 instead and got 300 back, you've only sold 1,700. . . . If you get too conservative, you can die. I guess I've been a big roller; because I believe in what I do, I've taken risks."[27]

One later employee, Peter Taylor, felt Jack's sense of gambling bore a dubious resemblance to a form of Russian roulette: Jack "didn't ask himself, 'How many copies of this book *will* sell?' He'd ask, 'How many *should* it sell?' Then he'd say, 'To hell with it. I'm a pipe-dreamer. Let's find those people who'll buy it, and promote the *hell* out of it.'"[28] In publishing, the difference between "will" and "should" is absolutely crucial because the key to success is making the right guess between the two verbs. Publishing on a "should" basis is a recipe for high blood pressure and constant agitation.

The journalist Marika Robert, who wrote an in-depth article on Jack for *Maclean's* in 1962, characterized him as "aggressive, extroverted, charming and colourful. Sitting in a bar or restaurant—where he conducts a good deal of his business—he looks more like a wealthy playboy. He says he prefers watching a hockey game to reading a critical essay and would rather discuss beautiful women than the beautiful books he publishes. The story once got round that he had never read a single one of his own books. Typically, the thought of a publisher who doesn't read manuscripts appealed to him and he likes to encourage the rumour." She added, "He sleeps little, smokes and drinks heavily and works hard. He thinks he may be deliberately killing himself, but seems to enjoy the idea—it fits the reckless publisher image."[29]

Jack was well aware that there was a distinctly Canadian approach to publishing, one best seen in terms of the editing process. In the States, books were overedited, he felt: "The American editor feels unless the book is rewritten he hasn't been doing a good job for the writer. In England, if the work requires much tinkering, the publisher feels he shouldn't be publishing the book." So what was the typical scenario in Canada? "Canadian publishing typically comes somewhere between these two concepts. Our editors are not the U.S. martinets nor as professional. They are much more involved, however, than the average British editor who really doesn't take that whole process too seriously." As in so much of his life as a publisher, finding his own path was the order of the day.[30]

Though he was criticized for it, Jack enjoyed publishing a wide variety of books. There was the mainstream best-seller, which delighted him. Then, there were the writers who aimed at "sheer literary quality, and a writer of this sort is not really concerned with the market for his book. Such writers are producing works of art." A good example of the second category was Douglas LePan's novel *The Deserter* (1964): "We don't think we can sell a large number of copies, but it is a beautiful piece of writing that will live and will sell over a long period of time. In the other category is the work of Arthur Hailey, who writes clearly for the commercial market. If he makes any pretensions to literary standards, he keeps it well hidden."[31]

In 1965, Jack confessed to Hailey, who was born in England but then resident in Toronto, how much his publisher side as opposed to his literary side admired *Hotel*. "I read it in one sitting without intending to do so. I should have been working, but I read it and enjoyed it. It moves quickly. It's readable as hell. I think it is damn well constructed, and although it ain't going to win you the Nobel Prize, it should sell a helluva lot of copies. It's [as] good a piece of commercial fiction as I've seen in a long time. From a book publisher, baby, that's the highest possible accolade."[32]

One part of Jack's personal search was for writers who could sell large numbers of copies and yet produce works of genuine merit. This is a rare combination, but in the early 1960s Mordecai Richler, Margaret Atwood and Peter Newman came his way.

Jack contemplated publishing Richler as early as June 1954, when on a visit to England he sent back a cryptic report mentioning that he had heard the novelist was living there. Richler had already published *The Acrobats* that year, to bad press in Canada. "He is a young graduate of McGill [in fact, of Sir George Williams University], and his book was reviewed in the Montreal papers quite recently. I have made a note to get in touch with him."[33] Jack did not make contact. In 1955, Jack was persuaded that Norman Levine had overestimated the young Montrealer's talent. Eight years later, in the wake of Jack's enormous liking for *The Apprenticeship of Duddy Kravitz* (1959), he made an about-face.

By 1962, he had again become in-terested in publishing Richler, although the author's Canadian rights were initially contracted elsewhere. However, he did have strong reservations that March about *The Incom-*

*Mordecai Richler*

*parable Atuk* in light of negative readers' reports and his own assessment of the manuscript. He was frank with the author: "I am not wildly enthusiastic . . . I am absolutely convinced it is your worst work to date . . . I would like the first Richler book on our list to be one we could promote with full enthusiasm, but this one isn't it." Somewhat apologetically he added, "Apart from stuffing it, let me know what you want us to do."[34]

Such frankness did not offend Richler. In fact, it strengthened the relationship between the two men. Richler withdrew the book temporarily, revised it and by October, even though it contained some unflattering references to two M&S authors, Pierre Berton and Leonard Cohen, Jack had become enthusiastic. He told Hugh Kane:

I have changed my opinion on this completely after reading this version twice. I like it very much. I think it is a real gasser, as they say. I think his revision has been completely successful. I think it might have a large sale.

Will you read it as quickly as you can? . . . I shall be most interested in your reaction. As of the moment we are committed to $1,500 if Richler insists, but theoretically we could still reject. No contract exists. His next book will be the short stories; then the second Duddy novel.

I have recommended only minor changes. Deletion of "shit" and "wiping the behind" references. The toilet syndrome (mine or Richler's? who knows?). Also reference to Face-elle and a very vicious reference to RCMP on page 73. Beyond that there are spelling mistakes . . . but I don't see much else that needs to be altered. I think he has covered himself as far as Berton and Cohen are concerned, although the latter still gets a very rough treatment.[35]

A bit later, there was a slight dispute about the book's title. The American edition was called *Stick Out Your Neck*, a title that did not appeal to Jack, who wanted to use the English one. Mordecai was indifferent, telling Jack to choose. Jack responded, "We have decided to call it *Stick Out*

*Your Atuk*, or perhaps, *Your Atuk and Mine*. If there's one thing we're good at, it's titles."[36] Mordecai's next letter was signed "The Incomparable Mordecai."

As he had done years before to Earle Birney regarding *Turvey*, Jack sounded a warning to Mordecai about language: "I would prefer to see you drop some of the references to the toilet and bodily functions relating to same. Believe me, this is not prudery or any form of censorship—and it's only a suggestion anyway—because we're now publishing books freely with all the four-letter words." However, he was concerned the potentially large market for the book would be reduced if the book stayed as it was; he was also concerned about the unflattering reference to the RCMP who, Jack maintained, could covertly arrange to have the book banned.[37]

Between 1954 and 1963, Richler, in addition to *The Apprenticeship of Duddy Kravitz*, had published *Son of a Smaller Hero* and *A Choice of Enemies*. *Atuk*—much more slapdash and surreal than his previous books—was a radical new departure for him. Its subject matter was extremely controversial: the inherent stupidity of Canadianizing American pop culture. Jack believed that satire, if it was sharp and funny enough, could promote nationalism.

Born in Montreal in 1931, during the Depression, Richler has written extensively of the working-class Jewish neighbourhood around St. Urbain Street and Baron Byng, the area's predominantly Jewish public high school. He attended Sir George Williams University (now part of Concordia University), worked part-time as a reporter, dropped out of school and in 1951 left for Paris, where he became part of the North American expatriate scene, which included Mavis Gallant and Terry Southern. He returned to Canada in 1952, worked for the CBC and moved to England in 1954.

Although correctly regarded as a relentless and scurrilous foe of philistinism in any form he encounters it, he is also tender-hearted. Like Jack, Mordecai has his shy, gentle side but can also be extremely stubborn and pernickety. One of his most vivid experiences with his publisher was in Cannes, where he had gone to report on the film festival in 1972 for

*Life*. Jack dropped in on him there—literally dropped in, for Mordecai returned one evening to his hotel, the Carlton, to find Jack, who had bribed a clerk, asleep on his bed. Jack's fantasy about Cannes had been tremendous, as he later sardonically recalled: "I had a mental picture of arriving at the Cannes Film Festival in a stretch limo, a Canadian flag flying in front and half a dozen starlets with me in the rear. The fact that I had little interest or knowledge of the film industry did not seem relevant."[38] The letter Jack wrote to Richler before Cannes is more comical and self-revealing:

> If I go to Paris, Elizabeth will be with me, which is fair enough, but I sure as hell ain't going to take her to the Cannes Film Festival and I don't want to be there when Florence [Mordecai's wife] is there. As you can understand, my purpose would be serious research because I have always been anxious to find out whether I made a serious error in not becoming the chairman of our Film Development Corporation [a post offered to him by Judy LaMarsh]. I plan to turn up with the official letter [from LaMarsh], which talks about the $10 million, etc. I'll change the date on it, have a blow-up made and post it on the outside of the door to your suite. Please get the information [on the festival] to me as quickly as possible because I would need a lot of time for preparation—like, I have to have business cards printed listing the assets of my new film company. I want to have my hair styled and get some new publicity stills made.[39]

Once he had wakened Jack, Mordecai casually mentioned he was having lunch the next day with the sexy actress Jeanne Moreau, the siren in *Jules et Jim*. Jack insisted that he go too. Mordecai refused, not wishing to share the spotlight, causing Jack to become outrageously angry at the missed opportunity. But Mordecai held his ground and went by himself the next day. When it turned out he was one of about four hundred journalists who had received invitations from the wily Moreau, he did not bother to inform Jack.

Jack and Mordecai had extremely roguish reputations, and of course they very much enjoyed each other's company, as can be seen in Jack's post-mortem of a party in December 1968: "Elizabeth didn't mind you taking the glass from our party. I am still trying to find out who took several cases of booze. We couldn't possibly have consumed that much. One of these days I'm going to learn not to drink at my own party so that I'll have some idea afterward what took place. Truthfully I can remember almost nothing. I went to bed at seven and am told that the party officially ended at seven-thirty, when a taxi came to remove Harold Town from the premises. I hope as one of the guests of honour you felt it incumbent on you to remain until at least seven o'clock."[40]

Jack was quite prepared to offer the younger man no-nonsense, fatherly advice. He did not like the author's photograph submitted for the dust jacket of *The Street* (1969): "Those are great pictures. . . . We'll give some thought to using one or the other on the back of the jacket. There may be some delay, the main problem being that I can't decide which of the snapshots would be more effective in killing the sale of the book completely. Who in hell would want to buy a book written by a snot-nose little brat who looked like that?"[41] He also thought Mordecai—whom he sometimes called Mordy—was wasting his time writing book reviews for London's *Spectator* magazine and sometimes being excessively negative: "To begin with, the pay is hardly worth it. Secondly, I don't think it does one's prestige as a writer any good— unless one plans to become a professional critic. It's an open invitation to other critics and novelists to slander the hell out of your future books when they appear. And also I can't help feeling that people who are able to write creatively themselves can devote their time to much better ends than reviewing other people's books. So to hell with it!"[42]

There were also exchanges about the supposed pornography in *Cocksure* (1968). On May 22, 1965, Mordecai told Jack, "It's getting to be a very dirty novel, and I'm wondering whether I should let you publish it, let alone read it. It could corrupt you."[43] Jack shot back, "You must be thinking of someone else. I like dirty novels. If I only had time, I'd write one myself. I'm particularly well qualified."[44] Another time he told the novelist, "Okay, so make your books sexy. You can't shake me. We are dedicated to sex."[45]

In his turn, Mordecai could be merciless in satirizing the inefficient way M&S was run. In September 1969, he told Jack, "I have long suspected that there are two versions of any given McCl & Stew contract, the one mailed to the innocent writer and the one kept in the basement at Hollinger Rd. for drunken directors to chortle over."[46] When Mordecai complained about major errors in royalty statements, Jack, despite the dash of humour he was able to mount, was mortified: "The only reason you haven't received a reply to your last letter before this is that I read about three-quarters of it and decided to go out and shoot myself. It's a grim world. The shooting was not entirely successful, and now your letter has emerged again from the bottom of a huge stack of unanswered correspondence. I simply turned the pile over and your cheering note came out. Oh hell . . ." As for the confusion in the royalty statements, he wrote, "I don't understand it. I ask for figures. I am given figures and then they don't relate. To hell with it."[47] There was the time Mordecai ordered twenty copies of one of his novels and received the same number of copies of *Adolescents in Society*, for which $1,000 was deducted from his royalties: "What the f _ _ _ would I want with them?"[48]

Jack's claim that he had no skills as an editor is proved patently false in his dealings with Richler. He took on this delicate job when he told him how much he liked *St. Urbain's Horseman* (1971), which he found powerful, impressive and extremely enjoyable: "I'm all for leaving editing to the editors. I can tell you, for what it is worth, that there were only two spots in the script that bothered me. The first is that I have a hunch that part two is too long, and because I didn't find its totality as relative to the whole as it might be, I concluded that it kept the reader too long from the main flow. For more or less the same reasons I couldn't really feel that the baseball game belonged. Relevant I guess it is, but I found it an unnecessarily lengthy interruption.

"So tell me how the professionals react and let's get on with it.

"Cheers!"[49]

Throughout his career, Jack resolutely maintained he was a publisher and not an editor, but his skills as a first reader and editorial commentator were remarkable, a talent that gave his authors tremendous confidence and himself great joy.

Early on in their relationship, Richler was candid with Jack about his life of self-imposed exile in England and the consequences to his writing life:

> I am even seriously thinking of returning to Canada to live, to stay, man, in a couple of years time. But how would I earn a living? I've got three kids. Ultimately, I fear my serious work will suffer if I stay abroad longer than ten years (eight already used up) but the truth is I can earn my nut—a good one—with three months' lazy work here. In Canada, where would my money come from? TV quiz shows? Not this boy. . . .[50]

> If I want to write non-paying books, that's my headache, not my children's. They are entitled to security, etc. etc. etc. Neither does Canada owe me a living. Believe me, that's clear to me. If I want to write and live there—again—it's my headache. I do not expect flowers to be strewn in my path.[51]

Maybe, he wondered, Jack could pay him a retainer to act as a fiction adviser, but Jack was frank: Mordecai should return to Canada but perhaps only after he had "hit it big" with one of his novels.[52]

The special nature of Jack's relationship with Richler is glimpsed in a letter from Gabrielle Roy to Jack, who had arranged for Mordecai to visit her: "I found him, as you had said warm-hearted, and what's more and which I did not expect in the least, sort of child-like, and even defenceless and vulnerable in a sense despite what is spoken of him. People will never cease to surprise me."[53]

In 1964, twenty-five-year-old Margaret Atwood, a doctoral candidate in English literature at Harvard, offered one of her first substantial pieces of fiction to M&S, *Up in the Air So Blue.* The reader's report was dismissive. "This is a piece of the Camus school. It begins and ends abruptly. . . . [T]he reader can find in it whatever symbolism or significance he chooses to see. It is very competent writing, but I do not think it is anything more than that." The novel was rejected. On her behalf Al Purdy submitted a volume of her poetry the following year, which Claire Pratt disliked. "This is negative poetry, dealing with not only the lost generation but the lost world. . . . I don't like this verse and found it monotonous and tedious. Her habit of overusing parentheses is very annoying. My feeling is that it is forced poetry, that she is not writing happily, and that she doesn't give a damn. She may have some talent, but this is not enough."[54]

An unusually canny student and writer of literature, Atwood published her first volume of verse in 1961 (*Double Persephone*), when she was twenty-two. Knowing intuitively that she was a born writer, she was not badly discouraged by the negative reaction at M&S to her fiction or to the verse, many of the rejected poems later finding their way into *The Circle Game*, published by Contact Press.

Further interest was expressed by M&S in another novel by her after the appearance of a story called "The War in the Bathroom" in James Reaney's magazine *Alphabet.* It was Jack's eye that was attracted by the story; he gave orders for her to be contacted. Somewhat reluctantly she sent the manuscript of *The Edible Woman* to M&S in October 1965. As she later put it, she did not know her way around in the publishing world. She was struggling in Boston, preparing for her Ph.D. comprehensive exams at Harvard.

The novel was read in late 1965 or early 1966, and two of the four readers were enthusiastic (Joan Walker and Kathleen Rhodes). On

*Margaret Atwood*

the basis of the first two reports, two "major" readings were commissioned: Joyce Marshall read the book "with great interest and pleasure throughout. I have to admit, however, that when I reached the end I wondered whether the book were really *about* enough, whether she is, in fact, ready yet to write a novel. . . . A flaw certainly is that the central young lady and her young man are a bit dim compared to some of the others. . . . The book is simply too young, I think, and that is all. Interesting but not publishable."[55] John Robert Colombo, an Atwood fan, was also not completely taken with the book: "Everything she has written to date bespeaks a strong imaginative bent but stumbles over an infirm metrical, social and psychological basis. . . . The novel is very much a pastiche in the tradition of pastiches. . . . I'm extremely unsympathetic to this kind of novel and feel there should be a narrative worth recounting before the author can expect a reader to spend three hours poring over so much prose.. . . . I certainly think the book deserves another reading, perhaps by a female reader who goes for Lawrence Durrell and Mary McCarthy and Doris Lessing. But I think the unconvincing narrative thread cripples it."[56]

Atwood, knowing her book's many strong points, had submitted the manuscript with a certain irony, as she remrked to an editor at M&S on February 26, 1966. "As you might expect, I am not wildly interested in revisions; I should be interested in hearing your readers' comments, though. But I have the usual arrogance of my tribe, i.e., I think I'm God." In spite of the reservations expressed by the readers, the book was deemed suitable for publication. Atwood accepted a publishing offer from the editorial director Jim Totton that February. Inexplicably, four months later M&S wrote to Atwood's agent in England, Hope Leresche—and not to Atwood herself—to see if the title was still available. The reply was affirmative, but once again nothing happened. In the summer of 1967, the author phoned M&S and left a message: she intended to retrieve the manuscript.

*The Edible Woman* might not have been published by M&S had not Jack become annoyed by the inefficient way the correspondence with her had been handled. In the spring of 1967, he became aware again of her growing reputation when he read "My First Interview" in *The Toronto Daily Star*, at the time she won the Governor General's Award for poetry for *The Circle Game*. He dictated a letter telling her how "enchanted" he'd been by what he'd read about her. She responded by asking after the whereabouts of her manuscript.[57] Jack then checked the M&S files to discover that she indeed had an accepted novel languishing in his firm's possession.

Jack informed Marge Hodgeman in July that "[the Margaret Atwood] file bothers me a good deal. It gives real evidence of the chaos and carelessness that existed for some time in our editorial department. I presume that is all in order now. However, what bothers me most is that the correspondence seems to come to an abrupt end with a letter from the author dated March 6, 1967. What happened then? [One editor] suggests the ms is being revised. How does she know? Was it returned? . . . All sorts of letters seemed to be missing from the file. I want to write Margaret Atwood. I consider it an urgent and very important matter."[58] He met with the author—who remembers wearing a brownish A-line dress with miniskirt of a wool jersey blend too heavy for that day's weather—the following month and reaffirmed his firm's decision to publish if she made revisions. While downing several Bloody Marys in rapid succession, he apologized for the careless handling of the manuscript. When she asked if he had read her novel yet, he told her, "No, but I will." He also said, "We publish writers, not just books."

He saw for her a "promising future and thought this particular novel more saleable than most first novels that are published."[59] The writer Clark Blaise, a colleague of Margaret's at Sir George Williams in Montreal, read the manuscript and made helpful suggestions. Her problem was time: she was teaching full-time and working on a series of poems based on the Canadian experiences of the Englishwoman Susanna Moodie in the mid-nineteenth century. When *The Edible Woman* finally appeared in the autumn of 1969, Atwood had her first book signing, which took place in the Hudson's Bay men's underwear department in Edmonton (she had moved to that city to teach at the

University of Alberta). "This is why we all love Jack," she explains with her customary brio. "He has given us some of the most surreal moments of our lives."[60]

Peter Newman (born Neuman) emigrated with his wealthy Czech Jewish family from Austria in 1940, when he was about eleven years old. Although some of his family's wealth had been stripped from them, his industrialist father prospered in his new life as a farmer in Canada. The shy teenage Peter was educated at Upper Canada College, where he was discriminated against because of his accent, and the University of Toronto, where he became a member of the "Untidies," the University Naval Training Division. In his early twenties, he became an assistant editor at *The Financial Post*. His first book, *Flame of Power: Intimate Profiles of Canada's Greatest Businessmen* (1959), attracted Jack's attention because of the author's ability to weave analysis with relevant biographical facts. The two men joined forces when Peter's original publisher, Longmans, Green, thought the idea of a biography of Diefenbaker "stupid" because the subject was still alive and his political future uncertain. That rejection brought Jack and Peter together.

From the outset the sometimes reclusive Newman saw himself as a far different kind of author from Berton and Mowat. He was insecure, afraid to put a wrong foot forward in public. He was also by nature a troublemaker, a journalist who was not afraid to confront the famous and powerful and to display their feet of clay. Newman was often discouraged by the task of taking on Dief. "I was on the point of giving up over and over again, but Jack would come to Ottawa four or five times a year and we'd have dinner at the Château Laurier, and he would make me feel that what I was doing was vital and important. I'd go back to the typewriter full of enthusiasm I didn't know I had. By showing he had faith in my ability to pull it off, he won my loyalty forever."[61] Jack's earliest discussions with Newman concerned the timing of the biography, eventually titled *Renegade in Power*. Would June 1962 be the best time to publish it? "Is this election going to give you what you need to finish up, or will it seem more desirable to wait until we see what really is going to happen to Mr. Diefenbaker?"[62] Diefenbaker's government was reduced to a minority in the 1962 election and was defeated by Pearson's Liberals the following year.

Although Newman had not planned to interview Diefenbaker, who was still prime minister in 1962, Jack insisted and the writer complied. He would ask some "genuine" questions and would incorporate any "genuine" answers on the galleys. If Diefenbaker were to become

*Peter C. Newman*

really angry, Newman said, Jack would have to publish his book posthumously. The final result was exactly what Jack was looking for: "I have read through the galley proofs (as far as they have been received)—a much more careful reading than I was able to give the manuscript—and I must say I am impressed by your accomplishment. I think it represents not only a fine piece of writing but a superb job of research. Unquestionably, Diefenbaker will be upset by the book, but it seems to me to be a pretty carefully reasoned and fair evaluation and I think he has no real right to be bitter."[63]

Within eight weeks of publication, *Renegade* had sold thirty thousand copies, assisted not only by the quality of the book itself but also by Diefenbaker: in defeat he was even more flamboyant than he had been while in power. In January 1964, Newman observed that "Diefie" had exploded at a meeting in Vancouver and promptly sold another thousand copies of the book. Sales eventually exceeded eighty thousand.[64]

A significant difference between the shy Newman and the outgoing publisher can be seen in their responses to the launch party for *Renegade*, which Peter left at about 11 p.m., at which point Harold Town and Jack were standing by the door trying to hang one another by their ties, each having the other's in his hand. "The idea was to see who either gave up or choked first. At least I think that was the idea. I don't think they noticed me going." At such events, Newman recalled, "the author is usually the secondary factor—the most important is that Jack is having a good time."[65]

In 1965, Gage (educational books), Macmillan (educational, fiction and non-fiction) and McGraw-Hill (educational and non-fiction titles) were substantially larger firms with bigger sales than M&S. With the Canadian centenary fast approaching in 1967, M&S seemed to have two choices: to consolidate itself simply as *the* principal Canadian publishing house in terms of quality, or to expand to become the principal Canadian house in volume as well as prestige. Jack chose the latter course, certain that if his firm consistently produced the best Canadian books and the market for Canadian books increased, the future would be extremely rosy.

Jack's vision was not shared by the more cautious Hugh Kane because such a move could only be realized by more heavy financial borrowing. Even if sales were exceptional, a huge backlist would be created, with the resulting problems in warehouse space and inventory expenses. Even an enormous increase in sales would be accompanied by all kinds of woes. When Jack did not want to know a bitter truth, he evaded it. And he did not wish to grasp the implications of Hugh's concerns.

Seven series of books, all proclaiming their nationalist identities, were begun in the mid-sixties: the Canadian Best-Seller Library Series (mass-market paperbacks of titles published earlier in hardback), the Canadian Centenary Series (an eighteen-volume history of Canada produced by professional historians for university use), the Canadian Centennial Library (eight titles), the Canadian Illustrated Library Series, the Carleton Library Series (history reprints), Curriculum Resource Book Series (for high schools) and the Gallery of Canadian Art Series. (There was another series: the Secret Circle Books, children's books published in association with Little, Brown.) In addition, from 1960 to 1969, fifty-seven titles were added to the NCL's original eleven volumes (1958-60). The firm was title rich but risking fiscal impoverishment. In 1967, ninety titles were published, compared with fifty-three in 1964. Such incredible expansion also meant that more staff—there were ninety employees in 1965—had to be hired in every division to deal with the resulting workload. This meant much more money had to be earned before M&S could show a profit of any kind.

For instance, the commitment to the Carleton Library, the first volumes of which appeared in 1963 and which can be seen as a nonfiction parallel activity to the NCL, was heavy. These volumes were mainly reprints of existing books dealing with various aspects of the history of Canada. The initiating editor was Robert L. MacDougall, whose high academic standards personally infuriated Jack. The English-born Diane Mew, who was responsible for the series until she left M&S in 1968, found the entire scheme a wonderful challenge and an exciting introduction to a subject she had previously known almost nothing about.

Jack also wanted M&S to increase its stake in the reference and text-book market, prophesying that this division could be responsible for two-thirds of his business in the future. (In 1962, its first year of publication, the concise Canadian French-English, English-French dictionary sold forty-five thousand copies.) Although this was an increasingly competitive field with steep development costs, it could help subsidize trade publishing. Jack personally found such work "dull," just as he had earlier lost interest in agency publishing, about which he said, "I'd rather distribute liquor. It's more profitable."⁶⁶ The publishing of reference and educational books became increasingly more narrow and competitive and, in the process, never provided M&S with the kind of backup support envisaged by Jack.⁶⁷ There was also a growing market in official company histories that could be underwritten by the firms being commemorated. M&S took advantage of this situation and published books on Massey-Harris, Molson and the Bank of Montreal.

Talk that new technologies could threaten the existence of the book in its 1960s form was not taken too seriously by Jack. He could foresee a machine about the size of a book into which a text in the form of a disk would be inserted, the text being projected from the front of a machine: "This won't affect the publisher. It will be a change in the product, a change in the type of firm, a change in distribution methods.

And of course it will cost more to enter the field. It is my opinion that the book *per se* has outlived its usefulness."[68] At the same time that he saw a very different form for the book, he was afraid that the Canadian education system was not producing good readers. As a publisher he obviously felt more threatened by this phenomenon than by technological advancement.

The Canadian audience, modest though it was, had to be attracted to his products, so Jack placed a great deal of emphasis on the appearance of books, particularly the dust jackets. At M&S, design was the domain of the Czech-born illustrator Frank Newfeld. *Love Where the Nights Are Long,* the collection of erotic verse selected by Irving Layton, was released in two editions: a trade paperback and a hardcover edition limited to 199 copies selling for $65. The text of the limited edition was accompanied by provocative illustrations by Harold Town (the paperback contained a selection of the Town drawings). Despite the high price, the hardback sold out. Jack did not own one of these: "Too expensive. I couldn't afford it."[69]

A. J. M. Smith, the poet and anthologist, was sorry he had agreed to have verse of his own in that collection: "Most of the [other poetry] is just plain crap."[70] The critic and academic Desmond Pacey told his friend Layton, "I believe Jack McClelland is exploiting you for his own monetary gain. There *is* something vulgar and phoney about *Love Where the Nights Are Long* and its Harold Town illustrations and limited signed editions and its general aim of 'look how shocking I'm being!' I am genuinely afraid that you are becoming a victim of your own cult. It's easy to be a big frog in the little pool of Canadian narcissism—but you've got to go beyond that if you're going to win the Nobel Prize."[71] Adding insult to injury, Pacey attacked Layton's 1963 volume of verse, *Balls for a One-Armed Juggler,* which sold more than two thousand copies in its first month of publication. Layton himself was amused by the prospect of a respectable woman from Westmount going into a bookstore and asking for his *Balls.*

In an attempt to raise much-needed money, Richler was considering, as he told Jack, a screenplay: "It's about a poet, see. He's very, very famous in Canada, although nobody ever heard of him elsewhere. He's a virile, sexy, garlic-eating ... well, parochial schoolteacher. The youngest fifty-year-old in Jewdom. I'm thinking of calling the flick *Balls for a Horny Pigmy*. What do you think?"[72]

Until the appointment of Pierre Berton's assistant Elsa Franklin, M. F. (Bud) Feheley, president of TDF Artists, and the writer Christina McCall Newman to the board of directors in May 1969, it had been mainly M&S staff and, earlier, family members, who had sat on the board: Jack, Jim Totton, Hugh Kane, Jim Douglas (sales), Owen Wilson (secretary-treasurer) and Mark Savage (educational division); Robert Martin, the M&S lawyer, and Pierre Berton were also members.[73] When Frank Newfeld joined the firm full-time in 1963 as art director, he received a seat six months later. Throughout John McClelland's tenure and Jack's, the board at M&S had little direct power in running the company. The only persons who ever really challenged Jack at such meetings were Hugh and Pierre.

Newfeld thought Jack's sleek appearance and aristocratic bearing were very much like those of a head prefect at an English public school. He admired Jack but found him impossibly bossy and capricious. Once there was a major crisis when $1 million was owed to the Verona-based printing firm Mondadori, which was refusing to release two books still in its bindery. Jack and Frank flew to New York to speak with the Italian firm's representative. The two arrived at dusk, went to their hotel and Jack departed for dinner. At two in the morning, Frank's phone rang. It was Jack. "Are you still up?" "I am now," Frank assured him. Jack arrived at Frank's room, said he did not know what to tell the representative but, in any case, was flying back to Toronto first thing in the morning. Frank would have to deal with the situation by himself. Without any guidelines from his boss, Frank, who was taken aback by Jack's insensitivity, attended the meeting the next day, fudged his way along and was finally informed the matter would have to be resolved in Verona. When Frank returned to Toronto and advised Jack of the outcome, he was told that was fine: Frank would travel to Italy the following week by himself to resolve the matter. Ultimately Mondadori was paid and the stock of the two books shipped to M&S.

Even books that sold well would be subject to Jack's criticism if he did not feel the author had lived up to his full potential. The Anglican Church commissioned Pierre Berton, an agnostic, to write *The Comfortable Pew*, which attacks the clergy and laity's complacency in the face of rapid changes in Canada. The intent was to shake things up. Berton succeeded admirably. In addition, the book made $50,000 for the Church, even more for Berton and much less than that for M&S. "Anglicans," Jack said, "are much sharper businessmen than I am." Of the book itself, he had no high opinion: "It's topical and timely, but of no lasting value except as an exercise in journalism."[74] Privately he had told Berton, "If the book were by a new writer, I would urge publication . . . the press would be kind . . . I have a hunch that a substantial element of the press will use this book as an excuse to crucify you. It's not a brilliant book and you are expected to write brilliant books."[75]

In 1964, Jack, who felt Berton's tremendous abilities had still to be channelled properly, invited him to take on the position of editor-in-chief of the Canadian Centennial Library (he was also editorial director of the Canadian Illustrated Library Series). Jack offered him a downtown office, a secretary and an editorial team. The CCL venture was co-produced with *Weekend* magazine, which would handle advertising and publicity. "It's easy work," Jack told him. "Won't take too much of your time." Berton accepted.[76]

Throughout Canada, more than three hundred titles appeared to celebrate the centenary. William French of *The Globe and Mail* observed, "Never before has this country—perhaps any country—embarked on such an extensive program of force-feeding its readers." Sales of the CCL, a mail-order venture, were extremely strong. The first title, William Kilbourn's *Making of the Nation*, appeared in November 1965; the rest shipped bi-monthly until 1967. One hundred thousand copies of each title were printed (the break-even point was seventy thousand); each title sold out (some were reprinted so that their sales were even greater). All kinds of promotional stunts were employed: a first free book followed by automatic mailings of subsequent titles, negative billing (the subscriber had to cancel subsequent books sent to him or her) and deluxe versions in simulated leather.

The consuming idea in the publishing world was that Canadians would buy more Canadian books in the centennial year and, even more crucial in the case of Jack McClelland's vision of the future, that Canadians, their appetites finally whetted, would buy more in the future so that such books would truly dominate the market. At about this time, M&S added the tag-line "The Canadian Publishers" to its colophon.[77]

Behind the scenes, Pierre and Jack had some angry disputes. Infuriated that M&S was eating up the time of designer Frank Newfeld, who had been seconded to CCL, Berton instructed him on July 5, 1965, to "sever" all connections with the parent firm. Jack, as he told Berton on July 7, was offended by this high-handed act: "I will be charitable and assume that you are wilting under pressure, sick or are suffering from a temporary mental derangement." Berton was also not happy with the way his own books for M&S were being handled, as can be seen in Jack's letter to him in late July concerning *The Cool Crazy Committed World of the Sixties.*

I am aware, perhaps more than anyone else, of the importance of getting the book out on time. Your book is under control, according to the information I have. Some delays have occurred, but they have not been the result of oversight or inefficiency on the part of our staff. . . . In your letter you refer twice to our supposed record of tardiness in getting out your books in the past. I suggest that you are labouring this point. Unless you can demonstrate otherwise, it is my opinion that it has been a very long time since we have been late with one of your books. If I am correct, then surely you don't need to continue to beef in perpetuity. Another one of our authors told me recently that he has been advised by you that we are slow and inefficient and that we must be bugged continually if one wants anything done. Thanks very much, but I really don't think that has been your experience.[78]

A few months later, the two were back on good terms when Jack proposed a scheme whereby a negative review of Berton's book could be turned to their mutual advantage: "My suggestion is that we . . . take a reasonably large ad in the [*Toronto*] *Sun* in which we say in effect that Barry Broadfoot says Berton book doesn't come off, etc. M&S say non-sense, Broadfoot is an idiot, etc. Therefore, in order to let readers of the *Sun* decide for themselves, we are going to offer free copies of the book to the first two hundred people who write and agree in advance to fill out a simple reader's report. . . . If it worked, it would be a first-rate publicity gimmick right across the country."[79]

Although commercially successful, Berton had, as he later recalled, the feeling that he had not, apart from *Klondike*, achieved anything really lasting. His job at M&S was spurious: Jack "was the real editor; I was only a traffic manager."[80] Financially he had been well rewarded by M&S: in addition to his salary, he received 2.5 per cent of the common stock of the firm. In 1968, he abandoned his involvement as editorial director of Illustrated Books, his official title at M&S, so that he could begin work on the railway books, a project, he assured himself, that would give him the fulfilment previously evading him. In spite of his complaints and Jack's often thin skin when he heard them, their friendship continued on a comfortable course. Jack always pushed Pierre to write books: "I'm counting on it," he told him. In turn Pierre pointed out, "Other publishers may be just as charming, but you can't get drunk with them."[81]

From authors with whom he had formed a close attachment, Jack's sensitivity to criticism was sometimes excessively high. In October 1964, he wrote to Farley Mowat about discontinuing their publishing relation-ship: "To put things bluntly, we have reached a point where it no longer makes sense to continue our business association. . . . The problem was initiated by your memorable comment at [Jack's cottage at] Foote's Bay.

It would be pleasant to think that it was a spur-of-the-moment thought. I know that you regretted the statement as soon as you had made it and it would have been out of character for you not to have regretted it. . . . You had come to Foote's Bay intending to say it. Whether you were right or wrong, whether you had justification or not, it is my view now (as it was then) that you had come to believe in the opinion that you expressed." The "memorable comment" that initiated this correspondence can no longer be recalled by either man, but it likely was something about Farley's enormous debt to Peter Davison, his editor at Little, Brown and to the fact that M&S, without much work, had hitched its wagon to a star. Davison was Mowat's primary editor. (Since Davison was the person who actually prepared Mowat's work for publication, no one at M&S would have had the responsibility of offering the author advice about the form and content of his books.) Nevertheless, if Farley had called Jack's attention in a hurtful manner to this fact of his literary life, he had not meant to do so. Jack was deeply hurt.

In one sense I don't feel you were entitled to that opinion. Spoken in jest, it would be fair enough. Spoken in seriousness, it was a negation of everything we have attempted to do. But you held the view and if you held it, you certainly had the obligation to express it. And if you held it, it had to mean either that I had done my job too well or too poorly. Either way it meant to me that we had outlived our usefulness to you. . . .

It is this, chiefly, that makes it necessary for us to go our separate ways. We started as business associates. We became friends. Perhaps the only way that we can remain friends is to forget the business. There is nothing revolutionary in that. I've told you many times that I consider publishing a service business. The publisher exists only because he offers a service to authors. If a Canadian author feels that he is losing money by publishing with us, then to hell with it. I don't wave the flag quite that much. It has always been my belief that Canadian authors make more money by dealing with us and by listening to our advice.[82]

In the same letter, the editor side of Jack could not resist comment on the manuscript of *Westviking*, Farley's new book, which he had just read: "None of the foregoing, Farley, has any relation to the Norse book or to any other book. I think the Norse book is a bad one. At no time have I been the slightest bit concerned about it from the financial point of view, or from the standpoint of it not being a potential best-seller. I'm aware, too, that many worse books are published. However, unless the revision has been extensive, I would be concerned about the effect of the book on your reputation. If it were published in anything close to its original form, it is my view that it would damage you to a degree that I don't even like to think about."[83]

In his turn, Farley was repentant, despite the fact he could not recall the remark that had upset his friend so much.

> Your letter shook me badly. I had not had any idea that you had been harbouring a dart in your vitals these past six months, and was annoyed with you for what I took to be a lack of concern with the problems I was having with the Norse book. I see that I was wrong. There is probably no point in attempting to disabuse you of your conviction that I have an abiding distaste for M&S. I can, however, assure you that I have not the slightest recollection of whatever heinous remark I evidently made at Foote's Bay. I recall getting very drunk, very gloomy, and busting a glass on the wall. . . . Whatever was said was not meant. I have no real quarrel with you, or the company, apart from the usual picayune bitchings which all authors indulge in. . . . I do not know (since you refrained from telling me) either what I said. . . . I like you as a business associate, quite apart from how I feel about you as a friend . . . I would be very sorry indeed to leave M&S and even sorrier to lose you as a friend. And despite what you may say, the friendship would certainly not survive the rupture.[84]

Jack's letter to Farley shows just how personal publishing was for him: he was quite willing because of a taunt uttered under the influence of alcohol to give up a very profitable relationship. His pride and sense of honour led him to make it quite clear that if his services as a publisher were not considered valuable, he did not wish to offer them. Even though he was quite serious about ending his business relationship with Farley, he could not resist the editorial chastising. Farley's apology was accepted.

Meanwhile, in the summer of 1963, Jack had to deal with Margaret Laurence, who, having separated from her husband, was living in England with her two children. In a letter that makes perfectly clear his priorities, he told her his reaction to the breakup of her marriage: "I don't really know what people want to hear when they have just recently decided to separate. Probably they don't want to hear anything, but for what it is worth, let me say to you that you have something that is more important than any marriage I've ever heard about. By which I mean your career, which I say in all humility should make you one of the great international writers in the next decade or so. I don't think you can afford to concern yourself about the dissolution of a marriage, no matter how serious a jolt it may seem at the time. So forget it. It's of relatively no importance."[85]

More central to Jack was his extreme annoyance with Macmillan in London because that firm was publishing three books by Laurence virtually simultaneously: her travel memoir, *The Prophet's Camel Bell*, her collection of short stories, *The Tomorrow-Tamer*, and her first novel set in Canada, *The Stone Angel*. He wrote her a no-nonsense letter telling her flatly that not only was her work being rushed into print but also that simultaneous publication of several works could prove disastrous.

> More often than not I find myself writing to you like a Dutch uncle. . . . What in hell goes on at Macmillan's? Have they gone completely berserk? They are rushing the short stories into print. They are rushing the novel into print. . . . Even if you were the second coming of Christ, it would be foolish to publish three of your books in one season, or even three of your books between this fall and next spring. . . . Please believe, even though Macmillan is one of the great imprints in the publishing world, that editorial policy in English

publishing houses is inclined to be too damn lax. . . . It may be that you have rushed it too much. It may be that it has flaws. I know very well that you won't make changes unless you agree entirely with the suggestions that are made, and I think this is the way it should be. But surely there is time to have *Hagar* [*The Stone Angel*] properly evaluated. This is going to be a key book in your writing career.[86]

He strongly suggested she phone her English publisher and editor, Alan Maclean, demanding production of the Hagar novel cease immediately. Of course she refused.

I am sorry to be nasty about this matter, but I resented your remark about the second coming of Christ so much that it was very fortunate for both of us that you were not present at the time; otherwise, I would have clobbered you with the nearest solid object available. I do not imagine that *Hagar* is without flaws, nor am I so lacking in critical perception that I delude myself about the quality of my writing. . . . Please, Jack, do not ever imagine that I am at this point overestimating my own abilities. My problem has always been the re-verse—to have enough faith in my own writing capacities to be able to go on, in some fashion, because the alternative—not to go on—would mean that nothing at all was any good anywhere, for me, since this kind of work appears to be a necessary condition of life.[87]

The next major quarrel between Margaret and Jack, whom she often referred to as "Boss," occurred a few years later when he had determined, at the time of the publication of *A Jest of God*, to make her name a house-hold one in Canada. Margaret was ambitious, but she was exceptionally shy when it came to public events. She just happened to mention that she wanted to visit Canada. This fuelled the imagination of the Boss. Well before the trip, exhausted by his expectations, Margaret unsuccess-fully attempted to set limits. Later, in a rather bemused state of mind, she reflected on just how much of a compromise had in fact been reached: "When McClelland said 'a working trip,' he sure wasn't kidding. In the two months, I did a total of 17 radio interviews, 15 newspaper interviews, 4 TV interviews, and gave 4 talks. How I ever survived is a mystery."[88]

Like many other writers, Margaret Laurence compromised with the Boss because she was aware he had her best interests at heart. For the same reason, Leonard Cohen agreed to be one of the four "Peripatetic Poets" who travelled across Canada in the fall of 1964 (the others were Layton, Birney and Phyllis Gotlieb). Birney was enthusiastic: "I'll be on a kind of four-man vaudeville team touring [six] eastern Canadian universities, two shows a day, each on a different campus," he told a friend. He added, "Sounds like a New York firm of Jewish lawyers with a junior goy partner thrown in to get the carriage trade. We will read our poems, autograph our books, appear on panels, be attended throughout by a film crew from the National Film Board." Attendance at the readings was excellent, but the volumes of poetry were often not available. "In one place we'd be without the Earle Birney book, in another we wouldn't have the Leonard Cohen book." As Jack recalled, "We did everything but sell books."[89]

A year before, Cohen had just finished his newest collection of verse, *Flowers for Hitler*. He modestly told his publisher, "If I may mention the truth, it's beautiful." He also informed Jack, "You know that I will side with French Canada when the Confederation disintegrates. I just want to let my Anglo-Saxon friends know. We can still be on the best of terms." Jack responded, "I am glad to learn that you will be carrying arms on the French side. I have been waiting to hear which way you would jump. My own decision will relate directly to the success of your novel [*The Favourite Game*]. If it becomes a raging best-seller in Canada and our own books don't sell this fall, I will be glad to see you join the Separatists and will probably go along too."[90]

Before Viking New York bought Cohen's novel (the originating publisher was Secker & Warburg in London in 1963), it had been rejected by Knopf, one of whose editors had called the book "distasteful," revealing simply little more than the "sexual education of a young man, a well-bred Montreal Jew, who delights in detailing all his exploratory amorous adventures. . . . The writing has the short staccato style of a poor translation." Another reader at the same firm found the book "dreary" and "insufferably egotistical": "I feel sorry for Secker & Warburg if this is what they regard as a first-rate first novel." When Alfred Knopf confronted Jack with this information, Jack replied, "I am surprised by your readers' reactions to the Cohen novel. I can only think that you must have seen it in the earlier draft we rejected ourselves. Certainly it is much improved as it stands today. If it is the current one [the assessors saw], then I would have to place myself squarely on the Secker & Warburg team. I think it's a beautiful piece of writing and probably the best first novel to come out of Canada in many years."[91]

Cohen was, as far as Jack was concerned, a poet—and should stick to developing his talent in that form. *The Favourite Game* was not published by M&S until 1970 in the NCL, but that was largely because of problems with Secker & Warburg. When the proofs of the Viking edition made their way to his desk that year, Jack was lavish in his praise.

It is, as you said so modestly yourself, a beautiful book. There is no question about it. It sings. It has rhythm, and pace and feeling. . . . Will you do me one very great favour—and yourself an even greater one. I'm a prude and I'm old-fashioned and I'm not an editor and I'm even a fink, whatever that may be, but please, Leonard, in the early part of the script . . . you have a very brief incident where you use a popular four-letter word in perhaps the hortative sense (or worse) in relation to God. It is my humble opinion that this is not essential to the book. It does nothing for the book, the author or the reader. It's in execrable taste—even appalling taste—and please, please, please, don't mar a fine book with such childishness.

Having admitted that I think this is a superb book, I can still say that I don't feel humble or embarrassed or in a mood to second-guess the advice we gave you several years ago. It's a beautiful book, but it's still a first novel and the fact is, friend Leonard, that you didn't have to write a first novel. So that's not much of a paradox. This may be one of the best first novels that's appeared anywhere (I think it probably is) in some time, but it's still labelled first novel from the very start in form, in content—but not in terms of thought and insight and feeling and sheer lyricism—so damn it, I bow and scrape and admire you and congratulate you, but I still don't think it's what you should have done. Sour grapes, probably, but I don't really think so. One of the great dangers in staying in this business is that you begin to think you know something about books. My greatest virtue as a publisher for years was that I knew nothing about books and I even admitted it.[92]

In fact, Jack had high expectations of Leonard Cohen the poet, pointing out to him that many of the poems in *Flowers for Hitler* were weak. He even suggested that the young man was coasting on his reputation. Cohen was co-operative in substituting poems, but he was quite fixated on matters of design. Jack became a bit peevish, especially as no one at M&S liked the title: "God knows," a somewhat exasperated publisher told the young poet then living in Greece at Hydra, "you're the last person in the world that I want to quarrel with. I have great respect and admiration for you, as you know. I don't tell you how to write your poetry. Now you are beginning to tell me how to publish books. . . . We went along with your title. There is not a person in our shop that likes the title . . . we conceded on the title . . . Having conceded on that, though, we find it is the title that is causing all the damn trouble with the design. . . . We have given the designs you submitted what I consider to be as fair as possible consideration. . . . We are proceeding with the second . . . design. . . . If you don't like it, sue us. Find another publisher next time. . . . I'm sorry that this is an unhappy letter, but every now and then one has got to face facts. . . . The book has got to come out on schedule."[93]

The bad-tempered letter amused rather than angered Cohen.

It's a historic Greek morning. Your peevish letter delighted me. Shiva is dancing. . . . The summer has been cool and bright. It is clear that you want to punish me for insisting on my title. . . . [The] second cover, besides being devoid of taste and meaning, is a successful attempt to humiliate the author of the book it pretends to advertise. . . . I must consider this second cover a personal affront (unconscious, no doubt). . . . Needless to say, I forgive [the designer]. I forgive you for your joylessness. . . . Nobody is going to buy a book the cover of which is a female body with my face for tits. You couldn't give that picture away. It doesn't matter what the title is now because the picture is simply offensive. It is dirty in the worst sense. It hasn't the sincerity of a stag movie or the imagination of a filthy postcard or the energy of real surrealist humour. It is dirty in the brain.

You invite me to sue you. You don't know how much just such an irrelevant battle tempts me. . . . What is more pleasant than a match between comrades? . . . Incidentally, Jack, you really don't expect me to travel all the way back to Canada to preside over the distribution of that crude hermaphroditic distortion of the image of my person. I'd really be ashamed to stand beside a stack of them at a cocktail party. . . . So why don't we forget about the whole thing? You never liked the book very much.[94]

The book was in production, so Cohen had M&S over a barrel, as Jack admitted. "Anyone who writes a letter like your last one, and at the same time cables detailed corrections to be made in the page proofs, must have been pretty damn sure that we would back down, roll over, wag our tail, etc. Well, I have news for you, my friend. Against my better judgment, that's exactly what we are going to do. . . . I would dearly love to be sued sometime. I only want that to happen when I'm in a position to defend my stand."[95] Frank Newfeld's proposed dust jacket design was scrapped in favour of one by Cohen.

Leonard's second novel, *Beautiful Losers*, was published by M&S in 1966. Jack was taken aback by it in a very positive way, even though he still felt compelled to warn the writer again about the hazards of turning from poetry to fiction:

Migod, it's a fantastic book. It astounds me and baffles me and I don't really know what to say about it. It's wild and incredible and marvellously well written, and at the same time, appalling, shocking, revolting, disgusting, sick and just maybe it's a great novel. I'm damned if I know. . . . It's the majority view at Viking that it's a very superior piece of work. All I can say is that I think it is an amazing book. I'm not going to pretend that I dig it, because I don't. So let us not pretend. I enjoyed reading it. I would like to reread it and will when I have a chance. Are we going to publish? At the moment I don't know. . . . I'm a little apprehensive about the reaction of the Catholic Church. . . . I'm sure it will end up in the courts here, but that might be worth trying. . . . You are a nice chap, Leonard, and it's lovely knowing you. All I have to decide now is whether I love you enough to want to spend the rest of my days in jail because of you, and even though I can't pretend to understand the goddamn book, I do congratulate you. It's a wild and incredible effort.[96]

Jack secretly approached Northrop Frye and Claude Bissell, the president of the University of Toronto, about the dangers of publishing such a potentially scurrilous book: "I have concluded that we must publish despite the fact that we are almost certain to run into an obscenity charge either in Ontario or in the province of Quebec. . . . I have to be truthful and say that I don't really understand the book. I think it may be a great novel, but I am by no means certain. I have great respect and admiration for Cohen, and undoubtedly I am influenced by this. . . . He does not consider it a novel as such, but rather a 'Confessional Prayer'. . . . I would be extremely grateful if you could find time to look at it, and to let me have your frank evaluation."[97]

Despite his trepidation, Jack went ahead with *Beautiful Losers*, which was not banned. (He was not aware that the novelist, perhaps displeased by M&S's inability to take on his first novel, had secretly offered his second to Mel Hurtig, who refused to "steal away" one of his friend's authors.)[98] Jack did become impatient when Cohen the iconoclast complained about the book's initial lack of success in the marketplace:

I understand that you are bitching because *Beautiful Losers* is not available in all stores. Certainly this is frustrating, but just what in hell did you expect? You may be naive, but you are certainly not stupid. Booksellers have a perfect right to decide what they will sell and what they will not sell. . . . I understand that you are whining about lack of promotion. I am delighted to look at that one too. . . . The book has had radio publicity from coast to coast, television coverage from coast to coast; it has been written about in *Time* magazine, *Maclean's* and the majority of major newspapers and the reviews in the little magazines will follow. . . . It is beginning to sell moderately well in some stores. If it is not a raging best-seller, it is not because the book hasn't been promoted.

And now a final message on the whole situation. I realize that the book is very important to you. I realize the total personal involvement and that you are particularly sensitive to everything relating to the book. That is understood, and I think the importance of the book is accepted and appreciated in the few important places where such could be understood and appreciated. But migod, Leonard, it is a bonehead time for you to lose your cool head on this thing. For God's sake, relax. Even though you wouldn't accept it in advance, it was completely predictable that almost no critics or reviewers were going to understand or identify with the book. . . . There is sound evidence for believing that the value of the book and the importance of the book have been recognized, and that the recognition will ultimately spread by degrees. There is no other way. People can't, and won't, be bludgeoned by it. My sincere recommendation to you as a friend is that you relax. Let the achievement of the book speak for itself.[99]

A year later, when Jack had dinner with Irving Layton, the discussion turned to Leonard Cohen, about whose work Jack offered a frank opinion. Layton was flabbergasted: "For a moment I caught a glimpse of the man behind the mask. You're not at all what you'd have the world believe you to be: a philistine who doesn't know the value of the books he's publishing. You shan't be able to sell me that article again, not after hearing your very shrewd and judicious observations and seeing for myself the way you penetrated into the core of a man's writing."[100]

Part of the problem for "the man behind the mask" was that he had little or no time to be, as Margaret Laurence put it, "essentially a private person." The middle of 1965 was particularly disastrous, as he told an author. He had developed a stomach ulcer, and other complications caused in large part by overwork followed: "I spent a very poor summer; didn't do much of anything; got sadly behind in my work, my promises, my commitments."[101]

In addition to the burdens of trying to run a growing publishing house, Jack had to be all things to all manner of men and women. He had to be the judicious yet critical friend of Farley Mowat; he had to keep the talented ego of Pierre Berton in check; he had to convince Margaret Laurence to market herself effectively; he had to mollify Leonard Cohen. He even quarrelled with Malcolm Ross about including *Beautiful Losers* in the NCL; it did not appear in that series until 1991 when Ross retired. (Ross was also extremely reluctant in 1961 to allow Richler's *Son of a Smaller Hero* into the series—it did not appear there until 1966.) Jack even felt compelled to tell William French of *The Globe* how to run his book section; the journalist "interpreted his criticism to mean that not enough M&S books were being reviewed favourably."[102] He also needled French: the book pages of the St. Catharine's *Standard* were the best in Canada, Jack claimed.

The sad truth was that Jack often found it impossible to know exactly who he was, so varied were the demands, so strenuous the pressures.

# 7

## BETWEEN ROCKS AND
## HARD PLACES
# (1966-68)

"I'M NOT PREPARED to go to a psychiatrist personally to solve our problems. I am prepared to arrange appointments for any of you who think it would help you or us. . . . We are not looking for a scapegoat; we are not interested in assessing blame. We are interested in the past only insofar as it is a guide to the future."[1] Jack's attempt at humour in this memorandum is subdued at best. Many M&S employees felt they were living in a high-pressure, crowded loony bin, where they were very much underappreciated. Despite such sentiments, they often happily worked long days to try to make the company operate smoothly. "We're all crazy" was a constant refrain, although spirits were frequently high. There was one very sour note. In June 1967, Jack, in response to the disruption caused by Mark Savage's alcoholism, fired him, although no satisfactory arrangement was ever reached with Savage on his shares in the company.

For Jack, both the "past" and the "future" provided no satisfactory guidelines to understanding the troubled present that confronted him in the mid-sixties. There were two basic problems: projects such as the Canadian Centennial Library, a joint imprint with *Weekend* magazine, were selling well but required huge capital investment and production costs; the backlist—the books a firm produces one year and keeps in print for a number of years—was not quite on the verge of returning the money invested in it. Jack had tried to make a commitment to the future: "A publishing house feeds on itself and if you take a sufficiently long-range view you do *eventually* achieve economic stability. The only interesting part of the McClelland & Stewart financial picture to me is that you see a steady upcurve in the sales of our back list. A lot of this is authors like Sheila Watson, Leonard Cohen, Irving Layton and others. When you publish them you're apparently going to lose money. But they make money in the long run."[2]

But it was the "short run" that was causing all the problems. Previously, McClelland had been in the process of building a relatively small firm and could raise money personally. In the early days, he had not given "too much of a damn" whether the firm was profitable: "If I paid my salary and paid the salary of my employees . . . then my attitude was, okay, we've paid our bills, we've done some good books, this is what the whole thing is about. We were building a publishing company, and a solid publishing company."[3] The backlist was now generating sales of over $1 million a year; the base was a solid one, and of course a backlist did not require expensive editorial or design costs.

Suddenly, Jack was in need of a large cash infusion and found that lenders were not eager to do business with a firm that, in comparison with other types of business, had a poor earnings record. He was honest about his predicament: "Money *doesn't* mean all that much to me, the books mean more to me than the money—it meant one hell of a lot to *them* [the banks]. And suddenly you discover, Oh God, if ten years ago I had followed the normal businessman's concern for a steadily increasing profit, then I'd be able to borrow money today. I wouldn't have the publishing house that I have today, and in fact I don't really believe that McClelland & Stewart would be as useful or as valuable to anybody. But you can't convince a Canadian banker of that."[4]

*Jack, circa 1967*

Idealism defeated by crass commercialism. That was one way of looking at it. Another was to see the firm as the victim of its own success. According to Hugh Kane, the first real trouble arose from the mail-order division created, on the pattern of Time-Life Books, to market the Canadian Centennial Library and the Canadian Illustrated Library. In retrospect, he reflected, "This was extremely successful. McClelland & Stewart doubled its volume in 18 months. Any firm doing that without an infusion of capital is in serious trouble. They expanded far, far too fast."[5]

Some endeavours, such as the Canadian Preview Book Society (for $10 a year a subscriber would receive six paperbacks resembling proof copies four to six weeks before publication), ate up money and were failures. As he revealed in a piece in *The Toronto Daily Star*, Robert Fulford received an announcement of this venture signed by Donald Stewart, director of Special Projects. Certain that there was no longer a Stewart at M&S, the journalist tried to get to the bottom of the mystery and discovered that there was of course no such person. In any event Fulford was not impressed by Stewart's "exciting" new project: "Quite frankly," the publisher's announcement claimed, "this idea will appeal only to those of above-average intellect and accomplishment. A group accustomed to being in the 'Inner Circle,' so to speak." The missive was slightly contradictory and even insulting, as Stewart observed a few paragraphs later, "No longer need your book-reading habits follow the crowd, nor be swayed by the critics."[6] A few days after Fulford's report of his investigation appeared in *The Star*, he ran into Jack, who said only two words: "You bastard."[7]

The planning of the new book club was done by a consultant from New York, Sherman Sackheim. After he returned to Manhattan, M&S had to put his ideas into action, which caused a great deal of trouble. Since M&S always experienced difficulty in getting books ready for their actual publication dates, having books ready four to six weeks in advance proved to be in the main impossible. Some "Preview" books were mailed to subscribers after they were readily available in stores. At the outset Jack told Bob Fulford that Sackheim's scheme was "the greatest single idea in the history of book publishing," but he later informed him that the specially prepared mailing list of potential subscribers had inadvertently been thrown out in the garbage.[8] (In the early eighties, the biographer Phyllis Grosskurth was devastated when some valuable papers she had asked Jack to store for her at Hollinger House were stolen or, more likely, chucked as trash.) Like many M&S schemes, this one had not been thought out completely.

Rumours about inefficiency at M&S became rife. Many of the stories were true. When photocopies of page proofs were mailed out to potential buyers of serial rights, there would always be something drastically wrong with the copies: forty pages would be repeated, chapters would be missing. In response to the continual plagues of errors, Jack would proclaim loudly, "I'm surrounded by fucking idiots." For a while, many people in the media would nod in sympathetic silent agreement, but later many of them would muse about the identity of the person who had hired the fucking idiots.

One anecdote from 1970 illustrates this problem. For a long time Jack had been pursuing Robertson Davies, whose novels were published by Macmillan. However, Davies had done several other projects with M&S and agreed in 1969 to write the book on Stephen Leacock in the

Canadian Writers series. In March 1970, when the book was published, he wrote Jack: "I am sending you with this a marked copy of *Stephen Leacock*. As you will see, the proofreading has been very much neglected and the general preparation of the book has been so careless that in two places substantial portions of the text have been dropped. . . . When the proofs of the book were sent here, they were very carefully proofread and returned with a list of at least thirty-three typographical errors; my secretary was assured, over the telephone . . . that the errors we were returning had already been corrected, but clearly this was not so. . . . The Leacock book is such a mess that I am ashamed to speak of it to my friends and could not dream of recommending it to students. It is humiliating to be associated with it."[9] The careless proofreader was fired, but any chance of Jack's obtaining a novel from Davies had been dashed (he did not give M&S one until 1991 after Jack had retired).

As Canada's Centennial approached, M&S's net sales per annum were nearing $5 million. Unfortunately the Canadian Illustrated Library—in the wake of the success of the Canadian Centennial Library—did not really meet the high expectations placed on it. Until 1966, M&S had not actually lost money, but in 1967 the loss was $67,000. As far as Jack was concerned, he had reached a turning point: the company had to expand yet again, and thus become genuinely profitable and not flirt with disaster, or it would founder. Jack thought that M&S's financial situation would improve if it became larger, and presumably took in more money. Many of his advisers thought the opposite: money had to be earned by publishing profitable titles, not by taking on a number of books, with the idea that the successful ones would pay for the losses of the others.

Late in 1965, he was in touch with Michael McCormick, vice-president of the House of Seagram. During the Second World War, that firm had paid the costs of independently publishing Leacock's *Canada: The Foundation of Its Future* (1941). As a Centennial project, Seagram was interested in finding a successor to the Leacock volume, a worthwhile celebratory project they could underwrite. Although Jack suggested a popular history of Canada written by someone like Pierre Berton or the historian Donald Creighton, he also observed that such a history was not really required. He raised the possibility of support for Farley Mowat's trilogy on the Canadian North.

Perhaps a substantial and beautifully illustrated book on Canada? It could be a project that he had discussed with Charles Bronfman "several years ago" (1960) and that Jack took responsibility for not following up on: a book (more specifically, an anthology to be edited by the historian and critic Reginald Watters) about Canada that would include selections from various Canadian writers with lavish design and photographs: "I'm thinking of the concept of a book that is so superb that it could not be produced by normal commercial sources . . . relatively low priced . . . [with the] widest possible appeal." Such a book, which would normally take about four years to do properly, could only be ready for the Centennial if a lot of extra money was spent on it.

Another possibility was a biography of Sam Bronfman, Charles's father and the founder of the House of Seagram, whose wealth was based on whisky. Jack was well aware that Terence Robertson, the author of the extremely successful Dieppe book (*The Shame and the Glory*, 1962), had been in touch with the Bronfmans about such a venture: "I know, of course, that Terence Robertson had several discussions (perhaps with Charles Bronfman) on the subject of a proposed history of the House of Seagram which would, in effect, be the story of Sam Bronfman. Robertson who is one of our authors has reported to me that he had an enthusiastic reception. He has not pursued the matter further because of other obligations." Jack considered it a better idea—more saleable—to do Sam's biography than a company history. Although such a book would not require a subsidy, it could be subsidized to ensure that the best possible person could be persuaded to undertake the task.[10] A year later, in December 1966, no decision had been reached on any publishing enterprise to be sponsored by the Bronfmans (although, at that point, Jack suggested a one-volume Canadian encyclopedia).

Earlier, in the autumn of 1966, Jack thanked Louis Melzack, the owner of the Classics Bookshop chain, for helping him set up a lunch with Leo Kolber, who managed the Bronfman-owned Cemp Investments. In December, Jack told Melzack, "I don't know whether Leo Kolber has kept you up-to-date on negotiations. Things seem to be proceeding reasonably well at the moment. He has been wonderfully helpful and I am grateful to you for making that possible." What Melzack facilitated was a whole new direction in the relationship between M&S and the House of Seagram.

In the wake of increasing difficulties in raising money through bank loans, Jack's original discussions in 1965 with Seagram regarding a Centennial project now became focused a year later on the possibility of a huge cash infusion in M&S to be made by Cemp Investments and by another prominent Montreal family, the McConnells (St. Lawrence Sugar, *The Montreal Gazette*), the owners of Starlaw, a holding company managed by Derek Price. After protracted negotiations, the cash-strapped publisher made a tentative arrangement whereby the Bronfmans and the McConnells would provide $1.2 million to M&S; a holding company would be established that would be "jointly and equally owned by the three parties." The capital was an investment, not one that was supposed to have any strings attached to the actual working of M&S as a publishing firm.

The "Basis of Agreement" of 1967 included these central statements:

McClelland would retain sole operating control of McClelland & Stewart Limited. This would be interpreted to include the sole right to determine policies and procedures, to appoint personnel, auditors, lawyers and to carry out all normal management functions.

The holding company would retain the right to determine policy respecting alterations in capital structure, capital expenditures over a fixed amount. . . . It would be understood that ownership of the holding company would not be divulged except by mutual agreement.

Although this agreement would convey to McClelland the sole right to manage without interference it would be understood that the holding company would have (a) full access to McClelland &

Stewart Limited records and books . . . (c) the right to assert full control over management of McClelland & Stewart Limited by majority vote of the holding company.[11]

According to this proposal, Cemp and Starlaw were obviously to remain silent partners, but the agreement was essentially contradictory. On the one hand, M&S had "the sole right to determine policies and procedures"; on the other hand, the holding company would have "the right to assert full control over the management" of the company.

Jack had something else on his mind during the first Kolber and McClelland lunch. Sandra Kolber's manuscript of her volume of verse, *Bitter Sweet Lemons and Love*, had been declined by M&S. John Robert Colombo had found it in the slush pile, the unsolicited manuscripts that accumulate at all publishing houses, and recommended that Jack at least think about doing the book. Instead, Jack wrote her a long, sympathetic and constructively critical letter on October 31, 1966, to explain the rejection. He suggested further work on the poems and a consultation with Irving Layton, a friend of hers. In her reply, Sandra told Jack that she had deleted some of the less successful poems and was not worried about the scornful reviews Jack predicted would come from the "little poetry magazines." She returned the shortened manuscript together with her "hearty request" that he publish the book. On November 7, Jack replied, "Fair enough. We'll publish it next year, and I'll see that a contract is sent along in due course. Meanwhile, we'll consider the short version and let you have our comments as soon as possible." Seven days later, Jack sent a memo to John Colombo informing him that M&S would publish the book and that Colombo would act as editor.

Jack's reasons for overriding his original decision are not hard to see: Leo Kolber was Sandra's husband; Louis Melzack was certain the book would sell well in Montreal and would give it window space; an editor at *The Montreal Gazette* was enthusiastic (although Jack suspected this person's reasons for liking it were identical to his own: the author's husband's prominence in the world of high finance). Colombo was told by Jack how he should handle the manuscript, given pointers on design and marketing and ordered to keep mum within M&S about the reasons for publishing it for fear it would be "destroyed in the house by talk." Before the book was published, M&S had been assured that Eaton's College Street store in Toronto would give it a window display. When a phone call to confirm this arrangement was placed, the befuddled, somewhat haughty manager said the idea was preposterous. Leo Kolber was phoned and immediately indicated he would handle the matter. About a half hour later, M&S received a phone call from the same official, now sounding a bit distressed. There had been a complete misunderstanding: of course Mrs. Kolber's book would have a window to itself. The initial order for a few copies became a few hundred. Mordecai was as irreverent as usual when he needled Jack about Mrs. Kolber's "ring-a-ding verses, namely, Me, Leo, and the Menopause."[12]

A far more sensitive matter was the breakdown of the Cemp–Starlaw deal. Years later, Jack summarized the events: "I went to a meeting to finalize the deal, only to find it had become a condition that most of the senior management be replaced. At that time the deal was all but signed, sealed and delivered. I got very emotional and dramatic, told them to stuff it and walked out on the deal without knowing where the hell the money I needed would be coming from."[13]

In January 1968, Jack provided this analysis of the difficult situation he had to deal with: "On December 1st, a condition was stipulated that was unacceptable to me. . . . It required adding to our staff a financial man senior to everyone but me. I cannot say that such a man is not needed . . . however, it altered the proposal . . . in several important ways. . . . I was prepared to sell 50 per cent of the company at less than its real value in order to gain the special long-term association and financial backing that this deal anticipated. But the insertion of one of their people at this stage meant simply that I was giving up control of the company. If that has to be done, I want to sell out completely, not be locked in to what could become an impossible partnership."[14] In effect, Jack had budgeted for this influx of money and was seriously hampered when the deal fell through.

Jack's annual publishing list was becoming impossible to maintain. He now felt he should have kept things short and simple, but he had always resisted such an approach to the marketing of Canadian literature. In January 1967, a worried Alfred Knopf had written Jack about the possible takeover of M&S by Seagram. At first Jack was flippant: he liked the Seagram product—whisky; he was less certain of his own: "Canada has reached the stage where one can publish here with moderate success, but I am afraid we are many years away from being able to take much pride in many of the books we produce. Perhaps I am just despondent because it is January and we have about sixty titles on our spring list. I wish we had ten. We couldn't live with ten, but I'm not certain we can live with sixty."[15]

Five months later, when he had seen the M&S spring list, a somewhat startled Knopf wrote Jack a fatherly letter urging him to cut back on the number of titles he was publishing. Of course Jack agreed with his mentor, but he still felt he was doing what was correct in the Canadian marketplace, where a proper book culture had not really come into existence: "You are right. We can't keep track of the titles and authors. We'd be far better off with a much smaller list, except that my current philosophy is that we can't survive in the Canadian market without a lot of titles."[16] The "current philosophy" was really Jack's "permanent philosophy"—and his Achilles heel.

A difficult situation was compounded by new market forces. By 1968, there were twenty Classic bookstores, almost all in Toronto and Montreal; Coles stretched from coast to coast with about fifty stores. These chains were able to make demands that the independents could not. (In any case, there were relatively few independents: in 1963, there were 900 stores in Canada that sold books, although only 125 were proper booksellers.) Jack Cole was frank about his profession: "Books can be merchandised like beans or peas or anything else." The department stores regarded books as low-profit, low-volume headaches.

"Experience means a lot in bookselling and the department stores don't have it," Jack McClelland reflected. "If a man does well managing the book department, he's promptly moved to dry goods or something else that needs a pusher."[17]

The only major retailer who shared Jack's enthusiasms and vision was Louis Melzack, whom Robert Fulford in 1963 called "the only really aggressive and expansionist bookseller in Canada." In addition to opening what was apparently the first store anywhere devoted to paperbacks in 1955, Melzack was famous for his love of books. His first Toronto Classic bookstore was opened inside the Deer Park branch of the Toronto Public Library. Like Bill Duthie, whose store was next to a public library in Vancouver, Melzack considered bookstores and libraries as necessary complements in each other's existence.

Once when M&S was desperately behind in paying its printers and paper suppliers, Jack asked Louis if he would "pay his bills" for him and this loan would be applied against the huge fall order that Classic placed with him. Melzack saw nothing wrong with this proposal. When Jack once made the same request of Jack Cole, a negative response was quickly issued. Melzack, who had gone into the business of selling books at the age of thirteen and had been tutored by one of his customers, Stephen Leacock, had, as Robert Fulford observed, Jack's "expansionist" fervour. Louis always considered Jack "quirky" but he liked quirky—in fact, he thought it a cornerstone in Jack's success as a publisher. Once when he was asked to negotiate the sale of a valuable manuscript, Jack, in asking Melzack's advice, observed, "I don't own it. I'm just trying to sell it. That's the trouble with this book publishing business. When I'm not acting as a pimp, I'm either a prostitute or a handmaiden."[18]

But even as Jack was feeling badly stretched, his example of encouraging Canadian literature was inspiring the formation of some small Canadian publishers, such as Coach House Press, New Press, House of Anansi and Lorimer, which nursed the young talents of writers like Dennis Lee and Michael Ondaatje.

Jack's fostering of Canadian writing—and his various publicity stunts—had finally bestowed a bit of glamour on the previously staid notion of the writer in Canada, a country that had for the first time fallen in love with a prime minister, Pierre Elliott Trudeau, and that all of a sudden saw itself as capable of creating popular international and national entertainers like Joni Mitchell and Gordon Lightfoot. And now there were also bright stars such as Pierre Berton, Farley Mowat and Margaret Laurence in the Canadian literary firmament.

Despite many successes, all kinds of other problems confronted Jack. As he told Hugh Kane in July 1968, he was sorely disappointed by Grace Irwin's novel, *Contend with Horses* (1969): "It is a shame this girl is such a prig because she really writes well and has a good deal of skill in constructing her fiction."[19] As the book stood, it was extremely old-fashioned and its print run was only two thousand. In the spring of 1967, Farley called to insist that *Sibir: My Discovery of Siberia* be published that autumn. But his call came too late: planning for the fall catalogue was already complete. There is, Jack told an employee, "a real probability that we shall have to indulge Farley."[20] In this instance Jack was lucky: the book did not appear until 1970.

Jack also had serious reservations about Adrienne Clarkson's novel *A Lover More Condoling* (1968), although he realized she was reaching a market that was elusive but perhaps financially rewarding: "This is not a great book, but it's not all that bad. It's a promotion item and we should get in and out of it quickly. . . . It should be an elegant, tasteful women's-type book. Although Adrienne would probably have a fit because she is a little further out than this, I can best describe the concept in my mind by saying that the finished product should look at home on the coffee table beside a copy of *Mademoiselle* magazine as distinct from *Vogue*. What I am trying to suggest is something a shade off the cold, high-style elegance of the latter, but that is still elegant and has a touch of the intellectual pretension of *Mademoiselle*." In a witty aside, he concluded, "Migod, we publish homosexuals and now I admit that I read ladies' magazines. It makes me nervous."[21]

Pierre Berton's *Smug Minority* (1968) was a sort of son of *The Comfortable Pew*. The earlier book subsidized by the Anglicans was followed by this one, which, as Berton recalled, the NDP asked him to write. "The only assistance the NDP would provide would be a series of weekly discussions with people chosen by the party and by myself."[22]

Books that centred on politics presented Jack with some difficulties because he wanted to avoid the appearance that the firm was taking sides. In November 1967, he told Peter Newman, "Your comments on our political publishing are both flattering and extremely interesting. I think you are probably overemphasizing the importance of this particular group of books, but nonetheless it has been an area of publishing that I have particularly enjoyed and sales have been modestly gratifying. I think, perhaps, the best book in this general category that we did was a small paperback by Judith Robinson called *This Is on the House* and published about ten years ago. It was no runaway best-seller, but it did reasonably well, and I had some feeling at the time that it played at least a small part in bringing about the change in the government. . . . As you are aware, we have been very careful to straddle the political fence thus far. I am a little nervous . . . that when Pierre's little blockbuster comes out in the spring, we may be forever marked as a left-wing house."[23]

For Jack, Berton's new book eventually presented him with even more considerable complications; according to a memo he sent Hugh on May 27, 1968, Pierre had "worked out an arrangement with the NDP whereby they will be using *The Smug Minority* as an election manifesto of sorts. . . . As far as my attitude is concerned, I don't mind saying that I deplore the fact that Pierre approached the NDP, but that's his business. In actual fact he would be willing to support any party or any candidate that used his book. From our point of view, I don't think it associates us with the NDP, and I think as far as book sales in the stores are concerned, they have probably dwindled to the point where the effect of this program can only be beneficial, not harmful." He also mentioned that Berton was to appear with Tommy Douglas "in a national TV free-time broadcast in a form of debate in which he will challenge Douglas on various points relating to *The Smug Minority*." The NDP "will supply books (within limits) to any candidate willing to support the Berton thesis and

*The Smug Minority.* To this end a questionnaire has been mailed to the candidates. If the questions are answered satisfactorily in Pierre's opinion, he has then agreed that he will support that particular candidate publicly and that that candidate will use the book." This initiative involved offering a free book on a first-come first-served basis to people who were prepared to go to the candidate to collect it. Jack thought as many as ten thousand copies would be used by this scheme (Berton had agreed to forgo royalties on this promotion; M&S provided books to the NDP "in quantities of not less than five thousand at 75 [cents] apiece").[24]

Much more interesting than the agreement between M&S, the NDP and Berton was the reason for it. Initially Jack had been so enthusiastic about the book's success that he announced the biggest advance printing in Canadian publishing history: 100,000 copies, the break-even point being 40,000. However, sales only reached 70,000, thus giving the impression that the book was a commercial flop, leading to rumours, as Pierre Berton recalled, "that its publication had nearly bankrupted McClelland & Stewart, that [Berton] had been forced to buy up half the printing so the book would not be remaindered. McClelland was said to have fifty thousand hidden away in his basement."[25] In fact, providing the NDP with copies of the book at rock-bottom prices proved to be a brilliant strategy in getting rid of the stockpile of 30,000 copies.

At the same time he continued on his roller-coaster ride trying to keep M&S solvent, Jack maintained his strong convictions about the place of authors in his scheme of things. He was concerned that authors were not being treated as well as possible by staff: "We are middlemen offering a service to authors. It is a service business. We serve well or not. If we let them down we hurt ourselves, just as in any other service industry. Satisfied authors are our most effective PR tool. Unhappy ones are our most expensive liability. Don't forget it.

"You can make almost any mistake at M&S and be given another chance—rudeness or arrogance in dealing with authors—no matter who they are—I will not tolerate." In the same directive, he even suggested priorities in the treatment of writers, always keeping in mind that "the author is king":

1. M. Laurence, Peter Newman, Farley Mowat can do no wrong. We indulge them. On a judgment issue, always balance in their favour. In doubt, ask for a ruling. Never be afraid to ask.
2. Lesser authors obviously are indulged to a lesser degree, without in any sense weakening the principle that we are performing a service.

Co-ordination was another key principle being overlooked at M&S, leading Jack to frame "McClelland's Laws":

(a) The inevitability of error or oversight at M&S is beyond comprehension.
(b) Anything you don't check personally will go sour.
(c) The fewer the loopholes for error, the greater the likelihood they will occur.
(d) Anyone in book publishing is basically a masochist.
(e) The inevitability of error is equal to the impossibility of pinpointing responsibility.
(f) Don't trust anyone who is foolish enough to work in a book publishing firm.[26]

Jack's defence of the rights of authors was uttered even as he saw the publishing enterprise in Canada as a bleak one. He was especially down on Toronto as the centre of such firms in English-speaking Canada, as can be seen in this tongue-in-cheek account: "There is little community of interest, no literary core, no literary establishment.... Toronto is a cold and dispiriting literary scene in other ways. Few notable authors live here. Indeed, so sparse is the literary population that we are frequently called on to round out the numbers at literary parties by sending staff members . . . [to] impersonate distinguished authors. As a result Torontonians on occasion find themselves unexpectedly encountering Stephen

Leacock, Bliss Carman, Ralph Connor and others who have long since gone to a better world. . . . Only in Toronto [could the manager of the Maple Leafs] Punch Imlach become Author of the Week."[27] In the wake of such indifference, Jack tried to make things lively. For example, the launch party for *Will the Real Gordon Sinclair Please Stand Up?* (1966) was held in the lion's den of the Riverdale Zoo (the lion was tranquillized).

Jack also maintained that the Toronto newspapers did not find books newsworthy. Given this situation, "We are forced to urge our authors to involve themselves in car accidents, rape, shoplifting and radical speeches in Allan Gardens, in order to bring themselves to the attention of the press."[28] So "soul-destroying" was Toronto as a book publishing centre that, according to Jack, "The most reliable coverage of important Canadian books—much as I hate to admit it—appears in the Canadian edition of *Time*." Despite the gloom and doom, he did not see everything as lost: "Some of the younger publishing houses like the Coach House Press, the House of Anansi, the New Press and others may yet create a literary scene."[29]

Although he deliberately cultivated the misapprehension on the part of many authors and book people that he was something of a yahoo in intellectual matters, this was pure facade, as Irving Layton had discovered earlier. In reality, Jack had "so much culture [he] could hardly walk." He was certainly well rounded in his cultural interests. On a regular basis, he read *The Globe, The Star, The Telegram, The Financial Post, The Financial Times, The New York Review of Books, Maclean's, Saturday Night, Publishers Weekly, Quill & Quire* and *The Canadian Forum*; he perused *Playboy* and *F. U.C.K.* He certainly was in touch with popular culture: he almost never went to the theatre, but he liked to keep up with the latest Hollywood films and was known to enjoy skin flicks. His favourite magazine was the American *Atlantic Monthly*.[30]

Authors continued to provide Jack with a wide variety of lively vexations. Pierre Berton reacted sensitively if he felt an author who did not approach him in sales volume was given more of the limelight, or if his name was being used to promote someone like Gordon Sinclair (he was furious when a small slip-in advertisement for one of Sinclair's books was inserted into copies of one of his own titles; Berton thought the process should have been carried out in reverse).

Farley continued to be an everlasting source of both delight and frustration, as Jack confided to the author's American editor, Peter Davison, in February 1967: "His next book will probably be about the goddamn whale . . . a huge finwhale—it may run to seventy-five feet and about eighty tons and is possibly pregnant—trapped itself in a small natural aquarium near Burgeo. It went in at high tide over a shelf, and it now appears there is no natural way for it to get out. Farley has been appointed Keeper of the Whale by Joey Smallwood and is administering a fund to feed it."[31] The whale's problem, Jack informed Farley, could have led to financial security for M&S: "My own scheme involved a huge plastic tank in which we would have floated the whale up to Expo. My theory was that at a dollar a shot we would have cleared $30 million at Expo. The cost of getting the whale up there might have been $2.5 million, so we could have netted $27.5 million, which, as a matter of fact, I could use right now."[32] As it stood, Jack had to be content with the more mundane (but quite lucrative) level of profits generated by *A Whale for the Killing*, not published until 1972.

Although it seemed in principle that Peter Newman could do no wrong, Jack found him a difficult person to like. Newman's reticence and shyness were incorrectly read by his publisher as some sort of signal that the author did not like or appreciate him. The clash was of personality types, not mutually opposing wishes. The first hint of discord can be seen in an internal memorandum of February 1966. A testy Jack McClelland is irritated because Newman wants to receive his full-time pay at *The Toronto Daily Star* but work half-time in order to write *The Distemper of Our Times: Canadian Politics in Transition* (1968). Newman's boss, Ralph Allen, informed him this could happen only if a substantial (sixty-thousand-word) serialization was turned over to *The Star* at the time the book was published. Jack was forced to negotiate such a solution, but he was not happy about it, obviously feeling the Diefenbaker biographer was being a bit greedy: Newman "is making well over $40,000 with the column now. He has acquired a taste for luxury and he's sort of trapped in the sense that to give up this rate of earning even for six months isn't the easiest thing in the world. Despite [this], Peter wants to do a book."[33]

A year later, Peter also wanted Jack to assist him in furthering the writing career of his wife, Christina McCall, who had edited and introduced *The Man from Oxbow* (1967) by Ralph Allen, who had died very recently. Newman insisted that Christina not be told that he had asked Jack to help her. Dutifully Jack wrote:

> I finally found time to read the full manuscript of *The Man from Oxbow*. Up to that point I had read only your introduction. I must say that delighted as I was with the introduction, I am even more impressed by the work as a whole. . . . You may wonder what has happened to Jack McClelland. I don't normally read the books that we are going to publish these days—there seems to be far too many other things to keep me busy—except perhaps for a new one by Peter, or Pierre, or Farley. Well, I read this one mainly because I am going to be talking about it at our sales conference. I am glad I read it, and I congratulate you again. All of which leads me logically to the point that I think you should now give serious consideration to doing a book that is completely your own.[34]

Jack and Christina discussed the possibility of her doing a life of the celebrated Montreal neurosurgeon Wilder Penfield, but she decided against the project: she had a hyperactive, very demanding three-year-old child and a hyperactive, very demanding thirty-eight-year-old husband.[35] Jack shot back, "We would be prepared to make a sufficient advance to look after babysitters, housekeepers, and even, for God's sake, a mistress for Peter if that would help."[36]

Newman's insecurity surfaced when he complained to Jack in June 1968 about the competition for sales that would be unleashed if Judy LaMarsh's *Memoirs of a Bird in a Gilded Cage* was released at the same time as his *Distemper of Our Times*, which also dealt with Canadian politics in the sixties. Jack attempted to reassure him: "Again let me confirm that the LaMarsh book will not be published until next January at the earliest. We did sign a contract with her and we do have control of the situation. She did agree that a head-on conflict with your book would not serve anybody's best interests."[37] Smoothing ruffled feathers was part of Jack's job, but in the process he could become miffed at the author who demanded such comfort.

Jack's temper was often in danger of going out of control. He was dismayed when Earle Birney informed him that someone at M&S had told a would-be buyer in England that they could not supply him with the single copy of a volume of verse by Birney that he required. When the poet complained, Jack informed him that "it is not true that Canadian publishers make no effort to find their authors publishers abroad. It is not true that Canadian publishers are financially unable to compete in foreign markets with the books they publish in Canada, if I correctly understand the meaning of that statement. And as to mailing a single book to a buyer in England, we won't even mail a single book to a person in Canada unless they are a retailer. We are supposed to be wholesalers, not retail booksellers. Why the idiot who handled the order didn't refer it to a local bookstore, I don't know. It's difficult to employ anything but idiots these days."[38]

In 1967–68, Jack exchanged acerbic letters with Irving Layton. The trouble this time was with two books on Layton's work that had been commissioned by M&S and that Jack did not feel were publishable. The author, a friend of Layton's, became distraught and, as far as Jack was concerned, difficult. Layton, who desperately wanted the books to appear so that his stature as a serious poet would be enhanced, defended his acolyte, leading to a sharp reprimand from his publisher:

> Are you really all that bloody insecure? I could vomit. Let's get a few things straight and on the record. Firstly, from the time we started publishing your work, my public statements (which have been many) and my private conversations (which have also been many) have been consistent and have followed only this line: that

you are probably the greatest poet this country has yet produced, that you are a great teacher and that you are a great human being, and that you have elevated the art of poetry in this country because your poetry is not academic exercise or acrobatic but that it represents the life, thoughts, feelings, emotions, sensitivities, strengths and weaknesses of a human being who writes and feels what he lives and lives and feels what he writes. . . . Certainly we have used, when we could, modern promotional methods to sell the books. . . . You tell me I should struggle with my conscience. Forget it, baby. You are the one with the problem and it is as simple as that. . . . Well, good luck. Enjoy yourself. Maybe you will get to have lunch with Norrie Frye. Another thing I should tell you, old friend, is that the most important thing that your poetry accomplished in this country is to make poetry respectably unrespectable. Or if you prefer, unrespectably respectable. Poetry in Canada used to be in the hands of old ladies and the odd gifted human being like Bliss Carman. . . . Okay, you are fifty-six and you will turn your back on all that you have accomplished. Let's pretend your concerns have not been really blood and guts and life and death and people as they are. . . . No, let's change the Layton image. I can curb my crass, commercial motivation. My avarice is not boundless.[39]

In the midst of everything else, two entirely new problems were introduced by Isabel LeBourdais and Scott Symons, authors who challenged the legal and moral laws of Canada.

In 1959, fourteen-year-old Steven Truscott was convicted in adult court in the Ontario murder-rape of twelve-year-old Lynne Harper. Isabel LeBourdais, the wife of Donat LeBourdais, who was an M&S author (*Metal and Men: A History of Canadian Mining,* 1957), and the sister of Gwethalyn Graham (*Earth and High Heaven,* 1964), followed the case and the trial carefully. Certain that a horrible miscarriage of justice had taken place, LeBourdais wanted to write an account of the entire legal mishmash. On May 8, 1961, Jack (in an unsent letter) told her that he was really "hooked" on the preliminary material, the thirty pages she had shown him. He himself believed Truscott was innocent, "but whether he did or whether he didn't [kill her], according to our popular view of justice he should not have been convicted." Like LeBourdais, Jack was keen on Steven taking a lie detector test, "even though the results would not influence my opinion that the book should be published. If the . . . test indicated he had not committed the crime, our position would be greatly strengthened. If it indicated that he probably did . . . I don't think that our point of view or thesis should be affected. It would still be true that he should not have been convicted, that he was not given a fair trial."

However, Jack had qualms about the legality of what he was thinking of publishing. He asked advice of Fred Hume, an M&S lawyer. Before his reply arrived, Jack drafted yet another unsent letter. He wondered if Truscott had indeed committed the murder. The trial had many troubling aspects. (Why did Truscott himself not appear on the stand—or his father or brother, or any character witnesses, for that matter?) Jack asked, "Why, if the parents believed the boy to be innocent, did they not get the best lawyer money could buy for the appeal? (And don't say they didn't have the funds; this is not a satisfactory answer.) . . . It seems to me, Isabel, that we are in complete agreement that it was not a fair trial. Of that I haven't the slightest doubt . . . Superficially at least, [my] theory seems to leave fewer unsolved riddles lying about than yours [goes on to use evidence that backs his theory] . . . If this theory were true, would any of these people admit it to you or to anyone else? I don't think so, because even though their action could be condoned morally, it could not be condoned technically and everyone could be disbarred, fined and possibly even jailed. All this is sheer conjecture, of course, and I hope you can show me that it's nonsense. . . . I am more than ever convinced that we must find the answer."[40]

By July 4, he had decided to publish the book, but he asserted that Isabel had to realize that her proposed book "presents complexities unlike any that we have encountered before. . . . I shall be candid and say that we are going to demand from you more faith in us than we are prepared to extend to you. We feel there is no alternative because of the intangible elements—interest and welfare of the individual, possible libel, contempt of court, etc.—that are involved." He spelled out details and asked, "We want to know whether you are prepared to give us the substantial control over the project implied in all the foregoing?" She replied, "I think I understand and am satisfied with your reasons for not caring for the title [*Who Killed Lynne Harper?*], introduction, first chapter and conclusion. A book of lasting value and wide significance is naturally desirable in both our views. I can see no reason why the interests of Steven Truscott would be in any way less served. The 'complexities' of our more formal agreement remain somewhat of a mystery to me, since from my point of view it is obvious that you wouldn't publish the book if you didn't approve of it. Co-operation between us cannot work to my disadvantage in any way I can conceive of, and I welcome it."[41] Everything seemed to be going well, as Jack's next letter to LeBourdais makes clear: "You are wonderful and I love you dearly. . . . The complexity . . . is simply this. When we make a contract, we like to make one that has some significance. . . . A contract that gives us the right to renege simply because we don't like the script is hardly a binding contract. In this particular case, there are so many legal reasons why we might have to decline—reasons that are not now apparent—that it makes it complex. In any case, it's not important since our joint approach to the whole matter seems to be completely compatible."[42]

Compatibility became a secondary concern when the manuscript was delivered the next spring. The readers' reports were unanimously negative, as was Jack: the book was poorly written, overemotional, frequently dull and possibly libelous. Jack told Ruth Taylor, the book's editor: "The editorial task defies contemplation. I can't imagine anyone directing her editorially in such a way that a publishable book could result. I wouldn't know where to start. The only possible hope now is to convince her that someone else must take over *or* [we must] reluctantly cancel the contract." Isabel refused to hand over her material to a ghost writer. She revised the manuscript twice more, at which time Jack felt the book might be publishable. At that point LeBourdais wanted Conway Turton to edit the manuscript. However, Turton was worried because the manuscript identified the person LeBourdais thought to be the killer.

Over the next year, fights about the book continued unabated. In August 1963, the enraged author told her reluctant publisher, "Whether you can get another book like mine, I doubt. I know I can get another publisher. . . . After all our association . . . I am left with only *one* reason for wanting to continue with you at all, and that is speed of publication. And unless I hear within a week that the stalling is over and you are going ahead in a far more businesslike and respectful fashion than heretofore, that reason will be removed. . . . If you are proud to be [the book's] publisher and are prepared to do a damn good job, get busy and prove it. And then you can count on me, all the way . . . or are you scared of it?"[43]

Many opinions were sought about the book's harsh, often a priori indictment of the justice system. Ruth Taylor, who visited the crime scene with the author and even accompanied LeBourdais to visit an uncomfortable, apprehensive Truscott, could not get LeBourdais to change the book's tone. The situation was nearly hopeless. Finally, on January 1, 1964, the author had had enough: "From the beginning you have shown no confidence in me and no respect for my experience or knowledge. You have consistently taken the opinions of any Tom, Dick, Harry or Jane who was a reader, or lawyer, or editor, or stooge and placed them ahead of mine or that of anyone who has been advising me. . . . Anyone can take the easy road and play safe." She ended on a very personal note: "My mother died on November 7. If you had published early in September as you said you would . . . she would have seen the book. As it was, she died without ever knowing that the book was published, or that I had succeeded in doing anything to save the boy she had grown to care about so much—Steven. I don't think I shall ever forgive you for that. I shall never mention this again."

Jack apologized, and the book was withdrawn. Over a year later, on May 10, 1965, unable to get the book off his mind, he approached her:

Seriously, Isabel, if you have not yet been able to work out a publishing arrangement with someone else, and if you are still interested in publishing the book, and if you are prepared to soften your position a little, we are still very much interested. Let me be quite straightforward about this. I am not suggesting a compromise, at least on our part. The position that we took—leaving aside any emotional outbursts on either side—was, in my view, the position that we had to take. We still feel exactly the same way. We would like to publish the book, but only if you will stick to the facts and not tilt at windmills. You may not think that this is much of a proposal coming from me. The fact is that I would feel very badly to think that this story is not to be published. If you have been able to make other publishing arrangements, that's good and I'm delighted. If you haven't, I do wish you would reconsider.

By this time, LeBourdais, who had tried unsuccessfully to negotiate with several other Canadian firms, had sent her manuscript to Ludovic Kennedy, the English journalist whose sensational *Ten Rillington Place* (1961) had proven that the wrong man had been hanged for the murder of his wife and baby. Kennedy passed LeBourdais's manuscript on to his publisher, the left-wing crusader Victor Gollancz. Deeply impressed by the book's passionate argument, he vowed he would flood Canada with copies, even if he lost money in the process.[44]

Fortunately Gollancz did not have to make good his threat. Assured by the English firm that the book in its present state would not attract a libel action, M&S published the book in Canada, paying a fee to Gollancz for permission to produce the book by offset printing. Within a few weeks after publication in 1966, almost sixty thousand copies (cloth and paper) were sold, making the controversial title a whirlwind success.

The book's influence went far beyond the events of the early 1960s, as the eminent politician Stanley Knowles told Jack: "I am both shocked and frightened by [the book]. . . . If the procedures followed in the Truscott trial are standard, there must be many miscarriages of

justice in this country. Something must be done to correct these procedures."[45] In 1967, the Canadian Parliament took the unusual step of
referring the Truscott case to the Supreme Court, which did not strike
down the conviction. After serving ten years of his sentence, the obviously innocent Truscott was released on parole.

In 1965, at the age of thirty-two, Scott Symons left his wife and son,
was fired (for insubordination) from his curatorship of the Canadiana
collection at Toronto's Royal Ontario Museum and went to live in
Montreal where he wrote his first novel, *Place d'Armes: A Personal
Narrative* (1967). Composed as a so-called combat journal, the narrative is printed in five typefaces and has two narrators, each based on
aspects of the author's character. The book's raw power derives from
its exploration of the division between heterosexual and homosexual
in himself and on his use of that division to talk about the split between
English and French cultures in contemporary Canada. As he told Jack,
he saw the book as "positive": "a young Canadian's plea for a relevant
Canadian civilization. . . . As you probably know, I have parted company with the Royal Ontario Museum . . . so that I can devote myself
to what is the number-one Canadian question: creative survival."[46]
Symons was well aware that his book, very close to the autobiographical bone, would be controver-
sial. In fact, he confronted his publisher with this issue: "You had the
courage to commission the book.
I'll be damn surprised if you don't
have the courage to publish it! No
one else that I know of in Canada
would have done either. . . . Wait till
you read it!"[47] To a fellow publisher,
Jack characterized the book in
restrained but positive terms: "It's an
offbeat piece of work, a little bit on
the shocking side."[48]

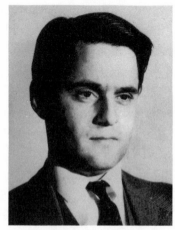

*Scott Symons*

Short, muscular, intense and charismatic, Symons has a background not completely dissimilar to Jack's: he had been educated at the Rosedale Public School and then at Trinity College School in Port Hope, Ontario, the University of Toronto Schools and Trinity College at the University of Toronto. Unlike Jack, whose personal freedom had been respected by his parents, Scott felt confined from boyhood by his parents and by society, largely because he felt compelled to suppress the homosexual portion of his nature, even though he did have a love affair with another boy at Trinity College School. As a youngster he was made to feel that his body and his erotic desires were "dirty." In an attempt to avoid such feelings, he became a gymnast, which was solitary, ritualistic and graceful. As an adult Symons was half in, half out of the fast track of worldly success. He was a rebel, but he remained within the system. Finally he escaped to Montreal, where he began to see more and more clearly that his country's duality reflected his own: "I guess I really reached the point at which I had to live out, enact, what I believe. I can no longer merely think it, or suspect it. . . . I have got to live my crisis. My crisis is a spiritual one, and it is inextricably bound up with the nature of Canada."[49]

Symons, a volatile combination of upper-class Tory snobbery and in-your-face gayness, once received his editor, Diane Mew, at his posh home clad only in his bathrobe. On another occasion he arrived at M&S accompanied by a sinister-looking young man, who, it turned out, was the taxi driver who had driven him and whom he was trying to pick up. When Diane visited Symons in a hospital ward, he loudly talked about a friend: "I told him he had no balls." At the launch for *Place d'Armes* held at his home, he invited Irving Layton, who in his customary way proclaimed himself loudly, and Earle Birney, who glowered in self-imposed isolation.

If Jack found Symons's work a bit shocking, he was careful not to betray this in his dealings with the author, to whom he was nevertheless extremely frank about his reaction to his next novel, *Civic Square*. With the non-judgmental compassion of a man who was aware of his own shortcomings, Jack provided Scott with an accurate appraisal of his work. Although supportive and imaginative, Jack came down on the side of revision, more revision and yet more revision:

> I have just finished reading about half of the new manuscript and thought I should write to you. . . . I probably won't get around to reading the rest of it in the immediate future, which is a lousy thing to say to an author, but the fact of the matter is that there is little purpose in my doing so. I don't, at the moment, have time to read for pleasure. Being a book publisher is not unlike being a wine merchant, I guess, in that you can't survive if you spend too much time sampling the merchandise. . . . So I don't have time to read the rest of your manuscript, which is a deftly turned compliment. . . . The exuberance you should keep, but having made your point, get on with the next one. I think it is too free. I think you spread your shots too widely and lose some of your targets because of it. Don't ask me for examples. It would be far better to ignore the point, but I think you should read through very carefully and continually ask why, why, why. What's this to the reader? . . . the too frequent use of word combos. If you find haircomb, handwash, flyzip and windpass (and I admit you don't) all in one sentence, it becomes a bit much, a bit affected, and it mars the style. I also think you are a bit liberal with your talk and with my favourite four-letter word, fuck. I think it is quite startling and immeasurably effective to read in a piece of serious prose that the country is all fucked up. But I am certain that you destroy its value when you use it too freely. This is not a censorship plea, God knows. What I guess I am trying to say is that you weaken the whole piece by coming on a bit strong on the emancipation bit.[50]

Since cutting did not come easily to Symons, the book was eventually boxed—not bound—and sold as a reproduction of 848 typewritten pages. The box itself was blue and was intended to suggest the packaging used by Birks, the fashionable jewellery company. Each copy of the eight-and-a-half-pound book was personalized by Symons: with a red felt pen, he drew birds, flowers and penises in every copy—his gift to the reader. In 1969, when *Civic Square* was published, the author sent this message—accompanied by a drawing of enthusiastic male genitalia—to his publisher: "Cocks are beautiful,/ All cocks are beautiful./ Not only in themselves (because some are more, or less)/ but more for what they do./ And what we do with them./ When we permit."[51]

In the process of acting as editor-publisher (a role he hated), Jack was drawn into the deep divisions within the author and within himself, something Symons noticed when he began to write letters to his publisher calling Jack's attention to some of those contradictions. If you are willing to publish my book, Symons was telling him, you are a much more complex and interesting person than you think you are. Symons was also aware of the connections between Jack and himself in their backgrounds and shared love of the greatness of Canada and what it had the potential to become:

> You must sense that somehow I am hitting deep into things that affect you—Jack McClelland. Jack McClelland as a guy, a man, a male, a husband, a lover and also lastly (and quite least in my order of interest) a publisher. Because I am deep into these things . . . Nothing in my mind is as disastrous as a man who is afraid of himself, his own cock—or his own wife, or another man's wife, or even another man. . . .
>
> What is, in my mind, great about you, is that you . . . are willing to let a guy like me get on . . . and publish it. And that takes conviction and guts. . . . I agree about finding an inexpensive (and non-gimmicky) format for the book. . . . I guess what I'm saying, Jack, is that if you can't tell another human being that you love them (without being suspected of every deviation in the book), then something is wrong with all of us. And if you can't say that, and know that, then we all have to be suspicious of conning one another. And I'm not. Love, Scott.

Symons's conviction of just how really committed Jack was to him led to a further declaration:

> the relationship which is growing between you and me is far from a "business relationship." It is much closer to the relationship that existed between Thomas Wolfe and [Maxwell Perkins, his editor]. A relationship that was one of profound friendship and love. In the case of Wolfe and his publisher-editor it became virtually a Father-Son relationship. . . . Our relationship is much more like that of a Prefect and a promising New Boy. . . . You recognize that this difficult courageous stubborn male lucid verbose guy called Scott is saying something. . . . And you're trying to help me say it. . . . You're holding a door open—and saying hurry up, ya little bastard . . . I'll help you, but make it quick; I can't guarantee it forever. . . . And that is our relationship: one of affection, admiration, twinges of deep shy love, and help mutually. . . . You're not a Big Daddy, or a Bossman, or a President . . . you're a buddy who is more than a buddy, a comrade who is a comrade-in-arms—if I can pun on dangerous delicate grounds, you're a Publisher-in-Arms. A militant publisher who is also a buddy-in-arms . . . with my image here being that of linked arms.
>
> Now I am on dangerous ground. But I'm going to thrust through. I am on dangerous ground because it can sound as though I am using homosexual imagery about you, Jack. Let me be clear about this. I do not believe you to be a "homosexual"—not at all.[52]

Although Scott gave Jack an assurance he had not requested, the two men were much alike in their ability to fly in the face of received advice, conventional wisdom.

Years later, in 1977, Symons recalled with startling clarity exactly what Jack's influence on him had been: "Do you remember the day when I came to you, and we discussed the first book I would write? . . . This was in 1965. And you agreed that, yes, I should write a book about being fucked by a city, by Montreal! And you stuffed an advance of

$500 into my trembling hand. And I sallied off. . . . Something else I would like to tell you now. For years the only psychic and emotional home I had was . . . McClelland & Stewart."[53]

In a wry aside, Jack vented his concern about allowing full expression of Symons's exuberant pronouncements concerning the high level of repression found in Canadian society:

This business of being his publisher is for us both joyful and terrifying. The problem with him as we see it is that his lack of discipline is killing him both as a man and as a writer. . . . P.S. Let me say . . . we are considering the propriety of adding a section in his new book in which he speculates in some detail on the relative sizes of the erect penises of such prominent Canadians as Lester Pearson, Paul Martin, Paul Hellyer and I guess Charlotte Whitton [mayor of Ottawa], to name only a few. Is Canada ready for this? Is it necessary? Desirable? Permissible? Do we censor him? Do we tell him he has already delivered this particular message more effectively in thirty other places in the same manuscript (which is true) when we know in advance that his answer will be that the important thing is that he be permitted to say what he feels at this particular point in this particular context or everything is lost. I can't help feeling that it must have been both easier and more profitable to publish Lucy Maud Montgomery.[54]

Symons may have had many axes of his own to grind, but he saw into the insecure side of Jack McClelland in a way few authors ever did. He beheld the man who was eager to publish good Canadian titles, even though they might be risky in terms of subject matter and style; he also saw the person who was run ragged by that ambition in the harsh business world.

In 1967, M&S published eighty books.[55] (Of course M&S in their role as agents for foreign publishers *distributed* many other titles each year.) This may not seem an inordinately large number of books for a major firm, but it did represent an enormous increase in the number published annually since Jack joined the firm: 1946: 15; 1950: 9; 1955: 21; 1958: 20; 1960: 30; 1962: 50; 1964: 53; 1965: 71; 1966: 75. Of course, not all authors will be equally successful in the marketplace, but the publisher may have made legal or personal commitments to every one. This results in a large infrastructure that takes a great deal of money to support.

In 1967, Pierre Berton's *Hollywood's Canada,* Irving Layton's *Periods of the Moon,* Farley Mowat's *Polar Passion* and Al Purdy's *North of Summer: Poems from Baffin Island* appeared. These were well-known writers whose careers Jack had encouraged. Many of the other titles reflected the fact that M&S was a general trade publisher catering to the needs of Canadians from all walks of life: Ivan Shaffer's *Stock Promotion Business: The Inside Story of Canadian Mining Deals and the People Behind Them, BP Canada Travel Guide 1967,* David A. Randall's exposé of the auto insurance business, *Dollars on the Highway,* Simma Holt's *Sex and the Teen-Age Revolution,* Richard Jones's *Community in Crisis: French-Canadian Nationalism in Perspective,* E. E. Rich's *Fur Trade and the Northwest to 1857,* Luella Creighton's social history, *The Elegant Canadians,* Eleanor Findlay and Margaret Capes's *Today You Are Pregnant: A Common-Sense Guide for Expectant Mothers,* J. M. S. Careless's *Union of the Canadas: The Growth of Canadian Institutions, 1841–1857,* Herbert Whittaker's *Canada's National Ballet* and Rabbi Gunther Plaut's *Your Neighbour Is a Jew.* Among the imports were *The Autobiography of Bertrand Russell* and A. A. Milne's *Christopher Robin Book of Verse.* There were two books centred on the indigenous peoples: *Eskimo Masks: Art and Ceremony* and Ronald Melzack's *The Day Tuk Became a Hunter and Other Eskimo Stories.* There were a number of high-risk items: David Lewis Stein's protest novel, *Scratch One Dreamer,* Peter Taylor's first novel, *Watcha Gonna Do Boy . . . Watcha Gonna Be?,* George Bowering's first novel, *Mirror on the Floor,* P. K. Page's volume of verse, *Cry Ararat!,* and, of course, Scott Symons's *Place d'Armes.* This listing, which is far from exhaustive but typical of the M&S list from 1960 to 1985, shows how seriously Jack took his nationalist ambitions.

Under Jack, M&S enjoyed great success in increasing its share of Governor General's Awards (GGs), which began in 1936. In 1948, two years after Jack joined the company, Hugh MacLennan won the Governor General's Award for fiction with *The Precipice* (Collins) and A. M. Klein for poetry with *The Rocking Chair and Other Poems* (Ryerson); Thomas Raddall's *Halifax: Warden of the North*, an M&S book, won the prize for non-fiction. Two Indian File volumes—James Reaney's *Red Heart* and James Wreford Watson's *Of Time and the Lover*—won for poetry in 1949 and 1950 respectively; R. S. Lambert's *Franklin of the Arctic* won the juvenile award in 1950 for M&S. No M&S titles received GGs in 1951 or 1952, but Douglas LePan, P. K. Page, Pierre Berton and Irving Layton were among those winning in the fifties; in the sixties, Brian Moore, Douglas LePan, Al Purdy, Margaret Laurence, Mordecai Richler and Leonard Cohen were successful. From 1973 to 1976, M&S garnered all four fiction awards; however, three Macmillan authors provided stiff competition by winning awards in the seventies: Alice Munro, Timothy Findley and Robertson Davies.

As the list increased in size and awards accrued, it was Jack's relentless dedication that inspired the workforce at M&S, although they did not appreciate being labelled "idiots" by their employer in public pronouncements. Many employees had caught the spirit of their boss. They were doing important work, and many were exceptionally dedicated, despite the constant threat of financial extinction facing the company, the constant worry that their jobs would vanish.

Being the M&S publisher meant taking even more risks than publishers normally do. Advances, which were never above industry standards, did not contribute to the company's financial woes. Rather, it was the sheer magnitude of Jack's commitment. The list, which had taken years to build, was simply too large and became even larger: 87 titles in 1970, 84 in 1972, 101 in 1973. Ultimately Jack saw himself as a Sisyphus who had created his own enormous stone—and in the process devised his own torture.

# 8

## BITING BULLETS

# (1968−71)

ALMOST IMMEDIATELY after the Cemp–Starlaw deal fell through in late 1967, Jack tried to secure a loan from the Toronto-Dominion Bank for $250,000. Soon afterwards, he asked the Royal Bank, his firm's bankers of long standing, for an additional $500,000 by June 1968 to "bring our payables to a satisfactory ... level" and for the January promotion of the Canadian Illustrated Library. (The Royal had lent Jack $150,000 in January 1967.) The Royal did not want to make a new loan, and, furthermore, jeopardized the T-D loan because they were unwilling to release collateral (twelve hundred M&S shares) pledged earlier to them (a condition of the T-D loan was that those shares be assigned against it). After some delay, the Royal released the shares, and the T-D loan was made.

At first, Jack thought M&S could survive—barely: he thought the firm would make a modest profit (it actually lost $123,000).[1] He expected (correctly) the various centennial projects to take a loss. In order to survive, Jack cut operating expenses by $350,000 and eliminated a number of titles from the autumn 1968 list. Even these measures did not prove sufficient. In a memo to the accounting firm of

Woods, Gordon, hired as management consultants to prepare a report on the financial ill health of his firm, Jack candidly told them that there was very poor communication within the company; there was no active budgetary control, no cash budget (commissioning editors made contracts with authors without really knowing if they had money to pay them or the printers); customer service was at an all-time low. The situation at M&S was as bad as it had ever been.

In the midst of this horrific crisis, John McClelland died on May 7, 1968. His son felt the loss keenly. John had been the type of publisher who had both the grit and the cunning to keep his firm alive, even in the precarious days of the Depression and later the Second World War. In 1968, Jack simply did not know if he had sufficient savvy to stay the course as his father had done.

By the beginning of 1969, when the degree of the loss at M&S for 1968 was clear, Jack had nowhere to turn but back to Leo Kolber and Derek Price. By March of that year, he had reached a new deal with them: Cemp and Starlaw were granted an option to acquire 50 per cent of the common shares of M&S (price if exercised: $500,000); in turn, they would guarantee the T-D $250,000 loan and arrange a further $600,000 in loans from the same bank. Larry Ritchie, the recently appointed "financial man," had been with the Clarkson Company when it was hired in 1968 to negotiate with M&S creditors to prevent bankruptcy. Ritchie was to report once a month to A. M. Ludwick, who worked for Kolber. (Most of the loans guaranteed by the two Montreal firms came due in 1971.)

Ritchie, who purchased 5 per cent of the four thousand common shares owned by Jack on November 5, 1971[2], was appointed to be a watchdog, but he quickly shed his image as a "suit." Very soon, as many fellow employees recalled, he wore loud clothing, drove an Alfa Romeo and in general imitated some of Jack's worst excesses. One day he permed his hair and wore a white safari suit to the office. He was not pleased when someone asked if he had gone into medicine.

Jack, who never really appreciated "numbers" people, had little respect for Ritchie, so what little influence he might have had in curbing his employer's wilder financial excesses never really became operational. The boss rode roughshod over him.

Years later, in the late seventies, Len Cummings would take on the same thankless job and be largely ignored, but he remained a financial overseer who tried to talk common sense to Jack and the editors, who essentially controlled the firm's direction. In a sense, Len would have been as happy selling beans as books. When he attended his first sales conference, he complained, "All you guys do is sit around and talk about the contents of books." At the very least Jack admired Len's acumen, whereas he was content to ignore Ritchie and, quite often, made fun of him at board meetings. Jack was particularly dismissive of Larry's increasing propensity to offer his opinion on what books should be published.

When Ian Adams was trying to sell his book *The Poverty Wall* (1970) to M&S, Jack quipped to Farley in February 1969, "I can't think of a more appropriate publisher for a book on poverty. If the rumours that he refers to are true—and they probably are—he can do his first chapter about M&S. As to whether the rumours are true, in the main they are, although it looks like we have been bailed out once again and I'm probably going to have to struggle with the goddamn thing for another year at least."[3] The "goddamn thing" was finding a way to keep M&S solvent. The issue of profitability was very much on hold. A dubious peace had been achieved.

Jack had now developed what Harold Town called his "harried-executive" look. As Elspeth Cameron wrote in her *Saturday Night* article, "He always manages to be dressed formally, but with a casual air, as if he's just descended from the Parnassus of Executive Wonderland. Then he takes off his coat and loosens his tie to dash over to the stockroom to make sure those thirty copies get shipped off to Ankleford in time. He gives the impression of someone who's barely taken care of trouble. Afflicted on all sides with chicanery, slightly splattered with flak, he's ploughing ahead and slaps down his report of yet another heroic action."[4] The businessman side of Jack wanted to be somewhere else. In fact, one of his favourite expressions was "Gawd! I could be down on Bay Street by now making a fortune!"[5] Of course his aversion to number crunching had kept him off Bay Street in the first place.

At times he displayed a strong streak of single-mindedness. On one occasion a meeting had been convened to decide on the illustrations for a calendar. After everyone else was satisfied and Jack still disagreed, he loudly declared, "I'm the owner of this fucking company and we'll do the pictures I want!"[6] He also had the tendency to hear only what he wanted to hear when requesting advice. At meetings he would tune out the words of anyone whose observations were of little or no interest to him. Many of his employees would disagree with him, but they were aware that there was a point beyond which they dared not challenge him. If someone had the courage to mention that there were many authors whose books never made money, he would remind them that he published authors, not books; if that failed to convince them, he would say he was "building for the future." If he was in a bad mood and someone asked him how to undertake a particularly onerous task, he would say, "I don't care how you do it, just fucking do it!"

Sometimes, at least on the home front, the tables got nicely turned on Jack. In 1968, eighteen-year-old Carol McClelland asked her father for permission to go to a party that was starting very late in the evening. Jack refused. Harold Town and Leonard Cohen, who were visiting the McClellands, insisted that Carol and her older sister, Suzanne, be allowed to go. Jack remained adamant in his refusal. The painter and the poet came up with a solution: they would drive the sisters to the party and chaperone them. Jack could not really say no. The four attended the party, and were then, with everyone else, thrown out by the host's elder brother, a ruthless maintainer of parentally imposed curfews, who had no respect for the celebrities he was expelling. When the quartet returned to the McClelland home on Dunvegan Road, Jack was waiting up for them, whereupon Harold proceeded to tell him about the "orgy" they had attended.

On May 7, 1969, Jack, in response to a series of "rumours" that had reached him via Charles Fannin of the University of Toronto Bookstore, wrote to him to put the best possible face on the crisis he had just overcome:

> For the past eighteen months many rumours about McClelland & Stewart have circulated both in and out of the book trade. It was reported that we were having financial difficulties; it was reported that we had been taken over by half a dozen different American firms; it was reported that we were about to declare bankruptcy and, indeed, as recently as ten days ago representatives of two friendly competitors actually announced the date on which bankruptcy was to occur. The only truth in all the foregoing is that we have been through a period when our cash resources were inadequate for our needs.
>
> Undoubtedly the rumours were fanned by the fact that we brought in management consultants; that we reduced and changed our personnel substantially; that we cleared a large inventory of books to a local dealer; and that we thought actions might be more effective than words in combatting these stories.
>
> Our actions included continuing to publish the best Canadian books available anywhere; continuing to promote more aggressively than our competitors; an improvement in our service to the trade; a number of major new appointments including a new general manager, a new comptroller, a new service manager, a new warehouse manager; and continuing to pay our authors (more than $350,000 in royalties and fees in the last six months).
>
> Let me announce quite clearly, then, that there has been no change of ownership and that we *do* intend to stay in business for many years to come. I make no secret of the fact that we have encountered difficulties. This resulted directly from a too-rapid expansion that was not sufficiently supported by capital and management resources. We have now acquired both to a degree that will permit us to continue as the major force in Canadian book publishing.[7]

"Aggressive" selling methods could lead to other sorts of problems. In response to an M&S warehouse sale to the public at Toronto's St.

Lawrence Market, which raised more than $150,000 for the cash-strapped company, George Ramsay, the president of the Canadian Book-sellers' Association, wrote a stiff letter to Jack in June 1969: "Booksellers have noted with concern your company's increasing predilection for bookselling methods which go outside the normal practices of the trade. Mr. Jack McClelland has often expressed himself on the subject of his company's first duties to authors. Is it part of McClelland & Stewart's du-ties to authors to throw their books onto the sales tables at one-quarter or less of the published price? To deprive them of their royalties, to advertise the fact by every means available, that in order to sell these books all the resources of a give-away sale are required? To virtually ensure that these books will not appear in bookstores?"[8]

In his turn Jack could have observed how expensive it was to run M&S. Unsolicited manuscripts were up to 2,500 a year, 95 per cent of these automatic rejects. Ten out of the remaining 125 would eventual-ly make their way into print, but the cost of processing so-called over-the-transom (unsolicited) submissions was $50,000 annually. If ten became books, the firm would lose money on five, four would break even and one would make a modest profit. "A sensible man," Jack spec-ulated, would "decide that no manuscripts should be read; pocket the $50,000 so saved and spend the winter in Florida."[9] As he himself rec-ognized, he could never be "sensible" in that way.

There was the real issue of print runs. "Authors inevitably feel that we instinctively print too few copies. Our bankers feel that we print too many. . . . It is almost impossible to be right. The tendency is to print too many." He outlined the tortuous process in detail by talking about a hypothetical book the publishing team decides can sell 2,700 copies. A first printing of 3,000 is ordered; the price is $5.95. Then things become really complicated. In the meantime, "the cost of book manu-facturing has risen 20 per cent. The manufacturing estimates come in, and one finds that on a 3,000-copy printing the retail price will be not $5.95 but $7.95. Everyone feels that this is hopeless, but if one prints 4,000 copies, the book can be sold for $5.95. Inevitably then the deci-sion is to print 4,000 copies and work a little harder. Inevitably the sales stop at 2,700, and any profit that might have been made is lost on the 1,300 copies that are remaindered at 20 cents a copy."

Then he imagined another possible scenario: a first printing of 3,000 is ordered. Six weeks before Christmas, sales have reached the 2,500 copy level at the rate of 300 copies a week. Another 2,000 copies are manufactured, which arrive three weeks later, when sales have evaporated (sale of five copies a week). The accountants are dour: there is enough inventory on hand for fifty-three years. The reprint should not have been ordered. If the publisher had said, to hell with it; let's make a profit for a change—there is no way we'll reprint the book, demand would have been unprecedented, there would be no stock left and the author would have been irate. As Jack said, this anecdote sounded "lighthearted" but it was an escapable, dire fact of life for him.[10]

Some books seemed like trouble from the beginning. During negotiations with the House of Seagram in 1965, when the possibility of M&S publishing a biography of Sam Bronfman had been raised, Jack had been interested in engaging the writer Terry Robertson, who had begun negotiations with Sam well before that date. On April 5, 1965, Jack sent an internal memorandum to Hugh Kane and Jim Totton, indicating he was well aware that any book about the head of the Bronfman family might be controversial: "Herewith Robertson's preliminary note re the rum-running book." (Jack is referring to gossip that the Bronfmans had been bootleggers, a fact not then in public circulation.) Three years later Robertson raised (and whitewashed) this issue in a letter to Jack: "[Sam] has been, in fact, handicapped by the sometimes questionable behaviour of his elder brothers, Abe and Harry. During the chaotic days of the twenties Abe and Harry succumbed on occasion to the temptations of the time in order to make a fast buck. In consequence, they sometimes found themselves walking close to a crooked line and ended up in trouble. Sam, whose whole character would be repelled by such tactics because they were neither intelligent nor far-sighted, felt obliged to rush to the assistance of his brothers at critical moments, despite the fact their lack of judgment and occasionally ill-judged escapades were foreign to his nature."[11]

Although Jack provided Leo Kolber with the names of other authors who could write the proposed life of Sam Bronfman, it was decided by December 1967 that Robertson would write the biography for M&S. The author was given an advance of $75,000 (exceedingly large by 1967 standards), and in a separate agreement at the same time Cemp provided a subsidy of $25,000, a third of the advance. The agreement carried this important provision: "The Publisher will direct and administer the Robertson Contract and will provide Cemp with complete information at all times concerning that contract. It being the intention that the Publisher will carry out the administration in such manner as it shall from time to time see fit; however, Cemp having the right at any time to make directions and recommendations as to how such administration is to be carried out."[12]

Robertson, as he told Jack, was well aware of the dubious ethical territory he was entering by agreeing to write a book in effect subsidized by the Bronfmans and over which they could exert a great deal of control. A month before the M&S contract was finalized, he was still not certain he would be the designated author.

That Bronfman should reserve the right to bank the book doesn't make too much sense. . . . But what presumably you and Bronfman want is the reputable writer who wouldn't waste a couple of years of his life on an unpublishable book. . . . The family could kick the hell out of him when his manuscript is complete, but until then their role should be to co-operate. . . . The most objectionable condition seems to be the method of selecting the writer. Apparently several are to be interviewed and the so-called winner will be taken on as hired help. This is a loaded venture for any writer, and you won't get the best that way. Bronfman should decide who he wants and approach the writer through his agent or publisher. . . .

I've done my homework on the subject—superficially, anyway—and I find the prospect challenging and exciting. But I'm not about to be nice to the Bronfman family just because the guy in the waiting room outside might get the job. I think you may find that this condition will prove more troublesome than any other. The question of a whitewash doesn't really arise. This is the era of the success story, and the more rough and tough its beginnings the better.[13]

Robertson's book on Dieppe (*The Shame and the Glory*, 1962) had been a very personal undertaking; he had interviewed many of the survivors and members of their families. Researching and writing that book may have touched him so deeply that he never fully recovered from the trauma. A vulnerable and charming man, he could be both self-important and overly ingratiating. His bravado would desert him as he became embroiled in this questionable undertaking, and Jack McClelland would be a major participant in the resulting tragedy, which would unfold in late 1969 and early 1970.

During her tenure as secretary of state (1965–68) in Lester Pearson's Liberal cabinet, the formidable Judy LaMarsh, MP for Niagara Falls from 1960 to 1968, established the Canadian Film Development Corporation. At her request, Ernie Steele, her deputy, had called to see if Jack would serve as head of this new organization: "I was tempted. The fact that I had little interest or knowledge of the film industry did not seem relevant. This occurred during the period when I was negotiating with the Bronfman and McConnell families of Montreal regarding an investment in McClelland & Stewart."[14] Fearing his potential new partners would be appalled by such a diversion, given the rocky state of M&S finances, he turned her down.

Although she was known for her frequently brash and acerbic pronouncements, there was also a deep shyness in this remarkable person, who as minister of national health and welfare (1963–65) implemented the Canada Pension Plan and Canada's medicare system. As secretary of state, she brought in the Broadcasting Act, established the Royal Commission on the Status of Women and presided over the Centennial Year celebrations.

Judy did not really get along well with Pearson, and she expected—perhaps rightly—that her political acumen would not be effectively used by his successor, Pierre Trudeau. She also became tired of being the token woman and suffering the consequences: "My weight, my age, my home, my cooking, my hobbies, my friends, my tastes, my likes and dislikes, all became public property to a degree suffered by none of my colleagues, including the Prime Minister."[15] Coupled with such difficulties was LaMarsh's recognition that there was very little room at the top for women, an issue about which she confronted Pearson. She was also a very ambitious person, whose motivation for leaving politics was inspired in part by Trudeaumania. As a letter from Jack to her reveals, in January 1968—before the Liberal convention that spring chose the Quebecker as the new leader—she entertained the idea of seeking that post and asked Jack's advice, which was forthright and supportive:

> As to running for the leadership, I honestly think you should. To be honest, I don't really think this country is ready yet to elect a woman as prime minister. I am even more certain that the Liberal Party is not ready to elect a woman as its leader. However, if you [were] a candidate it would do two things: it would hasten the day when a woman could be the head of one of our political parties and prime minister; it would also do a great deal to enhance the image of the Liberal Party. It would stir up the convention: it would create a fantastic amount of public interest. As I think you know, I am completely amoral politically. I am a Canadian first and a publisher second. To be a publisher in the proper sense of the word, I avoided party affiliations. As an independent, then, I tell you sincerely that I am concerned about the impact of the Liberal convention and I hope sincerely that you will give the matter more consideration. If you are really going to leave the political scene, it could be a spectacular way to do it. . . . Alternatively, if you are going to stay on, which I sincerely hope you are, it could do nothing but enhance your image.[16]

At the age of forty-three in 1968, Judy decided to abandon politics. She settled in Vancouver, where she established her own radio phone-in show. She also decided to write her memoirs and, of course, she chose Jack, a kindred spirit, as her publisher.

Previously Judy had known Jack as *a* publisher. As soon as he became *her* publisher, he had to assure her that he would be doing everything in his power to make her book a success. He was annoyed to hear from John Colombo that she had informed him she was certain Peter Newman was receiving preferential treatment over her (earlier, Newman had been worried that LaMarsh's importance would be greater than his). Jack was baffled, although he was well aware of the special arrangements he had made a year earlier regarding Peter Newman's work schedule. He told Colombo, "I don't understand the reference to Peter Newman. . . . What in hell is she referring to? Thus far, Newman has received no special treatment that is apparent outside our office. None of the promotion or publicity has been launched. The details of that are known only to our own people or to trade customers who have now been exposed to the book, and as far as the special treatment he is receiving editorially, again it is a private matter."[17]

Like many authors, Judy was worried that her book, *Memoirs of a Bird in a Gilded Cage*, was not being sufficiently publicized. However, the book sold very well, and everything was going smoothly until a lawsuit for libel erupted over this passage: "A brash young radio reporter, named Ed Murphy (heartily despised by most of the Press Gallery and the members), had somehow learned that Maurice Lamontagne (the Secretary of State, and a long-time friend and adviser of the Prime Minister [Lester Pearson]) had purchased furniture but had not paid for it."[18]

Murphy sued. Jack considered paying him off, but LaMarsh would not apologize: "I don't particularly want to enrich this guy, but if the publishers are prepared to pay the $1,500 [the amount Murphy wanted in damages] and I do not have to make an apology, it doesn't matter to me whether you settle. I do not want to be in the position that I have to admit publicly that I paid him anything at any time."[19] So the case was heard. Peter Newman was supposed to be roped in as a defence witness, although he ultimately did not testify. As Jack reported to the law firm representing himself and LaMarsh:

Newman is prepared to say that he, too, was disliked (possibly despised, it's a question of terminology) by most of the members of the Gallery simply because he got good stories that other people didn't get. He refused tō be a member of the Gallery "club." . . . Newman will say in court that Murphy did a lot of digging; did get a lot of original stories by fair means or foul; and did not share them with his fellow members of the Gallery. It is for this reason that he was despised. Newman's contention then is that Judy's comment is perfectly valid. It would be supported by him and other members of the Gallery, provided the connotation is not necessarily that he was despised personally. In fact he was, but I think it is not necessary for us to take that position unless we are forced into it. . . . I think if we follow this angle we should be able to convince Murphy's lawyers that he really doesn't have a case.[20]

The lawsuit was heard in January 1970, Jack's first libel case that actually resulted in court proceedings. Judy LaMarsh, who had trained as a lawyer, sat in front of the courtroom with the defence counsel. As Jack recalled, "I sat in the back until I was called as a witness. As I walked up to the witness box, Judy rose and spoke in a stage whisper that could be heard by everyone in the hall: 'Don't be nervous and for God's sake, Jack, don't use the word "fuck." They don't like it in court.' Actually, it broke up everybody, including the judge who ducked behind the bench. I think her motive was to inject a touch of levity into the solemn atmosphere in the courtroom."[21]

During her testimony LaMarsh revealed that Murphy's name had not been in her original manuscript; she had seen his name in some book and added the reference in page proofs. Murphy, who in 1970 had an open-line show on radio station CKWX in Vancouver, professed to think LaMarsh a "very fine person, a very Christian woman. She did once call me a bastard but then she was quite partisan." He also mentioned that she had once, in Moncton, New Brunswick, invited him into her motel bedroom for an interview, which he had conducted sitting on the edge of her bed. During her testimony, Judy rebutted this: "I deny it. I have no recollection whatever."[22]

What is certain is that Judy's editor, John Robert Colombo, had warned her, when the book was in page proofs, about the passage that caused the lawsuit: "You're libelling him in his line of work." She calmly replied, "I can justify this." During her testimony, Judy attempted to give the impression that the mention of Murphy was for her an unimportant, incidental detail. Colombo's recollection contradicts this.[23]

On the stand she also noted that Murphy's name had appeared in a mere thirty-five thousand copies of the hardcover; there was no reference to him in the paperback. The judge found in Murphy's favour and assigned damages at $2,500. Although Jack did not wish to launch an appeal, Judy insisted M&S do this on the grounds that the judgment was "dangerous" in that it interfered in what matters of opinion could be uttered in a free society. The B.C. Court of Appeals dismissed the appeal, and later the Supreme Court would not hear it.

In 1969, there was a problem with another title, *The French Kiss* by Eric Koch, a political satire about the French president Charles de Gaulle and Quebec, which was already in bookstores when legal advice was received that some members of the family of the late Quebec premier Daniel Johnson might have been libelled (members of the family were in fact thinly disguised). The three thousand books were recalled, small slips pasted over the offending passages and the copies then returned to retailers. Jack only learned of the potentially disastrous situation at the book's launch at the home of the book's editor, Pamela Fry. He called her aside, told her the book would have to be recalled and acted quickly and decisively to prevent a lawsuit. According to Fry, she was the only person at M&S who had ever bothered to read the book.

Another publication that should have sold well was a flop: *The Day I Invented Sex* by Larry Solway (1971). One day after listening to the sometimes coarse Solway on the radio, Jack came into the office and asked his secretary, Marge, "What kind of an orgasm do you have? Clitoral or vaginal?" Taken aback by his own boldness, he explained that he had just heard the popular host interrogating a caller to his show. Immediately Jack decided to ask Solway to do a book devoted to the subject of sex. "The fact is," Jack later recalled, "we couldn't sell it. It bombed."[24]

In a letter to a journalist in May 1963, Jack, compiling a list of authors he especially liked, had made this remark about Terence Robertson: "favourite drinking companion, unpredictable, given to vast enthusiasm, and I believe one of the top non-fiction writers working today." He did not yet know just how meaningful the epithet "unpredictable" would become.

Throughout the late sixties, the survival of M&S was linked in various ways to the Bronfmans, Leo Kolber and Cemp Investments. (In 1969, M&S published yet another book by Sandra Kolber: *All There Is of Love*.) Well before Robertson began work on the Bronfman book, Jack knew the author was a heavy drinker. Robertson was certain he could do an excellent job, so rich and varied was the material: "My reaction to the Bronfman story is that the writer who can't produce a vivid, responsibly written book ain't tryin' at all."[25]

One condition of the contract was that Robertson provide Jack with monthly reports (just as Larry Ritchie provided Cemp with monthly reports on M&S's general financial status). From the outset, Robertson, aware of Sam's early life as a bootlegger, started to be drawn in to the elderly patriarch's sometimes skewed view of the world and began to see him as someone more sinned against than sinning. Realizing that the project might be more complex than he first envisaged, he warned Jack in April 1968 that the book might take longer to write; he might not be able to meet his deadline of April 1, 1969: "Sam believes he has founded a dynasty. His children believe the reverse, that is to say they each reserve the right to go their own way independently. . . . The snags, obstacles and the danger areas are beginning to appear as they always do in projects of this kind. . . . [As we go along] the greater becomes the chance of the timetable being extended."[26]

For Jack, the faintest suggestion that this book might be even slightly delayed became a matter of grave concern: "Eliminate from your mind any thought of extending the timetable. I don't want to be told again that

I am rushing you to completion of an inferior product. The time available is ample, providing you firmly resist the temptation to go further afield, dig deeper and see more people. . . . Please, please, please plan your remaining months carefully so that you come in ahead of the game, not behind."²⁷ Jack wrote so imploringly only because of his own worries about displeasing Leo Kolber. The publisher's letters to Kolber on the matter are breezy, but Jack was very anxious to assuage him, especially when Kolber became aware that Robertson was drinking heavily:

> I have had several conversations with Robertson since he sent in this report [April 30], and my best judgment at the moment is that he is going through a normal period of writer's despair. . . . Obviously we want a good book whether or not it takes him an extra six months or a year. I still feel that he has more than enough time to give us a good book within the stipulated limit. . . . Writers like to feel sorry for themselves and they get very temperamental, as I am sure you know.
>
> I was shaken by your reference to his heavy drinking because this is a problem that we have never had before. Temperament, yes, and all sorts of other problems. Although he drinks a fair amount (I guess about as much as I do, which is enough), I have never seen him drunk more than perhaps once or twice in the more than ten years I have known him. I have never known it to interfere with his work. I will try to keep in closer touch with him than I normally would at this stage and will take some action if it seems necessary.²⁸

By June, Robertson was making good progress on the book, but one problem was developing: "that of Sam Bronfman emerging as a three-dimensional character. . . . He is a brilliant, wonderful, nice person who hardly ever went wrong and hardly ever made an enemy. This is obviously not true."²⁹ The Sam Bronfman Robertson was getting to know was a genius but one with a guilty past. Robertson beheld all this but felt forbidden to write about it and, in the process, realized he might not be able to write a good book because he was being forced to write an untruthful one. Paradoxically, he became both a willing confidant and an intimidated journalist.

The biographer was slowly bewitched by his subject, spent a great deal of time with him and became part friend, part assistant. Jack, realizing what was happening, attempted to put a stop to this by asking Kolber to intervene: Robertson "looks on himself as personal guru to the Bronfman family, which is not my affair. I look on him as the author of the Bronfman book and I don't want him to have any excuse for not doing it and not doing it well."[30] That autumn, Robertson was desperately struggling with the manuscript's early parts (dealing with Prohibition) and knew a book that neglected Sam the bootlegger would be panned by the critics ("I am convinced that critics would be scornful of a book which blithely ignored what the Bronfman story is really all about"). Also, he was very attached to him: "Sam also needs diversion. He's got gout and for the first time in his life he's not allowed to drink. Life's bloody difficult, ain't it?"[31]

With an increasing sense of despair and fear, Jack—as he admitted to Kolber—was certain things were going very badly with the book: "All my instincts and experience as a publisher tell me that Robertson should now be cut off from all outside contact, including Mr. Bronfman . . . and he should be concentrating on nothing but writing the book."[32] Increasingly the author himself realized he was trying to complete work on an impossible book, so many unforeseen and contradictory forces having been put in place:

My progress is governed to a large extent by the many whims of Samuel Bronfman, who at one time can totally concur with what I am doing and at others violently oppose it. . . . If Sam is going to blow up and apply the right of veto, it is going to be on this [first] part of the book [dealing with Prohibition]. . . . It surprises me that it should even be attempted to render into a manuscript so massive a project, and one fraught with so many difficulties. . . . He [Sam] will not accept anything but the best book possible, and as we have discussed so many times I am not writing (1) a book which could be termed "bought" or (2) an unpublishable book. If you doubt my logic, then please discuss with Leo Kolber and if you can both convince me that I am wrong, I will be prepared to change my approach. . . . If [Sam] likes most of the draft, he may be more ready to compromise on changes. If he gets uptight about the draft, he is likely to be extremely tough to deal with. Enough said.[33]

In a subsequent letter, Robertson was even more direct about the literary mess into which he had been drawn: "Main problem remains the same, which is attempting to reconcile what I would like to write with what Sam would like to have written. . . . I think the predicament is best described by a remark of Sam's: 'What does it matter if people say this is a bought book? After all, they've been saying nasty things about me for years.' It is only recently that he has begun to understand that I cannot afford that type of public reaction."[34]

By January 1969, Jack tried once again to take Robertson in hand: he was to concentrate solely on writing the book. He was not to anticipate a hostile reaction by Sam or Leo. He was to finish the book by the end of March. No manuscript arrived on Jack's desk, but as he told a colleague, "One of the frightening aspects of this Robertson situation is that while we have been paying him, I now have reason to believe that he has not been paying his own bills."[35] Suspicious about where the money actually went, Jack hired Bolland Evidence Consultants, a detective agency, to follow the married Robertson to the Bahamas, where he was seen meeting a girlfriend. Jack did not tell Robertson what he now knew.

By April 16, Jack informed Kolber that the Bronfman biography could not appear in 1969; on the same day, he encouraged Robertson to soldier on but told him that M&S would now fund only "essential expenses." Robertson himself remained worried: "I think considerable rewriting is necessary to inject more warmth and humanness where at present the manuscript seems too cold and impersonal. . . . Finally and most importantly I do not myself believe that Sam has been captured as a person the reader can clearly visualize and come to care about very deeply."[36]

By May 2, an incomplete manuscript was submitted. According to Jack, it was dismal but possibly redeemable. The readers hired by Jack hated the book. One of the reports—by Peter Gzowski—reads in part: "Since this note is for your eyes only, I see no point in hiding the fact that I think this book is awful—even on its own terms. It's not even good prostitution."[37] By the end of June, Jack assured Kolber that the manuscript was "substantially improved," although Robertson's "personal life is such a mess it will be something of a miracle" if he completed the book satisfactorily.[38]

Things now went drastically from bad to worse. Robertson disappeared for long periods of time: research papers associated with his book were left at various hotels, he rented cars that he did not bother to return, he spoke of suicide. On September 9, 1969, Jack told Leo, "There is still no word as to Robertson's whereabouts. He seems to have disappeared for the present at least, which as far as I am concerned is a good thing."[39] A month later, Jack reflected on the whole sorry situation: "I don't think the Robertson experience proves anything except that I seem to have made a lousy choice. Hindsight aside, I don't think even God could have predicted this particular outcome."[40]

In December 1969, Robertson attempted several times to talk to Jack on the phone. Jack, who was usually at the beck and call of authors, declined to speak to him. On the evening of January 29, 1970, Robertson tried to reach Pierre Berton, who was out of town. In her husband's absence, Janet Berton spoke to Robertson. He told her that "he felt that he had been very badly treated by [Jack] and by Mr. Bronfman's associates and that it had been his intention to relate the story to Mr. Berton. He told Mrs. Berton that it was his intention to commit suicide."[41] A very worried Janet Berton phoned Jack, who contacted the New York City police. When Jack contacted the police the next day, they assured him that they had called on Robertson at his hotel and that everything was in order.

On the following night, January 30, Robertson called the McClelland home and spoke to Elizabeth. He told her he was very annoyed that Jack had dispatched the police to his hotel the night before. On the same night, Robertson called Roderick Goodman of *The Toronto Daily Star*'s editorial department to explain that he had been commissioned to write the history of the Bronfman family but that he had "found out things they don't want me to write about." According to Graham Murray Caney, another *Star* editor, Robertson had told him his life "had been threatened and we would know who was doing the threatening but that he would do the job himself." While he was still on the telephone, Caney had the call traced and alerted the New York Police Department. Detectives burst into Terence Robertson's room just minutes before he died of barbiturate poisoning.[42]

Robertson's manuscript was incomplete and never published. Only years later in 1978 would Peter Newman publish a true portrait of the liquor magnate, *Bronfman Dynasty*. In his Author's Note at the beginning of his book, Newman states that he found it difficult to accumulate factual evidence that would dispute or confirm the gossip surrounding Sam's enigmatic past:

> The mystery that has been deliberately created to shroud the Bronfmans' early careers in bootlegging through Canada's West was not simple to dispel. Fortunately, I managed to track down several of the surviving associates during the Bronfman brothers' adventures in the Saskatchewan liquor trade. Now mostly in their nodding eighties and lodged in old people's homes on the outskirts of small Prairie towns, but still remembering vividly how they used to "run the booze for the Bronfmans," these valiant survivors shared their memories with me. Among them was Ken John, a hale and articulate retired accountant now living in Estevan. He was there the night Paul Matoff, Sam Bronfman's brother-in-law and operator of one of Saskatchewan's busiest "boozoriums," was killed by the blast from a sawed-off shotgun poked through the window of the CPR station at Bienfait.[43]

Robertson was a first-rate journalist who compromised his skills at the behest of his magnetic subject. To a certain extent, Robertson fell apart because of the task he had undertaken. While his life had most probably not been threatened, as he claimed it was, he must have felt that his professional life was indeed in peril. There is also a great deal of evidence to suggest that his personal life was unravelling at the same speed as his conflicts about the Bronfman book were escalating. Both situations fed into each other and no doubt contributed to his suicide. Jack was more severe with Robertson than he might have been with other authors in similar predicaments because he had so much riding on his involvement with the Bronfmans, Leo Kolber and Cemp.

In addition to Cemp, another important investor in M&S was Pierre Berton, who had put some of his own money into the Canadian Centennial Library; he also served as a director of the firm. Ultimately, Berton's great contribution to M&S was his books, and their outstanding sales potential. In *My Times*, he gives some general impressions surrounding the appearance of his magnificent railway books, the first of which was published in 1970:

> *The National Dream* received unqualified praise from those critics who reviewed it. Some ignored it, thinking, apparently, that it was just another potboiler. *Time*'s Canadian edition, which reviewed most major works, was silent. The most influential review came from John Bassett in the *Telegram*; he said the book should be in every Canadian schoolroom. The academic community was grudging, but the fact that its members noticed it, reviewed it, and took it seriously was enough for me. The scholars, of course, said there was nothing new in the book. . . . These natterings didn't affect the ordinary readers, who began to buy the book in astonishing numbers. Jack McClelland had announced a first printing of ten thousand, a huge quantity for a hardcover selling at $9.95, a fat price in those days (*The Smug Minority* [published only two years earlier] was priced at $2.95). Jack was so jubilant that he insisted on having a cake the size of a pool table and covered with ten thousand candles made for the launch. Every restaurant in town, including

the CPR's own Royal York, turned him down. Jack finally found his man in Pierre Moreau, the smiling maitre d' of Les Cavaliers on Church Street. A former French Resistance fighter, Moreau wasn't afraid of anything, and certainly not a cake. As the media gathered for drinks and speeches, the monstrous confection was trundled in and the candles lit. The result was spectacular.[44]

The candles were doused by a fire extinguisher, the smell of charred cake filling the air for some time.

Behind the scenes, things were not quite so sunny or comical. Well before the publication of *The National Dream* in the autumn of 1970, Berton was upset when Michael Bliss of the University of Toronto's history department wrote a negative report on the book. In trying to offer genuine comfort to the aggrieved author, Jack called the professor's assessment "horseshit," but he tried to put the matter into perspective: "I think you should take care not to be too confined by the inhibitions of the academic historian. . . . He may be a sound, academic historian, but I think he is somewhat lacking in practical judgment."[45] On another occasion, Jack advised the thin-skinned author: "Don't read the reviews! Measure them!"[46]

Perhaps more than any other author, Berton knew how vital publicity was for the success of a book in the marketplace. Concerned that Catherine Wilson, the head of publicity at M&S, would not do as good a job as he wanted, he insisted, by special arrangement, that his friend and agent, Elsa Franklin, be solely in charge of promoting his new book. It was she who "canned" Jack's publicity scheme whereby Pierre was "to dress up like a train engineer and cross Canada flogging" the book.

Jack did not object to Elsa's taking charge of publicity, but Catherine was still responsible for invitations to parties and posters. On the day after the launch party for *The National Dream*, Pierre told Jack exactly what he thought about what he labelled a disastrous event. He did not appreciate what he considered to be Catherine's casual approach to publicity; he also felt she was prone to carelessness in writing copy.[47]

To what he sensed was justifiable criticism, Jack responded, "I can't really disagree with any of the points you make."[48] Most authors who worked with Catherine considered her outstanding. A single parent with three small children, she had joined M&S in 1968 at the age of twenty-six as a copywriter. Within a month, she fell afoul of Pierre when she rewrote a few sentences of a blurb he had submitted for *The Smug Minority*. Jack, whom she had not yet met, called her into his office and gently told her that no one ever rewrote Mr. Berton's copy.

For Pierre, Jack's problems were compounded by the fact that he sometimes did not take well-meaning advice, such as the time Pierre suggested that Jack publish the first novel of the young, struggling writer and former actor Timothy Findley. (And Irving Layton always held it over Jack's head that he had not pursued, at the poet's instigation, Stephen Vizinczey's *In Praise of Older Women*, which was published by Contemporary Canada Press in 1965.)[49]

Earle Birney was in complete agreement with Berton about the incompetence of some M&S employees. In fact, he had to distinguish between Jack the publisher and Jack the owner and chief executive officer of M&S:

My dear Jack, when I've been using the word "you" and "yours" in this letter, I've been talking about the firm M&S, not you personally. They are very different entities, though it's part of your own genius, your charm and effectiveness, that you almost persuade everybody that your firm is as well meaning, clearheaded and generous as you, personally, are. The thing is that over so many years, I have been losing more and more of my confidence in M&S as a firm. What you personally want, and even what sometimes you promise, has a way of not happening, because of the intricate nature of the firm itself. . . . [He goes on to complain about remaindering, advertising, publicity and permissions. Of proofreading he says,] There is a massive incompetence or laziness or arrogance. . . . It sometimes leads to the perpetuation of errors, now in school textbooks, which originally appeared in poems through the incompetence of that bird-brained alcoholic your firm assigned to be proof-editor of my *Selected Poems*. . . . With genuine personal wishes as ever.[50]

Jack was not quite sure what to say in reply: "That's quite a letter. I can't say that I enjoyed reading it. I can't even say that I agree with all of it, but I agree with many of the points that you make. I'm not going to attempt point-by-point reply because the only purpose of doing [that] would be for the benefit of posterity, and if your letter were ever published it would ruin McClelland & Stewart." He ended his reply by sending the angry poet "Love and Kisses."[51]

The failure of some staff members to do their jobs properly added to the difficulty of running M&S. In the summer of 1969, Jack suffered a different kind of blow when Hugh Kane, with Jack's support, left M&S to become president of Macmillan. In his new job as the competition, Hugh hoped to "make Jack's life a little more interesting." In his casual, offhand and witty way, Hugh told Peter Sypnowich of *The Toronto Daily Star*, "I might say there's no truth to the rumour that Pierre Berton owns McClelland and Stewart. There's no truth to the rumour that Seagram's owns it. There's no truth to the rumour that General Motors owns it." Thinking ahead to what the future might hold for Jack, he added, "Knowing Jack as I do, I don't think he'd accept American money. He might in a crisis sell the company to Canadian interests. But I think he'd close it down rather than see it out of Canadian hands."[52]

But Hugh did indicate to Sypnowich that he was a "large shareholder" in M&S. In fact, he considered himself to be the owner of 24 per cent of M&S, based on the share agreement he had made with Jack in 1956. On the day the piece in *The Star* appeared, an angry Jack wrote Hugh that such a statement was not good for Macmillan or M&S because of a possible conflict of interest, and furthermore it was not really accurate: "What is correct is that I now personally owe you a sum of money, the amount to be determined on the basis of the value of your share of our agreement at the time you left. The payment of the sum, which was to be determined, will, of course, depend on the way things go and my ability to pay it. I think, perhaps, you should reread that letter, but certainly you are not in any sense a shareholder of the firm either officially or unofficially at the present time."[53] There are a couple of other letters discussing this matter, with Jack finally concluding, "It's all bloody complex, and there is no simple answer, but it will get sorted out eventually."[54]

At about the time Hugh left, Jack made a crucial appointment of someone who could assist him in running the firm. Peter Taylor's novel *Watcha Gonna Do Boy . . . Watcha Gonna Be?* had been published by M&S in 1967. His background was in newspaper reporting and in public relations/advertising. Jack met Taylor in Ottawa at the time the book appeared. During a lengthy conversation, Jack told Taylor that four departments at M&S were completely out of sync with each other: publicity, sales, advertising and management of the sales representatives. Taylor informed him that the four divisions had to be placed under one umbrella with a manager who had the skill and know-how to make them talk to each other. Two years later, Taylor, who had joined a firm in Halifax, was phoned by Marge Hodgeman: "Jack has been looking for you for over four months. We thought you had vanished." When the two men finally spoke again, Jack flew Peter to Toronto and offered him the job he had dreamed up on the spur of the moment years before.

Peter loved Jack, although he thought of him as a "juvenile delinquent dressed up as a businessman."[55] They were kindred spirits, particularly in the ways they allowed their imaginations to run wild in dreaming up promotion schemes. When M&S published Barbara Froom's *Snakes of Canada* in 1972, Peter had small flat boxes constructed and stuffed with excelsior; the outside read, "The little fellow in this box is but one of the hundreds of species described in . . ." There was a small puncture made on the side of each box, indicating that the supposedly enclosed reptile had eaten its way through. This item was sent to booksellers, newspapers and various other media. The switchboard was inundated with complaints about the insensitivity of sending live creatures through the post. Other callers were disappointed that their snakes had escaped: could replacements be provided? And some were threatening: "If the little bastard loose somewhere in this office even shows its face, we're going to sue."

Another of Peter's stunts was the stand-up cardboard man who looked like a flasher. His query, "Psst—do you want to buy a Canadian book?" was answered when his raincoat was lifted to reveal a list of NCL titles. There were the junior-size jockstraps sent to every radio and television interviewer in Canada (including Betty Kennedy and Adrienne Clarkson) to promote LaVerne Barnes's *Plastic Orgasm* (1971), a look at the sleazy side of Canadian professional football. While at the cottage in Muskoka, Jack had organized his children into a giggly, dock-side assembly line to produce the little protectors, known at M&S as "JACKstraps."

In their relentless drive to sell books, Jack and Peter used a wide variety of locales for launches: one week the Granite Club, the next Gross-man's Tavern. (Even before Peter's arrival, some zany schemes were wisely abandoned, such as the idea to send out fortune cookies to accompany advance copies of Adrienne Clarkson's novel *Hunger Trace* (1970) or the plan to put real estate signs reading *Your Neighbour Is a Jew* on lawns to promote Gunther Plaut's 1967 book of the same name.)

During his eleven years at M&S, Peter gladly worked exceedingly long hours, so much was he taken with the manic energy that infused M&S. Never a great fan of print advertisement for books, he moved M&S in the direction of radio and TV interviews for authors and rein-forced the commitment previously made to touring.

As time passed, Taylor recalls, M&S's once elegant Hollinger House building began to deteriorate. Since there was no genuine air condi-tioning, employees sweltered on especially humid days. On such occa-sions, Jack would strip to the waist, his bare chest on display.

Finances may have been bad, but spirits remained high. One day, some young designers mummified one of their group in toilet paper and pushed him down the hall on a trolley. Paper airplanes routinely flew between cubicles. There was a lot of laughter, some of it nervous, most of it genuinely hearty. In a mischievous moment, Taylor came up with a brilliant money-saving scheme: henceforth, all employees, especially secretaries, had to refer to people only by their initials when writing memos. Since someone else in the firm with the initials JM came alphabetically before Jack, he was henceforth to be referred to as XX1. A few days later, Peter came across a distressed secretary tsk-tsking the notice: "It's not fair to treat Mr. McClelland that way." When Catherine Wilson was rapidly elevated to director of promotion, publicity and public relations in 1970 (in spite of Pierre Berton's earlier criticism), she was given a company car. The only problem was that she did not drive, although she had indicated on her application that she did. She confessed her problem to Roy, the warehouse manager, who lived near Hollinger House. That night, he drove Catherine to his house, parked the car there overnight and she took public transportation home to central Toronto. This charade—morning and night—lasted the few months until Catherine received her licence.

Although Jack was never around to fire people (his heart was simply too soft, so this was one responsibility he did not mind delegating), he continued to be readily available to any employee who poked his or her head in at his door. His warmth and kindness were legendary, and this explains in large part the strong sense of community—of shared purpose—that enveloped the beleaguered company.

Jack was a famous hypochondriac, but the reputation is not fully deserved. One evening, he was enjoying a boisterous order-in dinner of Chinese food at Judy LaMarsh's home; another woman author, LaVerne Barnes, was present. Judy left the room to go upstairs, and when she returned, she was startled to see Jack clad only in shorts, lying in front of the fireplace, gagging. Barnes was on top of him, pounding his chest. He had succumbed to something in the food (probably a sauce with a touch of lobster in it); he recovered only after the fire department had been phoned and he was rushed to hospital.[56]

In 1969, M&S recorded a profit of $83,750, which rose to $107,325 the following year. This good news was overshadowed by the huge debt load the firm was carrying, debts guaranteed by the Bronfmans and the

McConnells, the last 30 per cent of which came due on March 15, 1971. In a very real sense, Jack was back where he had started in 1967: he was carrying a large debt and he had never really obtained the new money he needed to support his earlier expansion of the company.

It was the best of times, it was the worst of times for the entire Canadian book industry. "Success has almost killed us," the House of Anansi's Dennis Lee truthfully asserted.[57] He meant that there was suddenly a huge public craving for made-in-Canada books but no capital investors willing to back the firms who wanted to produce titles to feed a hungry market. One American publisher told Jack, "With the public attitudes towards your firm, the attitudes of your authors, the publicity that's been attached to this—if you were operating in the United States, you could go into an American bank and I can guarantee they'd give you two and a half million dollars without much argument. And you can't get a damn thing from Canadian banks." Jack's comeback: "And there *is* that difference. This country has all the advantages, we have everything going for us, but we have this goddamned stupid shortsighted conservative banking and business community, who are a real drag on the potential."[58] Another publisher quipped, "We made a profit last year. I could take you out and buy you a cup of coffee with it."

There were many other impediments. In 1969, U.S. subsidiaries did 59 per cent of the dollar volume of book sales for a total of just over $113 million. In the same year, only two of the new Canadian fiction titles bore the imprint of an American subsidiary. Canadian firms had less than 20 per cent of total sales, yet they published 87 per cent of the Canadian fiction, 88 per cent of the poetry.[59] There was also the inescapable, sad fact that "fine novels by Brian Moore, Mordecai Richler, Leonard Cohen and Margaret Laurence [published by M&S were] selling very poorly" in hardback. It was the age of trash, specifically Jacqueline Susann and Harold Robbins.[60]

M&S's payment of its printing bills was in a constant state of arrears; in March 1971, Doug Best of T. H. Best Printing, which had been extremely patient and loyal to M&S, complained of the shabby treatment his firm had received: they were owed $220,000 and a promised cheque in the amount of $36,900 had been withheld from them. If such behaviour continued unabated, "we have no alternative but to cease work on M&S orders now in progress."[61]

In the late sixties, M&S was not the only Canadian firm in serious trouble. In Quebec, Le Centre Educatif et Culturel was taken over by Libraire Hachette; Le Centre de Psychologie et de Pédagogie was bought by Encyclopedia Britannica of Chicago; W. J. Gage's trade division was sold to Scott Foresman, also of Chicago; Clarke, Irwin was for sale— unofficially.

The big blow to Canadian-owned publishing came in the fall of 1970 when the Ryerson Press ($2.8 million in debt) was sold by the United Church of Canada's Division of Communications to the American firm McGraw-Hill. William Heine, the editor of *The London Free Press* and the chairman of the division, said that competition "was becoming fierce; management was in many respects still operating under nineteenth-century conditions; unwise purchases of machinery compounded efficiency problems; the impact of extensive borrowings for new equipment was not fully assessed; and the firm gradually became what is known in business as a sick outfit."[62] Two serious offers for the beleaguered outfit surfaced: from McGraw-Hill and Maclean-Hunter, whose losing offer was $1 million less than its American competitor.

The small presses—House of Anansi, New Press, Tundra Books, Fiddlehead Books—which had emerged in part in the wake of the interest generated by M&S, Ryerson and Macmillan in Canadian-made material—formed an emergency committee to try to block the sale. The poets Eli Mandel and Al Purdy urged Ryerson authors to tear up their contracts. The premier of Ontario, John Robarts, met privately with representatives from Ryerson and McGraw-Hill, but the sale was allowed to go forward.

Jack McClelland, who had helped to create the climate responsible for the small-press movement in the 1960s, was painfully aware that these new firms—and not M&S—were able to take on the kind of experimental fiction by young Canadian novelists that he wanted to publish. His overhead was simply enormous—and growing. Of course, he sarcastically explained, there was a way to make everything work: "All you have to do is fire all the editorial and design people, who cost $200,000 a year, keep one copy editor, publish ten or fifteen books already in the schedule and milk that $2 million worth of backlist sales for all it's worth."[63] On the other side of the coin, M&S was publishing 110 books a year, making hasty marketing and editorial decisions and allowing its inventory to grow by leaps and bounds. One situation that could not be remedied was the collapse in the textbook market after the province of Ontario decentralized its textbook buying in 1969; across Canada, photocopying machines were flagrantly used to disobey copyright laws and thus shrink the textbook market even further. Jack had once hoped that textbooks would be his salvation, but they led nowhere and Jack had no real interest in that kind of publishing.

Taking the bull by the horns, Jack appeared on the *Pierre Berton Show* on radio criticizing Ryerson as a "sick" firm that had published nothing of importance in the previous ten years. Some of Jack's feelings about the Ryerson Press can be seen in a letter to Mordecai Richler in January 1968: "This . . . is to inform you officially that I have just accepted the appointment as editor-in-chief of the Ryerson Press. There were several conditions attached. I told them that a few of our important authors (Richler, Norman Levine and [the hockey star] Eddie Shack) would move with me and this is part of the contract. . . . I must tell you that it will mean some change in your writing style. All four-letter words must be omitted, and in future, please, no references to screwing, buggery or to any perverted acts. I admit that won't leave you much to write about, but that's the price of loyalty."[64]

When pressed by Berton on whether he would ever sell his company to American interests, Jack replied, "No, I wouldn't. But there is only one reason for that. We publish Canadian authors. They publish with us because we are Canadians. We are a Canadian firm. I wouldn't sell under any circumstances and the answer is yes, I would go bankrupt first but I hope we won't face that and I don't expect we will."[65] A few months later, Jack was no longer certain about keeping the firm.

In 1970, he became co-chairman of the Committee for an Independent Canada founded by the former federal Liberal minister of finance Walter Gordon, Peter Newman and the economist Abraham Rotstein as a citizens' committee to promote Canadian economic and cultural independence. The Quebec journalist and politician Claude Ryan was Jack's co-chair of the committee, which was launched on September 17. Nine months later, this group had 170,000 signatures on a petition to Prime Minister Trudeau demanding limits to foreign investment and ownership.

In many ways, Jack did not really believe in the principles of the group—at heart, he was a free trader. On the other hand he had been so burnt by American domination of the publishing industry that he had become certain that effective control over foreign incursions into the Canadian cultural marketplace might help to make publishing more financially viable.

Walter Gordon recruited Jack because of his reputation as a workhorse and because he was not attached to any particular political party. In the five years since he had published George Grant's seminal Red Tory diatribe, *Lament for a Nation: The Defeat of Canadian Nationalism,* Jack had learned the hard way just how accurate the McMaster University professor's cautionary, bombastic broadside had been. (Grant's book had been a very special project to Jack. John Robert Colombo was summoned to a hush-hush meeting at eight-thirty one morning with Grant, whom Jack had met at a conference. In an aside, the publisher told the editor, "We might lose our shirt on this book, but it's a great book and we have to do it." Jim Totton, who did not think M&S should publish such a "negative" book, also considered Grant's title deplorable and told Colombo to find a better one. This was a task Colombo was happy to fail at.)

Despite his continuing commitment to a publishing program inspired by the nationalist tract *Social Planning for Canada,* a pervasive weariness had overcome Jack. On the morning of February 18, 1971, his face its usual ruddy colour, his clothes rumpled, nursing a hangover, he gunned his aging Mustang convertible at perilous speed along Highway 401 to arrive only a bit late for a meeting of the CIC he was chairing at York University's Osgoode Hall Law School. Reeling off a mass of statistics, he made his point abundantly clear: "There is no other country in the developed world that has sold out more of its birthright to foreign ownership [than Canada]. There is no other country in the developed world that has fewer controls over it. And there is no other country that is selling out its economy as fast. We must have some regulations to prevent foreign interests from having this sort of power over our economy and ultimately our culture."[66]

Three hours later, he assembled his staff at Hollinger House to say that his sixty-three-year-old family firm was for sale. Jack, at forty-nine, had, as Pierre Berton put it, "eaten, slept and drunk publishing" for twenty-five years. Physically and emotionally drained, he had come to the end of the road. The resulting shock waves of disbelief and grief were not shared by Elizabeth McClelland: "It's been a big decision. I think I'm delighted. He's been married to the business for so many years. I guess I'm just the jealous wife."[67]

9

# THE PERILS OF
# NATIONALISM

(1971–72)

"A CANADIAN is someone who drinks Brazilian coffee from an English teacup, and munches a French pastry while sitting on his Danish furniture, having just come home from an Italian movie in his German car. He picks up his Japanese pen and writes to his Member of Parliament to complain about the American takeover of the Canadian publishing business," said Campbell Hughes, president of the Canadian Book Publishing Council in 1971.[1] (Shortly after making this statement, Hughes moved to an American-owned firm.) From first-hand experience, Jack knew just how true Hughes's wry observation was. He remained deeply emotional about parting with M&S; he was not just offering a smart quip when he said, "It is like selling your wife."[2]

Farley Mowat spoke for many other writers when he lamented the desperate situation M&S had reached: "McClelland & Stewart is one of the last bulwarks of Canadianism in this country. And it is being forced to the wall by a total lack of interest by people who pretend to govern this country and who are no more than spokesmen for U.S.

interests in Canada. If we allow McClelland & Stewart to be destroyed [by being sold to the United States] we deserve to become second-class citizens of the U.S."³ The prominent Toronto bookseller Roy Britnell echoed those sentiments: "I share with everybody in the book trade the hope that he will remain in publishing. The publishing he's done is just wonderful."⁴ Mordecai offered to send a telegram to Ottawa: "SAVE MCCLELLAND & STEWART, LAST GOY PUBLISHER IN THE WEST."⁵

Perhaps the most far-reaching comment came from Marshall McLuhan, the media guru who was a professor of English at the University of Toronto (in 1969, M&S had published a revised edition of *Counterblast*, an earlier work from 1954): "Things like magazines and publishing houses are far more central to the Canadian identity than the CBC could ever be. The CBC is not an identity image builder. If Canadians have any concern about identity they should care about Jack McClelland. He's one of the most picturesque publishers on this continent. He's got style. He's got a lot of flair and dash."⁶

Unlike radio and television and even magazines, McLuhan was pointing out, books are, like buildings and paintings, permanent identifying marks of a culture. They are essential in the establishment of a national personality. If the Canadian identity is difficult to define, the demise of the country's major nationalist publishing house would be a heinously self-destructive act, making even the most tentative attempt at self-definition that much more difficult.

There were the many "ordinary" Canadians who knew the value of keeping M&S alive: some of these people wrote directly to Jack expressing their support and in many cases enclosing cheques and money. Strangers approached him on the street, inquiring where they could send contributions.

Mel Hurtig, the bookseller-turned-publisher who succeeded Jack as co-chair of the CIC in December 1971, stressed the unwillingness of the banks to provide loans: "In fact, the book publishing industry is the epitome of free enterprise—in taking a lot of risk capital and investing it in something that might only sell a dozen books. A publisher is only successful if he can develop a backlist. To do that he must build up an inventory. And to do that he must get expanded credit facilities." Otherwise, publishing in Canada would be swallowed up by American interests.[7]

In retrospect, Pierre Berton provided his own analysis of the situation: "The company . . . had been calling itself *The Canadian Publishers.* Now that imprint was about to be hawked to the highest Yankee bidder. Here was an anomaly. Thanks to the new nationalism, authors like me were making a good living from our work, while the big chains, Coles, Smith's, and Classic, were raking in the profits. But best-sellers weren't enough to balance the losses from the small, if worthy, works that Jack was gambling on. His own enthusiasm and philosophy had put him in a Catch-22 position. As a confirmed nationalist and one of the founders of the Committee for an Independent Canada, he had already jettisoned many of his American connections, at considerable cost."[8]

Jack's own disagreement with some CIC policies in the area of publishing, and the steadily increasing problems at M&S, had led him to resign as chair in December 1971 and later give up membership in the organization itself. Specifically, he objected to Abe Rotstein's policy paper on publishing, which was adopted by the CIC. That document advocated excessive taxation of, and other restraints against, foreign publishing houses operating in Canada. Jack was outraged: "Knowing the industry very well, I knew this to be about as stupid a policy as one could adopt. I became concerned about the committee in terms of ill-conceived, ill-informed policies. I said to myself, Migod, if they can have a policy like this proposed and approved for an industry that I do know something about, what about the policies they are adopting for industries I know nothing about. . . . I decided that the CIC was great in principle but dangerous specifically, and I quietly dropped out."[9] Jack was strongly anti-American; in part, his commitment to the CIC had been engendered by such feelings. Philosophically, and somewhat paradoxically, he disagreed with the exclusionary, pro-Canada policies of the CIC, which, he felt, tied his hands as a businessman. Ironically, he was now not averse to telling nationalistically inclined publishers how thoroughly he disagreed with their pro-Canada emphases.

Jack's disdain for young publishers like James Lorimer was both gener-ational and territorial. Jack saw himself as the elder statesman, a position he did not wish to be displaced from. He also saw himself as the true Cana-dian publisher and did not want to be accused of not being Canadian enough by the new nationalist brand of publishers who wanted foreign products to be second string in the marketplace in this country. Although he claimed to have no political biases in the acquisition of titles, Jack turned down Marcel Rioux's separatist tract *Quebec in Question*, which, when published by Lorimer in 1971, sold twenty-five thousand copies.

The dispute between old and new was enacted between the older Canadian Book Publishers' Council (CBPC) and the newer Association of Canadian Publishers (ACP). With the exception of M&S's presence, foreign-owned companies dominated the CBPC, whereas the ACP, to which Jack's firm did not belong, was run by more nationalistically inclined smaller houses. Jack resented the domination of American and English publishers in CBPC, but he did not like the scene-stealing antics of the ACP. Furthermore, since he ran M&S as a one-man show, Jack saw no reason to be overly involved in any kind of publishing asso-ciation. If he had a problem with the federal or provincial government, for example, he would call the appropriate minister to discuss it.

The selling price of M&S was $1.5 million, and Jack wanted the sale completed within two months. He would not sell to Americans, he said. Then he wavered slightly: ". . . only as a last resort will [M&S] go to a foreign buyer." There was another case of double-think: "The firm is in no immediate difficulty but my personal financial commitments on behalf of the firm are close to $2 million. I don't have that sort of money." For one thing, since M&S's reputation was based on its Canadian list, not many foreign interests would want to buy such a firm. Second, M&S was starting to show a slight profit, but it was heav-ily encumbered by financial obligations.

The federal trade minister, Jean-Luc Pepin, said he would "consider" using government funds to save M&S, but this hardly seemed necessary since the company would be a sound investment in the private business sector in Canada. He added that McClelland's determination not to sell to Americans made government action unnecessary. Outside the Commons, Pepin said, "He's talking about $2 million [in debt]. I can't believe that there's not $2 million in Canada. I can't believe the private sector in Canada have lost interest in that kind of property."[10] Pepin's suave assurance that M&S was a desirable commodity at its selling price was immediately countered by Arnold Edinborough, the former publisher of *Saturday Night*, and the publisher William Baxter: no such "risk capital" was available to the publishing industry. The NDP's Doug Rowland urged the Liberals to provide long-term, low-interest loans to book publishers and to set up a "Canada book development corporation" to keep the industry Canadian.

Jack was convinced that loans from either the Canada Council or the Industrial Development Bank were necessary to save companies that dealt with national identity and culture. For instance, two hundred Canadian authors who received royalty payments from M&S were affected. Yet, he claimed, publicly at least, he was now more concerned with the future of an independent Canada than the survival of M&S: "I have great hopes and dreams for Canada but if Canadians don't insist on action from their government it will be too late. We will be puppets, and we have too much going for us for this to happen. I feel sure I'll solve the company problems. I wish I could be as sure that the Canadian problems will be solved."[11]

Jack was throwing down the gauntlet, in the process making it crystal clear that he expected some form of government assistance to come his way. He was slightly embarrassed when university students throughout Canada attempted to form a consortium that could purchase his tottering firm: "I'm grateful for their interest, but a publishing company can't be run by a committee."[12] There was, however, the "nice kid" (otherwise unidentified) from the student council at the University of British Columbia who phoned Jack when he was in Vancouver:

"We'd like you to have dinner with us tonight and meet a group who are—"

"Well, I'd *like* to," Jack interrupted him, "but I really—my time is just *completely* booked. I'm trying to sell the company. I've got all these people to see."

"Well, we want to *buy* the company."

"I realize that, but can't we talk about it again? I'll be back here, and I really don't think this is the time . . ."

The student was not about to be put off. "You're not taking us *seriously*," the student protested.

Jack was cornered. The student continued: "Well, if I told you I was calling from a five-million dollar building that we own and that we financed, would that impress you?"

"It might," Jack agreed.

"If I told you that our income here at the student council is close to six hundred thousand dollars a year, would *that* impress you?"

"What time do you want to have dinner?"[13]

Reluctantly, Jack had come to the conclusion that a publishing firm relying almost exclusively on made-in-Canada products had to be subsidized in the face of the high costs incurred in producing and distributing books for a relatively small population in such a large country, one that was literally attached to another with more than ten times the population.

One response to M&S's difficulty, in the letters column of the Canadian edition of *Time*, was decidedly unsympathetic. This correspondent pointed out the

> inability of [Jack's] employees to fill orders, the absurdly high prices of some of his publications and the unresponsiveness of his sales force to appeals for information. Yet McClelland is, in Canadian terms, a master of the publishing game. . . . None of the proposals thus far made to bolster the industry will do more, I think, than guarantee annual incomes of pleasing proportions to publishers unable to set their houses in order—editorially and otherwise. What

is needed is a smaller, more aggressive industry run by businessmen-publishers of the type that has succeeded in the U.S. and elsewhere.

Publishing is no more a game for amateurs and dilettantes than is wildcatting for oil—to which it bears a very close resemblance.[14]

*Time* itself might have been interested in buying M&S, but it had just acquired Little, Brown of Boston, represented in Canada by Jack's firm. Maclean-Hunter, having lost out to McGraw-Hill in an unsuccessful bid for Ryerson, decided not to make an offer.

In a very dispirited way, Jack had left the door open to not being able to sell the company by saying he might have to struggle along by borrowing money "on a painful basis."[15] Cemp and Starlaw were prepared to purchase shares in M&S if stocks in the company were publicly traded. As Jack told Wood Gundy Securities, those firms had remained committed to assisting him: "They are, as I think you realize, the guarantors of our loans and have been helping us behind the scenes for some time. There has been some suggestion in the press that they are crowding us at the moment but this simply is not true. We are crowded by the fact that we don't have enough working capital."[16]

Earlier, in the wake of the outcry over the Ryerson sale, the Progressive Conservative premier of Ontario, John Robarts, decided to establish a Royal Commission to examine the Canadian book publishing industry. The lawyer-novelist Richard Rohmer chaired the commission; the other two members were Marsh Jeanneret, the University of Toronto Press publisher, and the political savant Dalton Camp. Their work had barely begun when Jack made his announcement.

As Jeanneret recalled, the three-man committee was certain that there was not any real likelihood of a buyer coming along: "One cannot easily auction off a liability. Yet the major role that M&S had played in supporting Canadian authorship—latterly largely thanks to Jack—was inescapable, and, in the absence of refinancing, its collapse was certainly imminent. This would have been a cultural disaster for the nation at that time. And so we issued the first of numerous interim reports, this one to recommend that the province acquire from M&S convertible debentures up to about a million dollars."[17]

In M&S's submission to the commission, the importance of a made-in-Canada publishing program was emphasized. There was, that document argued, a vital link between national identity and national culture. Without the latter, the former would be eradicated. And great writers almost always came into being in "close association with a great editor or publisher."[18] After Lorne Pierce, the Ryerson Press had become rudderless; on the other hand, M&S was resolutely committed to Canadian titles. The report pointed out that there seemed to be a consensus that Canadian publishers could not run good, effective businesses, as if what was lacking was sound commercial sense. What *was* true is that because of the vast physical size of Canada, its small population and the domination of the field by the United States and Britain, Canadian publishers required governmental assistance.

In mid-April 1971, William Davis, who had succeeded Robarts as premier, announced in the Ontario legislature that on the recommendation of the Rohmer commission, the province would grant M&S a $961,000 virtually interest-free loan (the federal government was asked to put up half the money). The offer was to purchase from M&S ten-year-term convertible debentures for one-third of the company's total assets of almost $3 million. The firm had to repay this amount over ten years, but the government would charge no interest during the first five years and a low rate after that. To safeguard its money, the province insisted that some directors be appointed to the M&S board by the Ontario Development Corporation, the agency granting and administering the loan.

In the short term, Jack had won an important victory. He certainly had persuaded one segment of government that Canadian culture needed to be subsidized in order to survive. Moreover, given the largely no-win situation he felt his company was placed in in the selling of its product, he regarded himself as a good entrepreneur. He was therefore stung when Stanley Randall, the former Ontario trade and development minister, accused him of being an inept businessman whose poor judgment was responsible for the woes at his publishing house. In December 1970, Randall revealed,

McClelland had asked his department for $1.5 million in loans. "Here's a guy who lost $2 million of his own money . . . and now he wants to borrow $750,000 from the taxpayers of Ontario to publish more books that nobody reads."[19] Jack's lawyer served a notice of libel against Randall and *The Toronto Telegram*, which had printed the story, but the matter was later dropped. (However, Randall's attack on Jack was in part a payback for the publisher's un-flattering references in CIC speeches to the politician as a "threat" to Canadian economic freedom from the United States.)

Not so easily dropped was Jack's conviction about the fragility of Canadian culture and government's role in protecting it. In an address to the Empire Club in February 1972, he warned about "The Threat from Within": "We have brought the Wooden Horse within our gates. Foreign influence has seeped into the very marrow of our society. Greed, self-interest, complacency, confused purposes—values not introduced, perhaps, but certainly encouraged by the presence of foreign capital— have replaced the self-sacrificing determination that built our country."[20]

That year, when Macmillan Canada was for sale by its parent company in England, Jack desperately wanted to buy it. Despite M&S's own precarious financial health at the time, he did not want a "powerful Canadian communications company" to obtain Macmillan, feeling such an acquisition might provide Macmillan with a new influx of money and thus impinge on his own company's turf. He wanted to acquire Macmillan Canada's trade list but also, more importantly, its lucrative educational division. Behind the scenes, Hugh Kane did everything in his power to help his former boss. Jack made a formal offer to buy Macmillan Canada, based on a public offering of shares in the combined companies. He was unable to guarantee the underwriting for a two- to three-week period, during which time an offer from Maclean-Hunter would have expired. Jack had even booked a flight to London but cancelled when the rival offer—not as large as his own—was accepted.

More than most executives, Jack knew first-hand how difficult it was to market made-in-Canada products when so many more made-in-U.S.A. wares competed with them. In April 1971, he was quite candid with Farley Mowat: "I am so goddamn far behind in everything that it is slowly driving me out of my mind."[21] In June, there was a sequel to the earlier crisis when a lot of red tape temporarily prevented the payment of the ODC loan. On June 7, Jack, knowing that a lot of good will on the part of his writers would be lost, told Larry Ritchie, "I have had enough calls and letters from authors to satisfy me that if we are not able to send out our royalty payments and resume normal business by June 11, all the efforts of the past few months will have been wasted."[22] Only at the end of the month did this tempest abate.

After the departure of Hugh Kane for Macmillan in the summer of 1969, there was no one left at M&S to curb Jack's often short-lived enthusiasms and to prevent him from overcommitting vital resources. The person who eventually assumed that role was the glamorous Hungarian-born Anna Szigethy, who graduated from the University of Canterbury in Christchurch, New Zealand, in 1964. Before joining M&S in 1969 at the age of twenty-six, she had worked for Cassell and Collier Macmillan in England and Canada. Anna, who married the lawyer Julian Porter in 1971, impressed Jack with her incredible organizational agility and her ability to make decisions in a calm and detached way. Those particular skills had always evaded Jack, and he admired anyone who practised them well. There had always been too few employees at M&S with those qualifications.

From the start, Anna noted the different levels that Jack operated on when she beheld a notice in the ramshackle company boardroom. It began, "The objective of all M&S employees should be to thoroughly analyse all problems, anticipate all problems." It ended, "However, when you are up to your ass in alligators, it is difficult to remind yourself that your original objective was to drain the swamp."[23]

Larry Ritchie, who had entered M&S a model businessman and who over the years got made over in Jack's much looser image, did not appreciate Anna's capabilities, or her quick rise to power. On March 21, 1971, Jack told him, "Anna Szigethy . . . is at least as valuable to us as [the manager of the college department]—probably more so because she is more mature and knows publishing better. The only problem with her is that she is still an unknown quantity as far as the future is concerned. As long as she stays with us, though, she is exceptionally valuable. She works very hard, is conscientious, but more important than anything else she knows what publishing is all about. Again, I am not certain about her salary. I think we increased her to $14,000 or $13,500 last fall. Under the circumstances I think her salary should be $15,000 or if Dave's [the manager of the trade department] is more, the same as his." Ritchie, whose written response to Jack no longer exists, did not agree with his boss's assessment. This led to Jack's blast on April 11: "I am completely baffled by your recent memo re A.S. Either you didn't get my earlier memo on this subject or I didn't see a reply from you. . . . As to the raise for A.S., it is my view that it is more than justified. To my certain knowledge she works as hard as anyone else in the firm—except perhaps for the two of us—and she does her job very well. But I'm not going to repeat the reasons given in my other memo."

Jack and Anna fought constantly, and creatively. They had a competition about who was working harder. He would stagger in one morning and announce, "I'm dying! I was up to three drinking with Farley!" She would raise the ante: "That's nothing: I was up to five reading three manuscripts!" Every time you told Jack how well he looked, she wryly recalled, he immediately said he was dying. She could not discuss any ailment with him: he immediately acquired the symptoms.[24] If anyone praised or criticized Anna, Jack had a standard, non sequitur response: "What do you expect? She's Hungarian!" To Anna's chagrin, he would also inform writers that her name rhymed with "spaghetti."

Despite temperamental differences, Anna, who became editorial director in 1972, was a kindred spirit, someone who shared many of Jack's ambitions for M&S. Like Hugh, she was not afraid to criticize Jack face-to-face about his short-lived enthusiasms and lack of follow-through.

Just as Jack had felt quite free to be snippy with Hugh Kane on numerous occasions, he did not spare Anna when he became impatient. Referring to the fact that Sinclair Ross was becoming "too bloody difficult," he told her in 1974, "To hell with it. . . . You straighten him out."[25] And regarding pricing for a Group of Seven calendar, he summarily informed her, "Your point is well made, although you might have made it equally as well by asking Larry [Ritchie] rather than addressing a pricing memo to three people. More to the point, your memo does not contain the sort of information that I should like to have if I were doing the pricing."[26]

Tact was one of Anna's particularly strong suits. For years, Jack and Earle Birney fought constantly. Jack once told him, "The problem, I think, is that you have too much time available and I have too little. Our paranoias end up the same, although the causes are different."[27] In December 1970, at the very same time Jack was wrestling with the possibility of selling M&S, the poet was irate when a quotation from one of his poems was cited incorrectly on a calendar:

> Getting onto McStew's Beautiful Canadian Calendar is like finding your name in the Obituaries. . . . The quote "The small firs like spun white candy" is not to be referred to as "Maritime Faces" but to the poem to which it belongs, on the next page of *Selected Poems*, titled "Arrivals," and what your request has disclosed is that McStew are still unable to inform even their own editors of the fucking fuck-up they did to my "Maritime Faces" in the *Selected Poems* [inserting three lines in the wrong poem; he goes on to explain how this error has been repeated over the years in anthologies]. . . . Use the line, but if the Calendar comes out with the line credited to "Maritime Faces," I'll fucking well come down with a Molotov cocktail for the whole of Hollinger House.[28]

Some sort of aggressive male behaviour seems to have overtaken the McClelland–Birney relationship, but a vastly different tone can be seen in a letter Earle wrote to Anna in the wake of two letters Jack sent in the midst of the calendar fiasco: "I hope you are well, my dear, and not working harder than you want to. I miss not having news of you, but I realize that you may be annoyed with me because I showed my feelings about jack mcc to you and you felt in the circumstances you had to be loyal to him. It would please me very much if he and I could be reconciled, but it cannot happen unless he apologizes for the two really filthy and demeaning letters he wrote me. They are so bad they seem calculated to force me to withdraw from his firm."[29]

Jack's "really filthy" letters concerned a long list of complaints Birney had sent to John Newlove, the recently appointed poetry editor. As he told the poet, Jack was boiling mad: "Are you trying to turn him against me? Are you trying to endear yourself to him? I mean, what is the purpose of the exercise?" Jack informed Birney that he was sick of his complaints about everything and everyone: "What in hell are you trying to do? My guess is that [Newlove's] only conclusion will be that you are a real horse's ass. Has it not occurred to you that John might have developed a little loyalty toward me?. . . On the record, I don't get mad all that easily, but you are beginning to get to me."[30]

Anna's intervention was such that Jack wrote a conciliatory letter to Birney, who told him on February 27, 1971: "Your great letter has blown away a personal cloud of gloom I'd been walking under ever since we began this quarrel-by-mail. . . . I'm mortified, too, that my wrangling had anything to do with your decision [to sell the firm], and that you were forced to take time, in such a crisis of your own life, to write letters to me." Birney, who had once been invited to dinner with Prime Minister Trudeau, even grandiosely offered to intervene with him on Jack's behalf: "But is there any point? Is it too late to help McC&S? As for helping you personally, I reluctantly have to admit that you are probably doing the right thing for your own health and future by getting out. You may end up as prime minister yourself, in consequence—or, alternatively, writing the best damn book of this century-we-never-quite-belonged-to. Already you are becoming the new Mr. Canada, and all this business has at least shown you, if you didn't know before, what a charismatic bugger you are, and how everybody loves you, including me."[31]

Anna's diplomacy, which considerably assisted the reconciliation between publisher and poet, would be put severely to the test in the years ahead.

On June 30, 1971, after the latest financial crisis had been solved, Jack wrote to all M&S authors apologizing for the delay in sending royalty cheques. This money had been held back in order to keep the firm solvent. He mentioned that the Ontario government would soon be adding two directors to the board, which at that time included himself, Berton, Mowat, Elsa Franklin, Bud Feheley, Frank Newfeld, Bob Martin (the firm's solicitor) and Larry Ritchie: "As taxpayers we welcome them. As publishers we expect to astound them."[32] Morale and efficiency had been affected by financial pressure. "It has created disruption, many changes and occasional chaos. Some authors have suffered as a result. I hope you are not one of them. If you are, I apologize." He did not anticipate that he could publish better books, he comfortingly assured the writers, but "expect improvement in our sales, promotion, publishing and marketing techniques."

Sam Orenstein of Perlmuter Orenstein Giddens Newman & Co. was placed on the board by the ODC to be a watchdog on spending. He found the challenge difficult: "Jack's a cuddly, beautiful man, but he's a little less practical than he might have been. The board met once a month, and Jack would throw out ideas and the others—Berton, whoever—would comment. I assisted the company in concentrating more on proven authors and advised Jack to cut down on the number of people he was encouraging."[33] Significantly, he added, "He is less attracted to money than to accomplishment, and he had to be reminded occasionally of the parameters money permits."

Chaos, it seemed, was not something that could be avoided at M&S, financial crisis or no financial crisis. In August 1972, Jack sent William Koshland at Knopf in New York a "collector's item": a 1972 reprint by M&S of Frank Russell's *Watchers at the Pond*, originally a Knopf book: "An idiot editor in our establishment thought that your famous Borzoi [colophon] was part of the illustration for the book. It appeared on the title page." Jack retained several copies of this curiosity: "If I ever do my publishing memoirs, this will make an interesting part."[34] There was also the time the name of the playwright, actor, screenwriter, novelist and biographer Ted Allan was spelled "Allen" on the title page of one of his books: Jack told the offended author he should be grateful to be published. The author was not pleased by such a dismissive attitude.

Peter Taylor recalled the "feeling that emanated from the accounting department every year-end that you'd probably be looking for a job in April. Stories were always floating around. There was a constant cloud of doom and gloom on everyone's face except Jack's. He seemed to believe instinctively that everything would turn out okay. He'd say, 'Look, we need a million dollars in sales to make it this season' and everybody would be wondering how the hell we'd do it."[35] Then, like a magician producing rabbits from hats, Jack would announce a big winner in next season's catalogue: a Newman or a Berton or a Mowat. Most times, Jack played the role of incurable optimist extremely well, but he was frightened that he might run out of conjuror's tricks.

Some younger writers—poets and novelists—indeed felt Jack had run out of magic. As far as they were concerned, he showed little or no interest in them. They were certain he had lost touch with "new" writing. This charge is to some extent justified because by 1971 Jack had an established stable of writers whom he knew well, many of whom were friends. Even in the sixties, Hugh Kane frequently handled authors Jack had little or no interest in. Without doubt, Jack cultivated writers who were celebrities or likely to become such. Even by the early seventies, much of Jack's time was occupied by trying to save M&S, and he had far less time to read, especially submissions from unknowns.

John Metcalf published his novel *Going down Slow* with M&S in 1972 but subsequently decided his needs would be better met by a much smaller firm, Oberon. He never dealt directly with Jack but spoke to him at ten one morning when he called to complain about late payment of royalties and the remaindering of his book without his having been informed by M&S. Jack irritably replied, "Look, if you stay with us, we look after you; if you don't, we don't."[36]

If Jack was afraid of getting out of touch, he took steps to protect himself. In Anna Porter, Jack discovered a substantially younger person who was "with it." He hired the young, also with-it David Berry, known for his T-shirt, jeans and shoulder-length hair, to deal with the slush pile, the entry-level editorial job at M&S. Shortly thereafter, David became an editor, dealing mainly with historical and current affairs non-fiction. He found the working conditions primitive: senior editors like Anna Porter or Linda McKnight, who was responsible for educational publishing, had windows; his cubicle was windowless, the stench of the binding glue from the new books in the warehouse was pervasive and most employees were, like Jack, chain-smokers. The furniture was in a bad state of repair. The blackboard occupying one wall in the boardroom was covered with graffiti, various profane statements constantly being added.

On Mondays, the entire day was consumed by an editorial meeting, which Jack, Anna and heads of the various divisions attended. One by one, the editors would be summoned to the boardroom to report on the status of all their projects. One warm day, in the midst of such a meeting, feeling an equal measure of frustration and playfulness invading him, David threw himself out the open first-floor window onto the grass.

Anna Porter undertook substantive editing on a wide variety of titles, especially those by the house's star writers. Many other books had little or nothing done to them before they were presented to Berry, who usually had to have them ready for the press within forty-eight hours. He became a specialist in what he called "typographic copy editing." After a while, he found his work depressing as well as exhilarating. His most productive day on the job was the one when he drank the Thermos of marijuana-enhanced tea he brought to the office. He quit abruptly when Jack and Anna took little interest in promoting C. Frank Turner's book on Sitting Bull, *Across the Medicine Line* (1973). Delays on the part of the author virtually killed a lucrative book club deal, and in any event, Turner was not the kind of person the media would lionize. Screw it! David said to himself. For him, Jack was a mercurial combination of an Italian Renaissance princeling and one of the "guys." The boss could be a know-it-all to avoid, but he was just as likely to pour Scotch freely on an evening David stayed at work to read final page proofs.[37]

Patrick Crean, who joined M&S in 1971, was given responsibility for the slush pile, all five thousand manuscripts. He remembers books on

UFOs, the Bible, masses of poetry, "everything under the sun." He made a "nut file" of the "crazies," 10 to 15 per cent of the fringe element who submitted their manuscripts. There was the poet from Guelph who hired a Brinks truck, complete with guards, to deliver his. There was another poet who wanted to recite his verse on the phone because he did not have any money for postage.

Crean soon developed a sense of what to expect: if a book was wrapped in a particularly odd way, it usually meant the contents were worthless. During his nine months at this task, Crean found one publishable book: Seymour Blicker's *Shmucks* (1972). Once he was short with a potential author on the phone; the would-be writer complained to Jack, who summoned Crean to his office for a dressing-down. He informed his young employee that the proper maintenance of the unsolicited manuscripts was a heavy responsibility, a public service. Feeling completely burnt out—"corroded"—by this task, Crean was relieved to be promoted to the Franz Kafka Memorial Room, inhabited by the juniors in the editorial department. Despite the drawbacks, Crean adored Jack, a true mentor to him. "It was a very lively place. I had a lot of fun."[38]

The big egos of some writers sorely contributed to Jack's problems, a good example of which can be seen in an Irving Layton letter to Jack of July 1971 concerning *Il Freddo Verde Elemento*, the translation into Italian of *The Cold Green Element*, first published by Contact Press in 1955: "Wow! I'm sure I don't need to spell out what this means. If vanity or ignorance doesn't mislead me, I'm the first Canadian poet to break the language barrier separating him from the continent. [The translator] assures me that publication by Einaudi means an almost automatic translation into five or six other European tongues. Excuse me, but is that the Nobel Prize I see gleaming before me? Anyhow it's a step, a very necessary one, in that direction."[39]

In the wake of such dazzling possibilities, Layton became concerned that the paperback edition of his *Collected Poems* (1971) be purged of the inconsistency in inking and typefaces that "along with numerous typographical errors makes the hardback something of a scandal—as

Robert Weaver noted in *The Bookman.*"[40] More irritated with Layton than Weaver, Jack nevertheless wrote the poet: "Who is Bob Weaver? As a matter of fact, fuck Bob Weaver! (He is right though—the book was assembled by madmen.)"[41] Also, Layton wanted to expand the text of the *Collected Poems* paperback. Such decisions were rightly those of John Newlove, the poetry editor, but Jack hung tough on this issue: "In the past we have agreed that we leave the poetry to you, and the publishing judgments to me."[42] The collection was not expanded.

The poet accepted the decision with good grace, and two months later, in July 1972, he was preparing to send from Greece the manuscript of *Lovers and Lesser Men* (1973) to Jack. "It's the sort of book I hoped I'd write one day and by gum and by golly I think I've done it. . . . I've been working like a bloody fool and slave since I got here. . . . All the lovely girls parading in nothing but their pubic hairs and here I am scribbling like a fucking medieval monk into my notebook. . . . I've dedicated one of the poems—one of the best, titled 'Poetry as the Art of Pugilism' to you."[43] Jack sent him a splendid reply, which shows the pleasure that publishing, despite its hazards, often gave him: "That's a great letter. . . . The last time I heard 'by gum and by golly' it was used by a small-town carnival barker at a fall fair somewhere in Western Ontario. He was trying to induce me (and he succeeded) and several dozen other people to go into his tent to see a genuine Aphrodite. We all paid our money and we all went in and we all saw a genuine Aphrodite. A few of us, I guess, were a little bit miffed because it turned out to be some microscopic creature rather than a human, but nobody said very much. It's a great expression. Whatever the hell made you think of it in Greece?"[44]

Al Purdy, whose first book of poetry appeared in 1944, began to publish at M&S with *The Cariboo Horses* in 1965. Born in 1918 in Wooler in Eastern Ontario, Purdy was raised in nearby Trenton and educated at Albert College in Belleville. As a young man, he had tried his hand at a number of jobs, including cab driver and factory worker, and he is in every sense of the word a self-educated poet, one who could try Jack's patience with the best of them. His initial quarrel with Jack was about "the Town/Purdy thing," an anthology of Canadian verse selected by Purdy, each of the participating poets to have a portrait by Town included in the book. In July 1970, Purdy asked that the number of poets be increased from twenty to twenty-two. Jack said no. Purdy was also preparing for M&S an anthology of poetry by young poets, *Storm Warning*, and Jack insisted that the age of thirty-two be the cut-off point for inclusion. The poet was only mildly—and teasingly— angry: "Dammit, you're taking the pleasure out of doing this book for me, and I don't like it. There was a great deal of fun dredging the country for good poems, emitting little twitters of excitement when I found one. So I shall hold this deprivation against Jack McClelland forever."[45] Jack's response was similarly even-handed:

> Migod, it's difficult dealing with sensitive poets. You ask me to pay a terrible price for my convictions: you are going to hate me forever: and in this case I must pay the price. . . . Although I am reluctant to do so—and it really isn't my style to interfere in editorial matters unless I have an absolutely firm conviction about something— I really feel I must take a strong position on the age limit for *Storm Warning*. As far as this book is concerned, your function is selection and editing. My function is publishing and marketing. I wouldn't presume to suggest that deletion of a single poem on the grounds of quality because that is entirely your problem. What I do say is that from the standpoint of marketing, it would hurt the potential of the book very seriously—at least in my opinion—and in turn hurt you and the poets involved were we not to insist on an age limit of thirty-two. . . . Someday you may forgive me.[46]

The poet was thrilled by the "shindig" book launch for *Storm Warning* held at the St. Lawrence Hall. It drew twelve hundred people to the facility, which seats five hundred: "If the book doesn't sell like deodorized and diamond-plated edible fishscales, you can sue Purdy," the poet told his publisher.[47]

Purdy had always been wary of Jack, but the two got along reasonably well until in 1972 the poet asked retroactively for a contract for the

Town/Purdy thing. Town was working on the book as much as his schedule allowed. He was of the opinion that there was a conflict of interest on Purdy's part because he wanted to include his own work in the anthology, and there was a money problem—Town wanted the larger share of the royalties, whereas Purdy wanted a fifty-fifty split. McClelland was placed in an uncomfortable position, but he was on Town's side:

> My position is that while I accept that it should have been settled in advance (though as I think back to the occasion, it's a wonder anything was settled), the fact is that it was not. I'm quite willing to accept the total blame for the fact that it was not settled, but that doesn't in any way resolve the problem. . . . Harold says he must have at least 75 per cent or the drawings can't be included. I must also be honest enough to say that I totally agree with his position, and I think that almost anyone would. His contribution to this book is the major one. . . . I pointed out to you that my opinion here is given as a book publisher and the fact that Harold is a close personal friend is totally irrelevant. What solutions are available? One that I hope for is that after consideration you will decide that Harold is right about the division. Failing that, the alternative is to abandon the project. This, as I see it, would leave you free to work with another artist and Harold free to work with another anthologist.[48]

Purdy told Jack he was stung by what he considered to be the injustice of the proposed solution.[49]

Jack had a great deal of difficulty responding to Purdy. He thought the poet was being unreasonable, but at the same time he knew he had unintentionally wronged him. He wrote a letter on June 2, another on June 16 and one on June 22, the latter being the only one finally sent. The first two letters were similar in the sentiments expressed and worried both Marge and Anna. In an extremely uncharacteristic move for her, Marge told her boss before he sent the letter of June 22: "Anna and I have again discussed the Purdy letter and the consensus of opinion is that [it] should be completely rewritten. It's not often that I feel very strongly about the letters you write because you are a master at the craft, but there is something about this one that really bothers me, and I wish you would reconsider doing it again."[50]

In his unsent letter of June 16, Jack made a distinction between the work of an anthologist/editor on the one hand and the artist/poet/novelist on the other: "It happens, Al, that creative writers—poets, novelists, etc.—happen to rank higher on my list than editors. It's that simple! . . . That has nothing to do with you. It has something to do with me." He mentioned that the art by Town was worth about $50,000, but that the work itself was not marketable separately from the proposed anthology: "Who is going to pay $2,500 for a portrait of, say, Raymond Souster, or as far as that goes, Earle Birney, Leonard Cohen or Al Purdy? I'm damned if I know. I sure as hell am not." He pointed out that Town, like the poet, was an artist who had "only so much creative energy and can only do so much first-class work." Why was Town prepared to occupy himself for so long on a book that would never repay his investment in time? "He is doing it because he believes in Canada and is interested in Canadian poets and because he thinks it is worth doing. The sacrifice is considerable. The contribution is considerable."[51] He then points out to Purdy—in detail—just how minuscule was his effort compared with the artist's.

The letter that was posted is much more equitable, sympathizing with the poet and validating his cause for anger. He knows Purdy may wish to leave M&S, acknowledges he has himself done a "lousy job"[52] of satisfying the poet but promises to do his very best to look after Purdy's interests in the future. He offers the poet $500 in compensation and later increased the amount—prodded by Purdy—to $1,000. The project was scrapped.

Another aggrieved author was the humorist, novelist and short story writer Max Braithwaite. He is perhaps best remembered for *Why Shoot the Teacher?*—which Jack published in 1965—an autobiographical novel about his experiences teaching in a Saskatchewan one-room school during the Depression. In 1972, Braithwaite was very upset about the sales of *The Night We Stole the Mountie's Car*, published the year before. He did not tell Jack about his discontent; he left this unpleasant task in the hands of Farley Mowat, who felt a bit awkward about broaching the matter with Jack: "He is very depressed [over low sales]. . . . Now don't get prickly and don't go all defensive. . . . He [Max] cannot afford losses due to inefficiency on production and distribution. As a result of very poor sales of *Mountie*, he is close to being strapped."[53]

Farley was expecting a hostile reply from Jack. He was very surprised by what his publisher told him:

> Max's book was not the only one that suffered from an incredible backlog in Canadian binderies last fall. . . . I can tell you that more money was spent on the promotion of the Braithwaite book than all but a handful of Canadian titles published in 1971. . . . . I know it to be a fact that retailers across the country lie like troopers to defend their own position when they haven't ordered enough copies of a goddamn book. . . . I am sorry that you and Max feel bad about it. Frankly I don't. I think we did our best by it, and I think it was a damn good best, and at most I think he lost the sale of a couple of hundred copies. . . . I have great affection for Max and great respect for him as a writer. His books are best-sellers by Canadian standards, but I think he must recognize that his books are not as popular as yours, as Pierre's and as those of a handful of other authors. . . . It was a self-indulgent book as he paid more attention to what he wanted to say than he did to the interests of the reader. . . . I am, by the way, sending a copy of this letter to Max. . . . I don't, by the way, blame him for bitching. Every writer does. It is part of the game. . . . I have been listening to author frustrations for twenty-five years. . . . I've never claimed to be the perfect publisher.[54]

A somewhat stunned Farley responded: "At least nobody can say you don't take authors' 'bitchings' seriously. Which is one of the reasons you still have a lot of good authors despite the obvious inadequacies of M&S's publishing organization."[55]

Mowat's confrontation with Jack about Braithwaite was a mild warm-up to the contretemps between Jack and Pierre Berton. For years, Pierre, a consummate professional, had been more concerned about the physical appearance of his books than most M&S authors. For example, in August 1971, he complained to Jack about the typesetting of *The Last Spike: the Great Railway, 1881–1885*: there was a great deal of broken type and bad register markings on the pages. A bit later, he informed his publisher that the finished copy he had just seen was fine, except for the fact that the spike embossed on the cover was to be in gold and on a slight slant.[56] McClelland's response was a terse "Great God, man."[57]

The art department at M&S was governed by two principles: Jack felt a book could be judged by its cover, and he knew what he did *not* like on jackets. There were three guiding precepts: (1) Green jackets prevent a book from selling. (Publishers often have these idiosyncrasies. Alfred Knopf hated yellow whereas Victor Gollancz thought the same colour was the key to success.) Therefore, Jack had to be argued into allowing paddy green on the cover of a book devoted to the Irish Rovers; he had the softcovers of Joe MacInnis's *Underwater Images* (1971) ripped off because they had greenish tones. (2) No book was to look as if it was science fiction or had a hint of pornography in it. Even the genre of the occasional science fiction book could not be suggested. Jack threatened to fire the entire art department when a rather lurid series of covers was produced for Marian Engel's *Bear*. (The design used for the M&S hardback—as opposed to the later Seal, which appalled Engel—was very tasteful.) (3) Books that win design awards are poor sellers. (Jack was not amused when his art director David Shaw won a major award for a book he designed on the side for Mel Hurtig, *Peter Gzowski's Book about This Country in the Morning*, which became one of the hot sellers of 1975. There is a fair amount of green on the cover.) Jack also had a prejudice against animals, especially elephants, on covers. He ordered Shaw to remove the heads of herons from the jacket of Margaret Atwood's *Surfacing*: "Get those goddamn birds out of there!"

*Dust jackets of major M&S titles*

Although Jack was often a demanding employer, the creativity of the art department was unleashed. The art department of M&S continued to comprise a rather zany assortment of characters, who never had so much fun in their entire working lives. (Most members of the rock group Luke and the Apostles belonged to that division.) They created a fictitious member of the department, Clayton B. Ashley, who sent and received memos. (For years, a photograph of Frederick Philip Grove was used on all the NCL editions of his work until his son notified M&S that this person was not his father. A photo of the real Grove was located, and the unknown man became Mr. Ashley.) For a time, the designers called themselves the Group of 58 because they were housed for about two years at 58 North Line Road, a block away from Hollinger House. On summer afternoons, they would buy bread, cheese and wine, pull their telephones out through the window and party on the lawn. If anyone from Hollinger Road phoned, they would pretend to be at their desks, working away. This practice was discontinued when Larry Ritchie caught them.

Contrary to Pierre Berton's beliefs, no one's books were given as much attention as his own. He was, however, one of the few M&S authors who knew how crucial design is to the successful marketing of a book. There were as many as thirty suggested dust jackets for *The National Dream* before a new art director reworked the very first one, changing the type from green to gold. In the process, he came up with the "look" of all future Berton books.[58]

Pierre's complaints about the physical appearance of his books were nothing in comparison with his increasing sense that publicity at M&S was poorly handled. In order to counter various kinds of M&S inefficiencies,

Pierre had his agent, Elsa Franklin, oversee the publicity campaigns for all his books. The problem was that Catherine Wilson and Franklin were frequently working at cross-purposes to promote the same Berton book because Wilson was still responsible for posters, print publicity and party invitations. Knowing what a perfectionist Pierre could be, Jack attempted in August 1971 to warn Wilson before things had a chance to get out of hand. He chose an extremely roundabout way of advising her to get things right this time: "Needless to say, the guest list for this [Berton launch] party submitted by Elsa bugs me in the same way and to the same degree that your average guest list for parties bugs me. I say that to make you feel good. Elsa will get the same snarly reaction from me that you usually get. I get more and more crotchety, I guess, but when the names of guests are improperly spelled, it absolutely drives me up the wall, and I wonder if any part of it is right and will be handled properly."[59] Berton's displeasure with Wilson erupted again when she scheduled a country bacchanal—Food, Poetry and Wine in the Woods—for John Newlove on the very same night Franklin was holding an event to celebrate the revised edition of *Klondike*, originally published in 1958. Pierre was on the verge of asking Jack to fire Wilson, who had been told nothing about the *Klondike* celebration.

Farley, on the other hand, thought Wilson had done an excellent job promoting his books and contacted friends in the industry to tell them Pierre had asked Jack to fire her. In turn, Pierre, who had not asked for Wilson's dismissal, was furious about Farley's interference and his passing on incorrect information about what Pierre had or had not asked of Jack. Berton demanded an apology from Mowat.[60] The dispute about Catherine Wilson obviously unleashed some pent-up antagonisms between the two men, both of whom were directors of M&S.

Jack, caught in a three-way conflict not of his own devising, fired Wilson before Berton asked him to do so. In this instance, as he told Berton, he was more on his side than Farley's:

I have no hesitation in saying that I agree with your letter and particularly with its moderate tone. I hope he will respond in an appropriate way. I have some reservations about your request that copies of his apology be sent to everyone to whom he has made statements. . . . I don't know how many people are involved, but I am concerned that a sort of round-robin apology might in fact have the reverse of the intended effect and exacerbate the situation. . . . Leaving aside all considerations that relate to M&S and publishing, I now find myself in the crossfire between two old and valued friends. Unless all three of us are extremely careful, there will be three losers. . . .

I am sending a copy of this letter to Farley. I think and hope you both know that regardless of the outcome, I won't take sides in the matter. Maybe I'll be the big loser. To me, the term "friend" is absolute, and degrees don't exist. I ask you both, as I have asked myself, what is the end-product here and what can any of us achieve. I am certain that not one of the three of us wants to do any hurt or harm to Catherine Wilson. I am equally sure that not one of the three of us wishes to destroy our mutual friendship because I handled her essential departure from M&S in a manner that left much to be desired. I suggest we cool the whole thing.[61]

The actual firing was done by Peter Taylor, Wilson's boss, and not by the tender-hearted Jack. The night before she was summoned to a breakfast meeting with Taylor, Wilson had been, together with Jack, at a party at Louis Melzack's home in Montreal to celebrate the publication of Mordecai Richler's *Shovelling Trouble*. Jack, who obviously knew she was going to be fired, said not a word to her about this matter. When she subsequently consulted the lawyer Sam Grange about the manner of her dismissal, he got in touch with M&S and Bob Martin, the firm's lawyer. Although she never returned to work, she was kept on the payroll for six months and received back the company car, which had been taken away from her. During the negotiations between lawyers, she was startled to receive a phone call from an inebriated Jack, who told her he was upset about what had happened. He claimed he had to do what he had done because Berton had him by "the short and curlies."[62] Quite often, M&S

was way behind in paying royalties to Berton. This did give him considerable power over Jack.

Farley felt he, along with Wilson, was an innocent victim: "I have read Pierre's letter and it just plain makes me mad. Somebody has done a hell of a lot of lying about the whole mess, and I'm damned if I'll take the buck. I phoned Pierre, but he was in New York. . . . He is an arrogant son of a bitch, and I am half inclined to photocopy the whole of the correspondence and distribute it to the authors concerned. . . . Well, chum, I won't initiate anything more (unilaterally), but neither will I grovel to Pierre. You might call it the Last Straw. As far as I'm concerned, any friendship I had with him is at an end. It now remains for him to decide whether we part on a basis of neutrality, or wage war."[63] This dispute blew over, but it left a permanent mark on the friendship between Berton and Mowat. Farley insisted that Wilson act as the publicist on a freelance basis for his next M&S book.

In 1971, the year before this dispute, M&S made a profit of $228,000 on net sales of $4.8 million, one-fifth of the profits generated by a single title: *The Last Spike*. The Wilson episode and the success of *The Last Spike* might have fuelled what Jack considered to be Farley's fantasy that Pierre Berton dominated M&S. It certainly intensified that author's feelings that he was the less favoured sibling in his pursuit of the approval of his father-publisher. Farley's fear that Pierre had too much power over Jack was a sentiment shared by many M&S employees.

Despite the discord, the promotional tour for *The Last Spike* seems to have mended the friendship between Jack and Pierre. Each stop featured a breakfast that members of the press were invited to, the idea being that they could write and file their stories soon after leaving the meal in order for the stories to appear while Jack and Pierre were still in town. The menu included various Canadian dishes and a special cocktail devised by McClelland and Berton in the bar of the Park Plaza Hotel: champagne, orange juice, bitters, Grand Marnier and a lot of gin. The problem was that the cocktail was so potent (and, of course, free) that most journalists left the launch in no condition to write at all. On Berton's next trip through Winnipeg, he was told by a slightly wincing reporter, "God, I hope you don't have any more of those drinks with you. We were down for twenty-four hours the last time you came through!"[64]

Margaret Atwood had a different view of her "familial" relationship with her publisher. In 1971, she was concerned when she heard Jack was not completely taken with her new novel, *Surfacing*. She had also been upset that he had not met with her agent, Phoebe Larmore, when she had been up from the States. She also thought that *The Edible Woman* had not been sufficiently promoted. Jack was upset. Why, he wondered, had Margaret not discussed promotion with her editor, Pamela Fry? "Have you any reason to believe I am disinterested? Has it never been indicated to you that we consider you one of a handful of major authors that we publish? Ours is an incredibly sloppy, inefficient organization. So is every other publishing house that I have ever had any dealings with. That's the way it is."[65] Having made this assertion, he assured Margaret that he wanted to do everything in his power to improve the situation. In turn, she was conciliatory but firm. She liked the title of her new book and was quite prepared to stand her ground on its contents, even though she knew Jack was not as keen on it as others at M&S were.

In 1972, another title by Atwood was mishandled—*Up in the Tree*, an illustrated book for children. In October 1972, Margaret requested the return of the manuscript (and that of another children's book she had written), which was, she observed, "currently sitting on John Newlove's desk. You have had them for a year and a half and I would now like to try them out elsewhere."[66] Jack wrote to assure her that there had been a misunderstanding: he was under the impression that the matter was "in cold storage at your end rather than ours."[67] *Up in the Tree* was finally published in 1978. All in all, Atwood was not bitter about M&S, whose failings reminded her of "an eccentric aunt to whom one is, inevitably, related and committed."[68]

Later, in 1974, when *Surfacing* had sold extremely well, Jack told Margaret that her book—and Richler's *St. Urbain's Horseman*—had encouraged a revival of interest in fiction. He could even imagine a time when fiction would actually outsell non-fiction.[69]

Some books that would prove enormous successes caused the publisher extraordinary problems at the outset. Such was the case with Richler's children's book *Jacob Two-Two Meets the Hooded Fang* (1975). The readers' reports were, as Jack told Mordecai, divided on the book's merits: "The first reader says, 'Hot dog! This is a winner. . . .' The second reader says, 'Very tedious and much much too long for the age group who would be interested. The little boy in it is two times two years old and a precocious brat. . . . It is the sort of thing one can put down easily, and not care if it were never picked up again, even to dust.' What the hell do you do when you get two reports as diametrically opposed as those two? I guess if you are a publisher you read it yourself. That's what I did, but it didn't make me all the much wiser. I am somewhere in between the two positions. I think it is very witty, it's clever and it should appeal to kids."[70] Nevertheless, Jack thought the book was too long but realized he was reading "just a draft" and might be "pushing the obvious." Once again, he expressed his reservations to Mordecai in a constructive and dexterous manner.

By the summer of 1972, Jack seemed to have made a good recovery from the financial crisis of 1971. Berton published two books that year (the revised edition of *Klondike* and a picture book about the railway) and Farley, *A Whale for the Killing*. But Jack was deeply depressed. His firm owed $1,610,000 (the ODC loan plus $550,000 to the Toronto-Dominion Bank). He tried to brush negative feelings aside by telling Farley, "The real truth is that it is just old age and we have not yet accepted the truth of the situation."[71] But Marge told Farley, "JGM is in such a state of depression at the moment that I am really concerned about him."[72]

During the previous year, Jack had had to endure being labelled a bad businessman. Sometimes, he could joke about this predicament: "I could have the greatest chain of funeral homes in Canada, and probably end up making half a million dollars a year. I've thought all that one

*Jack, early 1970s*

through; it's the most profitable business concept imaginable to me. And then sell it to the Mafia—for a *huge* capital gain."[73] One of Jack's competitors said, "Canadian publishers have built-in handicaps. For Jack to do what he's done within those limits is an astonishing achievement. He's an excellent businessman."[74] Jack himself had countered the criticisms of the Ontario politician Stanley Randall: "I think I'm an incredibly good businessman; I think that to have been able to keep the company alive has been no minor achievement in a business sense."[75]

Jack contended that publishing was essentially a high-risk, low-yield industry and thus was really a young man's game. He was no longer young. He maintained that he had outlived his usefulness—and his creativity—as a publisher. He felt he had never really had the opportunity to make his own decisions about the course of his life. Publishing was the family business, and he had accepted the mantle of his father, to whom he was deeply attached and whose death continued to gnaw at him.

The break in the continuum between the private, shy, reclusive Jack and the flamboyant public figure he presented to the world increased markedly. In the midst of personal and professional insecurity, he clung to his ideal for his company:

> But in the final analysis, product itself—the literary product—is paramount. All the other factors are important, even essential, but even the best organized publishing house in the world . . . is dead if it runs out of good product. . . . For this reason the author will always remain the most important person in the publishing cycle. I'm talking here about mainstream publishing as opposed to what might be called commercial publishing or house-created publishing. Good mainstream publishing is more rewarding, financially and in

every other way, than commercial publishing. The top houses have a good mix of the two. Ours really needs both because you can't depend on enough good product from mainstream authors to keep in business, but the real success, the real satisfaction, relates to the mainstream. The most important asset of this company is our list of mainstream authors. Nobody in the company is as important as a mainstream author. All of us can be replaced. You can't replace a Margaret Laurence, an Irving Layton, a Leonard Cohen or a Mordecai Richler. We must remember that at all times.[76]

"Mainstream" and "commercial" publishing were, according to Jack, very different enterprises. Commercial books, which had the potential to generate substantial amounts of income, were fleeting in their appeal; mainstream authors produced enduring literature affirming the national identity.

Mainstream publishing may have been fraught with difficulties, but it was precisely what Jack had committed himself to twenty-five years earlier. In 1972, he was not certain he could carry on that mission effectively any longer. His shaggy, now largely silver mane of hair and narrow face gave him the look of an alert, high-strung thoroughbred, but his eyes, always watchful, betrayed his profound tiredness.

## I O

## GEMSTONE

# (1973‑74)

"I HAD A mild collapse several days ago, and although it is not a serious matter, my doctor is concerned. . . . I have had the feeling for some months that I have not been able to work as effectively as I should have, and so I guess we have to accept the fact that there is a considerable psychosomatic element in the whole situation. If the body is fatigued, the mind is fatigued and so on."[1] Jack's comment from the spring of 1973 shows how overwhelmed he felt by work. Some days, assisted by cigarettes and booze, he coped; other days, inertia prevailed. He told publisher friends at Atheneum and Knopf in New York, "Did I say I was going to be away for three weeks? Yes, by God, I am. I'm taking a holiday. It has become a question as to who is going to win. This

*Jack, circa 1975*

damn foolish business or me, and I finally decided to swing the odds in my favour."

In the early summer, after returning from a holiday in Bermuda, he tried, in what were supposed to be a series of personal reflections given the code name "Gemstone," to place the problems confronting him in some sort of priority. He wanted Marge, the only other person to know of the existence of these documents, to be quite sure that not even Elizabeth was apprised of their existence: "I think you have a growing tendency to treat my wife and me as one person. I realize that you don't do this in areas that would be considered dangerous, but nonetheless from reports that I have had of discussions between you and Elizabeth, I have some concern that you may feel that I disclose everything to her. I don't. It is not because I don't trust her. It's simply that I disclose many things to you . . . that are not at least at this point the business of Elizabeth."

Unfortunately, only the original six-page Gemstone memo has survived. What was wrong with the company? he asked. "My own analysis of the fundamental problem in the company has not changed now for two or three years, and it has not changed even after several weeks of serious concentration on various aspects of the problem while I was in Bermuda. I think the key to the difficulty is that we are a company without any heritage. By that I mean simply that although the company has been in business for sixty-five years, nothing but its historical record and its reputation has been handed down to the present management." There were many people in managerial and executive roles whose competence was open to question, but beyond that, there was the whole problem of Jack McClelland and where exactly he fitted into the scheme of things: "In one sense I am the only person in the company who has any real feeling of personal security. Here I emphasize the word 'personal' because I own the company . . . I can't be fired.

"For that reason I don't have to compete with anybody or I don't have to impress anybody. I don't have to prove anything. In another sense, however, I may have the worst feeling of insecurity of anyone in the company because my insecurity relates to the very existence of the company itself. . . . Even with the largesse of the Ontario and federal governments, our continued existence hangs by a very slim thread. We have to be right more often than we are wrong in everything we do." Even with his years of experience in publishing, he found it impossible to always make the "right" decision—and, he asserted, this might be "the real root . . . of the overall problem."[2]

The history of the company was fused with the McClelland family, and he was now the head. If he proved unworthy, the ship would likely sink. His deepening sense of apprehension was the worst imaginable: if he failed, everyone failed. Yet Jack, even with associates he trusted as much as Hugh Kane and Anna Porter, still found it difficult to delegate authority. In a very real sense, he carried the enormous burden of his firm squarely on his own shoulders.

Jack's refuge from M&S was provided by his wife and five children. In 1973, Suzanne, the eldest, was twenty-five, Rob, the youngest, twelve. Well before John McClelland's death in 1968, Jack and his family spent their summers at the Muskoka cottage that John and Ethel McClelland had bought after the Second World War. After his father's death, Jack and his family often spent their Christmases there. Jack, who was very much a "traditional" father in the best, old-fashioned sense of the word, always insisted that presents be handmade. He himself tended to be a bit tardy in making his own and on occasion called the art department at M&S to his rescue.

Once he arrived at Harold Town's place the day before Christmas Eve with balsa wood to build a boat for one of the children. "Suddenly," the astounded artist recalled, "he was Leonardo, holding this thalidomide thing up and admiring the lines, and I was the resident assistant, bringing the drinks down and offering praise at appropriate intervals. When he finally left it was close to dawn and I was schwacked."[3] There are also photographs of the entire family organized in a chorus line rollicking in homemade flannel pyjamas.

One visitor to Muskoka—Claire Mowat in the early sixties—remembered being in the boathouse with Farley and Jack early one summer evening. From their vantage point, they could look down at the dock where young Carol was visibly upset because there was no room for her in a boat that was to take family members for a cruise around the lake. Jack excused himself, walked down to the dock and sat down beside his daughter. He placed his arms around her, talked to her in an animated fashion and soon the two of them were joking. Jack may not have been at home as much as a man with a nine-to-five job could be, but when he was, he was wholly attentive to his family.

One of Jack's most prized possessions was his handsome Greavette mahogany launch. He loved to take it out in the dead of night, have a drink or two, smoke and sometimes ponder the M&S situation. Harold Town was a bit traumatized the time he and Jack were out late one night in the autumn, both a bit worse for alcohol: "We thought we saw lights in an empty cottage down the lake, and we headed over at once . . . to make a citizen's arrest. Jack looked like Captain Bligh at the wheel and sounded like an officer landing on the coast of Normandy. 'Don't scratch the boat! For God's sake, be careful! Jesus! Watch out!' He had no regard for *my* commando-like leap off the thing. All he cared about was his goddamned bloody boat!"[4] Once the two arrived at their destination, they realized that the mysterious light was a reflection of the moon on one of the cottage's windows.

Back home in Toronto, Jack was, despite his killing schedule, an attentive father, as all his children remember. He insisted they be up-to-date on current affairs: there were frequent quizzes at the dinner table. He was quite willing to help with homework. In general, he was not an intrusive parent, but he was a careful one. When teen-age Suzanne demanded her curfew be lifted, he readily consented but insisted she be at the breakfast table at the usual time the next morning. Anyone who knew Jack's domestic life was struck by how traditional it was, in contrast to the flamboyant public image he projected.

The McClellands' most important social contacts were with the "*Maclean's* gang." Its nucleus was a group of freelance writers and their wives and partners who had once worked together at the national magazine: June Callwood and Trent Frayne, Pierre and Janet Berton, Scott Young, and Max and Aileen Braithwaite. Other members included the broadcaster Fred Davis, Arthur and Sheila Hailey, Farley and Claire

Mowat, the architect John Parkin, Harold Town and later Anna and Julian Porter. From the late fifties and well into the sixties, this large group would gather on weekends during the summer at the McClelland cottage, the Hailey cottage or the Davis cottage. Jack, Pierre and Farley would often begin imbibing at breakfast time. June Callwood recalls an extremely unflappable Elizabeth, the steady centre of Jack's turbulent life, preparing breakfast one morning for an unusually large number of guests: she was trying to make something suitable using twelve bananas. During the winter, members of the circle would take turns holding casserole dinners at each other's home. Jack's and Elizabeth's personal and professional lives were largely given over to writers. They made many strong friendships. However, if all your friends are in the same business you are, in a sense you are never truly off duty.

In his role as a "hands-on" publisher, Jack dealt with most of the major complaints directed against himself and his firm. In September 1964, Irving Layton sent him a postcard: "Have you seen the McGraw Hill–Ryerson A. M. Klein *Collected Poems?* Why couldn't *you* have done something like that for me? It's a really handsome book—type, paper, format—and sells for less than $6. A paperback of my *Collected* would have swept the country like a forest fire fanned by a mistral wind. Really, I'm disappointed! But let's meet and talk about a new *Collected.* You'll find me reasonable—as always."[5]

Simma Holt, disappointed with the promotion and sales of her *Sex and the Teenage Revolution*, demanded the book's publishing rights be returned to her. Jack agreed to this. She told him her book would have sold better under a different imprint and also observed, "Maybe when you get back to the shop and are interested in people beyond the few in Toronto's 'in' group, you will realize there are 'in' writers beyond the Ontario border. . . ."[6] In his reply, Jack told Holt, who lived in Vancouver, that he feared she had become a "Western separatist." If she looked carefully at the M&S list, she would find relatively few Toronto-based writers.[7] Five months later, in July 1975, he congratu-lated her when she was elected to Parliament: "Although you were an extremely difficult author from a publisher's point of view, the very qualities that make you that should make you a great member."[8]

Pierre Berton continued his complaints, this time about the lack of hardbound copies of *The Secret World of Og* in Toronto bookstores. Farley Mowat, who had been edited by Peter Davison at Little, Brown in Boston, was now, finally, having the same function performed at M&S by Lily Miller, who had worked as an editor in New York City at Macmillan, McGraw-Hill and Lothrop, Lee and Shephard before joining M&S in 1972. The largest audience for Farley's books was in Canada, and it seemed appropriate to him to make this change; in addition, Davison was now a publisher rather than an editor. There were a number of necessary adjustments to ensure that this new arrangement worked, but it ultimately functioned very well. In *The Snow Walker* (1975), Farley thanked her for her "unremitting, gentle but implacable persistence" in improving that book. Lily, who abhorred office politics and found it impossible to edit at the company office, preferred to work at home. Other M&S editors disapproved of her apparently rebellious attitude, but she received Jack's unremitting support.

As was now becoming their wont, Berton and Mowat had another major fight. Berton was publicly critical of Farley's supposedly unsympathetic response to the arrest by the Soviets of the author Aleksandr Solzhenitsyn. On December 20, 1973, Farley told his publisher, "Hope to talk to you today about Pierre. I am really outraged by his actions and I will have nothing to do with him, nor will I sit on any board with him until he has publicly apologized to me. Either he or I will have to leave the board [of directors at M&S], and since I am aware that he isn't going to be the one to leave, then I shall have to do so. He is a megalomaniac son of a bitch."[9] This situation was remedied when Berton offered a full, eloquent apology: he was sorry he had given the impression that he felt Farley's stance was conditioned by the fact he had been a guest of the Soviet Union.[10]

Jack then had to calm Peter Newman when *Books in Canada* hired a person fired by Newman from *Maclean's* to review his *Home Country: People, Places and Power Politics* (1973). Newman asked Jack to write the offending magazine about this instance of obvious editorial partisanship.[11] Jack was hesitant: "The problem is that M&S and Peter Newman are the 'heavies.' We always have to lose in any confrontation because the confrontation, regardless of the facts, will be twisted by *Books in Canada* and a few other people in the book world, and whatever action that we take, I want to be sure that it is useful, not merely something that is going to lead to criticism of you and ourselves."[12]

Jack had another problem regarding Newman. In about 1968 he had advanced the writer $10,000 for a book called *Anatomy of Canada: A Study of Canada's Power Elite.* Concerned about the advance and the book, he met with Peter and Christina in June 1973. They agreed to do the book together. Jack agreed to pay Christina $14,000 a year for two years (she was reducing her hours at *Maclean's* to write the book); an additional $25,000 would probably have to be given to Peter, who might also go on leave. The total made available to the Newmans would be $53,000, $45,000 as an advance and $8,000 for expenses. Jack was very keen: "Apart from Pierre's western project, this is probably the safest and largest book in preparation in Canada at the moment. The only thing I don't like about bringing it to the board's attention is that I would hate to have Pierre and Farley thinking that we should be advancing them up to $50,000, although I do believe (not with these two in mind, of course) that this is going to be the general trend of the future just as an inevitable parallel of the signing of major athletes has skyrocketed." In advancing $63,000, Jack thought the book would earn at least $77,000, more likely $100,000.[13]

Eighteen months later, as Jack told Anna, things were not going well with *Anatomy*: "I had lunch with Peter and Christina Newman on Thursday. They have reached the mutual conclusion that they are unable to work together on the book. Apparently when they get down to the nitty-gritty of putting it together, their points of view are at variance and it just isn't working."[14] A bit later, an apologetic Christina wrote Jack to thank him for his patience and understanding.[15]

Other writers, such as the journalist-turned-novelist Sylvia Fraser, were elated by the graceful attention Jack gave their work. He published her first novel, *Pandora*, in 1972. She had felt extremely vulnerable when she handed her friend and would-be publisher this novel about an eight-year-old girl from a working-class family in Hamilton. He responded intuitively to the book. At that time, Fraser also noticed that Jack had the remarkable ability to see the merits of a book and to ignore shortcomings that could be eradicated.

At the sales conference for the 1974 list, he told his sales reps how much he recommended Fraser's new novel *The Candy Factory*, a highly symbolic story about love and lust, the chief characters including a tramp and a spinster: "Most of you have been here long enough to remember when we published Sylvia Fraser's first novel, *Pandora*. At that time, Mrs. Fraser had all the advantages and disadvantages of one who was known to be a friend of the publisher's. It meant that her book would be given some priorities; it meant too that her book would suffer slightly from the minor resentments from some of the less professional members of our staff. She lived through it. So did we. The book was well received—with almost no exception—by the critics." He added that *The Candy Factory* was not an "easier" book than *Pandora*. "Basically there is no easy way for Sylvia Fraser. Perhaps if I tell you a little about her, I can tell you even more about her book. She is an extraordinary person. Her mind quite literally does not range on the same level of consciousness as yours or mine. Her sensibilities, her intuition, her awareness of more possibilities than most people would find tolerable. Her familiarity with the symbolic, illusions, literary or psychological, her involvement in detail with all the nuances of the mind and soul—these set her apart. Formidable. Yes. In some ways I think of her as a Canadian Ayn Rand and I believe that she will ultimately be universally recognized as one of the truly major Canadian literary talents of her time." The book's subject matter was strong, certainly not for small-town public libraries or closed minds; the real question was whether the reps would like reading it and thus sell it effectively: "Will you enjoy it? If you are a good reader, quick to cope with contemporary fiction—and I don't want to frighten anyone—if, for example, you enjoyed *Beautiful Losers*, you will have no problem. If you don't really dig serious contemporary fiction, then I suggest that you don't read this one. Just take our word for it."[16]

There were plans for another project involving Sylvia Fraser. In the early 1970s, Jack hosted a TV interview show called *The First Team* on Metro Cable. In 1972, it was to be broadcast in colour for the first time. He planned thirteen shows. Guest authors included Richler, Atwood and other M&S notables, as well as Morley Callaghan and Northrop Frye.

Two years later, in 1974, Jack and Sylvia proposed to the CBC that this program be made into a half-hour national weekly TV show, to be called *Best-seller*, on books and the book industry, co-hosted by Jack, who would "provide a bookman's knowledge of the industry," and Sylvia, who would "provide a writer's knowledge of other writers and of writing." The aim was to produce a "fast-paced, extroverted show on Canadian books and writers that entertains and informs . . . and presents Canadian writers as figures of glamour—Canada's movie stars." The proposal was turned down by Knowlton Nash, director of TV Information Programs for CBC, who liked the idea, but stated that "our air time and our financial commitments are such that we are not able to undertake a special series in addition [to the CBC's existing reporting of book news]."[17]

Despite Nash's unwillingness to supplement CBC-TV's book coverage, the publishing scene in Canada seemed on the move: Longhouse, the Canadiana bookstore, opened its doors in central Toronto in 1973; Yousuf Karsh's iconic portrait of Margaret Atwood seated in a large high-backed wicker chair was constantly reproduced; CBC Radio's frenetic *As It Happens*, which debuted in 1971, often dealt with books; artists such as Christopher Pratt, Alex Colville and Michael Snow were making waves internationally. The cultural climate might have seemed auspicious for publishers, but Jack's daily grind at M&S remained exhausting and exhaustive.

Complex and difficult publishing problems arose in 1973 and 1974 concerning Margaret Laurence's last adult novel, *The Diviners*. Although she had acted as Margaret's American editor since *A Jest of God* (1966), Judith

Jones at Knopf in New York took a greater role in shaping Laurence's work in the following years. By the time of *A Bird in the House* (1970), Jones had assumed principal responsibility for Laurence's work within the Knopf–McClelland & Stewart–Macmillan continuum.

Judith had expressed serious objections to *A Bird in the House*, but these turned out to be trivial in comparison with her worries about *The Diviners*. As an editor, she liked experimental fiction that pushed the reader in new directions through the use of unorthodox narrative. (Her favourite Laurence book was *The Fire-Dwellers*. She especially admired its enormous technical risks.) However, Jones was not willing to allow a writer to put into print material that was unfocused and undisciplined. When she read the manuscript of *The Diviners*, she was certain of two things: it bore the mark of genius, and it was an utter mess. During that first reading, she was certain that within the chaos was a far more compact and coherent book waiting to be liberated.

In April 1973, she did not shirk her editorial responsibility when she wrote Margaret requesting a meeting, which took place in early June. Since no early draft of *The Diviners* survives, it is impossible to compare the completed novel with the material originally sent to the publishers. What is very clear is that all three houses wanted radical surgery performed before allowing the book to go into production, and that Judith Jones had the full backing of Alan Maclean of Macmillan and Jack McClelland when she met with Margaret. Judith Jones's charm, diplomacy and intellectual rigour worked beautifully during their lengthy meeting because she was able to communicate her enthusiasm for the book at the same time that she laid down the law.

Laurence's response to the critique she was offered can be seen in a long letter she wrote to Judith less than a month later, on July 2, two and a half pages of which are devoted to "MAJOR CHANGES." Most of these involve paring the narrative down so that subsidiary stories (by the characters Skinner and Christie) do not interfere with plot coherence.

In the summer of 1971, while Margaret was working on *The Diviners* at her cottage on the Otanabee River near Peterborough, Jack, who had just received the substantial loan from the government of Ontario, had a single poster printed for Margaret's benefit, complete "with a comic takeoff on the Ontario coat of arms. It stated: 'No visitors allowed between Monday and Friday. An important work is going on.'" On June 12, 1973, almost two years later, Jack, himself apprehensive about what was happening to Margaret's work-in-progress, wrote her an uncharacteristically long (six-page) letter, in which he expressed sentiments similar to Judith Jones's: "Let me start by saying that the manuscript contains some of the greatest writing that you have ever done. I have told you before that you are the only author who has improved every time out, and I think you have kept your record intact. I read the manuscript in one sitting from about nine o'clock at night until four in the morning. It's a very moving experience. I ended up in tears during the last half hour. . . . This is not to say that I think everything is right about the novel. I don't. I am totally in accord with [your] plan to work directly and solely with Judith Jones in bringing the script to its final form." He went on to underscore the crucial point being made by Judith: "The problem with the novel is essentially that you have larded the script with material that impedes the flow and that really is unnecessary in terms of what you are trying to do. I read every page, but I can be honest and tell you that it bugged me as a reader to have to do so because too often I was taken away from the narrative, from your own beautiful writing and characterization, and forced to read background material that I really didn't want or need." Her encounter with Judith and Jack's letter galvanized Margaret. On August 28, 1973, Judith, delighted to have had full support from Jack, told him, "You will see that there has been some major surgery performed—all for the good, I'm convinced—and the fact that Margaret feels the novel is much the better for it reinforces the conviction. . . . Your long letter to Margaret was wonderful, Jack, and a great help to me because we saw eye-to-eye on just about everything. . . . I hope we can all get together sometime to celebrate the launching of this book. I am very excited about its possibilities and I feel strongly that Margaret has brought together some very powerful elements here and created a tremendously moving and dramatic story."

Judith Jones's optimism was short-lived. Although the book was a major best-seller and received the Governor General's Award, it was not reviewed well in Margaret's opinion in, for example, either *The Globe and Mail* or *The Toronto Star*. More important, the book was subjected to two banning controversies that hurt the author deeply. Later, she could joke about the matter, as in her letter to Jack McClelland, in the midst of a fight with him about her forthcoming collection of essays, *Heart of a Stranger* (1976): "My first reaction [to your suggested revisions], not unnaturally, was one of incredulity and rage. However, my normally calm and indeed incredibly patient personality has once more reasserted itself, and I am able to look at the situation with my usual tolerance and cool assessment. What a good idea about making the book a 'great gift item'! Had you considered the vast possibilities of selling each copy individually wrapped in pink tissue paper, tied about with a wide pink ribbon? Or perhaps a tiny tasteful bunch of plastic forget-me-nots? This village, you know, has numerous gift shops—perhaps I might start one myself, handling only two items . . . this book plus *The Diviners*. I would, of course, call the shop . . . Porn 'n' Corn."[18] In his response, the Boss told her he was going to write *The Peterborough Examiner* "suggesting that they are on the right track; that all your books should be banned forthwith; that all your awards should be withdrawn because you are corrupting our children." Only someone Margaret trusted completely could jest with her about such a vital and sensitive matter.

Jack also treated Mordecai Richler's 1973 pronouncements in a lecture at Carleton University with a pinch of salt. The headline in *The Toronto Star* of March 26, 1973, summarized the contents of Richler's assertions accurately: "An author warns art isn't good just because it's Canadian." In general, Jack, who was well acquainted with much of the dross that constituted Canadian material, agreed with Richler, but, he told him, "There are a lot of individual points to which you have not given sufficient consideration."[19] However, he reflected, he had no objection to Richler's rejection of the stringent, punitive publishing policy of the Committee for an Independent Canada whereby non-Canadian firms were excessively penalized. He himself, as he pointed out, had resigned from that group because of their extreme position on that issue.

At about the same time, he urged the historical novelist Thomas H. Raddall, then seventy, to allow M&S to publish his autobiography, *In My Time* (1976): "It is a particularly fine record of the struggles of a professional writer in Canada. There are so many insights and comments of value for other authors, for editors, for publishers, for all people concerned with the book and magazine industry that for this reason alone it would be very useful for others to read of your continuing financial concerns, the struggles that you had and simply the life of a professional writer with the many intrusions and influences that make it so difficult to write."[20] Of course Jack knew those struggles from the point of view of the publisher in Canada and made a reflection that was as true about himself as it was of Raddall: "The calm, controlled, unruffled, charming exterior as contrasted with the struggle and the inner concern. I would suspect that many people, in fact most people, who have known you only casually will be astounded to find that you share the same sort of problems that they face themselves."[21]

Jack was perhaps not always as appreciative of some women writers as he might have been. However, he was certainly inveigled by Margaret Laurence into publishing Adele Wiseman's second novel, *Crackpot*, in 1974. In a strange, somewhat contradictory letter introducing a book that had been rejected by several houses, Margaret began by explaining that Adele was the type of writer who was "very sensitive about editorial criticism and has never really had a first-rate editor whom she trusted. . . . I think she'd like to submit the novel to you, but is a bit shy owing to your not having published [Wiseman's first novel] *The Sacrifice*. I told her (at no extra charge, Boss) that you might be a nut in some ways but you most definitely were not of an ungenerous spirit and would certainly not hold a grudge against her on account of her first novel. However, I think she'd rather you wrote to her about it, if you feel so inclined." Having attempted to arouse his interest, a somewhat embarrassed Margaret made it quite clear that Adele, unlike herself, would not tolerate major editorial intervention in the event he was inclined to publish: "The thing is this—as I understand the situation, she would *not* be willing to do major structural changes."[22] He eventually published a book that did not have the editorial attention it could have used.

Jack was less hospitable to Claire Mowat, Farley's wife. He felt she had a duty to act as a handmaiden to her celebrity husband and should forget her own ambitions to pursue a career as a writer. His apology— a very genuine one—still betrays his real feelings about *The Outport People*, which he would publish in 1983.

> I've been brooding about the fact that I seemed to have caused a stoppage of progress on your manuscript. That wasn't my intention. I wish we had taken the opportunity to discuss the whole thing at greater length the other night. . . . My comment was that of all the careers you could have selected, writing, it seemed to me, would perhaps be the least suitable. . . . But, for God's sake, this does not mean that you should, having started a book, be discouraged from finishing it.
>
> I came to understand that evening that the writing of this particular book was not really the start of a separate career for you—as I had first understood it—but rather something that you wanted to do to occupy your time and to tell a story you wanted to tell. That's fair enough. . . . My concern is related to the long-term prospect of a wife developing a career that parallels her husband's.

Very much concerned about the comfort and security of one of his best-selling authors, Jack offered Claire very different advice from that he had offered Margaret Laurence years earlier when her marriage dissolved. Nevertheless, Jack had the grace to tell Claire, "After [your book] is published, you can then decide whether I am right or not. . . . It's a matter of record that I have been wrong once or twice in my life."[23]

There was one author Jack was to be wrong about on a number of occasions: Roloff Beny, the painter turned photographer from the Prairies who wrote a brilliant short account of his emotionally turbulent origins: "My parents were constantly apologizing about me to friends, relatives and employees. Chuck [Beny's brother] was already following in the family footsteps, first laid down by our grandfather who had prospered and started a family of respectable and respected citizens. And now, cropping up from nowhere, a shy, skinny child who painted pictures and set his own strange fashions in dress. A painter, more than half a century ago in western Canada, was a creature unheard of. I grew up against a background of loneliness, feeling myself an oddity and an outcast."[24] From the time of early childhood in Medicine Hat and Lethbridge, Alberta, Roloff Beny had a sense of himself as an artist that set him apart. His father, who owned the local General Motors agency, his kindly mother, who suffered ill health most of her life, and his one-year-older brother, Chuck, were never cruel and unsympathetic to Wilfred Roy, who, born in 1924, eventually adopted his mother's Russian surname as his given name. Despite what could be termed a bad fit between Roloff and his family, he intuitively knew his own destiny: "When I was five years old, Mother took up a hobby painting luminous slogans on velvet pillows. One day she came home to find that her small son had borrowed her colours, and after decorating his face and body, had started an enterprising experiment with abstract murals on the dining-room wall. Thus began, somewhat spectacularly, my career as an artist."[25]

After completing high school, Beny attended Trinity College at the University of Toronto, where he was "intoxicated" by the academic gowns, the Sunday high teas and even the compulsory running. He even found the perfect retreat: the neo-Gothic belfry of the college's central tower. Beny also became extremely successful: he exhibited paintings at Hart House and became "The Father of Spiskopon," Spiskopon being the college's secret society. After Trinity, Beny was supposed to return home, but he went instead to the State University of Iowa, where he specialized in printmaking. In the winter of 1947–48, he moved to New York City to pursue a doctorate in art history at the Institute of Fine Arts of New York University. Manhattan reinforced Beny's desire to be an artist, not an art historian: "I wanted to be . . . in touch with and reflecting the tensions of the age, not fleeing from contemporary life but facing it."[26]

After a year in New York, Beny went to Greece, the transforming experience of his life, an "unashamed and deep collision" between his soul and a classical past still very much alive. Shortly thereafter, he met Peggy Guggenheim, the great collector of modern art; she became his "soul sister." At that time, he had a sexual crisis, coming to terms with his homosexuality: "Life had made up my mind for me, and I ceased struggling. I found that what I really loved was not limited by gender, but rather defined by beauty."[27]

In 1951, Beny started to take photographs of architecture and nature. Immediately, he discovered his affinity for photography. In the wake of the success of his first book, Beny settled in the heart of Rome. His penthouse, Tibor Terrace, was an engaging collection of contemporary art and fake Etruscan statues, tigerskin rugs and velvet cushions, which one close friend called "tacky." Luminaries from the film world at Cinecittà flocked to see Beny, including Vivien Leigh and her husband Laurence Olivier, the novelist Alberto Moravia and the soprano Leontyne Price. Beny's photos appeared in English *Vogue* and *Queen* and in *Chatelaine* and *Maclean's* in Canada. Beny never learned to speak Italian, although he lived in Rome for twenty-five years. Once, while attempting to give a speech in the presence of the doge of Venice, he thought he was giving thanks for "twenty-five glorious years in Italy"; unfortunately, he gave thanks for "twenty-five glorious anuses in Italy."

In Canada, Ted Browne at Longmans was Beny's publisher. In 1967 that firm published, under the patronage of Signy and John David Eaton, his magnificent *To Everything There Is a Season*. At a party held by the Eatons, Beny met Jack, who had vivid memories of the occasion: "My first reaction to Roloff was that he certainly looked the part of the committed artist. I thought his apparel was a bit on the bizarre side, but if there is one thing that Roloff made clear on our first meeting [it was] that he was not your normal human being."[28] For some time, Beny had been at odds with Browne, and in 1968, he turned to Jack for advice. He told the photographer to get an agent: "It is true that agents make it a little rougher for publishers. . . . In my view, they're a necessary evil, in the same sense that unions are a necessary evil. A glance at these contracts absolutely convinces me that you very much need one."[29] Jack tried unsuccessfully to obtain the paperback rights for *To Everything There Is a Season*, but he did become Beny's Canadian publisher when Browne died.

Beny was an extremely good—not a great—photographer, but he had a strong conviction of his own importance. Able to charm the super-rich, he was very comfortable in his role as self-appointed emperor of his own marzipan world. Incapable of being alone, he relentlessly surrounded himself with friends, admirers and flunkeys. He fainted constantly and lived on a wide assortment of pills. Jack and Roloff were very different men: Jack was a guy's guy, whereas Roloff was effeminate. Both were supreme showmen, hucksters who believed in what they were selling. More essentially, both refused to believe in limitations—their own, especially.

The first M&S title by Beny was *India* in 1969. Jack now found out a few more things about Beny: "He lived in a different world and his interests—all artistic—were on a different level. . . . Roloff, as a general rule, showed very little interest in anybody but the boss, and as a consequence there was an overwhelming tendency at Longman's to treat him as a 'pain in the ass.' To a degree, the same thing happened when he joined M&S, except for the fortunate fact that we had a few key individuals who genuinely admired his work and were sensitive to his needs and his somewhat unique way of life."[30]

Jack was soon fielding complaints from his new author, to whom he replied, "Re misspelling, misaddressing and so on, that's standard around here. It makes publishing more exciting. How do you think we get our kicks?"[31] If he needed something, Beny could be extraordinarily pleasant. To the film and opera stars he numbered among his friends, he was always the epitome of charm. To underlings, he could be brusque and cold. As Jack found out, Beny wanted to deal only with him: "Please, Jack, without in any way wishing to be critical, I do wish that Mrs. Hodgeman rather than just dropping me notes that you are out of town and that my letter will be answered shortly [she did this for all authors, not just Beny] would, I humbly suggest, in such letters itemize what has been done in your absence."[32] In turn, the photographer saw his publisher as a true mentor.

There was soon a strong bond between these two men. In May 1970, Roloff told Jack, "I am sorry to continuously send you so many things to think about, dear Jack, but I feel so frustrated that I continuously dream up new projects, and I feel you are the one person I can discuss them with quite openly—strangely enough, with even more enthusiasm than I can with Thames & Hudson [his English publisher].[33] Is this because you are also Canadian and as adventuresome as I?" Once, when Jack would not accede to a request, Beny regretted that Jack could not visit him in Rome, where, he claimed, "I could really put you under my spell."[34]

Beny provided M&S with a potentially lucrative, possibly prestigious and thus important opportunity to originate an expensive, original project that could be offered to other publishers worldwide. This was a new venture for Jack, one that could truly open up a fresh direction in Canadian publishing. Negotiations about this project, which would have been centred on Rajasthan, India [not published until after Beny's death], were halted by plans for a book on Persia. In 1962, Beny had been to Iran and photographed the Shah and Shahbanou, Farah Diba; five years later, he was invited to an elaborate ceremony, where he found himself inside the Golestan Palace. He felt he was drowning in a sea of diamonds. "Overwhelmed, I lurked behind potted palms. The visual feast was staggering. . . . I think even then that I was being given a unique opportunity to become part of that strange world of power and beauty. Everything I'd ever dreamed of was there, in such profusion it took my breath away."[35]

When his friend James George was posted to Teheran as ambassador, Beny acted decisively. He discarded Thames & Hudson as his originating publisher, made a tentative deal with M&S to assume that role and arranged to be given an audience with the Shahbanou, or Empress, who, looking over some of his books, wanted him to do a similar celebration of her country. He was completely ecstatic: "I felt like that character in the *Arabian Nights* whose caravan had finally arrived: Iran was my pomegranate to open and extract its hidden garnets."[36] Jack was to be not only the publisher but the "guardian angel" of this new venture.

The guardian angel was summoned to an audience with Her Imperial Highness in November 1973. At first he did not know "whether I should take this seriously. A round trip to Iran would cost about $5,000. If it really involved a business meeting with the Empress, it would be worth it. But if it was another Beny peccadillo?" But he made the long journey. During that visit, Jack helped negotiate an agreement for the photographer to receive a fee of $25,000, unlimited first-class air travel within Iran, a generous subsidy to ensure the book would be produced to the highest standards and a guarantee that twenty thousand copies would be bought by various government agencies. Jack was overwhelmed by the Empress:

Many of our "audiences" involved Roloff and the Empress studying photographs over a light table in her office while I stood in the rear and leered at this beautiful creature. Hidden television cameras were everywhere in Iran in those days, and I hadn't any doubt that they had many photographs of me stalking the unsuspecting Empress.

*Jack McClelland, unidentified man, Roloff Beny and the Empress of Iran*

Roloff, or Dr. Beny as he was known in Teheran, gauged his success by the number of minutes the Empress granted him in the "audience." Thirty minutes represented failure, fifty minutes was promising, an hour and ten minutes a triumph. I was Dr. McClelland to the Empress. Among this international set, one had to assume this title.[37]

Jack's negotiations for the Iran book also meant meeting with representatives of the Empress in New York City, where he distinguished himself one evening by dancing with "their belly dancer. I had some fear that my picture [was] going to wind up in the New York daily newspapers."[38] Dealings with the Iranians were complex, often pitting Beny against various factions within the court circle. In their letters, Jack and Beny referred to the Shah and Empress under the code names of George and Martha, presumably in honour of the Washingtons.

Beny was also a notorious cheapskate who never willingly parted with a cent. His considerable fortune was not so much derived from his work as a photographer as from inheritance, property in Toronto's Yorkville and, at her death, the proceeds of the sale of the jewellery left him by Peggy Guggenheim. The one person at M&S feared by Roloff was Bob Wilkinson, the comptroller. "Please, Mr. Wilkinson, can I have a cab slip to take me back to downtown Toronto?" he would plead. "No!" the outraged money man would bellow. The photographer would be devastated, but Wilkinson was about the only person at M&S he could not cajole or charm. To his own considerable cost, Jack was to find out just how difficult it was for a Canadian firm to market a book for a worldwide audience.

In the autumn of 1972, Jack asked Gabrielle Roy to travel to Toronto at his expense to be interviewed on his weekly half-hour cable-TV show. This venture, he told her, provided him with the perfect opportunity to plug the New Canadian Library series. She declined.

Two years later, Jack asked Joyce Marshall to prepare a retranslation of *The Tin Flute*, a project that he felt deserved top priority. He was sad to hear from her that the novelist was not well. He also responded sympa-thetically to Gabrielle's request to have a new introduction written to the NCL *Hidden Mountain*, to replace an introduction by the academic critic Mary Jane Edwards published earlier that same year. In that intro-ductory essay, after censuring the style, the use of the omniscient narra-tor and the characterization of Pierre, the book's main character, Edwards concludes, "Despite its stylistic and technical weaknesses, how-ever, *The Hidden Mountain* is illuminating."[39] Roy did not appreciate such grudging backhanded compliments and wanted them removed. Jack wrote, "I share your reaction to it totally. I wish—and it may be hard to understand—but I really wish that I had the opportunity to read all these introductions before they appear in print. The fact of the matter is that I just don't seem to find enough time available. . . . You can be totally frank with me. I feel that our relationship over many years has earned us both the right to be perfectly candid."[40]

Early that autumn, Jack wrote Gabrielle a letter in which he shows a side of himself often kept out of his letters even to those authors with whom he was closest: "At the moment, then, I am in a very good mood, sitting watching the sunset over the lake. The trees here [in Muskoka] are just beginning to turn—although they are mostly pines, spruce, etc. along the shoreline—but it is absolutely beautiful."[41] That revelation led to even more reflective—intimate—remarks in his next letter to her that December: "Have I ever told you that you write the most beautiful letters that I ever receive? I am often tempted to bother you with a continuing stream of letters just so that I can have the replies. Why should I be surprised, though? As I have told you so many times, you are the greatest writer in the country, and it is not surprising that you should write such lovely letters."[42] He spoke of another link between them—asthma: "We talked once about asthma but only very briefly. My own guess is that it is the most terrifying of all ailments. I contain my own through constant use of inhalers to a degree that would shock my doctor if he knew about it, but I have always believed in the principle that immediate survival is more important than long-term survival."[43]

In the midst of these exchanges, Gabrielle Roy obtained exactly what she requested: Malcolm Ross wrote a new introduction to *Hidden Mountain*. Jack, however, feared that Ross, as shown by his decision to publish that novel with Edwards's introduction in the first place, was no longer in touch with the pulse of Canadian literature. In fact, earlier, against Jack's wishes, Ross had been unwilling to allow books by Leonard Cohen and Mordecai Richler to be included in the series. For example, on September 18, 1968, Ross gave Jack his candid response to Cohen's *Beautiful Losers*: "He cannot avoid or deny the dirt of our life in a time of disintegration. But it doesn't do to take a bath in a dirty tub! . . . The book turns my stomach." Jack was now afraid that he too might be out of touch, so unliterary were the problems that passed over his desk.

Jack knew one thing—he needed to sell more books. In an attempt to clear out a portion of the inventory of paperbacks filling up his warehouse, he held a ten-day sale in February 1974. To publicize the event, Jack handed out free books at the corner of Bay and Bloor in Toronto. In a wry column in *The Globe and Mail*, William French pointed out that M&S "was usually on the other end of the handouts. But while it may not be more blessed to give than receive, particularly for book publishers, a little well publicized charity once in a while doesn't hurt the public image, or, in McClelland's case, his reputation as a stunt man."[44] The actual sale was a buy-two-get-one-free (the lowest price of three) affair for consumers. Although M&S hoped to clear 600,000 paperbacks, more than half were printed solely for the sale. Many bookstores across Canada were delighted: when the sale was over, they were allowed to keep at no cost the stock given to them.

Not all was sweetness and light, however, with Jack and the book trade. At a talk at Hart House in January 1974, Jack slagged the Association of Canadian Publishers. The issue was subsidies, which M&S received and many other publishers did not. In particular, Peter Martin, of Peter Martin Associates, thought Jack had attacked him unfairly and was not amused: "It is entirely possible that McClelland's statements were, in part, slanderous. . . . I think it is fair to conclude that the remarkable Mc-Clelland is calling me an idiot. . . .He inherited his publishing company from his Daddy. Most of the rest of us have had to start from scratch."[45]

Earlier, in September 1973, a subsidiary company called McClelland & Stewart West Ltd. was formed in Calgary. With a staff of two—a promotion manager and an editorial director—this offshoot acted as the official publisher of the Glenbow Institute, publishing exhibition catalogues and books relating to Western Canada. One story involves Jack's daughter Sarah, who was a student at the University of Calgary in the seventies. Most of her friends had learned of her high-living father and decided to pull a prank on them both. While Sarah went to the airport to meet Jack, her friends removed the entire contents of her room to the outside of her residence and decorated the place as a harem, complete with a man sleeping in her bed. Although startled, father and daughter enjoyed the joke.

Sometimes, Jack's strife-torn spirits were capable of inspiring him to moments of great merriment, as in his letter to *The Toronto Star* of March 27, 1973: "I knew we Canadian publishers were in trouble but I had not appreciated the gravity of our problem until I read Alexander Ross' column on Monday night. . . . When the paperback manager of Canada's largest 'books only' chain [Classic Books] makes disparaging comments about three of Canada's most distinguished authors—Margaret Atwood, Pierre Berton and Farley Mowat—while drooling over [the American prostitute-turned-author] Xaviera Hollander it is time to call a halt. . . . I propose that we use the term 'koob,' book spelt backwards, to describe the sort of impressions from a police blotter that Ms. Hollander writes. . . . Please don't misunderstand me. I like junk reading. I've sold a lot of koobs in my day and plan to continue to do so, but I do respect books and I think a distinction must be made."[46]

# I I

# A MODERN CANADIAN
# FOLK FIGURE

# (1975-76)

"HE IS SURPRISINGLY OLD-FASHIONED, this
modern Canadian folk figure. Isn't he, after all, associated with a lot of
trendy things? Isn't he a jet setter, a darling of the Beautiful People, a hero
of the new Canadian nationalism? Yet here Jack is with his tie at half-
mast and a cigarette dangling from his mouth, wheeling his car down the
parkway one-handedly like a 1940s-style private eye."[1] As Robert Stewart's portrait in *Book-of-the-Month Club News* implies, Jack in 1975 was
as contrary and quixotic as ever. In the first two months of that year, his
activities in the publishing business were more extreme than ever. In
January, he staged a protest against Coles Bookstores' practice of selling
remaindered U.S. editions of Canadian books; in February, he suggested
that Canada's university students might wish to purchase M&S. Publishing no longer excited him, he professed, but true to form, his actions
belied the claim.

So angry were Jack, Pierre and Farley at Coles that they were on the
verge that January of entering one of the stores, destroying the American

editions of Berton and Mowat titles from which the authors received low or no royalties, and getting themselves arrested. This alliance would have been surprising, considering that the two writers often felt like throttling each other. In the past, booksellers in Canada, notwithstanding the glaring loopholes in the Copyright Act, had usually respected publishers' contractual territorial arrangements and obtained their stock of a book from the legitimate Canadian rights holder. Coles had successfully challenged this arrangement in court and won. As far as Jack Cole was concerned, the issue was cut and dried: "Being retailers we feel an obligation to represent the interests of the public by offering books at the lowest cost. The publishers are trying to create an artificial price situation. How long will they be allowed to continue operating at the public expense? The taxpayer has to pay to subsidize the publishers and pay again through artificially high book prices. I say that's desperately wrong."[2]

"Desperately wrong" for McClelland was the importation into Canada of American Penguin paperbacks of *A Whale for the Killing* and *Sibir* (American title *The Siberians*). On the Penguins, Mowat received a royalty of 4 per cent of the retail price as opposed to the 15 per cent he would have received from M&S. His loss of earnings on these two books, Jack estimated, could be as much as $50,000 in 1975. The Berton case was even more complex—and ludicrous. In the United States, *The National Dream* and *The Last Spike* were published in a one-volume abridgement called *The Impossible Railway*. The American railway book was a remainder (unsold stock sold at a cut-rate price), for which Berton was not entitled to a cent. To add insult to injury, Berton pointed out that Coles was "creating confusion and anger among book buyers who think *The Impossible Railway* is a new book, only to discover that it's an abridgement of what they've already read."

Ultimately Jack's anger was focused on the federal government, which he wanted to amend the Copyright Act. André Ouellet, the consumer and corporate affairs minister, claimed to be sympathetic, but he would do nothing to assist Canadian publishers in the short run: "Mr. Ouellet," Jack reported, "has replied that he intends to revise the entire Copyright Act rather than make a short-term amendment. But the revision could take two to three years to get through Parliament. That's too long to leave Canadian authors and publishers unprotected at the very time when large sums of public money are being spent to ensure the industry's survival."³ The Liberal government in Ottawa was taking away the financial aid the Progressive Conservative government at Queen's Park had given.

Jack felt his own time was running out when he offered his firm to the university students of Canada for $3 million. The resulting non-profit foundation would not, he stressed, have actual administrative control of the company; any profits would provide scholarships and bursaries. "I don't want to sell to foreign interests, and I don't want to be taken over by government." In a particularly sardonic moment, he said, "I'm not all that fond of Canadians, either, though that may sound odd coming from a past president of the Committee for an Independent Canada. I don't really like Canadian businessmen." He added, "I like this country and its potential. . . . I want to be sure there will be one large option open to Canadian authors because the other publishing houses are going to become increasingly commercial." By "commercial" he meant that his competitors would become more and more agency publishers for American imprints. In a real pie-in-the-sky moment, he concluded, "I can't think of better owners of a major publishing house than a group of student unions."⁴ Jack even had a semi-serious discussion with Anna about the possibility of his going into partnership with her lawyer husband, Julian Porter.⁵

Back in Toronto that March, Jack felt refreshed after a gruelling business trip: "I did survive the tour. As a matter of fact, I enjoyed it. The thing you keep forgetting is that existence at 25 Hollinger Road is such an appalling strain that to get away on a trip—even if it involves only two or three hours' sleep out of every twenty-four—tends to be a blessed relief. I worked my ass off. Had a great time and really enjoyed it, and as a matter of fact, I learned more about Canada on this recent trip than I have known for a long time. The change in the book business—for the better—was one of the really astounding phenomena that I encountered. If I weren't too old for it, I would even think of staying on in the book business."[6] Despite Jack's intentions to the contrary, publishing remained very much in his bloodstream.

Sometimes it was possible to be bowled over by a new book, especially one that seemed to come almost out of nowhere. Up to 1975, Marian Engel had written two children's and four adult novels. An intense, deeply serious writer, she took on many feminist issues in her writings, which were uncompromising, forceful and critical of matrimony as an institution. She had also had a blazing fight with Jack one night at a party at Anna Porter's in the early seventies. She admitted to him that she had sold the paperback rights to her first three novels for $750, whereupon he berated her so heatedly that she broke down and wept. In 1975, Adele Wiseman, delighted that Jack had published *Crackpot* the year before, took it upon herself to act as peacemaker and to press Engel's new book on him, a piece of "damn fine serious fiction": "Briefly, it's the story of a physical relationship which a lady has with a bear; I state that baldly to get it over with, because that, though crucial, is only a concrete vehicle, and a damn good one at that. What is, from my point of view, so fascinating about this book is that she's really saying something that goes beyond the apparent 'grossness' of some of the action. . . . Of course the physical stuff will provide the public furor and delectation which I've suggested above, but you will see for yourself it actually evolves as an absolute, inevitable necessity of a beautifully controlled, balanced narrative." If Jack looked into this matter, she was sure he would be very grateful to her as his "little literary Goody Two-shoes."[7] Margaret Laurence also told Jack she was quite taken with the book. Engel, as she confessed to him, was delighted by his interest: "Adele and Margaret had warned me they were taking action, but I didn't expect a call from the Man Himself."[8] As he informed Anna, the publisher was extremely excited by the prospect of *Bear*: "Unless Margaret Laurence and Adele Wiseman are both out of their minds, it's a very important and very saleable book. The fact that it is basically about a lady being screwed by a bear is beside the point."[9]

Not wishing to be carried away by a feminist wave of enthusiasm and knowing that such a controversial book would need support within the writing community, Jack asked Engel for a copy of the manuscript and sent it to Robertson Davies at Massey College. Within two weeks, the author completed his report. Davies, one of Canada's premier humorists and novelists, adored the book. "It reminded me of Margaret Atwood's *Surfacing*, because it explores the same ground—the search for healing in the wilderness—but I thought it a much better book as a work of art. I am not surprised Margaret Laurence and Adele Wiseman urged you to publish it: it is, in the best sense, a woman's book, and they know what they are talking about. But—this must be delicately stated—neither Margaret nor Adele, who are both dears, labour under the burden of a strong sense of humour, and when the book is published you had better prepare yourself for some explosions, not of outrage but of ribaldry." In a wonderful comic turn, Davies imagined the critical reception of Engel's remarkable creation:

Writing from my own recent experience, I think you may run into a few things like this: [Roy] MacSkimming [from *The Star*] will like the book and understand it; French [from *The Globe*] will not like the book and won't understand it, and will be vulgarly jocose about it; [another critic] will complain that it is elitist (not every woman has a bear, so why should any woman have one?) and will hint that bears are well known to be homosexuals (like all sensitive people). . . . All critics, everywhere in Canada, will tell the whole plot in the course of what they think of as reviews, thereby spilling the beans. Gordon Sinclair will declare that he has never slept with a bear, but served under a sergeant who was a bear in the First World War. Pierre Berton will have an evening of *The Great Debate* on the theme Why Not Bears? Peter Newman will discover and publish the bear's income tax file. . . . Peter Gzowski and ninety-nine other TV and radio interviewers will lure Miss Engel to their studios and after a lot of humming and hawing, ask, "Now, Marion, I hope you'll take this question as it's intended, but did you ever . . . really—let me phrase this carefully—*you know what I mean* . . . with a bear?" Judy LaMarsh will ask a similar question, but not having read the book, will think it was a porcupine. . . . All of this you and Miss Engel will have to endure philosophically.[10]

When Jack told Engel of Davies's letter, she thanked her fellow author: "He sounded a bit worried that my reputation would be ruined. As I am under the impression that it has been ruined for years, I am not very concerned!" Well before sending the manuscript to Davies, Jack knew he had a winner: it "is not only a saleable book, it's a good one—damn well written. I am astounded because I never suspected M.E. had this sort of ability."[11]

In turn, Engel was glad to have Jack as her publisher. "I want to say now that I really appreciate your efforts for this book. I'm not sentimental: I think you took it on because it's commercial; I gave it to you because I think it's a really decent piece of fiction."[12] Worried about the public's reaction to a story about a woman's love affair with a bear, M&S produced a dust jacket that, as Sandra Martin deftly put it in an article in *Saturday Night,* was "more appropriate for a philosophical treatise on the existential meaning of Eskimo sculpture."[13] When a truly garish cover graced the paperback a year later, Engel was shocked, but Jack claimed he thought this new effort was too tame: "If I had really been in a bitchy mood that day, I would have made the cover raunchier."[14]

One of Jack's major regrets as a publisher of serious fiction was that Margaret Laurence had not written since the publication of *The Diviners.* In an attempt to capitalize on her enormous reputation, he urged her to gather together a collection of her previously published short nonfiction pieces. This led to a series of squabbles based on his wish to have some pieces omitted and his opposition to the various titles she proposed for the book, including "Where the World Began." When she suggested *Heart of a Stranger,* he knew she had at last hit on the right title. The trouble with the book was not its contents—travel essays, journalism originally published in *The Vancouver Sun* and *Maclean's,* philosophical and autobiographical reflections—but the expectation of a reading public that did not really want this kind of book from this writer. The situation distressed Laurence: "What worries me is that I'm not supposed to have light words, or so some critics seem to think. When my essays . . . came out, some reviewers said that it was pretty light stuff and not to be compared with a serious novel."[15] Privately—to Anna Porter—Jack maintained that the public would buy anything by Margaret Laurence, even if it was printed on toilet rolls.

In the midst of *The Diviners* banning scandal in 1976, Laurence had agreed to join the board of McClelland & Stewart. When she accepted, she informed Jack that her agenda would be to get more books by young writers published. Soon she was at loggerheads with the Boss. Certainly, she found herself in a distinct minority, thinking she did not have much in common with the captains of industry she met there. She also felt—correctly—that Jack and Anna orchestrated all the workings of the board well in advance of meetings.

If Jack at times was more than a bit chauvinistic about women writers, he could, even if it was in the interests of political correctness and market demands, take it on himself to be certain they were well represented on his list. In July 1975 he was quite firm with Al Purdy about the contents of his new anthology, *Storm Warning 2*: "Leaving women's lib aside and chauvinism aside, there are probably more female poets than male poets in this country, and if it is at all possible, without endangering the standards, they should be given at least some sort of reasonable representation. I wouldn't ask you for a minute to damage the quality of the book for this purpose. I would ask you to be fair about it because I don't think there is any doubt that the book will do a little better if women are adequately represented. . . . We can't add to the length, however."[16]

Earlier, in January, Jack received a disturbing memorandum from Larry Ritchie: "Peggy Atwood, as you probably know, is completing her third novel [*Lady Oracle*]. Unfortunately, I hear, she thinks you are not interested and would prefer not to consider it for our list. It would be a shame if rumours were unfounded, or she presupposed your lack of interest if you have different feelings or if the feeling emanates from an intermediary, like Phoebe Larmore [Atwood's agent]."[17] When Jack approached

Atwood, she immediately told him that the gossip was without foundation of any kind.

There was an additional tension between Atwood and Jack, which cannot simply be explained by the fact that both had strong, competitive personalities. When she began living with the novelist Graeme Gibson in 1973, Jack seemed to take this as an affront. Earlier, in the late sixties, Jack let it be known he was going to publish Gibson's first novel, *Five Legs*. However, no contract had been signed. At a weekend cocktail party at the Park Plaza Hotel in Toronto, Gibson, egged on by Farley Mowat, confronted Jack: when would his book appear? "You'll know on Monday," Jack assured him. On the appointed day, Hugh Kane called Gibson to decline the book. Subsequently, Gibson's acclaimed first novel was published by the House of Anansi in 1969. On one occasion, Graeme "rubbed it in" when Jack tried to pretend someone else at M&S had made the mistake of not publishing him, whereupon the novelist reprimanded Jack: "You're responsible for the decision."[18]

Over the succeeding years, Graeme heard that Jack had made uncomplimentary remarks about him. The rift was healed when Gibson himself auctioned *Perpetual Motion* in 1981. M&S was not offered the book. A deeply offended Jack called to complain. The novelist immediately allowed him to bid, and Jack promptly topped everyone else. He published the novel in 1982.

Jack's love of publicity was undiminished, whatever other problems he encountered. In February 1976, he was in Saskatoon because he thought his special skills were desperately required there: the year before, in July, while dressed as Santa Claus on an oppressively hot day, he was horrified when only one in four persons he approached would accept a free book in the M&S giveaway of paperbacks (this was in startling contrast to the citizens of Toronto, who eagerly snapped up the books). He was going back to find out why he had been so unsuccessful the year before. "We believe," he observed, "books are addictive, so if we can get Saskatooners to read one, they'll start buying them."[19] As soon as he returned to Toronto, Jack was at City Hall, where he weighed Mayor

*Jack in Saskatoon, February 1976*

David Crombie and the Maple Leafs captain, Darryl Sittler, and donated their weight in books to the charities of their choice. Then he skated around the rink in Nathan Phillips Square, bestowing free books on his fellow skaters.

One marvellous coup for M&S in the early part of 1976 was the sale on a firm, non-returnable basis of virtually the entire first printing (100,000) of *Between Friends,* the National Film Board's bicentennial gift to the United States. (A separate presentation edition of 20,000 copies was given to heads of government, and a copy was deposited in every major public library in the United States.) This book was ultimately the most commercially successful of all M&S projects during Jack's forty-year career.

A tender had been held to determine which Canadian house would acquire the rights to the commercial edition of the book (as opposed to those specially bound copies given as state presents). M&S and another firm committed themselves to printing 40,000 and were thus in a dead heat. To break the tie, Jack offered to do 90,000. The actual print run was 200,000 (two runs of 100,000 each). Jack had some difficulty with the first batch since Ashton-Potter, the printing company—worried about M&S's frail financial fortunes—wanted $11 a copy to be paid to them before the books were released from the bindery. Elsa Franklin was called in to help out: she formed a consortium of investors who provided M&S with about $1 million to gain possession of the otherwise imprisoned copies.

*Between Friends* ultimately took in close to $7 million in revenue; it was also the first collaboration between Jack and Lorraine Monk, the feisty, domineering visionary who ran the Still Photography Division of the National Film Board. Their other books included *Canada with Love* (1982) and *Ontario: A Loving Look* (1984). Once Jack said of her, "Throughout her career she has always managed to lead the audience."[20] To Monk the new art of photography held the key to an understanding of the world. She wanted Canadians to be aware of this art form and to contribute to it. In a wonderful accolade to her, Jack quipped, "Her family is already aware that she is incapable of taking a decent family portrait. I also hope they are aware that living in a home where one can seldom move without disturbing transparencies, prints and layouts has been more than worth it."[21]

In 1975, the year before the publication of *Between Friends*, M&S had recorded sales of ten million, an impressive increase of 22 per cent over the previous year. Still, in what was now in danger of becoming an annual ritual, Jack announced in January 1976 that he was "talking to some interested parties" about selling the firm. His "personal" deadline for such negotiations was July 1. Four days after the deadline, he informed his 135 employees that he had "withdrawn" the company from the market. One of the two prospective mystery buyers, Torstar, apparently made an unsatisfactory offer; the other did not bother to submit one. "I varied back and forth in my thinking about selling," he claimed. "In a way I would have preferred a clean break, but that wasn't possible because my conditions were not met. I'm perfectly happy about the outcome. Now I'll regroup my thoughts and carry on. The agony and indecision are ended."[22]

Sylvia Fraser advised him, "Don't be too upset that you didn't get any definite purchase offers. You've built up an important and complex business. Take it as a compliment that your shoes aren't so easy to fill. Don't give up your dreams, dear, and *don't* withdraw. As for all the rest, the best I can do is to offer you the enclosed. The key statement is the last one: 'The path of human progress is never straight, but obscured with much backsliding. We've just had an obfuscation. No more, no less.'"

The "enclosed" Fraser referred to was a nine-page fable she had written, titled "The Lion and the Flea,"[23] which tells the tale of the friendship between a flea, named Gesundheit, and a lion, Great Warrior. The flea offers the lion sage advice, and the lion becomes revered for his knowledge. Gesundheit gets tired of hearing his own words "quoted, without copyright" by his larger friend. Things become unpleasant between the two. Great Warrior stops listening to the flea, and Gesundheit leaves, the lion being "too proud and too stubborn" to ask him to stay. The flea returns eventually and finds the lion, now named Wise Warrior, eloquently addressing a council meeting at the watering hole. At first, Gesundheit is jealous and thinks the lion has a new flea in his ear. Upon discovering he does not, the flea realizes that the lion never really needed an adviser. "He [the flea] had just been a very noisy sounding-board—a first-class pain in the ear!" At first, the flea panics, but when he catches hold of himself, he feels overwhelming relief. He then settles down on the lion's paw to listen.[24]

As Fraser realized and was trying to tell Jack covertly, his thinking about his future and M&S's future was always in flux. One part of him wanted a clean break, another part imposed stringent conditions. The agony and indecision were far from over. In her fable, Fraser is also hinting that Jack's lion side is accompanied by a corresponding vulnerability: he can understand and appreciate himself only if he accepts himself as a composite of seeming opposites. She was also telling him to use his own heart and mind, that if he heeded those proddings, he would do the right thing.

As a father, Jack remained a constant presence in his children's lives. From the time his son, Rob, was six years old, he was an avid hockey player who, like his father, was a goaltender. Every Saturday morning Jack took his son to practice. He would sit as far away as possible from the other parents and on the drive home would review his son's performance—what went wrong, what went right—in an extremely tactful, helpful way. In 1972, when Jack had just acquired a new Mustang convertible, he and his son were loading the car with hockey equipment when Rob accidentally put a hockey stick through the car's canvas roof. Jack cussed a little bit, but he took the entire incident in stride. Rob understood that to his father his eleven-year-old son's feelings were more important to him than any automobile.

When Rob was fifteen, he borrowed an old M&S book published by his grandfather and lost it. Jack was upset, but he was overjoyed when Rob soon found a duplicate of the same book in a second-hand shop in Toronto with his grandfather's signature on the fly-leaf.

Increasingly, the Muskoka cottage became the focus of the McClelland family's life together. There, the children could have full access to their workaholic city father. Elizabeth, who sometimes chided Jack for not being involved in disciplining the children, could relax and share parenting duties with her husband.

Drives up to Muskoka could be hazardous to comfort. Jack's various cars, usually Mustang convertibles and almost always pale green, always had their tops down in sunny weather. Jack, cigarette in hand, would drive very quickly, oblivious to the fact that his passengers were freezing.

The many inefficiencies of M&S continued to irritate Pierre Berton, who fired off a complaint to Larry Ritchie. The author was unhappy with the royalty situation; there was simply no excuse for a publishing company not paying its authors promptly. In his capacity as a director of the company, he found the situation a precarious one, since it endangered the company's relationships with authors.[25] In a memorandum of August 21, 1975, Jack told Patricia Bowles, the director of publicity, that she was not to "give up" on handling the promotion of Berton's new book, *My Country* (1976): "Firstly, don't be critical of Pierre and don't, please don't, tell me that you want no part of future promotion of his books. I can understand your reaction to his letter—and I can't quarrel with it—but that particular response just ain't a very sensible one at M&S. I will defend anyone at M&S from unreasonable complaints of PB or any other M&S author. I would also defend the right of authors to be critical. Pierre is a senior author and a valuable one. He is also a director of the company. He is extremely demanding, but not unprofessional or unreasonable."[26] Use your best diplomatic skills, Jack was suggesting to Catherine Wilson's successor. However, his own patience wore very thin that August when Pierre complained about the dust jacket of *My Country*. The final result was a botched compromise. He especially did not like its pink and feminine look.[27] Some days, in the wake of such complaints, Jack felt it was not worth getting out of bed, but when he did, alcohol and a good number of cigarettes helped him get through the day.

In the sixties and seventies, non-fiction sold consistently better than fiction. Jack also found it much easier to develop non-fiction than fiction: the Laurences, Atwoods and Richlers were few and far between. Books like Walter Gordon's *Choice for Canada* (1966), René Lévesque's *Option for Quebec* (1968), Ken Adachi's *Enemy That Never Was: A History of the Japanese Canadians* (1976), Richard Gwyn's *Northern Magus: Pierre Trudeau and Canadians* (1980)—all defining moments in the history of M&S under Jack's leadership—had the capacity to influence the daily lives of Canadians in a profound way. Three non-fiction writers—Pierre Berton, Farley Mowat and Peter Newman—were consistently M&S's most lucrative money-makers.

In November 1974, the Newmans had decided they could not work together on their study of Canada's elite. In June 1975, Jack and Christina reached agreement over lunch concerning a three-book package. She was elated: her publisher's understanding and support made the writing of books a less onerous task than it otherwise might have been.[28] A few days later, a very angry Peter Newman wrote Jack. First of all, he had been assured from the outset that no Berton and Mowat books would compete with *The Canadian Establishment* when it appeared that year, and Mowat's *Snow Walker* was to be published the same season.[29]

Second, he was furious at what he perceived to be Jack's preference for Christina. He even wondered if there was any point in continuing with *The Canadian Establishment* series. He and Christina were no longer a couple, and he did not relish the prospect of being in second place. Almost taken aback by his own vehemence, he concluded the letter in the most amiable terms he could summon up on that day: he and Jack should have a pleasant lunch together to iron out their differences, and thus pave the way for future titles.[30]

In lieu of payment of the advance of $9,000 due to her as part of her contribution to *The Canadian Establishment*, Christina chose to receive ownership of Peter's files on government, which she had largely amassed. However, she felt her considerable work on the book was not recognized financially or in any other way. Despite their earlier agreement about a three-book package, she decided against making any agreement with M&S about another book.

A year later, in 1976, the bad feelings between Peter and Jack had not been resolved. On July 9, 1976, Peter wrote to say that Jack had not complied with a request for information. Among other things, did Jack think Peter should be using an agent? If there was a failure in communication between them, perhaps author and publisher should indeed part ways?[31] Jack was outraged at Peter's suggestion that he had deliberately failed him:

> What you would not get from the best agent on the face of the earth are answers to questions that require their own particular timing and that don't lend themselves to answers on demand. Frankly, Peter, the best suggestion I can make is that you stop worrying and treat yourself to a holiday. I have had one. I came back from that holiday to find what I can best describe as a petulant, accusatory and somewhat unreasonable letter from you. I didn't like the letter. Perhaps you should reread it to find out why. Because I have always felt that friendships and/or business relationships are two-way

streets, I chose to delay my reply. . . . In summation, then, Peter, let me suggest two possible courses of action. You can hire an agent. I won't be offended. . . . Alternatively, we can forget that this particular correspondence took place and you can believe we do have your best interests at heart.[32]

Three days later, Peter, touched by the letter, responded by suggesting that they put the past behind them,[33] but the relationship between publisher and author had been too badly scarred to survive indefinitely.

In the autumn of 1975, *The Canadian Establishment*, as Jack told Cass Canfield at Harper & Row, became "the top best-seller of all time in Canada. Based on its first season's sales, it did even better than *The National Dream* or *The Last Spike* by Pierre Berton."[34] The book did have some problems, however. Louis Rasminsky objected to this sentence: "One successful attack on anti-Semitism took place at the Rideau Club in 1964. Louis Rasminsky, the Governor of the Bank of Canada, had already been denied entry." Rasminsky told Jack, "The inescapable implication of the statement that I was 'denied' entry before 1964 is that I sought entry. This is untrue. It is seriously damaging to my reputation to suggest that I would so demean myself as to seek admission to a club which it was well known did not then welcome Jewish members."[35] In response, Jack was extremely polite but very firm: "Certainly you have read into this reference much more than was intended by the author. In being critical of the Rideau Club, Peter Newman did not intend to reflect on you in any way. . . . There are only two remedies I can suggest. . . . First is to delete the reference from the book. As it happens we are on press with the second printing and immediately on receipt of your letter, I made arrangements for that reference to be deleted. . . . The second step is to apologize to you for whatever embarrassment may have been caused. This I do on behalf of Peter Newman and myself."[36] Rasminsky accepted the apology.

*The Canadian Establishment* originally contained a passage about a Toronto socialite who had her chauffeur's uniform dyed to match the colour of the lining of her swimming pool. She took M&S to court, and when the matter was to be heard before the Supreme Court of Ontario, a furious Jack threatened—to the chagrin of his lawyer, Julian Porter—to attend the proceedings wearing a white toga, "because white is the colour of my bathtub." It was with some difficulty that Newman and Porter convinced Jack that this would be unwise.

More complicated was the reference on page 74 to Paul Desmarais, head of the Power Corporation of Montreal. Soon after the chapter on him was excerpted in *The Financial Post,* he threatened a lawsuit if a particular paragraph remained in the printed book. That posed an extensive problem since all seventy-five thousand copies of the first printing had just come off the press and were sitting in the printer's warehouse. At $14.95 each, the stock was worth $1,121,250. At once, Jack began Operation Paste-Over: a new paragraph was written in place of the offending one and printed, and twenty people were hired to paste it in.

Six months later, Newman met a mollified Desmarais, who was even willing to do a TV show with him. As Peter confided to Jack, Desmarais told him that there was a way of getting the sticker off the page: you put the book in a deep freeze for two weeks and it would become so brittle that it dropped off. Desmarais now thought the whole incident was very funny and apologized for his strong overreaction.[37]

In a gesture aimed at improving their relationship, Jack, in his response to this "very funny" turn-around, even invited Peter to join the Naked Potato Society, which he described for him in press release style: "The founder and chairman, somewhat improbably, is Jack McClelland the book publisher. The purpose of the organization is to eliminate the practice of serving baked potatoes in tinfoil in the better restaurants and dining rooms across Canada. JM claims that eating a baked potato in tinfoil is almost as horrid as making love to a beautiful woman wearing a condom. The one practice is obsolete, he claims. Why not eliminate the other?"[38]

Jack was also in high spirits when he agreed to waltz around the stage at the St. Lawrence Centre at a fundraising event for the Writers' Development Trust: the melody accompanying him was "Jack the Knife." He added wax vampire teeth to his costume and was very convincing in the role. In other notable performances, Marian Engel was chased offstage by a bear, and the Farley Mowat Dancers—Engel, Margaret Atwood, June Callwood, Alma Lee, Judith Merril and Sylvia Fraser—stomped across the floor in snowshoes.

One Johnny-come-lately to the Canadian literature scene raised Jack's blood pressure inordinately. While Edmund Wilson's *O Canada: An American's Thoughts on Canadian Culture* (1965) did a great deal to promote the writing of Marie-Claire Blais, an M&S author of long standing, Jack thought the book by the famous critic fatuous (in part because Morley Callaghan, only an M&S author in NCL, was the English Canadian author singled out for high praise) and in 1975 informed Anna Porter in no uncertain terms that Malcolm Ross's desire to include it in the NCL was to be rejected. "I spent a drunken evening with him [Wilson] while he was in Canada doing his two-week survey, and after listening to him politely for a couple of hours, I told him he was an ill-informed, egotistical old bastard. And he didn't know what he was talking about. . . . In about two weeks he undid most of the good work that Malcolm himself had been doing for the previous fifteen years. The answer is a categorical no!"[39] In general, Jack had little patience with theories about Canadian literature: he did not admire Margaret Atwood's critical book, *Survival* (Anansi, 1972), which, in a letter to Margaret Laurence, he labelled "uninformed, half-baked."[40] This landmark book sold extremely well, and, in this case, he may have lamented that M&S had not obtained the title for its own list.

To Jack's own sense of Canadian identity in the seventies was added a fiercely anti-American sentiment. Moreover, sensing that the nationalist fervour he had previously embraced and helped to create was now dormant in Canada, he began to refer to himself somewhat ironically as a "post-Nationalist."


A refreshing break from Jack's usual routine was provided by his trip in the spring of 1976 around the world in twenty-eight days, which included his first trip to the Orient and "my first (and probably last) trip to the People's Republic of China." He decided to practise a "conservative regimen" before starting out, which consisted of drinking all night with Mordecai Richler until eight-thirty in the morning on the day of his departure. Marge provided her usual extraordinary assistance by obtaining eye drops, tranquillizers and hangover tablets. His travelling companions were his wife and Janet and Pierre Berton. In Tokyo, Jack attended the International Publishers' Congress, where he distinguished himself by "being the only person who objected at the plenary session to any of the twenty-seven-odd resolutions that were unanimously endorsed."

The landscape of Japan appealed to him: "I was impressed by the fact that the countryside looks very much as it looks in Japanese art. Particularly the trees standing out look so much like their art that it is uncanny. It makes one realize how important the Group of Seven are to Canada because the Group of Seven really did reflect the distinctive nature of our own landscape." Professionally, he was awestruck by the enormous size of many of the publishing houses and their efficient distribution systems.

On arrival at Shanghai airport, he was astounded to see a large group from Cape Breton: the Men of the Deep, the Cape Breton miners' choir. Having heard that the Chinese considered excessive questioning rude, he announced in advance to his three companions that he would, at the conclusion of the trip, award a prize for the dumbest question. Janet, when she asked if any of the priceless heirlooms in the Central Pagoda of the Forbidden City were for sale, won this dubious distinction. Pierre, who asked few questions, was "a great success in China. The Chinese people to begin with were staggered by his size. He was also our party leader—nominated by me because I really didn't think there was any choice. This gave him the opportunity to talk almost without cessation from the time we arrived until our departure without asking many questions. Pierre, who is an expert on almost every subject known to man, was able instantly to identify every bird, every flower, every plant, every vegetable, each dish in every meal, every custom and he did so with great enthusiasm and conviction." Jack and Pierre themselves became objects of curiosity; their blond hair caused many Chinese to drop their jaws in amazement. Overall, Jack was impressed by Chinese medicine, the reverence paid to Norman Bethune, and the violent Chinese hatred of the Russians.

Publishing was completely state owned and controlled—in some ways, he observed, an ideal system. The country itself looked "like one huge market garden. There are people working in the fields and there are vegetables growing everywhere you look and on every available square foot of space. If there is one thing I am certain of, it is that nobody starves in that country and if Chairman Mao has accomplished no more than that, he has transformed a land where the vast majority of the people were literally starving into a country that will before very long be an exporter of food." He was a bit startled by the contrast between Red China and Hong Kong, "a land of hucksters, great wealth and great poverty." In concluding his twelve-page account of his journey, Jack noted with considerable satisfaction that Mr. Yu, their Chinese guide, had brushed up on M&S and was well aware of the firm's flair for publicity. As a parting gift, Jack gave him a special M&S cigarette lighter, "an example of capitalist promotion. He was very pleased by the gift, although he was one of the few people we met in China who didn't smoke."[41]

Subject as he often was to severe criticisms of various kinds, Jack was deeply touched in the winter of 1976 when Hugh MacLennan, whose novels were published by Macmillan, wrote to tell him that "with Alistair MacLeod's *Lost Salt Gift of Blood*, you may well have published the finest book ever written in this country." MacLennan did not think the book would sell well, but he thought it might ultimately be placed side by side with James Joyce's *Portrait of the Artist as a Young Man.*[42] Jack, who still liked to play the role of the ignoramus publisher with no inclination or time to read, let his hair down in his response to the Montreal-based novelist: "Migod, that's a great letter re Alistair MacLeod and I am grateful to you for it. I agree with your evaluation totally. The publication came about as the result of my reading one of the stories in *Tamarack*. I was totally turned on by it, and I got in touch with MacLeod who, as you say, is a very modest man, but he certainly is a major talent." Lily Miller remembers the day a very elated Jack came running into her office, waving a copy of the magazine: "Read this! It's wonderful!"[43]

In the same letter to MacLennan, Jack asked him to read *Une chaîne dans le parc*, by André Langevin, which M&S was bringing out in English as *Orphan Street*. Jack thought this might be the most important novel out of Quebec since Roy's *Bonheur d'occasion*. In a comment that speaks volumes about his real attitude to publishing in the Canadian context, he added, "I am tempted to get really carried away on this one and really try to force-feed the market. We don't do that too often, but there is some justification for it because, as I am sure you know, French-Canadian novels in translation almost inevitably bomb in English."[44] Langevin's might just have that special combination: literary appeal combined with commercial appeal.

Jack's championing of MacLeod and his desire to "force-feed the market" with Langevin show just how committed he remained to good publishing, no matter how risky the project might be. He was also determined that writing by Quebeckers should be available to all Canadians. Roy put the matter well when she told Jack in December 1975: "You are one of the few left of the breed of friendly publishers who genuinely love their writers."[45]

# 12

## SURVIVING COMMERCIALLY
## (1977-78)

"I AM NOT AN INTELLECTUAL. I am not a pundit. I am just a book publisher trying to survive commercially. I am civil, polite and a good listener in dealing with authors because that is my function. I am otherwise in my public life opinionated, rude, cantankerous and often vulgar."[1] This is Jack's comment on the business and personal sides of his personality. As usual, he was putting himself down, but by 1977 a certain gloom had set in. The sad truth, he told Farley, was that he was not functioning well: "As usual, I am up to my ass in problems, in backlog."[2] Jack was also aware of his own limitations: "Anna claims I am a person of short-lived enthusiasms and that I don't maintain my interest in things long enough. God knows she may be right, but more and more I think thirty-two years is long enough."[3]

Anna Porter was correct, but the "short-lived enthusiasms" were a by-product of trying to make his publishing program work, finding any realistic, occasionally far-fetched, way of earning profits. He had also become sensitive, perhaps overly so, to the needs of his authors. In May 1978, he upbraided a publicist, Glenda Ray, when Pierre Berton returned to Jack a form letter she had sent him and all authors on the fall list. He appended a note: "Jack—confidential, even a minor author shouldn't be getting crap like this." Jack told his erring employee, "I must say, Glenda, that I agree with his criticism. We don't publish all that many authors. You can do better than this. It should be a personal letter. It should be more friendly. If you want me to dissect it for you, the first paragraph is terrible. No author likes to hear about 'what promises to be our best fall list ever.' Authors are interested in only their own books. Ours is a PR business. Authors are our most important people. They keep us in business."[4]

In this instance, Jack supported Pierre, although, as in the past, the gifted historian could enrage him. At about this time, Jack had a "Bullshit" stamp made and sometimes used it on missives received from Pierre. In March 1977, having just read the manuscript of *The Dionne Years*, he was blunt with the author: "It contains more information about the Dionne years and the Dionnes than I personally care to have."[5] He also offered Pierre some no-nonsense advice a few months later: "It is my feeling that you should pick your subjects very, very carefully."[6]

Remarkably, the Berton–McClelland friendship survived all manner of disagreements, in large part because they were able to separate personal from professional issues in their dealings with each other. In February 1978, Jack was displeased by Pierre's proposed design for the dust jacket of *The Wild Frontier* and decided to have his own input as the publisher. He told Bob Young in the art department to make a dummy of Pierre's "revolting" idea but also to have ready one with some rich, expensive-looking colours, since Pierre's "colour combination will almost certainly produce a gift book that will look as if somebody has just thrown up on it."[7]

A little more than a month later, Jack wrote Pierre, emphasizing his author's tremendous organizational skills and urging him to run for Parliament as an independent nationalist. Jack was part of a group— including Peter Newman, Margaret Atwood and Mel Hurtig—making this request, though he did not completely share their political point of view: "As a post-nationalist, I am by no means certain that I could share the specific aspirations of this group. I believe in Canadian unity and the survival of the country, but I am no longer satisfied that it can be achieved with the freight of any consideration of economic and political independence."

As he makes abundantly clear, Jack was apolitical to the point of indifference: "Because you know that I do not admire our political system, that I do not support or belong to any political party and, in fact, that I abhor party politics, you may well believe that I am routinely passing on a request that was made of me."[8] However, Jack assumed that there would be a minority government and that someone of Berton's stature could, especially under those circumstances, make a considerable difference in the scheme of things. Berton did not run.

Jack, who was averse to making any kind of public statement about politics, was unreserved in his disdain for René Lévesque's threat to Canadian unity when the Parti Québécois won the election in November 1976. In March 1977, Jack, who had published Lévesque's *Option for Quebec* in 1968, branded him "as much a threat to Canada as an enemy invader."[9]

Farley Mowat presented an unexpected problem when he announced that he wanted to publish a volume of verse and had his American publisher's complete support in this undertaking. Jack fired off a letter on August 15, 1977: "Surely you're joking! Have you and Peter [Davison] both gone out of your minds at the same time? . . . I've only glanced at a couple of the poems. . . . It may be possible to destroy your whole literary reputation with one slim volume. The whole thing sounds suicidal and masochistic to me. I don't mean the poems—I mean the whole activity." Two days later, after he had read more of the poems, he was a bit more temperate in his response: "I'm honestly baffled. This type of thing isn't my cup of tea exactly—and never has been—but I don't think a book of these poems would be the crowning achievement of your literary career." Three weeks later, Jack took a slightly different but nevertheless sarcastic tack: "How could I have been so wrong? The material is fabulous. . . . Complete the manuscript as soon as possible. I am negotiating with Picasso at the moment re illustration. So it is my fault and I am sorry. I think you should [also] do a book about rabbits fornicating."[10]

By the end of the year, a very relieved Jack teased Peter Davison, whom he suspected had not been completely serious in backing Farley's poetry: "I think we'll never know whether he [Mowat] has abandoned the verse because you encouraged him or because I told him it was outright crap. It could become a problem that literary historians wrangle over for centuries. Who cares—the important thing is he has abandoned the verse."[11] However, Farley threatened to undertake a biography of Jack: "The truth is you are yellow. Scared to death that the truth will out. . . . Fuck you, it has to be done. At any rate, please do start getting some of it down on tape. . . . Otherwise I'll have to make the whole thing up, and you know what that will mean."[12]

In the summer of 1977, Jack quarrelled with Sylvia Fraser about the title of her new novel, which he wanted to call *A Casual Affair*: "You probably won't like it. You will . . . think it is trite. Let me say this about it. It is a good selling title and I am not aware that it has been used—at least by a major book."[13] Her preferences were: *Love and Unicorns— An Adult Fairy Tale* or *I Love You: A Modern Fairytale*.[14] When he wrote to Sylvia, who was on holiday in Egypt, Jack was firm about the title: "Please, Sylvia, stop worrying about the title for your novel. It has been agreed by all knowledgeable people here that the right title for the book is *A Casual Affair*. . . . We have decided that *Unicorns* must go. Please forget the title and enjoy your trip. It is now beyond recall. Should you be kidnapped, highjacked or otherwise done away with on your trip, we will relent and publish under the title *Untitled Last Novel* by Sylvia Fraser. What more reassurance could you possibly have?. . . Anna tells me that you are now travelling about with a Greek multi-millionaire who has a thing for camels. The combination sounds irresistible to me. . . ."[15]

The book describes the on-again, off-again relationship between a married male protagonist, a businessman, diplomat and politician, educated at Upper Canada College and the University of Toronto, and a woman illustrator, also married. She relentlessly analyzes his behaviour, urging him to face up to his emotions. Any argument about the title of *A Casual Affair* was mild compared with Jack's displeasure when he heard *The Toronto Sun* was about to publish the "rumour" that "the male protagonist [of the novel] is Jack McClelland." According to Jack's information, the female journalist circulating this story had been successful to the degree that *The Globe and Mail's* review had made this assertion before it was killed at the editorial desk. Jack insisted that Douglas Creighton, *The Sun's* publisher, do the same: "First, the story is untrue. Second, it is extremely damaging to the literary reputation of the author, who is a serious author. Third, and obviously most important to me, it could cause a great deal of embarrassment to my family." He added, "The worst part . . . is that if such a story appeared, no apology could undo the damage. I would be bound to sue. . . . Obviously it is not easy for me to write this letter. I am not interested in circulating the story any further. On the other hand, my lawyer has advised me that since I could not accept an apology, it is wise to state in advance that I would consider any reference to me in connection with the book as malicious." He requested Creighton's assistance, which was forthcoming, in averting any references to the matter in his newspaper. "The simple fact is that an unavoidable action would be brought into being that would be extremely damaging to me and even more damaging to the newspaper. Needless to say, it is embarrassing to have to write this letter."[16]

Coming up with the right title for a book could often be challenging. Al Purdy wanted to call his new one *The Crossword Mapleleaf,* a title his publisher found abominable: "In fact, I more than don't like it, I dislike it intensely. It's a rinky-dink title. It is light, gimmicky and unrepresentative of the book."[17] The title was changed to *No Other Country.*

Their next quarrel centred on Purdy's negative review of Leonard Cohen's *Death of a Lady's Man.* Purdy felt insulted by what he perceived to be his publisher's protective stance toward another poet: "I'm sorry you feel so personally affronted, as you appeared when I met you briefly at Hollinger House. Whether you know or believe it or not, I have quite a lot of admiration for you—for reasons I don't intend to specify. And I do hope we can be more or less civil to each other most of the time."[18] In response, Jack tried to make his own position clear on a thorny issue:

> For years I have been told that few people can tell when I am being serious and when I am not. It has even been suggested that I should carry a sign in my pocket which I could hold up and which would say something like "I'm only kidding. . . ." In my trade, reviews are of little significance except for any effect they may have on the psyche of the author. . . . I measure the value in column inches. The only type of review that irritates me is the lightweight, silly review. . . . Yours was anything but silly, and of course you had some kind things to say about Cohen.
>
> It is true that I don't agree with your evaluation of the book. So what else is new? I seldom agree with other people's opinions anyway. I happen to think this is one of the finest things Cohen has ever written. . . . Why do important writers like yourself risk their own personal relationships [with other writers by publishing negative reviews]?. . . Although Leonard would be one of the last people in the world to harbour a grudge because of a review . . . it would be so much easier to read the book and tell the paper I don't want to review it . . . say no . . . unless they [writers] can be positive about the book by one of their peers. . . . Life is too short.[19]

Jack did not bother to tell Purdy about the enormous difficulties that Cohen's new volume of poetry had presented to him. When Cohen first told him the title, Jack quipped, "Christ, Leonard, *Death of a Lady's Man!* With a title like that we don't even need a manuscript." Jack rued those words when the book was announced twice and withdrawn twice because the poet revised and added to the collection. Finally, it appeared in 1978.[20]

Poets did seem to give Jack headaches out of all proportion to their sales figures. In April 1977, an exasperated Jack told Anna that Earle Birney "is a pain in the ass; he wastes a lot of your time . . . and God knows who else's time; his market is declining; his writing and publishing plans for the next few years are formidable; he's almost certain to lose us a lot of money. I really think the time has come to call his bluff; it may not be a bluff and we may lose him. Fair enough—I for one am prepared for that."[21]

Birney's complaints were old ones—complaints about contracts, about delays in receiving proofs, about publicity. In response to all this, Jack wrote what was for him a very stiff letter:

> I don't really understand the point of all this shit, Earle. I don't know why you persist. You can't undo the past. What you are complaining about has absolutely nothing to do with contracts. I personally don't ever remember a dispute about a contract where we haven't been willing to amend or waive a clause. If you are doing this for some future historian, it has now been done thirty times over. It is not going to help you or me or anybody to keep bringing the goddamn thing up.
>
> Let me put it to you this way. If you really want to leave M&S, then I for one am not going to stand in your way. Anna objects to my saying this, but I am going to say it nonetheless. If a publishing relationship has to be this damn unfriendly, then let's put an end to it. . . . [My motivation] has always been what I once called "enlightened self-interest" and now call "ill-conceived self-interest." Of one thing I am certain. The problems in this business are enough without adding to it the problems posed by holding an author who is persistently unhappy and dissatisfied. It is simply not worth it. . . .Should you decide to stay, I am not going to ask you to stop complaining . . . I am going to ask you to try to find some new subjects to complain about. The fact that we have not done an effective job of selling some of your books in the past has registered. Everyone in the firm knows about it.[22]

There were many other fires to put out, such as the unreadable manuscript of Judy LaMarsh's first novel, *A Very Political Lady* (1979). The novelist Matt Cohen, himself an M&S author, was hired to fix the book, but he allowed words such as "perfricationing" to survive intact. Jack told

Jennifer Glossop, the book's editor, "I want you to give Matt Cohen a serious blast for [allowing such language in the book]. . . . I have never heard anybody use that expression in my life, except . . . in very bad English fiction."[23]

Adele Wiseman's *Crackpot* had been published by M&S in 1975. Three years later, Wiseman submitted the manuscript of her book on her mother and her mother's doll making, a book that presented all kinds of difficulties, as he told Wiseman's editor, Linda McKnight: "It is a very important work to Adele. She has been at it for a long time. Her mother means a great deal to her. . . . Her mother is dying of cancer. It is a bad scene. The scene is made even more difficult because of two additional problems. First, as we have known from the start, it requires extensive colour illustration. . . . An even more serious problem is my personal assessment that it is a very bad book. At best, I find it pretentious, self-indulgent, somewhat amateurish and in many places downright boring."[24] When he wrote to Wiseman, Jack was honest about his reluctance to do the book, due to high production costs and his own strong reservations: "You really have given me the toughest publishing problem I have ever tried to cope with." However, he was extremely clear about how he viewed his role as her publisher: "As a publishing house, we are faced with a dilemma. Our policy has been to publish authors, not books, and thus to publish imperfect works by an author we have confidence in when they are given to us. However, our responsibility is to the author as well. Thus, when we feel a manuscript might be damaging, we have an obligation to say just that. So, I do think that publication of *Old Woman at Play* in its present form could receive a very unfriendly press."[25] Wiseman withdrew the book from M&S; it was published by Clarke, Irwin in 1978.

This situation led to some sort of animus toward Jack; on May 17, 1978, Wiseman, three years after the publication of *Crackpot*, wrote him a vituperative letter about the fact that the remaining 750 copies of hardback stock were being sold off by Smith's at $1.99 each. When she called M&S, she was informed that they were getting rid of "overstock"; as far as Wiseman was concerned, she was being deprived of potential earnings. "Of course, this goes beyond the merely personal gripe. . . . Unless you inform me shortly that what I have said is factually inaccurate, I will be passing this on to the Writers' Union." Wiseman, who peppered her letter with the phrases "hostile behaviour" and "callous indifference," wanted to purchase the entire remaining stock in order to provide herself with the "opportunity to make up my royalty by doing the selling job you obviously didn't feel up to doing yourself."[26]

On May 29, a very angry publisher responded to the writer who had wounded him: "There may be people who react well to threats and intimidation. I am not one of them. If you wish to bring this matter, or any other aspect of your dealings with M&S, to the attention of the Canadian Writers' Union, or the press or anyone else, by all means do so." He explained why he was not willing to allow her to sell M&S stock and why the books had been disposed of through Smith's. He pointed out that *Crackpot* was readily available in the NCL in paperback. This version of the book, he called to her attention, "was published largely at the instigation of your friends," who "pointed out that its unavailability in an inexpensive format made it inaccessible for study purposes." Having established the fact that he had done her a long series of favours well beyond the call of duty, he concluded:

> I will add to the foregoing something that would have gone unsaid had it not been for the tone of your letter. Because of my respect for you and your work, we undertook to publish *Crackpot* to the best of our ability despite obstacles [Wiseman's unwillingness to revise the manuscript] that were thrown in our path. I think we did a reasonable job. For the same reason, we made what we considered to be a fair and reasonable proposal on the Doll manuscript. I came away from that experience with a strong feeling that you knew nothing about book publishing, that you were oblivious to economic realities, that you had come to believe that the world owes you some very extraordinary consideration as an artist. I came away from that interchange depressed, and your recent letter has done nothing to lessen that depression."[27]

Wiseman shot back: the world did owe her "extraordinary consideration"; she was sorry he was depressed but perhaps he had "value conflicts" that had led him to be depressed about the heated exchange
between them.[28]

Jack the reluctant editor can be glimpsed in a memorandum he sent
to Anna Porter when she asked him for his "very frank editorial opinion" of Margaret Atwood's short stories. Margaret herself had asked for
the unvarnished truth from her publishers. His response was both deft
and compassionate: "I think there is a wide divergence of quality in the
stories, although they are all well written; they all have the Atwood
trademark and could be written by no one else. She is incredibly good
on detail and incredibly good in terms of human sensibilities. The only
problem that I had with any of them is that her people all seem to be
semi-mad—at least in my terms—but that is undoubtedly the way
Peggy is herself and that's probably what makes a great writer. She is a
bit like Sylvia Fraser in the sense that her mind sure as hell moves on a
different level of sensitivity than mine—every gesture, every word,
every expression made by any of these people has some interior meaning. It terrifies me." He proceeded to discuss the stories in considerable
detail before concluding, "Okay, having given you my serious analysis,
I stand with my editorial fly totally unzipped. I won't be surprised if
I am told that you disagree violently with everything I have said."[29]

In 1978, a great deal of tact was needed to deal with the proposed
book of critical essays on Atwood by Cathy and Arnold Davidson.
Within M&S, there were varying degrees of opinion on the likely success of such a venture—one person thought fifteen to twenty thousand
copies would sell, another estimated two thousand. Jack did not think
this was the "right" book on Atwood; besides, there was the whole question of house policy, as he pointed out to Anna:

> I've taken the position in the past—specifically in relation to Layton
> and Birney—that we can't be all things to all people. We are essen-
> tially the publishers of a primary author. There is no reason why we
> should be the publishers of scholarly or academic books about those

authors. . . . A collection of critical articles about one of our authors—whether it's previously published material or not—I don't think that's our bag. As I think you know, it always pains me to say no to a book that is in a really practicable sense publishable. This is, but I think we will have to say no to it. If I felt that our saying no would be upsetting to Peggy, I'd say the hell with it, let's do it. I don't think this will be upsetting to her. . . . I think you should explain our position on the matter to her before you actually reject the proposal.[30]

Margaret Atwood herself was not sure where she stood on the thorny issue of the proposed collection. She realized the book might be too academic and that M&S might not be the right publisher: "It does seem at times rather heavy, rather like an elephant trying to fuck a flea; however, if other people believe I'm worthy of this detailed scrutiny, who am I to protest?"[31] Anna ultimately decided that Margaret would be offended: "Looks like Peggy will not take it lightly if we reject."[32] Jack, who felt he had a good understanding of the novelist's generosity and understanding, stood by his original decision. Anansi published the book in 1981.

In 1976, the year before she separated from her husband, Jack had given Margaret Trudeau detailed instructions about writing her memoirs when the time came. In fact, he'd sent her a blank diary: "I hope you will use it. I deliberately chose a blank diary so that you wouldn't look on it as an albatross around the neck and feel compelled to make an entry every day. In that sense, it is a form of diary that doesn't weigh too heavily on the conscience. That is not to say, however, that I don't feel you should take it very seriously. I do think and hope you will be conscientious about it. Notes made now will be extremely valuable when you come to do a book, and I am convinced that you can and should do a book when the time is right. This is an essential preparation stage. Let me know when you fill this one and another one will be en route immediately."[33] Two years later, Jack instructed Anna Porter, who was attending the annual Frankfurt Book Fair, to bid on Margaret

Trudeau's ghost-written *Consequences* (1982): he was prepared to go up to $75,000 in order to secure the book, which he had helped to bring into being.[34]

As usual, critical scrutiny and the purchase of expensive book rights had to give way to the acute financial distress in which M&S wallowed. In January 1977, when the number of employees at M&S had reached 150 and the cubicles allotted to most employees had become smaller and smaller, Jack tried to find a way to create a larger market for Canadian books by forming an association with an American publisher, a mass-market paperback house. Bantam Canada, a division of the American paperback company, had been forbidden in 1976, by the Foreign Investment Review Agency (FIRA), to act simply as an importer of books from the States. According to Statistics Canada, 95 per cent of mass-market paperback titles sold in Canada were works of foreign authorship.

FIRA suggested Bantam continue to distribute its paperbacks in Canada on the condition that it become a partner with a Canadian house to publish Canadian paperbacks. The year before, in 1976, the Canadian division of Simon & Schuster's Pocket Books had been sold to General Publishing, creating Paperjacks. So Jack was following a trend when he announced that he and Oscar Dystel, president of Bantam Books, New York, had formed a similar alliance. M&S owned 51 per cent of the new company, McClelland & Stewart–Bantam Limited.

Bantam had twelve thousand paperback outlets in Canada, many in non-traditional settings like drugstores and supermarkets, and their distribution system was extremely efficient. In a cautious article in *The Globe and Mail*, William French pointed out that the success of such a venture might be a real breakthrough: "If the new company achieves its aims, the works of Canadian authors will be readily available [in a way never before possible], the way Irving Wallace, Leon Uris and other American writers have been in the past. The Americans will still be there, however: Margaret Laurence will co-habit with Norman Mailer, and Peter Newman will share a rack with Jacqueline Susann. Canadian readers will thus have easy access to their own authors, at paperback prices."

The Canadian titles were to be called Seals and would be gradually streamed in with the American Bantams. Why Seal? Jack got "the idea on a plane to New York. We'd been kicking around a lot of names and none seemed appropriate. Suddenly I thought of seal of approval, and the seal is a Canadian animal."[35] Jack hoped that the logo—a seal balancing a book—would soon become as well known to readers as the Bantam rooster.

The first Seal was Peter Newman's *Canadian Establishment*, which was published on April 14, 1978, with an initial printing of 100,000 copies at $2.95 each. *A Jest of God* by Margaret Laurence followed in May, *Separation* by Richard Rohmer in June. Jack was extremely buoyant: "We're going to feel our way, and then we'll proceed on a program that will astound everyone in Canada." He added that he would not simply be producing paperbacks of his own firm's titles. He joked, "We've been snobbish about our past books, but now we'll publish 'good' or 'indifferent' books." He also pointed out that Canadian authors would be allowed to keep their full share of royalties (they would be paid the usual, higher rates of royalties instead of the lower mass-market rates), their books would be edited by Canadians and distributed by the best system in place in Canada.[36]

As far as Jack was concerned, the formation of Seal Books demonstrated the triumph of a made-in-Canada policy. At the press conference that heralded the launch of Seal Books, held at the Royal York on January 18, 1977, huge quantities of Scotch were flowing, prominent M&S authors—including Earle Birney, Marian Engel, Sylvia Fraser and Peter Newman—were in attendance, and Oscar Dystel did not sound like a man who had agreed to a gunshot wedding. He thought Bantam Canada was already more efficient than its American counterpart; moreover, he was impressed by the knowledge of the Canadian wholesalers and retailers; he cited his company's sensational success in previously distributing the Bantam edition of Margaret Laurence's *Diviners*: "210,000 copies in Canada alone—that opened my eyes."[37]

Jack claimed that the new imprint would promote books that were more commercial than literary in emphasis, leading one journalist to label him a "popcorn" publisher. Another important new development in the Canadian marketplace, and against which the Seal agreement must be seen, was the further growth of the bookstore chains—Coles, W. H. Smith and Classic Book Shops—which accounted for 50 per cent of retail (as opposed to mass-market) sales. The chains posed both a threat and a challenge: "Because of their bigness, they have become very important to the publishing trade. We are selling many more copies. But the chains tend to be selective in buying. Those titles that are not selected have relatively little market potential."[38]

In general, the formation of Seal, headed by Anna Porter, the former editor-in-chief at M&S, with offices on St. Clair Avenue East in Toronto, seemed to augur well for M&S. Various M&S documents reveal exactly the opposite.

The first was an "abbreviated version of a report" prepared for the executive committee of the M&S board.

1. The company is not earning sufficient profit to sustain growth or manage its current debt load.
2. Given even moderate inflation and the increasing cost of money, we can no longer project a change in that without a drastic alteration in our current level of operation.
3. Merger or sale do not seem to be viable possibilities at present.
4. Our cash shortage is critical. Additional loan guarantees of $500,000 are essential to virtually any form of continuation.
5. Bankruptcy would be a very costly route and must be avoided under any circumstances.

The options in the wake of the above observations were unpalatable: (1) bankruptcy; (2) voluntary liquidation that would lead to the survival of Hollinger House and a new, much smaller publishing company (loss could be as much as $2 million and 125 people would lose their jobs); (3) a continuation of the existing company in its present form. In any event, Jack hoped to curtail his publishing program severely: "In 1979 we will publish ninety books. For 1980, we project currently thirty titles for spring and perhaps twenty for fall. Under this program, we would expect to be at about forty titles level by 1981."[39]

No such reduction was ever reached, and no firm decisions were made, but the results of the above deliberations were enlarged and made more upbeat in a document intended for the eyes of a potential private investor, Bertram Loeb, whose family owned grocery-store chains: "Basically," Jack assured him late in 1977, "I have never been more optimistic about the long-term potential of publishing. The market for books is expanding steadily. . . . My basic hope for McClelland & Stewart would be a fairly rapid expansion or a merger acquisition . . . up to a level of about $20 million per year from our current $11 to $12 million position. I believe such a move, if properly financed, would make an immediate substantial change in the potential level of profitability." The "bottom line" of the prospectus was to attract new cash into the beleaguered company, but it also reveals Jack's general philo-sophy that only by creating a larger company could market dominance, and above-average profitability, be achieved.

Any real hopes of profitability resided with M&S's writers, who were capable of generating books with huge sales. The first volume of Peter Newman's *Canadian Establishment* had been a rousing success, so much was expected of the second. But while researching that book, Newman got sidetracked by the Bronfman clan, about whom he began to uncover the kind of facts that had years earlier caused Terence Robertson so much difficulty.

On May 12, 1978, Newman broke the news to Leo Kolber: the Bronfman saga had come to dominate everything else about the second volume of *The Canadian Establishment*. He and Jack had finally decided that a new approach was inescapable. The book would now deal solely with the Bronfman family, their position in business and society, tracing both the development of the Seagram Company and Sam's amazing career as well as the current generation. As a matter of courtesy Newman was writing all the Bronfmans to inform them of this development.[40]

His polite letter was written three weeks after he'd had lunch with Leo, who presumably did not know the new focus of the book at that time. When he read the letter, Kolber kidded the author: "You better bloody well be kind to us in your book. Or I'll cut your balls off."[41]

Newman's letter was inspired in part by a long memorandum from Jack dated March 6, 1978, which begins very dramatically, "I have been giving this matter a great deal of thought over the last several weeks. There is no doubt about it: we are dealing with the most powerful adversaries—should they decide to be that—that exist. Should they decide to interfere with publication of the book, they may succeed regardless of any determination on our part."[42]

Pressure could be brought against Newman through Maclean-Hunter, which owned *Maclean's*: he was editor-in-chief of the magazine, from which Seagram could threaten to withdraw advertising. M&S itself, Jack reflected, was "frail financially": "We don't owe Cemp any money directly, but we do owe them a relatively small amount of money through the T-D Bank, but this is on a stated basis of repayment rather than on a demand basis, and I don't think they could do much about that. If they were really serious, however, they could either influence or buy up one of our major suppliers and threaten corporate survival that way." On balance, however, Jack regarded the Bronfmans and Leo Kolber as realists:

> If enough good things are said about them, they are sensible enough to accept a very substantial amount of bad. I think that we may have to avoid—on the grounds that it has been and still is impractical— some minor details that while they may be sensational are going to make the whole thing unacceptable to them. It is a fact that Kolber didn't like the Robertson because it was a whitewash. . . .
>
> I think the real key is to make it a typical Newman book. Praise where praise is due. Hard facts of a negative sort where they are incontrovertible and where we have the documentation. We take no chances. We check everything legally. . . . I think we may find that what you are writing is the book that Robertson would not have had the guts to write. A book that [the Bronfmans and Kolber] are going to privately like but publicly oppose. In other words, a sensational

book that is going to do them a lot of good because it fixes their image even more than it is fixed today. . . .[43]

In conversation with Newman, Jack suggested the Bronfmans be given the chance to read the completed manuscript. On March 23, Newman was adamant. He had been a journalist since the age of twenty-one and had never shown a manuscript to anyone he was writing about to get approval. Such a gesture would compromise his integrity. He would be selling his soul if he changed course at this point in his career. He knew how explosive his material was, but he wished to proceed in the fashion he had long ago established.[44]

Less than two weeks after his letter of May 12, Newman met with Kolber, who was frank: he was too much of a realist to attempt to stop publication or to withdraw advertising from *Maclean's*, but he insisted that some of Newman's information had been obtained under false pretences. He "demanded," as Newman told Jack, that he and Charles Bronfman be allowed to come and read the manuscript in a closed room. When Newman turned him down, he finally gave up.[45] Or so it seemed.

Three months later, Leo Kolber and Charles Bronfman obtained a copy of the proofs, probably leaked to them by someone at the Book-of-the-Month Club. Jack met an extremely angry Kolber, and many of the issues raised at Kolber's earlier meeting with Newman were gone over once again. Jack mentioned to Kolber a further claim of Newman's: "Peter says we [Kolber and Jack] suppressed [the Robertson book] and were, in effect, responsible for Robertson's death."[46] (Of course, Robertson was the author of his own destruction.) In a lighter vein, Kolber threatened Jack and Peter by saying that if the book were published, the Bronfmans would "buy out McClelland & Stewart," whereupon Jack "leapt across the table with a look of joy upon his face."[47]

Newman, understandably outraged by the leak, had spoken out of turn. Yet he was afraid his publisher might succumb to the power of the Bronfmans.[48] Newman refused to budge. However, a list of "errors" in the book was prepared and adjustments were made to the proofs before the book was published. In an internal memo of September 8, Jack was worried about the possibility that news of the changes would be made public: "Peter has written a new preface relating that the Bronfmans have offered corrections. He gives up nothing in this new preface. I don't want any rumours started from this house that the Bronfmans have interfered. In other words, we have made some corrections for legal reasons and this is all I want anybody from this house to say to anybody and I mean period. That's it."[49]

*Bronfman Dynasty: The Rothschilds of the New World* may have been a major best-seller, but it produced all kinds of negative side effects. Michael McCormick had been Jack's first contact with the House of Seagram in 1965; Newman interviewed McCormick when he still envisaged his new book to be the second volume of *The Canadian Establishment* rather than a portrait of the Bronfmans. In 1976, he had told Newman that he was writing a book about his own experiences with the Bronfman family and wanted to reserve certain anecdotes for his own book.[50] On the grounds that Newman might use that material, McCormick threatened to sue when he learned the direction the book had taken.[51] (Eventually Newman and M&S settled out of court when McCormick did bring an action against them.)

Not only did Newman and McClelland have a lawsuit hanging over their heads, but there was also a problem with the selling of the book when a price war erupted between Coles and Classic, who were both selling *Bronfman Dynasty* as a loss leader. In an unusual move, Jack wrote to retailers across the country about what he saw as a "personal affront": "There are many ways to compete . . . better service, better displays, better selection, knowledgeable staff, even seasonal specials and sales are a few methods that come to mind. But using a best-seller that will contribute close to $2 million in retail sales as a loss leader is dumb, wrong and ultimately bad for our business."[52]

During the last phases of the production of *Bronfman Dynasty*, Newman had asked Jack if there was a possibility of adjusting the royalty rates on the book. He received a firm no: "Some major authors in the past have said . . . you are going to make a lot of money on my book, and you should take a smaller profit and use a lower factor. In theory this is true. In practice it is not. The publishing house that does that with the big books is a publishing house that gets into financial trouble. I for one can guarantee it because I have been along that route too many years in the past. The truth is that the publishing house already takes less on the major books. We spend much more money in percentage terms on promotion, for one thing."[53]

By September, Newman, as a result of Jack's response about royalties and what he considered his publisher's overeagerness to allow the Bronfmans to see his new book, wondered again if it was time for them to part ways.[54] Eight days later, after the two had lunched, Newman wanted to stay with M&S, but there were to be some changes. The two men were bound together, Peter argued; he did not want to go elsewhere, but he had asked a lawyer, Jerry Grafstein, to look after all his business interests.[55]

In November, Peter had planned a new book, one that could seriously rival Berton, and hoped to arouse Jack's interest: a big volume on the Hudson's Bay Company, which might have the potential of the railway books.[56] This project would finally sever Newman's connection with M&S.

In the meantime, Roloff Beny's dealings with Jack were byzantine. *Persia: Bridge of Turquoise* was published in 1975. The sales of the book worldwide could have been better, but there were several factors that worked against any genuine profitability: a succession of quarrels with Thames & Hudson; Jack's unfamiliarity in dealing with subsidiary rights to such a book; the exorbitant costs of producing it; and, of course, Beny's insistence that only the best would do.

Beny's plight in Canada was not helped by hostile reviews, such as Marci McDonald's in *Maclean's*, wherein she elaborated on the photographer's sycophancy: "Can a poor boy from Medicine Hat find happiness in the court of the last great despot-king? Sure, if he plays his cards right. . . . What use is pomp and ceremony and progress without the ultimate eye to capture and enshrine it in time? . . . Poverty, ugliness, discontent, all signs of a military or police presence—these things are not part of the Shah's vision, and so they will not find their way into official records, just as they must not find their way into Roloff Beny pictures."

*Saturday Night* compared Beny to Leni Riefenstahl, the photographer and filmmaker who had glamorized the Nazi regime. Despite—or because of—the notoriety, the book lost money.

In late 1976 and early 1977, the Empress, worried about the insurrections that were threatening to topple the Pahlavi regime, wanted Roloff Beny to produce a new kind of book about her country, as Jack's notes from his audience with her in January 1977 reveal:

> It is not necessary to represent all important industries, all ministries, all aspects of life in Iran. It is to emphasize the human side and the concern she feels for people, their environment and lifestyle—quality of life. . . . It is specifically not in any way to look like a chamber of commerce or ministry product. . . . She expressed delight at success of *Persia: Bridge of Turquoise.* She is genuinely pleased to have a best-seller on her hands and is delighted about the prospects of editions in other languages. . . . She was also apparently pleased at the review of cost for *Bridge,* $250,000, *Destiny* [the proposed book on Iran; published as *Iran: Elements of Destiny,* 1978], $400,000. . . . In summation she was vitally interested in all aspects. Wants the books to be superb. Wants RB to have freedom to make it a really exciting volume.[57]

However, the photographer—whom Jack sometimes called "Rip-Off Beny"—was becoming increasingly difficult to deal with. Jack wanted to be sympathetic to Beny, who had managed to infuriate all the Iranian officials he was dealing with, but the publisher found it difficult to keep his temper in check, as he told Peter Scaggs, the production manager, and Lily Miller, the new book's editor:

> I think we are all agreed that he is personally under a tremendous amount of pressure at the moment. He is running. He is tired, almost to the point of killing himself, but he keeps running. He is paranoid to begin with, and we are now faced with [the] last month or so on [this] project. He is very nervous. He is blaming everybody else. The pressure is really beginning to mount, so what the hell. . . . Unless we

make a helluva lot of money out of this one—which we may but which is still a doubtful possibility—my inclination is to think we can't afford to work further with this strange, driven character. I have great admiration and respect for him, as I know both of you do. He drives himself very hard. He is a perfectionist. He is also an unreasonable son of a bitch.[58]

Unwisely, Jack offered to act as Beny's agent with the Empress and everyone else who had a commercial interest in the new venture. Early on, he realized the book needed a subsidy of $500,000, in part to compensate for the losses on the first book. During Jack's visits to Teheran, he learned that there was no relationship between time and money: a great deal of his time was spent waiting by the pool at the Inter-Continental hotel for an audience with the Empress. In a peripheral way, he got caught up in court intrigue. One day, the Empress told him and Beny, "I'm going to give you the name of one of my close woman friends and a number that you can call. If you have to contact me for any reason, if you run into blocks, unconscionable delays or any serious problems, don't hesitate to call." Jack phoned once; of course, Beny, who had a tendency to manufacture crises, abused the privilege.

Ever the romantic, Beny saw things very differently from Jack. His second book was to be primarily "a paean of praise to the vision of the Pahlavi dynasty. Perhaps it was in a sense another of the Shah's *coups de théâtre*. I confess, despite my unwavering admiration and even love for the Shahbanou, I was growing rather uneasy about certain aspects of the work, and what I had seen and experienced during the preparation of the work. . . . Elsewhere, however, something was going wrong, and as I studied my layouts, I sometimes thought I caught a glimpse of disturbing, even dangerous undercurrents."[59]

When Jack met with the Empress in October 1977, she made it clear to him that "she doesn't like anything that costs money; that people are always trying to spend her money for her." Her proposal was simple and direct: she would purchase ten thousand copies of Beny's new book, which she would market on behalf of her foundation. Jack conceded, maintaining, "This lady is about as sharp as anyone I have ever met." Jack had also encountered fierce resistance from other publishers at the Frankfurt Book Fair to the high cost of the book: he desperately needed to sell foreign rights in order to make the Beny book profitable. Jack quickly became violently ill during this trip, later telling Peter Scaggs that he could not take any pills because he would not be able to have alcohol: "There is no way I can survive at this stage without drinking. I deserve a fucking medal for this trip."[60]

Throughout 1977, Jack still felt it possible that M&S could earn a profit of $100,000 on *Elements*, the second Iran book, but hope soon vanished. In June 1978, there were delays in payments of production costs due from the Iranian government; in August, there were severe earthquakes in Iran and violent demonstrations against the Shah; in October, forty-eight hundred copies of *Destiny* and ten thousand of the Persian-language edition of *Bridge* were shipped from the bindery in Wales via two Iranian Air Force 747s to Teheran. All disappeared. On January 16, 1979, the Shah and Empress went into exile. M&S's last adventure in the desert lost more than $150,000. Beny did not do too badly: before he fired himself as the photographer's agent, Jack had obtained for him a fee of $75,000 plus expenses. From Jack's perspective, things had gone very badly: the Iranian government subsidy for the two books never materialized, and thousands of copies of the book—never paid for—vanished.

In one of his last stays in Teheran, Beny went with Jack to a lavish bar at the Inter-Continental. Jack, although he was fascinated by the Empress, had nothing but contempt for the Shah. When he started to mouth these negative sentiments, Roloff told him to keep quiet: "The walls here have ears." Jack, who had had a lot to drink, got up, walked over to the curtains and shouted into them, "The Shah is a fucking asshole!" Beny, afraid for his own safety, sashayed out of the room, noticed he had forgotten his drink, walked back, grabbed it and only then made his grand exit. The next morning the men had an amicable breakfast together.[61]

In March 1978, nine months before the abdication, Jack was not pleased by Gary Dunford's column of March 21, 1978, in *The Toronto Sun*:

SHAKING DOWN THE SHAH?

This is the item that asks the question: What is publisher **Jack McClelland** doing this week in **Iran?**

Is he "attending a party"?

Is he showing the Shah and the **Empress Farah Pahlavi Shahbanou** the final plates of photographer **Roloff Beny**'s second book on Persia?

Or is he trying to collect—gulp!—**$600,000** that their terrific highnesses owe McClelland & Stewart for 20,000 copies of a Beny book that they haven't paid for? ... [T]here is a nasty rumour about that the Shah and Farah have not paid for 20,000 copies of the expensive books, leaving McClelland about $600,000 in the red. That kinda loot is probably pin money for the jet set. It sure can break up a balance sheet for a publishing house.[62]

Usually Jack welcomed publicity. This time he was appalled. In a private letter to the editor, Peter Worthington—accompanying a letter to the editor that was actually printed—Jack voiced his fear that the story would be picked up by the Iranian embassy and transmitted to Teheran, thus making collecting the money due M&S even more difficult.[63]

In his column, Dunford referred to the Shah's original willingness to subvent a book on modern Iran because it would "wipe away talk of the *unphotographed* things that go on there." In March 1977, Margaret Laurence, a recently appointed director at M&S, voiced her strong disagreement to the publishing of a second Roloff Beny book on Iran, which she argued was an extremely repressive country. Elizabeth, who had accompanied her husband on one of his last trips to Iran, was startled by how all of Teheran was an armed camp, with soldiers toting submachine guns to be seen everywhere.

Sometimes Laurence found Jack himself a bit dictatorial. In September 1977, she went behind Jack's back and sent a letter to members of the board concerning the Writers' Union of Canada, an institution Jack was extremely hostile to. He felt that such a group, from the time it was founded in the early seventies, might make it even more difficult for him to carry on with the publishing of Canadian titles, and might not wish to live in the "real world" of cutthroat publishing in the seventies. If, for example, contracts were scrutinized by the union with the intent of reforming them from authors' points of view, he might be even more tightly squeezed financially than he already was. In his eyes, a union was a threat when he was already facing an uphill battle to keep his company afloat. Jack's gut feeling was that since the author always came first with him, there was no need for an organization to dictate to him the conditions under which he already laboured.

As Margaret's letter to Al Purdy of September 28 makes clear, she did not enjoy being part of a process at M&S that was meaningless and depressing: "Every time I attend a board meeting, I come away feeling so depressed I think I can't stand to remain on the board. I don't think I will, either, after the year I promised is up, in the spring. What good do I do? None. The board is only a figurehead. . . . Jack [has] already decided exactly what to do. Every time I raise my voice, or write long letters to Jack, he listens attentively or replies in an equally long letter and pays not a scrap of heed. All the news seems bad, financially, which means they will take fewer and fewer risks with first novels, or with anything remotely experimental or difficult."[64]

In 1978, Margaret had yet another quarrel with Jack. Like many other writers, she thought that the conference held at the University of Calgary in February 1978 to determine the hundred greatest Canadian novels had been a tawdry experience. She expressed the feelings of many others when she complained about an M&S "takeover" of the event, despite the fact that her own novel *The Stone Angel* had topped the list (Gabrielle Roy's *The Tin Flute* was a close second). Although she realized that Jack was publicizing the New Canadian Library and trying to commemorate Malcolm Ross's achievement just as he was about to retire from this post, she thought the entire process demeaning and cheap. All in all, she was reminding him, there was a perception that Jack and Anna Porter had stage-managed the entire event and, in the process, excluded other publishers and writers who published with other firms.

Jack, bristling with rage at the accusations and rumours following the conference, wrote a conciliatory but firm letter to one of his favourite authors, refusing to take the entire blame for what was now being widely viewed as a fiasco. He had not excluded authors from other houses; in fact, he had personally invited Robertson Davies, Morley Callaghan, Hugh MacLennan and Alice Munro. The ballot had been prepared in a straightforward, honest manner. The University of Calgary had been heavily involved in the decision-making process. He was certainly not ashamed of having had a hand in an event that popularized Canadian writing.

1. I have absolutely no regret or remorse about anything I did to create and push this conference.
2. If the conference appeared to be pushing M&S authors and M&S books, it is mainly because the conference was about Canadian literature and the Canadian novel, and M&S authors just happen to form a very substantial part of what is Canlit.
3. If pushing the list lends support to my detractors and lends credence to the suspicions raised by a lot of small people, I can't for the life of me think why that should trouble me. Margaret, I am not running a popularity contest and never have tried to do so except with the people we publish. To hell with these people who resent M&S.

He offered her some final words of rebuttal: "Novels should not be classified? That's a joke. I may be a publisher, but I did study English literature at the University of Toronto. Novels shouldn't be compared with each other? That, too, is a joke. We don't have a large enough body of literature? That's a joke. It is a McClelland & Stewart promotion? To me, at least, that is a joke."[65] Jack's defence of his position is a sincere one, but the Calgary conference had largely come into existence to promote the NCL. And most NCL titles were M&S originals or titles from other publishers that could be bought in at affordable prices. Malcolm Ross was furious at the various ways in which the ballot had been manipulated. On March 17, 1978, he told Jack that the fracas was "the most painful experience of my entire career."

The more personal side of Jack's commitment to Canadian litera-ture can be seen in a letter to Gabrielle Roy soon after the conference: "I had one great disappointment in Calgary. Although I partied most of Friday night, I dragged myself out of bed at six-thirty in the morning, was in the lobby by twenty to seven to see you and Roger [Lemelin] depart, and to my horror and great disappointment, you had already left. . . . Gabrielle, how can I thank you enough for making the trip? I hope you didn't find it too arduous. I had promised that the Calgary air was good for asthma, and I hoped it proved to be that way. A num-ber of people remarked on the fact that you looked so much stronger and better at the end of the conference than you did at the start—and I felt that myself—and I just hope it was true."[66]

A year before, in a philosophical mood, he had told a Belgian pub-lisher, with whom he had negotiated regarding Beny's book, something about himself and his way of doing business that has the ring of absolute truth: "I believe that I may be one of the few totally honest people you met in the book business. It is my impression that you are honest too. We should have no problem. It was perfectly clear at the meeting that you are a better and tougher businessman than I am. I think you won every point and should be well satisfied. . . . I stand by our deal. We will live up to it in every detail and in every respect—bar-ring reasonable delays that are totally beyond our control—and we expect you to do exactly the same."[67] Unfortunately, "beyond our con-trol" was becoming more and more the hallmark of Jack's brand of publishing.

In 1978, Jack had to deal with yet another "rip-off," this time by his friend the historian and Toronto city politician William Kilbourn who, together with Robert Bothwell, had been commissioned by the C. D. Howe Institute to write a biography of Howe, the celebrated engi-neer-politician. Jack was disappointed by Bothwell's effort, but he was compassionate because Bothwell had little writing experience. Jack was furious with Kilbourn, as he told Anna: "I have been in the publishing business for a long time. In thirty-two years I have not witnessed even a remotely comparable dereliction of duty on the part of commissioned authors."[68] The letter to Kilbourn of January 23, 1978, is remarkable for its constrained fury: "While I am accustomed to being disappointed in manuscripts that I have looked forward to, nothing really in my past experience had prepared me for this. It is totally disappointing. It is not even remotely close to being ready for publication. It is a dismal performance by almost any standard that could be applied. . . . [Kilbourn's contribution] is light. It is trivial. It is lacking in depth and interest. . . .Given your background, it reads as though you haven't taken the project seriously at all, that you made no effort."[69] The biography was eventually whipped into shape by the two historians and published in 1979.

Commissioned company histories and biographies underwritten by corporations and foundations were a routine way for M&S to earn much-needed cash. One disastrous situation occurred when a supposedly reputable M&S author approached Jack: he had uncovered the secrets of one of Canada's great business dynasties. Jack, informed of the nature of the revelations, immediately sounded a note of caution. The writer assured him that the family would be so eager to have their secrets presented in the best possible light that they would co-operate with him and M&S. So Jack arranged an appointment with the patriarch, during which it became obvious that the author did not really want to write a book. He wanted to blackmail the family, his proposed book being only a fall-back position if no money could be shaken free. The patriarch was rightly outraged and refused to co-operate. Jack, who had known nothing of his writer's real intent, was badly shaken by the incident. No such book was ever published.

The general inefficiency that continued to invade M&S is evident in a vitriolic letter from the Alberta writer, Rudy Wiebe, of February 3, 1978. He was furious about the way his novel *The Scorched-Wood People* had been edited and published, particularly angry at the copy editor: "some Grade 9 grammar teacher who 'corrected' the punctuation to the point where it took me a month to get it somewhat back into shape— it's still not exactly as it should be—so that the whole book was delayed at least ninety days." To add insult to injury, the public-relations people at M&S had been more interested, it seemed, in promoting Charles Templeton's novel *Act of God*. Wiebe was also certain that he himself could have arranged more effective publicity if he had spent a half-hour on the phone doing so. He concluded, "I don't think I need to be treated as if I didn't know how to punctuate what I write, and I don't appreciate being treated like the country bumpkin."[70] Not surprisingly, Jack was mortified and readily admitted that M&S had "botched it up." The company had grown, he could no longer maintain "the same personal interest" that was once possible, and, in the process, Wiebe had become "nobody's baby." He mentioned another cause: "The squeaky wheel gets the oil. . . . It is sad but it is true that the authors who complain, interfere and demand most consistently are those who get the most attention."[71]

Bad days at M&S were becoming routine for Jack. He missed seeing Anna Porter on a daily basis. He had not really wanted her to go to Seal, but he knew that, like himself, she had strong leadership instincts and was the type of person who would not simply remain as editorial director at M&S. Some days, however, did seem worthwhile, as he told Gabrielle Roy in October 1977, recalling a recent encounter he had had with her: "It was one of the happiest days of my life. I got lost. Our time was much shorter than it should have been, but it was absolutely marvellous to see you. You are such an extraordinary person that I can tell you in all sincerity that a few hours spent with you is such an extraordinary indication of all the hard work that I have put into more than thirty years of book publishing that I can't believe it. To put it all differently, Gabrielle, you make it all worthwhile."[72]

# 13

## TREMORS

( 1 9 7 9 – 8 1 )

WHEN HE WAS A CHILD, Jack's allergies had seriously interfered with his schooling; as an adult, he had to avoid all wheat products and shellfish; cats, horses, dust and feathers were other hazards. Dogs did not cause him any distress, so the family pets were a succession of sleek Afghans. Asked once about drinking and, in particular, about smoking, he replied, "Your system gets used to it and would resent being cut off. I smoke at least fifty cigarettes a day. First thing in the morning, last thing at night. Sure I worry about lung cancer. But what the hell, I also worry about cirrhosis of the liver, heart attacks, strokes, car accidents, plane crashes and slipping on a bar of soap in the bathroom. *Living* is injurious to good health."[1]

*Publishing*, he might have added, was also an impediment to good health. At the end of 1979, in the wake of flat sales, he was forced to chop 15 people from his staff of 130—the infamous "Black Friday"— and to shave twenty titles from his 1980 list (eighty-four were published compared with a hundred the previous year). As he told Ken Adachi, an M&S author and the publishing reporter for *The Toronto Star*, "These are lean times, not only for publishing but other businesses because of inflation, the high level of interest rates and the downturn in the economy. We're, therefore, moving into the 1980s in a lean state. I look at these decisions as cautious and prudent steps in the light of what looks to be a very rough period of Canadian publishing." But he added, "It's not quite accurate to say our company is in trouble."[2] At the same time, Macmillan, owned by Maclean-Hunter, was losing money; there were major shuffles there as well.

There was also, in the words of *The Globe and Mail*'s William French, "a drastic clean-out" of titles at the M&S warehouse. Although this may have sounded to some like "prudent housekeeping," he claimed Jack had pronounced "a premature death sentence on 179 titles by 69 writers" (including Atwood, Berton, Engel, Mowat, Newman and Richler). The Writers' Union and the League of Canadian Poets donated ten copies of each remaindered title to the library at University College, University of Toronto. At a "wake" for the "dead" books, June Callwood, president of the Writers' Union, remarked, "A book is born, has a life and dies. . . . Death is called remaindering." The poet and academic Dennis Lee added, "The formula for popular fiction is that it should return its cost in the first six months. Every other kind of book is likely to be excluded [from that formula]. If all we'll get is Pablum, there's no point in preserving every publisher in the country."

Outraged by what he considered an overly sentimental response to what was an essentially economic issue, Jack fought back in a long letter to *The Globe and Mail*, starting with the list of twenty-three prominent writers: "At a conservative guess, this group has at least 150 titles actively in print. As a result of our action, a grand total of three titles will disappear." The remaining ones would be available in paperback. What kind of an emergency was it, he asked? Had French never been in a Coles, a Classic or a W.H. Smith, where "bargains" were readily available? "The Writers' Union, of course, is trying to raise an issue. The union believes that serious literature is threatened in Canada. It may have a point." The real culprit, however, was fickle "consumer taste [which was] not an exclusively Canadian problem. It is an international phenomenon stemming from a wider reading public and the multiplicity of titles that the industry churns out every year. . . .What Mr. French is suggesting is that we are banishing Darryl Sittler to the minors when we are actually allowing Carl Brewer a graceful retirement."[3] Bill French recalls that Jack had become much more "snappish" during this time than ever before.[4]

There was another, relatively new, problem haunting the industry—competition among the chains to lower prices. For example, Margaret Atwood's *Life Before Man*, listed at $12.95, was being offered at $8.99 or less by the chains and the department stores. Then, there were "returns." Traditionally publishers have accepted back and credited booksellers for unsold copies. Returns begin in January and can seriously cut into publishers' profits from a season's sales. Jack lamented: "We suffered from from a heavy rush of returned books last spring and next spring could be particularly bad. The price war is having a terrible impact on small retailers and ultimately the publishers. Too many people are being hurt. In fact, we got a huge return the other day on one of our books that is still No. 1 on the bestseller list."[5]

A related difficulty was that the chains, which controlled about 40 per cent of the retail trade, were only interested in best-sellers and would not touch the less-publicized books. The independent booksellers, whose sales were down because of the price cuts, were not, as Jack observed, "picking up the slack either. So our decision to reduce the number of titles in 1980 is, again, a reflection of the times."

Still, sales were expected to exceed fourteen million, and poetry and first novels were still being published by M&S, whereas Macmillan had axed poetry. In 1980, some titles were expected to make a lot of money: Berton's *Invasion of Canada*, Peter Gzowski's *Sacrament*, Mordecai Richler's *Joshua Then and Now* and Charles Templeton's *Third Temptation*. Jack told Ken Adachi, "I'm excited about our forthcoming list—the list is the strongest we've ever had—but not about the economics. We're being very cautious. It's not my normal style, but I've been burned too many times."[6]

"Burned" was the operative word. In 1977, a new children's division, called Magook Publishers Ltd., had been formed at M&S to sell

*Magooks*, a cross between a magazine (sixteen pages of poems and comic strips) and an original thirty-two-page book. The first issue included "The Cottage at Crescent Beach" by Ann Blade and a poem by Dennis Lee; the last *Magook* (number 8, published in 1979) contained, among other items, "Shakespeare and the Flying Bed" by Mark Côté and an interview with the ballerina Karen Kain. *Magooks* were available in bookstores but also in grocery and convenience stores; Air Canada distributed them; there were redeemable coupons for them printed on various Kraft food items. The series, which had been linked to a move by M&S into children's books from 1977 to 1979, was quickly discontinued because of poor sales. The same fate befell M&S West, the earlier initiative launched with the Glenbow Institute in Alberta.

Another important new venture was the establishment in the spring of 1977 of an annual competition worth $50,000 for the best first novel by a Canadian. The winner had his or her first book published in hardcover by M&S in Canada; Little, Brown in the United States; and André Deutsch in England. Paperback editions would follow from Seal Books in Canada, Bantam in the United States and Corgi in England. The actual prize was $10,000 with a guarantee of $40,000 in royalties. The hope was that this contest known as the Seal Book Award would provide further publicity for the establishment of the Seal-Bantam paperback imprint.

The first winner was *Judith* by Aritha van Herk. It was launched with a special promotion: any woman in Canada with the same name as the heroine could claim a free copy of the book. M&S printed thirty-five hundred special paperbacks for this purpose and received forty-five hundred requests. So great was the rush for free copies that in addition to the thousand disappointed Judiths, many imposters tried to inveigle copies. When the Seal prize was presented to van Herk at the Montreal International Book Fair, Peter Taylor with his customary elan had the cheque printed on a huge flip-flop billboard. The media were assembled outside, the billboard flipped to the cheque, Jack and Aritha mounted a ladder to reach it on an extremely precarious-looking scaffold, she endorsed the cheque and was then given a real one by the nervous bank official accompanying author and publisher. (Another Seal first-novel stunt had Brinks guards delivering $50,000 in silver dollars to William Deverell when *Needles* won in 1980. Earlier, the publicity department at M&S enclosed a hypodermic needle with each of the press kits for this book.)

This first-novel competition was also part of a new strategy on Jack's part to attract commercial fiction to his list (there were over five hundred submissions for the Seal prize and six additional manuscripts were accepted for publication). Although it had taken him significantly longer to build the fiction portion of his list than the non-fiction one, he had by the mid-1970s published important, best-selling novels by Margaret Laurence, Margaret Atwood and Mordecai Richler; in terms of commercial fiction, there was Charles Templeton. In 1979, Jack was trying to lure more of the Templeton kind of book to his list, and he also wanted to add more mysteries, science fiction and adventure stories. His attempts to diversify the list led to the perception by some that M&S was "selling out" with regard to literary titles.

In April 1979, Jack, in an interview with journalist Martin Dewey, had spoken of the problems of publishing a serious novel such as *The Sweet Second Summer of Kitty Malone* by Matt Cohen, with a retail price of $12.95 and a print run of five thousand. The costs were heavy: $2,700 for typesetting, $3,000 for paper, $1,000 for printing, $5,000 for binding, $2,500 for jacket design. Full production costs would ultimately rise to $15,000 or $3.00 a copy. The author would receive approximately 10 per cent of the retail price, and each book was sold to the trade for $7.13. This left the publisher with under $3 for promotion, warehousing, shipping and overhead. (All of the above figures were provided to Dewey by Jack.)

The advance paid to Cohen was $7,500 for hardback and paperback rights. Thirty-five hundred (not five thousand) copies of the book were printed, according to Cohen's knowledge, of which three thousand were sold. Based on these figures, the gross proceeds would have been $38,850, giving M&S itself only $21,390 before any expenses were subtracted. This would seem to mean a substantial loss, except that the sale of the paperback rights—in this case to Seal (later NCL, Penguin and Quarry)—would eventually augment M&S's original investment. Nevertheless, the hardbound version of this book would have cost M&S about $23,500 ($22,500 in manufacturing costs and advance royalties; an additional $1,000 for promotion should be added; this figure does not take the firm's overhead into account) to produce against income of $21,390.[7]

Jack's own feelings about publishing a brilliant young literary writer like Matt Cohen are contained in his frank, heartfelt letter to him on January 13, 1977, in which he makes crystal clear the distinction between a literary writer and a commercial one: "Stop worrying about how many copies your books sell, and stop, until the time is right, going across the country competing with the Pierre Bertons, Farley Mowats, Charles Templetons, etc. in a media exercise that really doesn't help sales. It takes valuable writing time away from you, and it really is a form of prostitution. . . . Concern yourself only with the concerns of a creative literary artist. . . . If you become widely admired by the handful of serious critics (as opposed to book reviewers), the market will eventually develop. It is a slow route but it is the only way it comes."[8]

When he received this letter, Cohen's mind might have wandered back to their first meeting ten years before, when the novelist was twenty-seven. He was a bit wary of meeting the "heavy-drinking, chain-smoking, crocodile-skinned" publisher who was said to have little or no interest in male writers. When he was ushered into the office, he beheld Jack talking on the phone, "shirtsleeves rolled up, collar open, and sipping a glassful of clear liquid which he kept replenishing from a Thermos reputed to contain straight vodka except when he was feeling ornery, at which times it was filled with grain alcohol."

"So, you're the new hotshot," he observed, as he squashed out the cigarette he was smoking into an overcrowded ashtray and began a new one. A very anxious Cohen tried to conduct himself with aplomb by rolling a cigarette of his own, but he ended up spraying tobacco all over the rug. "Well," Jack continued, "I haven't read [your book], but I hear it's great and that's all I need to know."[9] In essence, this was the relationship between the two men. Cohen found that Jack could, in his decision making, be as flexible as the Great Wall of China. He could also be "vengeful, unpredictable, irascible" but, in the ways that really counted, generous and supportive. Cohen would complain, as most M&S authors did, about inefficiency and bad publicity, but he knew at base that his publisher thought he was "great." There could not be a stronger basis for a solid publishing relationship.[10]

In November 1979, Timothy Findley, on behalf of the Writers' Union, lectured Jack about the conflict between commercial and literary fiction: "Writers of 'serious fiction' must *not* be driven from the marketplace simply because their time has not yet come or because they do not write for the mass of Canadian readers."[11] Jack, who obviously shared many of Findley's concerns, pointed out to him that there was something extremely paradoxical about the entire situation, since Margaret Atwood and Margaret Laurence were paid higher advances than either Charles Templeton or Richard Rohmer. He could not deny, nevertheless, that the market for "serious" fiction was bleak: the chains, more and more the dominant market force, picked the books they brought into stock very carefully, with an obvious bias in favour of those titles with a broad appeal. Price cutting, which had become an accepted fact of publishing life, lent itself to popular books as opposed to those for a more select audience. The independent booksellers, the real marketers of literary fiction, were suffering from competition by the chains. The new Book Publishing Development Program from the Secretary of State was based on sales: "It encourages publishers to produce books that will sell well, not books that necessarily have any intrinsic merit." The Canada Council block grants to publishers were a boon to the industry as a whole, but they did not assist individual, serious writers.[12]

For these reasons, Jack wanted to move to fiction that could appeal to a large market, a market increasingly being supplied by the chains (by 1979, Coles had 152 stores, Classic 76, Smith 44). If commercial fiction earned substantial profits, those profits could help to underwrite the cost of serious fiction. In an attempt to be sure that fiction and other literary books at M&S did not become too commercial or popular, Dennis Lee was hired in 1981 as the firm's top literary adviser or consultant, meaning, it seemed, that Jack had agreed that Lee had to approve anything published in the serious literary category. As William French reported in *The Globe and Mail*, Jack "promised that 20 per cent of the books he publishes in the future will be the kind of quality literature that usually loses money in the short term."[13] Jack put it this way to Lee: "What we want is a pied piper to lead the top artists out of the morass that has developed, and we want you to lead them out of the morass under our imprint."[14]

The agreement reached with Lee, whose book of poetry *The Gods* had been published by M&S in 1979, was much more fluid than French imagined. Lee, who had just returned to Canada from a year in Scotland, agreed to assist M&S in the selection of poetry (initially eight titles a year) and fiction. Lee suggested to Jack that he first concentrate on poetry (very necessary in the wake of the poet John Newlove's departure from his editorial post at M&S) but eventually direct his attention to fiction. But as things transpired, Lee found the poetry program more than enough, and he never did take on responsibility for literary fiction. With Jack's full backing, he created a new series of retrospective editions (the Modern Canadian Poets) for selections by established poets such as Layton, Purdy, Milton Acorn and Margaret Avison; fostered the talents of younger poets such as Robert Bringhurst, David Donnell, Don McKay, Paulette Jiles and Christopher Dewdney; and supervised the publication of new volumes by the established M&S poets. Lee also edited *The New Canadian Poets, 1970–1985*. The arrangement with Lee lasted until 1984, at which time the duties of poetry editor were taken over, in turn, by Russell Brown, Sam Solecki and Stan Dragland.

Of course by appointing Lee, Jack was merely promising to do for poetry what he had been doing with fiction for a number of years. Nevertheless, he hoped this "move [would] be hailed as a stroke of genius on my part by a wildly enthusiastic literary community from one end of Canada to the other."[15]

Promises or not, M&S had managed to lose money on a wide variety of books. Patricia Bowles, who worked as a publicist for Jack, feels he never resolved his "schizophrenia": "On the one hand, he's wanted to be known as a publisher of good literature; on the other hand, he's wanted to draw manuscripts that are commercially viable."[16] Jack did not see a conflict between commercial and serious: *the* Canadian publisher had to have a list that welcomed both kinds of books.

He certainly tried to pay attention to the demands of the market-place. In 1980, when Aritha van Herk's second novel, *The Tent Peg*, was about to be published, Jack had a dispute with her over the advance, which she felt should be substantial. Jack, who had never been guilty of chequebook publishing, was stunned: "There are only two novelists in Canada that I know of who receive advances in Canada of the sort you are talking about—Richler and Atwood. The only other novelist who could, if she wanted, receive that type of advance is Margaret Laurence." The publicity surrounding *Judith* may have generated larger than normal sales for a first novel, but essentially Aritha was at the beginning of her career. "The absolute maximum offer we would make for Canada for hardbound and mass-market Seal rights would be $12,500, and I think the offer is much more likely to be $10,000. So think about it very care-fully. I hope you decide to join the real world."[17]

Much to the annoyance of the Writers' Union of Canada, Jack had another massive sale from the company's warehouse in 1979. Whether the union was annoyed was of little concern to him.

The cutbacks at M&S did not work any magic. Four years later, Jack analyzed the situation from a vastly different perspective: "We tried cutting back in 1979, and we quickly discovered that cutting back is the worst bloody thing you can do in an inflationary period. That gets you into a cash-flow crisis. After a year and a half, we were advised that if we went on that way, we would die."[18]

In 1981, yet another new M&S policy caused even more problems in the public perception of the company. This was the War on Returns. In a letter of February 10 to all authors, Jack outlined the severity of the problem: "Of all the new books we published in 1980, only one title had a positive sale, net of returns, in the first six months of 1981." Therefore, the new experimental policy, applied only to new Canadian titles published in 1981: "We are offering the retail trade two choices, (a) our normal 100 per cent returns policy without penalty, or (b) our War on Returns plan, whereby if by November 15 they opt to go with this plan, they cannot return any of their 1981 books. As of December 31, we will credit them with 50 per cent of the dollar value (previously billed to them at the customary 40 per cent discount) for the inventory of these titles that they hold in stock." Booksellers would get a much larger discount on anything they sold, and M&S would have guaranteed sales. Some authors might object to this because they would "receive only half your regular royalty on copies that we credit in this way. Remember, these are the copies that would normally be returned for full credit and no royalty would be paid."

Peter Newman, a best-selling author who might suffer from such a policy, voiced serious objections to it: he asked to be exempted.[19] Although Jack refused, he tried to be conciliatory: "First, you are one of the people with whom I have already discussed the plan in detail and you expressed no reservations about it. I think we are talking about second thoughts. . . . It is a complex situation. We reviewed it very thoroughly. It is an experiment. It is a calculated risk. It is our opinion that it will earn you more money than otherwise would be earned. I think we have to see what happens."[20]

One measure of just how evasive success could be can be seen in Jack's February 1979 trip to London and then Egypt. In London, he met with the Raj Mata (Queen Mother) of Rajasthan about Roloff Beny's *Rajasthan: Land of Kings*, not published until 1984, the year the photographer died. In an attempt to recoup money lost on the Iran books, Jack attempted to reach a deal with President Anwar Sadat for a Beny book on Egypt.

Jack arrived in Cairo (all expenses paid by the Egyptians), but then nothing happened. Sadat did not seem to be available. Various officials talked to Jack, who had to cool his heels at the Hilton. He was taken on a private trip to the pyramids and other antiquities, but he became restless, finally announcing his intent to leave within forty-eight hours. He packed his bags, said goodbye to Beny and left for the airport. His luggage having been checked in, he was just about to board the plane when he was paged on the public-address system: a meeting had been scheduled with Sadat for the following day. He was confronted with a new problem: how to meet the president in the casual clothing he was wearing to travel? Airport officials rushed him into a jeep, which sped to the about-to-depart 747, from which all the passengers' baggage now had to be unloaded. Miraculously Jack's suitcase was the first to appear at the top of the ramp. The next day, Jack and Roloff were put in a stretch limo and driven to Sadat's retreat. The president greeted them warmly, gave them a pleasant lunch and the group of three formulated a deal on the proposed book. All might have turned out well except for Sadat's assassination two years later.

In July 1980, Farley was not working as productively as his publisher wanted. Jack told him, "You should be fucking well writing a book. I have it scheduled for 1981. . . . I have decided that you had better stay [at your summer home in the Maritimes] through October. . . . Things are lousy here. The weather is terrible. The business pressures are beyond belief. I am drinking myself into an early grave. I like the drinking but I don't particularly want the early grave, so for Christsake, Farley, hang in."[21] In a later note to Farley, he provided an excellent character assessment of himself: "I have never been a superrealist. I have been an enthusiast, an optimist, a problem simplifier—never a super-realist or even much of a realist."[22]

In August 1979, Jack wrote to Pierre Berton about his new book, *My Country: The Remarkable Past*. He began with compliments: "The manuscript is everything that I hoped it would be. I haven't any doubt that it will have a greater impact than the railway books. It is a pity that it probably comes too late to help Canada much in terms of identity. Misguided expediency governs the nation, I fear, and I doubt that even the book can turn the clock back on that one. In any case, it is a staggering work, rich in detail and incident." Next came Jack's objections to the book, which are deftly stated; he even takes some of the responsibility for the book's failings: "Having said that, let me tell you that I think you must do further work to turn a good book into a great book. . . . My problem is clear. The least interesting part of the book to me was a substantial portion of the first 150 pages. . . . I read the manuscript in a tired and somewhat depressed state of mind. My concentration and my attention span are both less than they should be." Having made his points, Jack imagines what an editor would say about the book; he is careful, nevertheless, to assert that he is not acting in that capacity. "I can't provide the solution. I am not an editor and I don't intend to act like one. If I were to give general instructions to the editor, it would be along these lines: I think pruning for clarity is needed, but please do not eliminate too much detail. . . . Watch carefully for both underwriting and overwriting and tread heavily on Pierre's toes if necessary. From time to time he uses some very tough words that seem to me to be pretentious, but this is an author who can say without putting the word in quotes that Washington was playing chicken."[23] The complimentary and respectful letter provided Berton with a beautifully articulated response to the book, one skilfully engineered to motivate the writer to improve the manuscript in accordance with Jack's editorial judgment. A month later, Jack upbraided an editor who was not quite as tactful as he was: "I can't pass on to him a report from you which starts 'I enjoyed this manuscript much more than I expected to . . .' I should warn you that although Berton is professional, he is also somewhat sensitive."[24]

In June 1980, Elsa Franklin, who continued to co-ordinate publicity for Berton's books, sent Jack a press release for *The Invasion of Canada, 1812–1813*.

### IT'S THE GREATEST THING
### SINCE SLICED BREAD!

*Yes!* That's what Jack McClelland, former boy *wunderkind* of the publishing world, said when he saw the manuscript of Pierre Berton's THE INVASION OF CANADA . . .

You, too, will want to thrill with Berton as he describes the sex life of General Isaac Brock, the weird puberty rites of the Shawnee Indians and the maidenhead-grabbing antics of General Roger Sheaffe . . .[25]

Elsa's accompanying note read, "Jack. Copy for flyer. Please O.K. if you approve." Jack's note to Elsa simply read, "I don't think it is coarse or vulgar enough for the current marketplace. Try to make it a bit more disgusting."[26]

In March 1981, he lamented that it was

hard to come up with original [publicity] ideas because we have done just about everything conceivable with Berton books before. Almost all new promotion ideas have been used on Berton books. What the hell can we do for an encore? . . . Under the ideas category I am con-vinced that the burning of the White House is the best one that has come up yet and I think you should get on to that one right away. . . . I can visualize a scene where we have a White House in every book-store window in Metro Toronto and by pre-arrangement we set them all on fire simultaneously by radio control. . . . Maybe burning the White House won't be popular in every part of Canada. Maybe in the West, they would prefer to burn Fort York. Perhaps we have to have a special model available for Western separatists and all Canadians who hate Toronto. . . . This is one of the sleaziest ideas we have ever had, but from past experience we know that sleazy ideas are probably the most effective.[27]

In a more serious mood, Jack was furious with C. P. Stacey's review of Berton's new book in *Books in Canada*. Jack shared his opinion freely with the editors of that periodical, whose raison d'être eluded him: "The editorial policy of *Books in Canada* continues to mystify me. I presume your target market is the general book reader, and yet to review a new book of broad general interest by Pierre Berton—a book already widely acclaimed by hundreds of advance readers—you have chosen a specialist in military history. Did you invite a former Nazi to review *Sophie's Choice*? Probably! It is a fair parallel. C. P. Stacey is all too representative of a body of scholars who think Canadian history should be reserved for historians. His petty nit-picking makes clear not only his envy but his concern that Berton might succeed in bringing the War of 1812 out of the dusty closet in which historians have enshrined it."[28]

A year later, in October 1981, Berton was angry at M&S's unaggressive policy in pushing *The Invasion of Canada* just as its sequel, *Flames Across the Border*, was about to be released. He was brutally frank. He had no sense of a guiding hand at M&S and was seriously considering placing his work elsewhere.[29] A month later, Pierre was not impressed with the two responses generated by his memo; a more aggressive sales approach was badly needed.[30] In his response, Jack pointed out that all marketing decisions for Berton books were made by Pierre, Elsa and himself. If things did not go well, the trio was collectively to blame.

What is even more interesting about the quarrel in the autumn of 1981 is that Jack had warned Pierre that largely to protect the book's commercial viability, *Flames* should be divided into two publications, making the books on the War of 1812 into a trilogy. "The point here is that regardless of the artistic merits of a natural story break, I do not believe that the Berton market in Canada will read a five- to six-hundred-page volume on the War of 1812. It is far too much. It was far too much for me, and I swear to you, no matter what any good reader or good editor may tell you, if I faltered, what percentage of your readers are going to finish the book?

"What, then, is wrong with the book? It is well written. It is well organized. It is full of colourful incidents and interesting people. What is wrong with the book is what was, in fact, wrong with the war. The canvas is too broad, the battles too disconnected and there is the lack of a strong, continuing central figure."[31]

Berton did not heed Jack's advice. In the second volume of his autobiography, he says, "I could not help suspecting a commercial, as well as an editorial, reason behind his plea. I could not, however, see any sensible way of breaking up the narrative further. Instead, to Jack's dismay, I cut out twenty-five thousand words. It sold well in Canada, poorly in the United States (where the myth of an American victory is still a part of American folklore). As usual, I got better reviews south of the border, where several critics remarked, not without astonishment, that I had been remarkably fair to the American side. That surprised and pleased me; I may have been writing as a nationalist, but never as a chauvinist."[32]

Roloff Beny continued to present Jack with new challenges. In early 1979, Jack was prepared to put up with the "strain, tension and all the other problems that Roloff introduces into our lives, providing we can control his projects in such a way that there is a reasonable return on the investment."[33] Just as Jack had an admiration and affection for Pierre even in the midst of horrendous disagreements, he had similar feelings about Roloff. As the publisher told Linda McKnight, who had become editorial director after Anna Porter became president of Seal Books, the photographer bestowed on M&S a special status:

1. The Beny projects are our most visible presence in international publishing; they maintain us in the field of international publishing in a way that no author does.
2. We cannot go backward; we can't retreat to being a strictly Canadian publisher. We must remain in the international field if at all possible.
3. I think it would be extremely foolish for us to drop Roloff at this point, for the above reasons, unless we had a comparable substitute. As far as I know, we don't.[34]

Although Jack's own relationship with Roloff remained fairly amicable, the photographer exasperated others. Lily Miller told Roloff she was not going to deal with his luggage at the airport; she was once so mad at him that she punched her fist against the wall. Harold Town made fun of him during at least one sales meeting. Typically dressed in an assortment of clothing styles—not unlike Sonny Bono—and a huge belt emblazoned with the initials RB, the photographer was introduced by Jack as the person who had come the longest distance to attend the meeting. Town whispered loudly, "The farthest with the least talent." Beny pretended he had not heard this insult and proceeded to give a description of the heavy equipment—four large cases—with which he travelled on assignment. Town quipped, "One for cameras, three for makeup."[35]

Jack's relationship with Peter Newman remained strained. The publisher was relieved when Michael Levine, also a lawyer, replaced Jerry Grafstein as Newman's principal adviser, but Jack now felt Peter distrusted him. Early in 1980, Newman undertook an anthology of *Maclean's* pieces for Macmillan to celebrate the magazine's seventy-fifth anniversary. Jack complained, he thought playfully, to Newman, but Peter was offended.[36] As far as Jack was concerned, Peter had missed the tone of his lament:

One of my problems in life is that apparently, more often than not, people have difficulty discerning whether I am being serious. I hear this from my family. I hear it from friends. I hear it from casual acquaintances. I don't really understand it, and to tell you the truth I never have. I have always assumed that a modicum of wit shows through. It is clear from your letter of February 8 that you took me seriously about the Macmillan thing. I really didn't intend it as serious, Peter. I was trying to bug you a bit. I have no question about your loyalty. I have no serious question about the appropriateness of Peter Newman being the author of this book. I think, too, that the book should do quite well if Maclean-Hunter is willing to promote it properly in the magazine, which it probably won't, but what the hell. Your letter was appreciated, but it was unnecessary. It is true I didn't speak entirely in jest. I would prefer that the book was not being published. I would prefer that the book trade had to wait for another book from Peter Newman, but it is not a big deal, it is not a big problem and it is not something that you should worry about. Least of all, you should not worry about it marring our relationship or our friendship. Its effect on that is zilch.[37]

Yet the essence of the relationship had been destroyed, as can be seen in Jack's memorandum of October 20, 1980: "He is in the hands of a show-business lawyer who is used to dealing in big sums, who is a wheeler-dealer type and who is also his money manager. Newman is committed emotionally to M&S, but it is a certainty that if we do not come up with the big deal here, Levine will shift him to somebody that does.... Peter Newman has heavy personal obligations because of alimony and other factors."[38]

Judy LaMarsh continued to be one of Jack's favourite authors, perhaps because their remarkable zest for life was so similar. When Judy, who had moved to Toronto from Vancouver, was dying in 1980, she was anxious to clear all her debts and called Jack for help. John Bassett, the former owner of *The Telegram* who had just set up CFTO television broadcasting in Toronto, had previously optioned the film rights to Judy's first novel (*A Very Political Lady*, 1979) for $25,000. Jack explained the situation to Bassett, who generously said another cheque for $25,000 would be on its way immediately for the film rights to her second (*A Right Honourable Lady*, 1980). It arrived the next morning. During the last two months of Judy's life, Jack visited her in hospital two or three times a week. One morning, she announced, "I won't be seeing you again." Later that day, she had her life support system removed and died within twenty-four hours. She told a friend that if she was going to die, she wanted to know what it felt like.

Despite serious reservations on the part of Linda McKnight and other senior editors, Jack was a fervent defender of Sondra Gotlieb's *First Lady, Last Lady* (1981), her account of her life as the wife of the Canadian diplomat Allan Gotlieb:

I found it fascinating insider material in terms of how our diplomatic service operates. . . . I think in terms of the picture she gives of the diplomatic service, she is pushing her husband's luck a bit, and I can understand why she doesn't want to go further on the inside-Ottawa bit just for the moment. The transitions are very awkward, [there are] timing problems and other things and yes, generally it is a bit sloppy, but migod, Linda, this should be a saleable book. It fits in with the *People* magazine syndrome today. I believe this is the sort of shlock that people want to read. I don't think it can be made into a great book, no matter how much time she spends on it because she is ultimately dealing with trivia. . . . It has the sort of colourful content and larger-than-life people that have made Judith Krantz very successful commercially. I don't think this is nearly as good as Krantz, but in a limited Canadian context, I think it is going to be even more compelling than Krantz to a great many people.

He also judged Sondra to be a "fairly tough, savvy person" with whom M&S could not afford "to mess around." After all, "there aren't many like her out there."[39]

In her endearingly curious and teasing way, Margaret Atwood asked her publisher to assist her research in writing *Life Before Man*: she needed help on determining whether a man's testicles would "shrivel" in response to fear. Jack's reply was "God knows. Cold water has that effect, but fear is another matter. I am prepared to believe some people can actually get a hard-on when faced with a fearsome situation."[40] Since it was a publisher's responsibility to be all things to all men and women, he offered to check with his doctor on her behalf.

If things were plain sailing with Margaret Atwood, they were not on an even keel with Al Purdy, who told him on May 15, 1981, "I could, by the way, publish just about anywhere in Canada. I assure you that is not boasting, which I try not to do, even when it's necessary to say something that sounds like it. I've had invitations from other publishers, but prefer to stick with the one I've been with for years, with the exception of small limited editions. But I have the strong feeling that M&S, in the person of the present recipient of this letter, remains fairly indifferent to my stuff and poetry in general. I know you will mention economics, but other publishers have to deal with economics as well."[41]

Irving Layton, who had had all manner of quarrels with Jack, was in a relatively good mood when he offered the following fantasy scenario to his publisher, who had assured Layton he would one day be the first Canadian to win the Nobel Prize for Literature: "I too believe that one day I'm going to helicopter to Stockholm to pick up the Nobel Prize for Literature and the wonderful loot that goes with it. I am, after all, and have been so for some time, Canada's only V.P.— Visible Poet. [He says he has support from abroad but not from Canada.] Ah, if my name were only Irvine McGregor and I didn't claim Jesus as my brother, or didn't say loud and clear that most Canucks are schmucks? Well, they can stick money and approvals up you-know-where—immortality is what I'm after. . . . I must give you my latest definition for a Canadian: someone, who, if you shoved an icicle up his asshole, it wouldn't melt."[42]

Jack's soothing attention to the often frail egos of his beloved writers survived intact, no matter how much he was put on trial. As Peter Gzowski once put it, "When you submit a book, it's not just your work, it's your whole life." In December 1979, the writer-broadcaster gave his publisher the manuscript of *The Sacrament* (1980), his account of a Saskatchewan couple who survived a plane crash by eating the remains of the woman's dead father. Gzowski dropped the book at Jack's Dunvegan Road home at six one evening and returned to his home in the country. At 1:30 a.m., the phone rang. "It was Jack who exclaimed, 'You've written a hell of a good book!' I was amazed. I thought, after all those years, all those debts, to sit around on a night there's a good hockey game going and read another manuscript—I was delighted by his essence of publisherhood."[43] At Dunvegan Road, Jack, who had always relied on Elizabeth to spend her "spare" time reading manuscripts, now extended this responsibility to the children, thus making M&S even more of a family business.

Jack's flair for publicity stunts had not deserted him. The most legendary and far-fetched of all was engineered by Peter Taylor for Sylvia Fraser's *Emperor's Virgin* on the Ides of March 1980. The writer herself has provided a hilarious account of what turned out to be in some ways a non-event.

One morning last March, Jack McClelland, the publisher, picked me up at my Toronto home wearing a Roman toga, gold laurels and floppy snow boots, by no means his usual morning attire.

I was dressed as an ersatz Roman empress, in a flashy silver gown from the back of my own closet—flotsam from the '60s, when some people wore that sort of thing.

The morning, as viewed through a slashing windshield wiper, was cold and blustery—a cause of more than casual interest, since we were scheduled to drive a chariot bearing my latest book, *The Emperor's Virgin*, to five bookstores staffed by togaed personnel.

We parked on Bloor St., where the parade was to assemble. Ahead of us was an enormous van containing our chariot. Across the road was a smaller van containing our horses. Running between them and a huddle of disgruntled photographers were assorted public relations people from McClelland & Stewart.

The long delay and their sober faces rimmed with snow did not augur well. At 11, the augury was confirmed. Our gold and scarlet chariot had a broken axle. At that point, we lost our chance of making the national news.

With the determination of Caesar invading Gaul, McClelland & I set out, by sandal, through what had developed into the winter's last blizzard, trailed by two shivering, bare-legged centurions toting books. After two bitter hours, we returned to our General Motors chariot, only to discover that Caesar had locked his keys inside and that all the imperial party had parking tickets delivered to them by the only other person afoot that day on Bloor St.[44]

Later that evening, there was a gala toga party to be hosted by five distinguished Canadian vestal virgins, although two of the vestals did not show up: Adrienne Clarkson was fogged in in Newfoundland and Doris Anderson was snowed in in Ottawa. Peter Taylor had been out of town on a business trip. When he returned, he was confronted by McClelland: "You fucking little prick! Where were you with your toga?"

*Sylvia Fraser and Jack promoting* The Emperor's Virgin, *1980*

The Roman escapade is regarded as the most outrageous of Jack's publicity bids. It is certainly a splendid episode, capturing as it does his public persona, but the other, more private side of Jack as publisher can be seen in a letter from a year before—January 1979—in which he spelled out for Sylvia Fraser what he considered to be the weaknesses of her manuscript of *The Emperor's Virgin*. It was certainly publishable in its current form, he assured her (Lily Miller, the book's editor, and Anna Porter viewed it very favourably), but Jack was certain that the writing did not meet her ability and that at this point in her career, she needed a "strong novel." This one was not measuring up. He made several detailed suggestions for improvement. "In summation, Sylvia, what I really want to say to you is that while you have all the ingredients and a fine setting and a good underlying power struggle, I do not think the execution, except in terms of style, is up to your best standard. I cannot predict a big market for the manuscript in its present form. I suppose it might be possible to 'hype' it in a sensational way and sell a fair number of copies. What it would not have, in my view, is very good word-of-mouth follow-up.

Reviews would be mixed."[45] Jack sent a copy of this letter to the American publisher, Sam Vaughan at Doubleday, who agreed with Jack. On March 12, Fraser told Vaughan, "I trust the feedback you and Jack have given me, and your willingness to carry through. . . . I see, now, that what I wrote was an outline for a book, rather than a book." The revisions she subsequently made, however, were not that well received, by either Lily Miller or Jack: many of the weaknesses were repaired, but somehow the book's spark was gone. Sylvia revised yet again. And a year later, when the "hype" was supposed to be sensational, the weather did not permit the event to have its full effect.

In the mid-seventies, when the province of Ontario instituted its program of guaranteed publishing loans at a subsidized rate of interest, M&S subsequently received additional funds to a total of almost $2.9 million (if one includes the original debenture from 1971). In addition, in 1981, the firm was using a substantial part of a $1.2 million operating loan plus $150,000 at another bank (the remainder of the $550,000 loan guaranteed for Cemp–Starlaw). In 1979, the Ontario government put Jack under pressure to reduce the size of its loan from them. With interest charges approaching $500,000 a year, he did not need much encouragement to comply. Thus, the cutbacks (staff layoffs and reduced number of publications) that year. Due to inflation, the cutbacks were not as satisfactory as hoped in allowing the firm to achieve a genuine operating profit.

Knowing something of M&S's position, the Alberta financier Peter Pocklington explored investing in the company as a tax loss. Jack told him: "Your expressed interest is in a tax loss and I do understand that certain advantages are available in this respect under Alberta legislation. It does, however, leave the question as to what happens after the tax loss, and that does not need a great deal of discussion. M&S is not currently a profitable operation, and as far as that goes, it never has been profitable at a level that would have much interest to investors in the short term. . . . I have said that we could provide about $5 million tax loss, but even this is not easy to visualize from our statements."[46]

The "tax loss" would be difficult to arrange because the firm had "a profit of about $400,000 for 1980 and a comparable profit in 1981, but in fact we are currently operating at a loss. The profit is artificial and directly attributable to the Book Publishing Development Program of the Department of the Secretary of State, which will have injected about $1.2 million into the company over a period of three years."[47]

Pocklington did not pursue the matter. In 1981, Jack, along with the best-selling novelist James Clavell, the Australian-born American screenwriter and author of mega-best-sellers like *King Rat*, *Tai-Pan* and *Shogun*, and Clavell's daughter, Michaela Krissman, discussed setting up a "new Canadian communications company" (book and film) using a substantial investment from Clavell, who was at that time negotiating advances between $2 and $3 million a book. As Jack put it, Clavell was "endowed with an excess of income," had Canadian connections and "for tax and other personal reasons" wanted to move ahead quickly with this plan. Jack had several strong opinions about such a partnership. "The Clavell income would free M&S from its obligation to the Ontario government," and also it might be able to "relieve me of my immediate obligations to M&S and enable me to devote perhaps 75 to 90 per cent of my time to our mutual interests."[48] When Krissman asked him about his other "interests," he replied: "That is a very good question. My first response is that I have been totally engaged in Canadian book publishing long enough. It does not excite me as it used to, and I want to do something else. I have said that I am prepared to commit at least 30 per cent of my time in the formative years, and that I would use the income from the new corporation to make that possible. It is an area that interests me because I can make use of my training and experience and because I believe it is a creative project that could expand rapidly and achieve all the things that your father wants achieved and that you want achieved on behalf of the family."[49] This initiative was Stanley Colbert's. The head of Dramatic Programming for CBC, he brought Jack and Clavell, who had once lived in Vancouver, together and was to have a managerial role in the new company. (Anna Porter, Pierre Berton and Elsa Franklin were also to be involved.) This project was put on hold in August 1981 because of complexities stemming from "Canadian citizenship or landed immigrant requirement . . . debt load and government obligations relating to M&S . . . [and] a mutual feeling that there is some easier and more straightforward way of achieving our mutual objectives."[50] This "solution" was obviously abandoned.

A year or two before the Clavell scheme, a retired billionaire friend of Peter Newman's wanted to buy a publishing house as a sort of hobby. "Jack and I spent the entire day together," this person recalled. "He gave me up-to-date financial statements and told me a lot about the company's problems. It was quite revealing. I took the information home and studied it. Frankly, I was surprised at the condition of the firm. I went through his warehouse and ran my finger along a shelf of books." Not knowing the full extent of the problem, he asked Jack, "Why don't you sell them off at high price? And what about all these people milling around; can't you cut back or figure out some early retirement plan?" Jack blushed. "I know we have more people than we need, but I've never fired anyone [face-to-face] yet, and I wouldn't know how."

At their second meeting, a boozy lunch, Jack outlined his plan: the businessman was to figure out how the bank and government loans could be paid off while Jack would conduct business as usual. The man did not want a partner—if he bought the firm, he wanted total control. "Finally," he recalled, "we talked numbers. With all those bank loans and government bailouts to pay off, [Jack] still valued the place at $3 million. Unbelievable! That meant a million and a half for me to keep a sinking ship afloat while he did exactly what he was always doing." He would have paid Jack $1 million, retired all the loans within ten years and kept Jack on for six months as a consultant. "But on top of everything else he had all these obligations to his authors. His strength is not in business—he has no ideas about budgeting, control of expenses, adequate sales targets, or proper marketing operations— and he has no intention of learning." He concluded Jack was only interested in the "romance" of the business and finally ended up informing him that the key to success in publishing was to have a soft heart *and* a hard head.[51]

During 1981, Jack decided, yet again, not to sell M&S. He wanted to place the company on a profitable basis without assistance from the secretary of state; he also wanted the Ontario government to forgive its various loans or agree to allow some form of conversion of the existing debentures. Therefore, he decided to ask Bill Davis's government to allow "(a) renewal of the debenture for a ten-year period, interest free; (b) conversion of the debenture to preferred shares on a non-cumulative basis; (c) conversion into a small percentage of common shares (probably not attractive politically); or (d) forgiveness (again probably not attractive politically)."[52] If the government was sympathetic, Jack proposed an orderly reduction in loan guarantees over the next decade, the reduction of his own shares (92½ per cent) in the company, which would allow additional equity into the firm's treasury (authors and employees would be encouraged to subscribe under this scheme).

And there was a new financial issue to deal with. After he retired from Macmillan, Hugh Kane had rejoined M&S in 1976 as president and managing director of the Natural Science Library of Canada Ltd., a subsidiary which published, among other things, the twelve-volume *Illustrated Natural History of Canada*. Kane's new responsibilities did not bring him into daily contact with Jack, as in the past. Kane did not enjoy running what was essentially a mail-order firm; he could not generate the expected profits. Four years later, in 1980, Hugh, who had just turned seventy and was retiring, wanted to recover his "shares" in M&S.

Jack, who had no resources of his own to draw on, offered Kane a pension of $1,000 a month. Hurt and angry, Hugh reminded Jack of some recent history at M&S: "I well remember your outrage when asked to agree to a reduction in [your] income from $54,600 to $35,000. Now, Jake, you are suggesting I try to adjust to a 'salary' of $12,000 p.a. when my 'Total Declared Income' before deductions has been . . . an average . . . of $43,901." He told Jack he could not get by on that amount, knew the pressures Jack was facing, but needed (and was counting on) his help, especially as it related to Kane's shares in

M&S: "All I am asking is that you and I together try to work out some fair and reasonable plan whereby you can discharge the 'personal obligation' you assumed with regard to my share holdings in McClelland & Stewart when I left to join Macmillan in 1969." He concluded, "And don't forget my recent admonition: 'Don't ever let us quarrel.'"[53]

*Hugh Kane*

Jack, who felt he could not do very much to alleviate Hugh's distress except to raise the monthly amount to $1,200, was extremely upset, especially as the two men had close emotional ties. The sad truth was that M&S—ergo, Kane's shares—was worth "zilch." Kane's response a few weeks later is filled with recrimination and sorrow: "What is being considered is the dissolution of a partnership, a partnership in which you owned 51 per cent and I owned 24 per cent. When you were still in school at St. Andrew's I had the responsibility for selling the company's products in one of the two most important markets in the country. I have been with McClelland & Stewart for about forty-five years, with two short absences."[54] Extremely embarrassed, Jack accused his old friend of being unrealistic.[55] In a subsequent letter, Jack lamented his entire involvement in the book trade: "Throughout my career, I thought I could turn all this around. So did you. You failed. So have I. I just don't have any magic solutions."[56] Late in his career, such agonizing personal disputes added to Jack's sense of defeat. The pension was paid at $1,000 per month and was carried on the company's books as a consulting fee.

In 1980, the journalist Judith Timson, in preparation for an article in *Toronto Life*, travelled with Jack to London, Ontario, when he was doing his "Canadian publisher shtick" as part of the National Book Festival. One evening, she observed him getting ready for an event: "He stood stripped to the waist in a room at the Holiday Inn . . . and although he said nothing out loud about it, there was a palpable weariness in the way he stood, and at the way he fumbled in his suitcase for the crisp whiteness of a fresh dinner shirt. His belly sagged gently over his belt. His face was a masterpiece of character and dissolution, with exploding red capillaries winning a narrow victory over noble features."[57]

"My hair is *not* white, it's blond," he assured Timson, as he ran his fingers through it, perhaps hoping he could prove his point in the right light. Having recently learned that M&S's increasingly crucial annual Canada Council grant of $95,250 had been reduced to $24,500, he claimed that nothing in his years of publishing had angered him more.

At public events, very much in the manner of a latter-day Jay Gatsby, Jack remained affable, expressing sentiments he felt compelled to utter. When reminded of some of them, he exclaimed, "Jesus Christ, did I say that? I mustn't have been paying attention."[58] One of the statements he regretted was the pronouncement that "the difference between Atwood and Templeton is the difference between a steak and a McDonald's [hamburger]." He paused. "Sorry, Charles. I'm only trying to entertain the masses."[59] Once a man who did not supplicate the gods but rather gave them orders, he felt defeated in the early 1980s.[60]

In 1981, the McClellands moved from Forest Hill Village to a house next door to the Bertons in Kleinburg, north of Toronto. A desperately tired Jack dreamed of achieving a semblance of breathing space from M&S if he no longer lived in the city. He and Elizabeth had always fantasized about living in the country, perhaps on a farm. Since Rob was the only child still at home, it seemed a sensible time to experiment, especially as there would be a financial advantage in selling their home in Toronto in exchange for a modern one in the country, although the Kleinburg house required a lot of work.

The hoped-for escape did not really materialize, as he told Farley and Claire Mowat: "The problem, you see, is that I spend all my time driving back and forth between Kleinburg and Toronto. It is a pain in the ass. . . . [However,] we have all the space in the world. It is much more comfortable than Muskoka. All it lacks is the lake, but Jesus, it has the Humber River, wildlife, birds, vistas." He added, "It is the season for author complaints. They are all mad at us for one stupidity or another and I don't blame them."[61]

The stupidities that surrounded Jack were largely not of his own making. More and more, he saw publishing in Canada as a barren pursuit and his own life as a crippling exercise in sheer frustration. He vowed to become "bottom-line commercial"[62] but somehow knew this was for him an extremely unrealistic goal. He began to feel very old and would have had a wry laugh when Mordecai Richler asked him, "What kind of rinse do you use for your hair?"[63]

# I4

## EMERITUS

## (1982-85)

IN CONCERT, at the beginning of 1982, Marge and Farley confronted an exhausted fifty-nine-year-old Jack, telling him he had to step down or step aside; otherwise, he faced the possibility of a complete collapse. Prodded by them, he determined he could best solve the problems at M&S if he handed over the day-to-day running of the operation to someone else. As chairman of the board, he would oversee the company's increasingly disastrous financial performance. He intended to free himself from the many impediments preventing him from giving monetary matters his undivided attention.

Jack chose energetic, bright, thirty-nine-year-old Linda McKnight, who had joined the firm thirteen years earlier (after three years with Copp Clark), as his replacement. Anna Porter, who might have been the logical person to succeed Jack, had established Key Porter Books with Michael de Pencier in 1980 and was obviously not available. Jack thought of approaching her but decided against it. Anna's own recollection is different; she suggests that Jack's love of drama led him to give the impression to the public that there was some sort of "showdown" between the two women. This does not seem to have been the case.

On a work trip to Bermuda, which also included Peter Taylor, Len Cummings, Marge and Jack, McKnight first learned she was being considered for the top job at M&S. (There was some talk of Peter Taylor's becoming president, but he was in advertising and marketing, which meant he had little or no experience on the crucial editorial side of publishing; in any event, he left M&S at about this time.) Later, back in Toronto, Jack poked his head in McKnight's office door at about eight one evening and announced, "By the way, I've decided to make you president." Stunned, she waited ten minutes or so before going to Jack's office. She told him what M&S needed was a "strong outsider," preferably a man and someone who would act "rigidly" in response to the firm's largely unorthodox approach to publishing. Jack had made his mind up and pushed her objections aside: McKnight was to run the company.[1]

Well before his decision to step down was announced, Jack sent McKnight a long memorandum offering his advice. In a way, he gave her a great deal of authority but essentially removed it as soon as it was conferred. He began by providing McKnight, whom he considered a more "conservative" and "sane" publisher than himself, with a realistic assessment of the situation:

> I want you to have full operational control of this company. I not only want you to have it, I want other people to know that you have it and that really is the starting point of this memo. You are not Jack McClelland. You did not inherit this company from your father. You cannot and should not, even for a moment, consider me as a role model. It is my guess that the worst thing you are going to face—primarily in the first year—is an attitude of disbelief. There will be a lot of people internally who will not believe that you are running the company.
>
> Anna Porter's chief problem when she was put in a position of authority at M&S stemmed from the industry stories that she got that way by sleeping with me. You probably remember the stories. Rightly or wrongly, I took the position that it was futile for me to deny these stories and instead said, of course it is true. This, of

course, infuriated Anna but it probably killed the stories faster than any denial would have done. In any case, you may be faced with the same thing or you may not. In your favour is the fact that I have enough miles on me now that people no longer worry too much about my supposed lechery. But that is a minor issue. The real issue is whether or not they are going to believe you are in charge.

Jack advised McKnight to hire a financial adviser (whose fee could be charged against her salary) and to plan her own agenda. Nevertheless, she had to start by being "tough. You must knock a few heads. You must, if necessary, make yourself unpopular with a lot of people but you must demonstrate what you expect. . . . Frankly, I think the firm and most of the people will react well to this sort of regime. If they don't, too bad. Too bad for them, I mean."[2] McKnight, who had suffered extreme culture shock when she left the more rigorously ordered Copp Clark, had gradually got used to the madhouse atmosphere at M&S; yet she was not completely prepared for the problems now confronting her on a daily basis.

McKnight had a far different approach from her boss's, although she claimed at the outset to be of "one mind" with him on long-range policy. "Five years from now," she predicted in 1983, "most of the older authors—though still Jack's intimate associates—will be closer to people in the house. I like to work as a team and have authors familiar with several editors, the director of publishing, and as many of the key staff as it's feasible to know."[3]

Teamwork had never been Jack's forte, however. From the outset, McKnight wanted to review properly the role of agency publishing in the eighties, something that might help to resolve cash-flow problems. This had not been a priority for Jack when he had purged the company of most agencies years before. McKnight and Jack were in substantial agreement on one issue: the book market in the early eighties was pancake flat; titles were selling at half the rate that could have been safely predicted in 1978.

After taking over from Jack, McKnight hired Jan Walter, formerly of Hurtig Publishers and Macmillan, to be "another Linda McKnight," asking her to take over her old duties as director of publishing. Very soon after settling in at M&S, Walter formed the impression that the publishing house was "a machine that had to be fed." It could also be compared to a combustion engine always on the verge of exploding. At times, she wondered if the crisis atmosphere helped or hindered the whole enterprise. There certainly seemed to be an abundance of employees and so, of necessity, it followed that there had to be an abundance of books. Jan, who had been used to the methodical and cautious way Mel Hurtig had costed books, was a bit startled by the wishful thinking that seemed part and parcel of M&S. Len Cummings was the only person who ever attempted to say no: if Walter came up with an idea he considered impractical, he would, in his very even way, point to his flow chart to show her how spending that kind of money would be useless or impractical. No one else at M&S voiced such sentiments. Although Jack no longer attended editorial meetings, she was impressed with his eternal optimism and his insatiable curiosity. He always seemed to see cloudless blue skies on the M&S horizon.[4]

The differences between Cummings and McClelland are best seen in Jack's memorandum of July 3, 1981, concerning Len's conviction that the fall 1981 list was too large: "I don't want this company to go out of business because our sales volume isn't enough to cover our overhead unless we can't find enough good books to publish. . . . One segment of the company, mainly the editorial planning committee, is determined to bulk up our sales and bulk up our list and save the company from inevitable extinction by default. Now you are in a mad panic about the size of our fall list. I simply don't understand it. You talk about the size of the gamble. Christ, Len, that's what this business is all about. Of course it is a lousy gamble. It has been a lousy gamble for seventy-five years."[5] Some gambles are not worth taking, Len was telling Jack; he was also making the point that businesses cannot be run in the expectation that future profits will wipe out vast debts. Jack added, almost as an accusation against Len, "You deal in figures and graphs. I am not able to do that. I have to deal with my own particular form of logic. It is too late for me to change my ways."[6]

In the early eighties, Jack's ambivalence about his own role in the publishing industry had reached enormous unresolved proportions. He wanted to leave; he did not wish to leave. He wanted to get rid of M&S; he wanted to hold on to M&S. Because he himself did not understand where he stood, he could not help circulating a series of mixed and confusing messages that trickled down to everyone at the firm. Some authors remained pleased by how they were treated at M&S; many were not. Roy MacGregor felt his novel *Shore Lines* (1980) received short shrift: it was "a shattering experience to realize that the man who was capable of moving mountains in the promotion game had not lifted a finger to promote my book." Silver Donald Cameron, who had written a very enthusiastic article about Jack in 1970, was outraged when Jack instructed him to "take out the fine writing" in his first novel, *Dragon Lady* (1980).[7]

Margaret Laurence's reaction to the news of Jack's new role at M&S, when it was announced in March, was typical of many M&S authors, all of whom saw this as Jack's first inevitable step towards retirement; she told the Boss how much he had meant to her, despite their various scraps. These included the fight over the title of *The Fire-Dwellers*: "At the time I didn't realize that the firm was in dire straits financially and you had a lot more on your mind than the title of one author's book. I also recall the famous battle over the Writers' Union contract, when I angrily wrote to all the board members. Ye gods, I now think the union contract is far too ambitious and complicated and needs to be simplified and made more realistic (I think this is being done). Also the fight re the Iran book . . . Well, we have disagreed a lot, throughout the years, Jack, but the main thing is that I have always felt I could express my views and that although you might disagree with them, you would always take them seriously."[8] Michael Ondaatje had never forgotten his gratitude to Jack for defending, in 1969, his use of words and phrases in his critical study of Leonard Cohen in the face of objections from Dave Godfrey, the editor of the Canadian Writers series: "You have always been very straight with me, and I value that greatly."[9]

Less typical was Mordecai Richler's response to Jack's "retirement," when he wrote him on December 22, 1982, concerning two forthcoming books, an anthology, *The Best of Modern Humour* (1983), and a collection of his essays, *Home Sweet Home* (1984): "If you are still allowed to handle anything more than the petty cash at the Feminists' Commune that was once the proud firm of M&S, you might want to apply your addled mind to contracts on these two books. . . . So I look forward to something written in your shaky hand from your bed in the Old Publishers' Retirement Home. Possibly, Marge visits you there and will take dictation, still able to understand you despite the clacking dentures."[10] In response, Mordecai received a reply from a very distressed "Marge Hodgeman":

> I have your letter . . . addressed to Jack, and I don't exactly know what to do with it. As I am sure you realize, he was institutionalized during the recent holiday period, and until further notice will only be allowed visitors on the third Friday in every month. That means he won't be able to deal with the content of your letter until I see him, I hope, on January 21. Regrettably there is even some doubt about that because of his precarious state—which has been initially diagnosed as hyper-senility—he has only been allowed three visitors a month. They tell me that this is done on a first-come first-served basis, and I have already made application on behalf of McClelland & Stewart, but I am concerned that some members of the family may want to see him and may be given precedence. Thus far, though, it is looking good because the family has shown an active uninterest.[11]

When Jack informed Mordecai he did not like collections of essays such as *Home Sweet Home*, the author promptly dedicated it to his publisher.

Later that year, Jack received the Molson Prize from the Canada Council. Earlier, in 1967, he had been presented with a Centennial Medal; in 1968, a doctor of laws degree from Carleton University (in the ensuing years he has received eight other honourary doctorates); in 1971, the National Award in Letters from the University of Alberta and the Banff School of Fine Arts. In 1976, he was created an Officer of the Order of Canada.

Unfortunately, Jack found it difficult to allow Linda McKnight sufficient leeway to create her own management style. She might have been captain of the ship, but he was the admiral. So anxious was he about the future of M&S that he simply could not give her the authority she needed. In a very real sense, he now had two jobs: chairman of the board and backseat president.

On August 13, 1982, Jack told McKnight how he was "managing" Conrad Black, whose book about the Quebec premier Maurice Duplessis M&S had published five years earlier. Peter Newman's biography of Black, *The Establishment Man: A Portrait of Power*, was to appear that autumn: "As I have already indicated to you, I have had to concede a little to Conrad Black. . . . Although the lawyers do not feel that Black can sue . . . our policy for the present is to calm him, get along with him as much as possible until we are into actual distribution." Six days later Jack told Black, with whom he had just had a meeting: "I thought I would let you know that I have, since our meeting, reviewed the proofs [of *The Establishment Man*] in their totality. It is, in fact, the first time I have had a chance to read the whole book in a continuous reading. It has confirmed my impression that it is a very good book indeed—in my view the best Peter has ever written. It presents an overwhelmingly impressive and favourable picture of you, although I do feel that it is sufficiently balanced to make it both credible and absorbing reading. I don't for a minute think you are going to like everything that is said, although on balance I think you should be extremely pleased."[12]

When McKnight became president of M&S, it was agreed that Jack would still continue to deal with some of his major authors, but such negotiations could be very time-consuming, especially in the case of Peter Newman. The relationship between publisher and author had not been good for a long time, but the presence of Newman's adviser, Michael Levine, exacerbated the already difficult situation. In January 1982, Jack told Newman, "I am sorry that I had to cancel out on our lunch at the last moment.

The truth of the matter is that I was not well. The impairment to my health was the result of anger over the most recent letter from Michael Levine. In my somewhat lengthy career as a book publisher I have never had the experience of dealing with an author through a lawyer. I have nothing against lawyers, and in fact I recommend to all authors that they regularly consult their lawyers. But I still deal with the authors. . . . I guess what you should be thinking about is whether or not you want to terminate our publishing agreement. If you do, I have no doubt it can be arranged on a friendly basis. We don't need legal games. As you might have learned by now, I am really not that hard to get along with."[13] Jack assumed that Newman no longer trusted him, but Newman, it could be argued, was simply following a new trend in the book world by hiring a lawyer-agent who would act in his best interests. Part of the problem was that Jack often played the role of agent in the marketing of some of his writers and felt one of his crucial roles as publisher was being usurped. For example, he had tried unsuccessfully for years to interest various American houses in Irving Layton's poetry.

In 1982, Newman wanted his work to be placed before an international audience and thus to reach many more readers than he could by simply devoting himself to Canadian subjects. Michael Levine, who had fulfilled this desire when he obtained an offer of $500,000 from Viking Penguin in England for a Newman history of the Hudson's Bay Company, asked Jack for a counteroffer. In refusing to make one, Jack was extremely forthright:

> That is a very interesting proposal. If it is real, and by that I mean non-conditional and outright over a specified payment schedule, then we think you should make a deal as quickly and as expeditiously as possible. . . . Our problem with the proposal is the fact that frankly we do not think that the Hudson Bay book is worth $500,000 or even close to that figure. . . . Peter Newman is very important to M&S, and I hope we are important to him, but certainly we would not want to stand between Peter and half a million dollars, no matter what the motives of the publisher are, no matter what its effect might be on M&S. Let me give you a realistic assessment. We think the Hudson's Bay

project is a very good one for Peter. We have over the last forty years done a number of HBC books and every one of them has been successful. None of them has earned $500,000 or even one-tenth of that amount for the author. None of the authors, of course, has been Peter C. Newman. . . .Obviously all this needs much further discussion. I hope at a minimum that it will indicate that we have nothing but the most supportive attitude toward Peter. If English publishers, in these terrible economic times, are really prepared to come up with $500,000 in hard cash, then we say for God's sake, grab it and run with it.[14]

When Peter Newman subsequently accepted the English offer, Jack was unequivocal in what he felt about the situation in an unsent letter to Levine.

Peter Newman had on many occasions expressed his ambition and desire to move into the international marketplace, and the Hudson's Bay Company book is his first international book. I hope, Michael, that you will appreciate my saying that because I understand and respect that particular ambition of Peter's. One of the things I admire most about him is his great drive and ambition. I do hope he makes it in the international marketplace. You and Peter have both been naive enough to believe that this is what has been accomplished, although I warned you that that was not my perception when I told you I did not think it was possible for us to make a deal with Penguin [which would allow M&S to be the Canadian publisher of his Hudson's Bay book]. . . . What has happened in fact—as I read it—is that you have come between Peter Newman and me. No problem—you have given him a $500,000 payout over the next four years but, Michael, I don't really think it is that simple. It is done, it is sealed, and I am no longer Peter Newman's publisher in Canada.[15]

Later, when Newman told Jack the Hudson's Bay Company book would be divided into two books (in fact, it ultimately became three), Jack told him that M&S had previously been paying him the equivalent of $250,000 a book and that, therefore, Newman had not really achieved anything by going to another publisher. The further irony is that the Hudson's Bay books sold well only in Canada and was a significant failure internationally.

Later, in April 1983, Jack, as he told Linda McKnight, met with Newman:

> This memo will surprise you as much as it surprised me. What I am passing to you is a new Peter Newman manuscript. I had dinner with him on the eve of my departure for [Jack's recently acquired condominium in] Florida—as you know a long postponed dinner—and he gave me the manuscript and asked me if I would read it and give him an evaluation. . . . It is a very important document. As a matter of fact, it is a document that absolutely stunned me as a Canadian. I think what it needs is a sexy title—something along the lines of *The Shame and the Neglect*. What it is, is a study of the world military position and Canada's current position in relation to that. . . . I think it will be widely reviewed, I think widely praised, editorialized, but regrettably I don't think it will sell all that many copies. . . . It is just the subject area that is unpopular.[16]

He then tells her he has been on the phone to Newman with a number of editorial suggestions. The resulting book was *True North*: Not *Strong and Free: Defending the Peaceable Kingdom in the Nuclear Age*, published by M&S that autumn.

Another glimpse of Jack's relationship with McKnight can be seen in his memo to her of April 20, 1983, a little over two weeks after his previous memo, in which he implies she is not acting fast enough on the Newman manuscript: "Linda, I have said repeatedly that I think Peter C. Newman and your meeting with Michael Levine is the single most urgent item on your agenda. . . . I want to know the result immediately thereafter. Whether or not it is in the middle of the night. I am not sure you realize it yet. Peter is already upset that he hasn't heard from you about the manuscript. . . . There is no problem as immediate as this one."

A year later, Jack reflected yet again about the Newman situation in a memo to McKnight. Newman was aware he might have made a mistake in following Levine's lead. The whole affair rankled with Jack.[17] The conflict between him and Newman was longstanding, although it had taken quite a while to come to a boil. The dispute between Jack and Levine is perhaps best understood as generational: Jack's way of doing business was in many ways courtly, extremely gentlemanly; Levine's aggressive defence of the best business interests of an important client simply did not sit well with Jack, who was used to dealing with authors on a more personal level, even when agents were involved.

There was also a generational conflict brewing between McKnight and Jack, who was consistently interfering with her ability to run M&S. At one level, Jack was certain the publishing industry was for people younger than himself. In 1984, he told his senior management, "I do not intend, ever again, to run this company. To put it in its simplest terms, I am too old to run a book publishing company, and frankly I am out of touch with the marketplace and I do not intend, ever again, to be in touch with it. It is that simple. Your problem . . . is to really dig that."[18] Of course there can be a considerable difference between being aware of an issue rationally and living it emotionally.

The dispute between Jack and Levine as well as Jack's constant supervision of McKnight has to be placed against the increasingly dire finances at M&S. In December 1982, a report by the accounting firm of Woods Gordon commissioned by the Ontario Development Corporation concluded that M&S was salvageable, but that Clarke, Irwin (founded in 1930) was not; that firm finally went into receivership in April 1983 when the CIBC called in its $1.5 million loan. Eleven years earlier, the ODC had bailed them out with $638,000; of the $34.3 million paid out to publishers by the ODC between 1979 and the end of March 1984, M&S had received just over $2 million.

Additional funds were raised by Jack in yet another "fire" sale, the notorious Atrium on Bay event where one-third of the company's $3.5 million in inventory, almost all of the twelve hundred titles in stock over the past twelve years, were sold at rock-bottom prices. More than 200,000 books were sold, the total take being $600,000. Gerry Ruby, owner of Lichtman's booksellers, disagreed "with the sale in principle. I wouldn't like to see other publishers do the same. . . . What happens when [all] the publishers start selling to the public in that way? It's the independent bookseller who's going to be hurt. This doesn't help the book industry." Bill Ardell, president of Coles, was even more vehement: "I sense a heckuva lot of annoyance. [Jack] had created a blemish on the relationship between the publisher and the retailer."[19]

Although M&S showed a small profit of $184,000 in 1983, the firm lost $777,000 in the first four months of 1984, was $5 million in debt with interest payable per annum of $600,000. After protracted negotiations with the province, which included a meeting in 1982 with Premier Bill Davis, Jack asked the Ontario government to convert into equity the total of $3 million in loans and loan guarantees held by the ODC, thereby making them part owners of the firm.

Ultimately, the ODC decided it did not wish to become a partner. The corporation, however, gave M&S a $1 million forgivable loan, $1.5 million in immediate cash and $500,000 in standby credit. The conditions: the firm was barred from receiving further provincial assistance, Jack had to raise additional equity by selling shares in the company to private investors and his own remaining share of the company was to be held in escrow as security against bank loans. That year, the company lost $2 million. Jack had was $1.1 million (there were approximately twenty-one private investors including Pierre Berton, Farley Mowat, Margaret Atwood and the real estate magnate Avie Bennett). As a result of this offering, Jack's share of the company declined from 92.5 to 64 per cent. One employee heard him say, "I'd fire any employee stupid enough to invest in this company."[20] The year before, Bantam, New York, lent Jack $241,000 to buy the controlling interest (75 per cent; the remaining 25 per cent was held by Bantam) in M&S–Bantam. Jack set up a family trust to hold the shares.

Nothing seemed to work, as can be glimpsed in Jack's very worried memo to McKnight: "We have not only blown $1,250,000 in cash flow— our current cash flow is still not comparable to [our] earlier picture. That scares the hell out of me. . . . At one point we are looking very healthy at the bank. Then, with $1.25 million additional cash we are looking unhealthy—all in, say, six months. Please understand there is no criticism of you, implied or otherwise. . . . There are several differences between your role in running M&S and mine when I did so. I was responsible to no one except myself (that was lucky, or may be unfortunate). You are responsible to the board, to the shareholders and primarily, because of the shareholding, to me."[21] He proceeded to tell her how to manage the situation.

McKnight herself had become convinced that she was being asked to do an impossible job; she also felt that her way of doing things was simply not Jack's. McKnight thought that Jack had a conflict of interest as majority owner of two publishing houses. In December 1984, he understood her position when she tried to make it clear to him that she intended to defend M&S interests, even though they might be in conflict with Seal, whose publisher was now Janet Turnbull. In a memorandum that was not sent, he reflected, "Forget shareholders, boards, everyone else—it is a simple fact of life that I do control both companies. It is also a simple fact of life that I believe these two companies better get along together and help each other, not hurt each other." He added (and crossed out in pen): "Furthermore, if I have to knock your fucking heads together, the three of you [McKnight, Turnbull and Norm Gervais, the new marketing VP at M&S] are going to be friends and work together."[22] Jack sometimes made it impossible for these three to collaborate because he gave them contradictory instructions.

Earlier, on August 29, 1984, at the time the shareholdings to private investors were being negotiated, McKnight told him exactly what she thought of the perilous situation confronting them:

The question [is] *not* "should you proceed with the share offering despite a moral dilemma" but rather the question is "can this company survive and if so, how can it survive?" . . . I want to have it clear, however, that in my opinion if we continue with our present style of operations, the firm cannot and will not survive.

You are the owner, chairman and CEO. What McClelland & Stewart is today reflects your work, your stamp, your particular publishing genius (and I use that word advisedly). Despite any expressions to the contrary, your influence extends to the lowest levels of the firm and your involvement continues to be significant. I sensed last night that you felt the long-term solution to M&S's problems is to continue to do much of what we have done before, only *better*. . . . I disagree. What will solve the problems is not personnel changes but essential and elementary changes in publishing philosophy. I would go so far as to say that the nature of McClelland & Stewart must change to survive. . . .

Examples.

1. We spend thousands a year on unsolicited manuscripts. We should curtail that abruptly, sending ripples through the writing and government community. No longer will we be perceived of as unusually supportive of the literary community.

2. We spend $1.1 million on marketing. To survive we will have to cut expenses radically across the board. Marketing is a prime target [for budget reduction], yet to cut the marketing budget goes against your grain, I know, and against all your experience.

3. Author relations. We will have to be far tougher on "star" authors, in some instances. [Roloff Beny should not be published by M&S in the future; she was also critical of Lorraine Monk's *Canada with Love* (1982) and *Ontario: A Loving Look* (1984), books of photography that, despite their apparent profitability, had huge production and thus infrastructure costs.]

4. Composition of the list. [A recent market survey] tells us bookstores can't move fiction and high-priced picture books. We must cut back in these areas, and expand in others. Do more bread and butter and less cake.

I think you feel the only hope is to do what we've been stellar at in the past, with new people and better people. I believe the market changes and economic changes are such that it is no longer possible to succeed with that style of publishing unless you have immense funds behind you.

[She does not think she, Len Cummings, the chief financial officer, and Jack are a] team for many reasons, some of which I suspect are irremediable. We lack the necessary degree of mutual trust and respect.

I cannot see any hope for the future unless you do two things:

1. Install senior-level management in whom you have confidence and trust.
2. And then, let go. Allow that management authority without interference. Like Alfred Knopf Sr., say to authors, politicians, booksellers, the world, "Alas, I am now emeritus and can only weep with you." Having said that, it follows that you may have my resignation when and if you feel you need it.

Letting go was exactly what Jack was unable to do; in most ways, his role at M&S did not change significantly. In a very subtle way, McKnight was also telling Jack that he might have created a great institution in M&S, but he was not greater than the resulting institution. To a large degree, Jack was the victim of his own success. He was trapped within the machinery he had invented.

Jack's concept of publishing had not shifted. When Len Cummings finally did resign in 1984, Jack wrote a memorandum that clearly shows the deeply conflicted sides of him as a publisher: "If you really want to leave, you have more than discharged your obligation to me, the company. . . . I will regret your departure." For Jack, the author still came first. Len "would kill the company by cutbacks and conservation. . . . I can't live that way—we not only prophesy, we predetermine our own failure." In his heart of hearts, Len did not believe that M&S could win. Jack was not so sure: "I intend to try." He also told Len, "You believe money management is a virtue. I do, but to a lesser degree. You are ambitious. So am I *now*, but only in a context of what I value."[23] What Jack esteemed was a vision of the publishing enterprise that simply did not make financial sense in the business world of the eighties. This was the continuing issue that Jack had faced throughout his entire career in the book trade.

Jack's belief in the author continued to be paramount. In 1983, Aritha van Herk, who had won the Seal Books prize for *Judith* and whose second novel had appeared in 1981, had submitted the manuscript of a third. Her editor, Lily Miller, considered the book basically unredeemable. She asked Jack to take a look at it. On May 12, he gave Lily his advice:

> If we go back to the starting block, what we have is a good writer, a proven writer, with a fine mind and a good track record. We have a writer who is steeped in literature, Canadian and otherwise. We have an individual who cares, who is determined to succeed, who is independent. . . . We can't say to her effectively that this is a mess. In fact, I think it is a mess, but having called it that, I think it would be totally wrong to think for a minute that it is without impressive redeeming features. . . . But what do we do about it? First, I think we tell her that she needs another six months, perhaps eight months, perhaps longer, of concerted work on this one. . . . You know and I know that it is the easiest possible course in publishing because of the economics and the pressures to be negative and critical. It is much more difficult to assess the odds properly and understand our total function. I am convinced that Aritha can ultimately pull this one off, but I am equally convinced that she desperately needs help and direction at the present time. So all you have to do is pull off a miracle. So what else is new?[24]

On the following day, a surprised—and very moved—Lily Miller responded, "Your memo about Aritha's manuscript is astonishing. Where do you find all that energy, that conviction. No one will ever replace you, Jack. You can be sure I will do my very best." The novel under consideration was *No Fixed Address: An Amorous Journey*, not published by M&S until 1986, when it was shortlisted for a Governor General's Award.

One M&S novel not shortlisted was *Masquerade: 15 Variations on a Theme of Sexual Fantasy* by an unknown "East European immigrant" named Lisa Kroniuk, whose agent was Elsa Franklin. Reviews were lukewarm, copies did not move from bookstores and prominent Toronto literati were surprised to be invited to a mysterious event several weeks after publication at the King Edward Hotel, where it was eventually revealed that Lisa Kroniuk was Pierre Berton. Jack was vis-ibly shaken by the rev-elation, although, like most of the book's readers, he had not in any way been affected by the novel's unerotic eroticism.

In January 1984, in a letter to Peter Gzowski guaranteeing a substantial advance on a new book, Jack himself seemed to be aware of the para-doxical nature of the deal he was making and the fact that he rather than McKnight was making it.

> I am a victim of my own current philosophies and must now rec-oncile that with an apparent aberration that would appear to be in direct conflict with policies that I have imposed and hope to see car-ried out in the future in both companies.
>
> I have, in appointing Linda, said, "Be a great publisher, enhance the M&S image but in so doing you must improve cash flow and bottom line. Don't take any risks, and be a much better business manager than I ever was." At Seal, I have said, "Let's improve prof-itability and forget anything 'worthwhile' or 'chancy.'"
>
> Now, along comes an author who says:
>
> (a) I want a bagful of money up front.
>
> (b) Don't bug me with deadlines.
>
> (c) I don't really know the shape or the form of the book yet.
>
> (d) It will be the best book I have ever written, if I can do it. If I can't, I'll give up writing.
>
> So what do I do? Great, I say! We will support you.[25]

Jack goes on to spell out why he will take such a chance—Gzowski's track record and his celebrity status being among the reasons—but the decision reflects Jack's great strengths and his great weaknesses as a pub-lisher. In a unilateral way, he is committing a great deal of money to a potentially impossible project; in his own unique way, he is expressing his belief in a writer who has already been extremely successful.

Loyalty to authors could obviously not be abandoned by Jack. He also retained his flair for publicity, when he stage-managed the Night of the 100 Authors for the Writers' Development Trust in the autumn of 1982 and pleaded with Margaret Laurence to attend:

> I want you at the dinner so much, Margaret, that I will, if necessary, drive to Lakefield to pick you up and bring you back, take you to the dinner, have you live at my place. . . . Your presence has been sold to businessman Donald Early, who has bought a table so that he will have Margaret Laurence as his guest. You may not remember Donald Early, but I hope you will. He is the chairman of the executive committee at McClelland & Stewart. You have met him at board meetings at days gone by. A very charming man. He is a partner in Greenshields and Company. You will like the people with him. It will be an old-home week. It will be a very pleasant evening. . . . Think back how many times I have laid a trip on you. Not very often. This time I am laying a real trip. Come. Please phone Marge on receipt of this letter and say, "Okay, tell the boss or old Jake that I will be there. I will be there reluctantly, but I will be there."[26]

Margaret, who had never liked Jack's publicity and fundraising stunts, succumbed to the Boss's charm. She and the other chosen writers were to parade into a large, glittering ballroom, where they were to be joined by their host or hosts. To her agent, John Cushman, whom she had seen in Toronto earlier that day, she related her experience that evening: "Thank God, I had lunch with you that day. . . . That was the only good thing that happened. . . . After the authors' cocktail party, we, the authors, were led as lambs to the slaughter, into what was apparently a long basement corridor connecting one kitchen with another. . . . The corridor was airless. . . . My feet hurt. I got more and more irritated. . . . 'If this line does not move soon,' I proclaimed, 'I AM GOING HOME,' [whereupon the publicist babysitting her offered to take her in before anyone else]. 'Are you out of your head? I'm a socialist!' "[27] Finally, when Margaret and the other writers reached the dining room, Donald Early was not there.

Mordecai Richler's involvement with the celebrated event was even more comical. He told his publisher:

Jack, I adore you. You're a fine fellow. A cherished friend. But this
sort of vulgarity really goes against my nature. I want no part of it.
I'm not a starlet, neither am I running for office, and I would be
appalled to enter any dining room "with appropriate lights and
musical fanfare." I don't want to dance to the Spitfires, whoever they
are. Neither do I wish to eat fruit salad and factory chicken with the
E. B. Eddy Company. . . . I prefer to dine with friends and pay my
own bill.

Such an evening is just not for me. I would only be miserable.
I would drink too much. I would be rude. I don't want to sign
posters or appear on TV. I'd feel like a fool. . . . Please don't phone
and try to convince me to come. I do not wish to attend. I will not.[28]

In such situations, Jack's powers of persuasion remained both remarkable and tough:

I share your view that it will probably be a horrendous event, that
you will get drunk (and so will I). I share all those perceptions, but
it is an event in a good cause and I am the one that will end up with
egg on his face if you don't turn up and I would resent that. Surely
to Christ you can go through a couple of hours of misery. If you
don't want to be introduced in the spotlight, then you don't have to
as long as you don't tell anybody else in advance.

Now, as to your table . . . you had agreed to sit with one of the
biggest assholes of all time. . . . He has to be in Europe—well, hell,
I think that is a break for you. I will send you information about
who will be at the E. B. Eddy table—they don't even know yet.
They will probably turn out to be thoroughly charming people,
and as I have said, you will only be with them for about an hour
and a half.

So look at it this way—you are doing it for me. Over the years
I have done some things for you—and you have done some things
for me—and it is probably a fair balance but I absolutely *do need
and insist on this one!*[29]

But Richler was able to resist Jack's considerable charm. He did not attend.

Jack was not able to summon up the same comical and genial tone in his dealings with Linda McKnight. His relationship with her became increasingly fraught, as can be seen in this snippet from a memorandum: "What I am giving you now is a direction. I have sworn that I will not give you direction, but this is a direction. . . . As I keep telling you, I think you are doing a terrific job in a lousy position. I did it without any policy guidance except policy guidance that I made up. I once tried to devise a policy book and get it approved first by our executive committee and then by the board. I got up to about twenty pages before I gave up because that took six months. Everyone is too opinionated in this fucking business."[30] So, of course, was Jack.

In the autumn of 1984, help seemed to be on the way when Norm Gervais was appointed vice-president, marketing and sales. Gervais had been instrumental in building Avon Books of Canada and had then become vice-president of sales for the same company in the States. His involvement with M&S began when he sold them the hardcover rights to Walter Gretzky and Jim Taylor's biography of Walter's hockey-playing son, Wayne—*Gretzky: From the Back Yard Rink to the Stanley Cup* (1984). Disenchanted with working in New York, Gervais was happy to return to Canada, although he faced a difficult situation: many M&S fall titles could not be published until mid-November 1984 because of delays caused by the firm's inability to pay various printers. Nevertheless, he immediately promised there would be no more Atrium fire sales, even though the company was planning to hold a nationwide sale that January.

Gervais, who was in his early thirties, was used to moving thousands of units of a particular book. He was a numbers man. Culturally, he was not prepared for the relatively low print runs of some M&S titles or for worrying about temperamental authors. Gervais was accompanied to M&S by his own personally selected sales force, a group of men who liked foil and embossed book covers. Their motto was to force retailers to take the product and sell books like "shit through a goose." Since his business world had nothing to do with M&S, Gervais's enthusiasm diminished rapidly. He felt defeated by his new job, and simply "lost it"; his health suddenly deteriorated. He and his team left within six months, obviously not having been able to accomplish the impossible. Once again, Jack, the eternal optimist, had expected great things: when Gervais was appointed, Jack told the board, "If he was only half as good as his track record and a third as good as he thought he was, he would be exactly what we needed."[31] Gervais, from the high-volume mass-market world, had been hired to sell books in the more modest M&S environment, whereas Janet Turnbull was required to make Seal a viable mass-market Canadian publishing firm. Linda McKnight, meanwhile, was in the uncomfortable middle—she was trying to turn M&S around while working with increasingly opposing signals as to the direction she should take.

Several years earlier, M&S had licensed to Seal, for a set period of time, the rights to six Lucy Maud Montgomery books. That licence was about to expire. M&S wanted to reissue those books as a set, along with two other Montgomery titles (*Rilla of Ingleside* and *Rainbow Valley*) by the same author, and rights had never been granted to Seal. Many years before, Ethel McClelland and Doris Stewart had purchased 50 per cent of the royalties from Chester Cameron Macdonald, the author's son, and so Jack controlled a portion of the rights to the Montgomery books personally and received the royalties from them.

Janet Turnbull had been hired by Jack to run Seal Books just as she was on the verge of becoming the managing editor of Collins Canada. Since she had committed herself to the Collins position, she tried to say no to Jack, who had launched "The Great Seal Hunt" to find a publisher to succeed Tanya Long, Anna Porter's successor. When he insisted, Turnbull said she would take the Seal job only if she would be the Seal publisher in fact as well as name. He agreed. Soon, Turnbull found herself caught between Jack on the one hand and on the other her Bantam bosses in New York, Alun Davies and Alberto Vitale. The Americans were not unsympathetic to Jack, but they wanted Seal run in a financially responsible way. Jack, Turnbull soon found out, had little understanding of the demands of mass-market selling; he wanted to promote Seal titles as if they were M&S hardbacks. Her firm did well, although its profits were not fantastic.

When Turnbull inquired about the rights to *Rilla of Ingleside* and *Rainbow Valley*, she was told by the M&S editorial director, Valerie Thompson, on March 14, 1985, that they were not for sale because of M&S's own plans to publish them. Turnbull subsequently spoke to Jack, who told her, "Consider them sold." Thompson was aggrieved and puzzled: "Evidently the books . . . have already been printed with Seal's imprint. . . . Will someone please tell me what is going on vis-à-vis M&S and Seal so I can do my job?"[32] When Thompson complained to McKnight, she made the point that not only had M&S lost rights that supposedly belonged to them but also they had heard of the loss from their competitors! On that day, McKnight sent Jack a memo:

> When we spoke briefly [this past] Friday afternoon on this subject, I presumed you were referring to the L. M. Montgomery titles already licensed to Seal and due either for retrieval or extension of license this year—not to titles on which we currently hold rights and which we had scheduled for reissue this fall. For me to accept this sale would be dereliction of my responsibilities. . . . The reality, Jack, is that we have another publishing house calling us and telling us we're selling them rights, in direct contradiction to our announced publishing program.
>
> Most important, though, is that we are losing income thereby. Seal will profit this fall, not M&S. . . . Jack, this is a difficult scenario for you, I appreciate, but I must act in the interests of McClelland & Stewart on this. I perceive it to be a clear conflict of interest situation. I cannot accept it.[33]

Eleven days later, not having heard from Jack but having learned that the Seal on-press date had been delayed a month, she wrote him again. He returned the memo to her with this comment attached: "Linda:

L. M. Montgomery will be Seal. Will discuss very soon but we need the cash. J."[34]

McKnight wrote again, summarizing what had happened and adding that the fee to be received from Seal was negligible. On May 8, she made this point to him yet again in a memo, which he returned with the comment that many more titles were involved, not just Montgomery. "The decision stands but let's discuss."

A document from the day before, written by Janet Turnbull, itemized other titles that Seal would be requesting from M&S. The list included "all titles" by Farley Mowat, Margaret Laurence, Margaret Atwood, Mordecai Richler, the popular novelist Charlotte Vale Allen and Peter Newman as well as Montgomery. For each title on the list, there are several figures given: annual rate of sale, royalty payment, licence years required, advance, royalty account status. McKnight was enraged, feeling that the money Seal was offering was insulting and thus demeaning (in the past, they had paid $125,000 for five W. O. Mitchell titles; now their renewal offer for six Atwoods was $38,000 to $40,000). "It is more than obvious that I do not have the authority to halt an action I consider damaging to McClelland & Stewart," she wrote to Jack. "I therefore have no option but to submit my resignation herewith to you and to the board of directors."[35] She obviously felt an unprofitable company was being forced to become even more unprofitable at the expense of another, prospering company. According to Jack, there was a world of difference—and therefore not much competition—between Seal's mass-market operation and M&S's low-key efforts in the same arena.

In reporting McKnight's departure, *The Globe and Mail* strongly implied that M&S was in a state of total disarray. A furious Jack responded in a circuitous way to the allegations: "First, that McClelland & Stewart is tottering! I say the term 'tottering' is ridiculous and totally inappropriate. That we are 'beleaguered.' Yes we are. We are beleaguered by *The Globe and Mail.* It has been suggested that we are 'financially troubled.' Let me say honestly that we had no material financial difficulties until *The Globe* launched its attack."[36] A few days later, Jack commented obliquely on the (accurately) reported reasons for McKnight's resignation: "Although it's common publishing practice to lease paperback rights whenever it's financially attractive to both the company and the author, everyone knows that a publishing house cannot simply transfer titles without the approval of the authors involved."[37]

What Linda McKnight and *The Globe* were not aware of was that Anna Porter and Jack McClelland had been discussing a merger between Key Porter Books and M&S during the winter of 1985, as a letter Jack wrote to Anna on April 3, 1985, reveals: "I am willing to remain as chairman but only on the condition that I will have no formal duties except to consult with you whenever you want. I really want to get out of active participation and responsibility in this trade. You would become chief executive officer. . . . That would give you time to decide about Linda's future. She could remain president and chief operating officer—which she is now—until you decide that." Key Porter would have had to invest $500,000 but would have been able to save a substantial amount of money in warehouse costs and other overhead. This venture was not pursued further.

Jack returned to the presidency of M&S, trying to put as good a face as possible on problems that never went away. In a letter to the nature writers Janet and John Foster, in response to their query about what happened with their book *Adventures in Wild Canada* (1984), which sold six thousand copies and then seemed to "vanish," Jack said:

Despite our very impressive history, it is a simple matter of fact that M&S was in disarray in the fall of 1984. We were involved in a major refinancing. That is how I spent my time. It took much longer than anticipated. It was not, in fact, completed until early October. This delayed our books—but meanwhile our marketing and sales staff were in disarray—quite apart from the late publication dates of most of the books. That disarray was compounded by the appointment of a new sales and marketing team who turned out to be not a minor but a major disaster. I could blame other people for that but I will not. I should have intervened and I did not. We went through an impossibly bad period and misadventure relating in my opinion to the mental and physical breakdown of one of the key new appointees to our staff [Gervais]. It happened. It was real and it was very unfortunate and very costly. That was followed by a major attack on the company from *The Globe and Mail*—the sources still undetermined—that cost us very heavily.

He goes on to say how strong M&S has since become, with more financial depth, more proficient sales staff. He himself was going to be around "for a long time. I am back at work full-time and you are going to see . . . many improvements and changes at M&S—all on the up side." He hoped they would "have faith" and want to continue with the firm: "I think you people are superb and we have let you down very badly. In recent years we have let a few people down, but I don't think it is ever going to happen again."[38]

*Jack, circa 1984*

But Jack's heart was no longer in publishing. Avie Bennett, the real estate developer who had invested in M&S in 1984 and subsequently become a member of the board of directors, helped Jack with some financial arrangement with the Royal Bank. Subsequently, Jack called him to say payment was due to the bank in a few days and M&S could not meet it. Bennett asked, "Do you want to sell the firm?" Jack responded somewhat despondently, "Yeah, I'm fed up." There was a subtle irony at work: Avie had recently performed as a stretcher-bearer in the National Ballet of Canada's *Nutcracker* (he would later celebrate his new profession by asking the National Ballet—he was an avid patron—to give a performance of *Don Quixote*, the story of a man who chases windmills).

Until that moment, Bennett had no idea he wanted to purchase M&S. According to published reports, the purchase price was $2.1 million: $1 million to Jack and the remaining amount to pay off the other private investors who had put money into the company. It is rumoured that Bennett immediately ploughed a further $1 million into the company. At the party marking the sale, a relieved Marge spoke of the end of an era: "I typed his speech this morning and I was never happier." Jack himself had mixed feelings: "I'm delighted to be able to turn over the albatross to a man I respect and a man who can afford it."[39]

Jack agreed at the time to stay on in some vague capacity for five years. Two years later, in February 1987, he realized this was a huge error: "When you sell a company, and are no longer the boss, you should get out. I don't like being second-guessed." He also said, "I made a mistake. If you no longer have complete control, you should get out. You shouldn't hang around. . . . I've had a love affair with Canadian authors. I have emotional ties which will still continue. I don't have a single regret, except for the fact that I never achieved my goal of becoming wealthy. I've had a fun career."[40]

The split between Jack and Avie was amicable. (Adrienne Clarkson succeeded Jack as publisher.) Bennett has an enormous reverence for Jack. However, there was a crucial misunderstanding: Jack thought he was staying on as publisher, essentially the editorial director of the firm now owned by Bennett; Avie's idea was that Jack stay on as a consultant to whom he could turn for advice when he needed it. Avie felt Jack was simply a senior adviser; Jack thought he was still running the show.

When Avie moved M&S from the wilds of East York to the building he owned on University Avenue, gossip said Jack was relegated to a small, out-of-the-way office. This is simply untrue: his medium-size office was only one door away from Bennett's. Whereas Jack was the showman par excellence, Avie preferred to work in a way suited to the shy, reclusive side of his nature.

Jack felt humiliated—as well as relieved—at having sold the firm in a money-losing position, as it was when he had handed it over to Bennett. As Avie became more and more a hands-on owner of M&S, he would become angry at old-time staff members who consulted Jack rather than him. "Why do you go to Jack?" he asked one startled editor. Gradually Jack sensed that the climate of the new M&S had changed: he was certain most employees were eager to please Avie. Jack felt he was a has-been. He really had no choice but to leave. At another level, Jack knew he was the world's worst employee; he also realized he had never been a team player.

In February 1987, Jack sold his controlling interest in Seal to Key Porter Books, although Avie had wanted to purchase it in order to develop an ancillary trade paperback arm to M&S's publishing program. At that time, Jack said, "When I sold M&S, I retained control of Seal. But publishing's a young man's trade and a full-time occupation. If you are leaving, then leave. Yogi Berra once said, 'It's never over until it's over.' Well, it's all over for me."[40]

Jack's next reincarnation was as a literary agent. Marge Hodgeman moved from M&S to work once again as his assistant, and two of Jack's daughters became involved: Sarah, who was her father's associate in Toronto, and Suzanne, his agency's representative in London. Nevertheless, he felt increasingly uncomfortable in his new role. In 1993, he summed it up this way: "The fact is I am no longer a literary agent. To tell you the truth, I don't know why I was foolish enough to get into the field after I sold and retired from McClelland & Stewart. The simple fact is that I hated [being an agent], hated being caught between slow-moving publishers who would take anywhere from four months to a year to make a decision on one hand and quite naturally the impatient authors on the other hand. Financially it could be very rewarding but not sufficiently so to justify the frustration of it all."[41] Some books were fun to place, such as Trent Frayne's *Tales of an Athletic Supporter* (1991). "For God's sake," Jack in the role of muse told his sportswriter friend, "get all that stuff down before you atrophy!" His other words of encouragement were in even plainer language: "Why don't you get off your butt and send me some athletic supporter stuff? You're a jock, aren't you?" As soon as Trent gave him two sample chapters, Jack sent them to a number of publishers and obtained a handsome offer from M&S.[42]

If being a publisher in the eighties and nineties was a young person's game, so was being a literary agent. As Jack himself ultimately recognized, he did not have the patience or the acumen of a Michael Levine. Jack felt a lack of control in his new profession: he was used to deciding what got published and what the advance would be. Now, he had to sell books to publishing houses who determined what a book was worth to them; once a book was sold, he had little effective control over it. To a man used to having a big say, his new calling was disastrous. To add to his difficulties, he became an agent just as the effects of the recession were being felt in the book world: advances were plummeting.

Later, Jack decided to write his memoirs, but this was not a task he found congenial, perhaps because his feelings about the whole publishing enterprise remained deeply ambivalent and profoundly conflicted. In many ways, he had been extraordinarily successful, but he also felt that he had been treading through a minefield his entire career, things having blown up in his face many times: "Re the memoirs. It's actually the wooden end of the rake that smashes the skull of the publisher. You have to step on the head of the rake and it flies up and slugs you in the back of the head. That is why, in fact, my memoirs are titled 'My Rose Garden.' I'm walking there in the moonlight when I step on the rake."[43] And so Jack's incarnations as an agent and as a memoirist turned out to be rather short postscripts to a long career devoted to Canadian writers, a career that really ended in 1985 when he stepped on the rake and sold M&S to Avie Bennett. It was a painful time for Jack but as a man now in his seventies, he can look back with pride and affection at what he accomplished, and while he no longer reads their manuscripts, he still counts among his closest friends writers he first brought to public attention at M&S.

Despite the many headaches he suffered during his publishing years, Jack took great joy in his work. He truly loved his authors, treasured their work and found enormous satisfaction in making their books available to the largest possible public. He was a true Canadian hero, a man who took on almost insurmountable forces in pursuit of his dream.

Jack was fiercely loyal. As Margaret Atwood once put it, "He'd go to the firing squad for you." Leonard Cohen claimed Jack liked to present "himself as a hell-raking, mean-assed guy, but he's adorable." He was a walking, talking example of all bark, no bite. He was also modest. Throughout his entire career as a publisher, Jack forbade authors to thank him in any list of acknowledgments.

Margaret Laurence, who knew the reverence Jack had for his authors, could have been speaking for all the other M&S writers when she said in 1986, "He is a Canadian pioneer. He has risked his life for us, Canadian writers. I think we have proved him right. Thanks, Boss."

Margaret Atwood maintains that Jack "swung onto the scene like a swashbuckling pirate." He did this at a time when Canadians "did not believe they had a literature, or if they did have one, it wasn't very good or interesting." In Jack's case, the pirate uncovered great treasure.

Canadian literature certainly existed before Jack McClelland, but he made it flourish. He did so by encouraging our authors, making their books available and of interest to the general public. He challenged the individual Canadian's tendency to think what was done outside the borders of this country more significant than what was accomplished here. He worked to sever the colonial ties that bound our country's culture to Britain and to distinguish Canadian literature from American. No single person has done more to raise the profile of Canadian culture to Canadians. A rival, James Lorimer, who disagreed with Jack's insistence on showcasing himself as the only significant Canadian publisher, recalls the immensity of Jack's contribution: "He provided a room into which other people like myself could enter and move."

Matt Cohen says Jack was "the man who decided Canada should have a literature made to its measure, invented it, published it, did everything possible to attract the spotlight to himself, his writers, their books until Canadians first started reading them, then wanted them." Jack, it can be reasonably claimed, did more to unite Canada than any politician.

Pierre Berton has truthfully called Jack "the last of the personal publishers." Indeed, Jack listened attentively to his writers, not to number crunchers. "Publishing was not a business for him; it was a calling," Berton has also observed.

Jack also made publishing fun. At the time Scott McIntyre resigned to launch his own publishing house, Douglas & McIntyre, he told his boss, "I wouldn't have missed McClelland & Stewart for the world." When Linda McKnight, now a literary agent in Toronto, speaks of Jack, her voice is filled with affection. And as another former employee, Anna Porter, has observed, he has also "given us all a great deal to live up to."

In 1993, Farley Mowat wrote a serio-comic elegy that puts everything in perspective:

> Friend, mentor, nurse and brother—
> In all this Nation there's no other
> Who has served writers as he has
> With faith, conviction and pizzaz.
> If CANLIT thrives, it is because of Jack.
> By God, I wish . . . I wish that he was back![44]

Jack McClelland's commitment to publishing constitutes the most sustained attempt by a single person to define and enhance Canadian cultural identity. He is our Prospero, the man who shared his love of books with his fellow countrymen. His legacy is enormous. We remain in his debt.

# WHO WAS WHO AT M&S,
## 1946−87

This list, which is not by any means a complete one of the persons who worked with and for Jack McClelland, is confined to those mentioned in the text. Because of the incomplete presence in the archives of M&S personnel and other files, it has not always been possible to definitively state when a person began and ended his or her employment, or to obtain, in some cases, more particulars.

**Bowles**, Patricia. Publicity manager at M&S from 1974 to 76.

**Brown**, Russell. Poetry editor at M&S, mid-1980s. Brown is the editor of, among others, *An Anthology of Canadian Literature in English* (1982) and *The Collected Poems of Al Purdy* (1986).

**Crean**, Patrick. Responsible for the slush pile, 1971–72; editor, 1972–75.

**Cummings**, Len. Cummings started with M&S in approximately 1978 and became vice-president of finance in 1983, assuming overall responsibility for accounting, data processing, administration and fulfillment operations. He resigned December 31, 1984.

**Dragland**, Stan. Poetry editor, M&S, 1980s. Dragland is the editor of, among others, two books on Duncan Campbell Scott: *Duncan Campbell Scott: A Book of Criticism* (1974) and *Floating Voice: Duncan Campbell Scott and the Literature of Treaty 9* (1992).

**Ford**, J. Wilfred. Appointed general manager and vice-president of M&S in 1940.

**Franklin**, Elsa. M&S board member, Franklin was described in *The Toronto Star* (December 19, 1982) as the "organizer of the multi-million-dollar marketing of Berton's books and wide-ranging TV interests (she's full partner in the company that owns a number of his shows)." She has worked as a TV and public relations consultant and was the originator and producer of the CBC television program *Under Attack*.

**French**, Donald Graham. A former teacher and newspaper man, French became M&S's literary editor and adviser in 1920; he was editor-in-chief when he died in 1945. French was an early promoter of Canadian literature and founded the Canadian Literature Club of Toronto in 1918. He edited several of M&S's most well known early books, notably, *Standard Canadian Reciter: A Book of the Best Readings and Recitations from Canadian Literature* (1918) and *Famous Canadian Stories Re-Told for Children* (1923, with subsequent revised editions in 1926, 1931 and 1945).

**Fry**, Pamela. Became a trade editor in 1966 and edited authors such as Margaret Atwood. Fry left M&S in 1971 to work on a federal government task force.

**Gervais**, Norm. Director of sales and marketing. Appointed vice-president in late 1984. Resigned for health reasons, 1985. He came to M&S from the American mass-market publishers Avon Books.

**Gilmore**, Christina. Head bookkeeper at M&S when Jack began working with the firm in 1946.

**Glossop**, Jennifer. Editor at M&S, late 1970s, working with authors such as Judy LaMarsh and Margaret Laurence.

**Goodchild**, Frederick D. John McClelland's original business partner. The two men, who had both been employed at the Methodist Book and Publishing House (later Ryerson Press), established McClelland & Goodchild in 1906 as a library supply house and published their first book in 1909. Goodchild left the firm in 1918 to start his own short-lived publishing house, Frederick D. Goodchild.

**Hodgeman**, Marge. Jack's long-time assistant, secretary and confidante. Born in 1929, she joined M&S in 1963, worked for Jack until his departure from M&S in 1985 and was a partner in Jack McClelland & Associates, Jack's literary agency, until her death in 1993.

**Hunter**, Tom. Warehouse boss when Jack joined the firm in 1946.

**Hutchinson**, Sybil. Editor-in-chief at M&S when Jack joined the firm in 1946. Resigned 1950.

**Kane**, Hugh. In 1936, Kane was the M&S sales representative for Western Canada. He was appointed production and advertising manager in 1946 and was elected to M&S board of directors. In 1953 he became vice-president, and in 1961 executive vice-president. Kane left M&S in 1969 to join Macmillan Co. of Canada as president. He was rehired in 1976 to serve as president and managing director of the Natural Science Library of Canada Ltd., an M&S subsidiary. Kane died in October 1984.

**Lee**, Dennis. Poet, essayist and editor, Lee was co-founder of the House of Anansi Press and worked as a literary consultant for Macmillan as well as M&S (1981–84). He won the Governor General's Award for poetry in 1972 for *Civil Elegies and Other Poems* and was the subject of the tribute *Task of Passion: Dennis Lee at Mid-Career* (1982), which was edited by a later M&S poetry editor, Stan Dragland.

**Martin**, Robert. Solicitor for M&S and long-time member of the firm's board of directors. Martin dealt with virtually all legal matters for M&S from vetting manuscripts for libel to representing the company in any actions against it.

**McGill**, David. McGill joined M&S in 1963 at the age of thirty-three after a stint as a manager in Eaton's book department. He was appointed manager of trade division in 1969. He became director of associate publishing, reprints, special markets and inventories in 1974. As vice-president of M&S in 1983, McGill was responsible for backlist sales, inventory control, associated duties in agency relations and special sales areas such as book clubs.

**McKnight**, Linda. President and publisher, 1983. McKnight joined M&S at the age of twenty-eight in 1969 as an editor, after working for Copp Clark. She held various other positions throughout her time with M&S, including senior educational editor, managing editor, director of publishing and vice-president, publishing. McKnight resigned in 1985 after clashing with Jack on the sale of M&S book rights to Seal.

**Mew**, Diane. M&S editor, 1961–68. Reponsible for Carleton Library Series.

**Miller**, Lily Poritz. Editor. Joined M&S in 1972 after working for various New York publishers. She edited many major M&S authors, notably Farley Mowat. Lily was one of a few key people to whom Jack sent drafts of his memoirs in the early 1990s.

**Myers**, John C. Manager of M&S's educational division, which opened in 1946. Was still active in the company in 1952.

**Nelson**, Robert J. (Bob). Was appointed director of sales in 1944 and was general manager of M&S when Jack joined the firm in 1946. Nelson was a member of the M&S board of directors from 1944 to 1952. He resigned in 1953 to form his own firm with George M. Foster and John R. Scott.

**Newfeld**, Frank. Designer, M&S. Appointed creative director November 1966, with responsibility for the design and manufacture of all M&S products, advertisements and catalogues. He became vice-president, publishing, in December 1969, in charge of the "conceptual planning and review of all [M&S] publications with emphasis on the visual and manufacturing side."

**Newlove**, John. Newlove was senior editor at M&S from 1970 to 1974, primarily responsible for poetry. A well-known poet in his own right, his books have been published for over three decades, several of them by M&S. Newlove won the 1972 Governor General's Award for poetry for *Lies*. He also edited (for M&S) *Canadian Poetry: The Modern Era* (1977). He has been writer-in-residence at numerous institutions across Canada.

**Porter (Szigethy)**, Anna. Named editorial director, 1974, Anna Porter joined M&S in 1969 at the age of twenty-six. She had completed an M.A. in English literature, and had worked for British publishers Cassell and Collier Macmillan. She became executive editor at M&S in 1970. In 1977, she was appointed president of M&S–Bantam Ltd., which published Seal Books. She resigned in 1982 to establish her own publishing house, Key Porter Books.

**Pratt**, Claire. Senior editor, 1957–64. An artist early in her career, Pratt ran her own book firm and was an editor with Harvard University Press. Her father was the Canadian poet E.J. Pratt.

**Rackliffe**, John (Jack). Editorial department, early 1960s.

**Ray**, Glenda. Publicist at M&S, late 1970s.

**Ritchie**, L. H. (Laurence). A chartered accountant, Ritchie was appointed vice-president and general manager of M&S in 1969 at the age of thirty-one. A statement in the files on Jack's father's estate says that Ritchie was an audit manager and management consultant with Clarkson, Gordon Co., which had been brought in to negotiate with M&S creditors to prevent bankruptcy in 1968 following the Royal Bank's decision in early 1968 to call its M&S loan. Ritchie was sent to M&S prior to May 15th 1968 to act as a full-time on-site consultant. He became a shareholder in the company in 1971. Documents in the archives indicate that he left M&S in 1978.

**Savage**, Mark J. Salesman in the educational division, 1948. Director, educational division, 1950. Sales manager for medical, technical and educational books, 1952, 1953. Elected to M&S board of directors in 1953 and was still a member in 1969. Appointed vice-president, administration, August 1966. His employment was terminated by Jack McClelland in 1967.

**Shaw**, David. Art director at M&S in 1970s.

**Solecki**, Sam. Poetry editor, 1980s. Solecki is a professor of English at the University of Toronto and is the editor of *Spider Blues: Essays on Michael Ondaatje* (1985), *Talkin' Moscow Blues/Josef Skvorecky* (1988), *Volleys* (1990), *The Achievement of Josef Skvorecky* (1992), *Rooms for Rent in the Outer Planets: Selected Poems, 1962–1996/Al Purdy* (1996) and *Imagining Canadian Literature: The Selected Letters of Jack McClelland* (1998). He was also editor of *The Canadian Forum*, 1979–82.

**Stewart**, George. John McClelland's business partner and co-founder of McClelland & Stewart. Stewart left Oxford University Press in 1913 to join McClelland and Frederick D. Goodchild, who had started McClelland & Goodchild in 1906. From 1913 to 1918, the firm was known as McClelland, Goodchild & Stewart, and became McClelland & Stewart in 1918 after Goodchild's departure. Stewart died in 1955 at the age of 79.

**Taylor**, Peter. Vice-president of M&S, 1979. After a career in journalism and public relations, Taylor joined M&S in 1971 as director of advertising, promotion and publicity. He resigned for personal reasons in 1982.

**Taylor**, Ruth. Joined M&S in 1960 as assistant to editor Claire Pratt and was Jack's executive assistant, 1961–64.

**Thompson**, Valerie. Editorial director, M&S, 1981, 1983. Handled acquisitions, supervising the manuscript evaluation process. Joined 1978 as executive editor.

**Totton**, Samuel J. Originally a teacher, Jim Totton joined M&S in 1951 as a salesman in the educational division. He was promoted to trade editor and in 1963 became editor-in-chief. In August 1966, he was vice-president and director of the educational division. Left in 1969 for a position at University of Toronto Press.

**Turnbull**, Janet. Publisher, Seal Books, May 1984. She also did editorial work for M&S in the 1970s.

**Turton**, Conway. Fiction editor, 1956. Along with co-worker Claire Pratt, Turton was instrumental in convincing Jack to publish the works of Marie-Claire Blais. Turton was still working for the firm in 1963 when she was involved in the editing of *The Trial of Steven Truscott* by Isabel LeBourdais.

**Walter**, Jan. Appointed director of publishing, April 12, 1982, she had previously worked for Macmillan and Hurtig Publishers. In her position at M&S, she was responsible for editing, design and production of all titles, and for the delivery of each season's list on time and on budget.

**Wilkinson**, Robert A. Comptroller, 1970 to at least 1974. Responsible for accounting and data-processing departments, including the preparation of royalty accounts and payments. A chartered accountant, Wilkinson began working for M&S circa 1968 at the age of thirty. He apparently left the company for some time, but had rejoined by mid-1976 (according to a letter sent by Marge Hodgeman to Mordecai Richler in June 1976). He was still with the firm in 1984.

**Wilson**, Catherine. Joined M&S circa 1967 at the age of twenty-six as assistant manager of the trade advertising department. Appointed advertising and promotion manager, August 1969, and promoted to director of promotion, publicity and public relations in 1970. Manager of trade publicity, 1972. She was championed by such authors as Farley Mowat and Mordecai Richler but was dismissed in 1972 after disputes involving Pierre Berton.

**Wilson**, Owen. Secretary treasurer and chair of finance committee, 1967. Member of board of directors, 1969. Resigned January 1969 to work at the Ontario College of Art.

**Yates**, Ross. Trade manager, 1952.

# SOURCES

*Archival resources*: This book is in large part based on the huge McClelland & Stewart Archives, 1948–1985, acquired by the William Ready Division of Archives and Research Collections, University Library, McMaster University in 1977, 1983 and 1985; and on nine accruals of the Jack McClelland Papers, acquired by McMaster between 1987 and 1997 and still in progress. Both are closed archives, but Mr. McClelland gave me and my research assistants permission to use them. All letters to and from Jack McClelland cited in this book, and all internal memoranda, company documents, reports, financial statements and other documents are from the M&S archives or the Jack McClelland archives unless otherwise stated.

*Books*: The bibliography devoted to Canadian publishing by Mark C. Bartlett, Fiona A. Black, and Bertram H. MacDonald, *A History of the Book in Canada* (Halifax: B. H. MacDonald, 1993) is useful; however, most of the entries cover publishing history well before 1946. Books by Canadian publishers include the following: John Morgan Gray, *Fun Tomorrow: Learning to Be a Publisher and Much Else* (Toronto: Macmillan, 1978); Mel Hurtig, *At Twilight in the Country: Memoirs of a Canadian Nationalist* (Toronto: Stoddart, 1996); Lorne Pierce, *On Publishers and*

*Publishing* (Toronto: Ryerson Press, 1951). The most important work on the history of McClelland & Stewart has been undertaken by Carl Spadoni and Judy Donnelly, *A Bibliography of McClelland and Stewart Imprints, 1909–1985: A Publisher's Legacy* (Toronto: ECW Press, 1994) and by George L. Parker, "A History of a Canadian Publishing House: A Study of the Relation between Publishing and the Profession of Writing, 1890–1940," unpublished doctoral dissertation: University of Toronto, 1969, and *The Beginnings of the Book Trade in Canada* (Toronto: University of Toronto Press, 1985). Other important works are Harald Bohne and Harry Van Ierssel, *Publishing: The Creative Business* (Toronto: University of Toronto Press, 1973); Delores Broten and Peter Birdsall, *Paper Phoenix: A History of Book Publishing in Canada* (Victoria: Canlit, 1980); C. H. Dickinson, *Lorne Pierce: A Profile* (Toronto: The Ryerson Press, 1965); Marsh Jeanneret, *God and Mammon: Universities as Publishers* (Toronto: Macmillan, 1989). I have found some books by and about English and American publishers to be extremely helpful: Bennett Cerf, *At Random* (New York: Random House, 1977); Tom Dardis, *Firebrand: The Life of Horace Liveright* (New York: Random House, 1995); Ruth Dudley Edwards, *Victor Gollancz: A Biography* (London: Gollancz, 1987); Desmond Flower, *Fellows in Foolscap: Memoirs of a Publisher* (London: Robert Hale, 1991); Sheila Hodges, *Gollancz: The Story of a Publishing House, 1928–1978* (London: Gollancz, 1978); John Lehmann, *Thrown to the Woolfs* (London: Weidenfeld & Nicolson, 1978); J. E. Morpurgo, *Allen Lane, King Penguin: A Biography* (London: Hutchinson, 1979); Charles Scribner, *In the Web of Ideas: The Education of a Publisher* (New York: Scribner, 1993); Wilfrid Sheed, *Frank and Maisie: A Memoir with Parents* (New York: Simon and Schuster, 1985); Fredric Warburg, *An Occupation for Gentlemen* (Boston: Houghton, Mifflin, 1960). The tribute volume *Jack McClelland: The Publisher of Canadian Literature* (Guadalajara: University of Guadalajara, 1996) contains some interesting recollections by various M&S authors. *Imagining Canadian Literature: The Selected Letters of Jack McClelland*, ed. Sam Solecki (Toronto: Key Porter, 1998) contains a generous sampling of Jack's correspondence, mainly with writers.

Any consideration of Canadian publishing must also take into account the reports by Royal Commissions and other federal and provincial agencies such as the 1951 Massey–Lévesque Commission on National Development in the Arts, Letters and Sciences, the 1957 Commission on Broadcasting and the 1961 Commission on Publications, centred on the magazine industry. The cultural history of Canada has been well served by a variety of diverse books such as Douglas Fetherling, *Way Down Deep in the Belly of the Beast: A Memoir of the Seventies* (Toronto: Lester, 1996), Robert Fulford, *Best Seat in the House: Memoirs of a Lucky Man* (Toronto: Collins, 1988), *The Arts in Canada*, ed. W. J. Keith and B.-Z. Shek, (Toronto: University of Toronto Press, 1980), Geoff Pevere and Greig Dymond, *Mondo Canuck: A Canadian Pop Culture Odyssey* (Scarborough: Prentice-Hall, 1996), *The Arts in Canada: A Stock-taking at Mid-century*, ed Malcolm Ross (Toronto: Macmillan, 1958).

*Newspaper and magazine articles:* Accounts of the day-to-day running of M&S by Ken Adachi, William French, Roy MacSkimming, Robert Fulford and other journalists in *The Globe and Mail* and *The Toronto Star* contain important pieces of information. The most considered accounts of Jack McClelland the publisher are to be found in the following magazine stories: Donald Cameron, "Jack McClelland and the Crisis in Canadian Publishing," *Saturday Night*, June 1971; Elspeth Cameron, "Adventures in the Book Trade," *Saturday Night*, November 1983; Susan Carson, "Jack McClelland: Valet, Wet Nurse and Publisher," *Globe Weekend Magazine*, March 10, 1973; Martin Knelman, "Business by the Book," *Financial Post Magazine*, October 1, 1983; David Olive, "Good Reviews," *Toronto Life*, June 1988; Marika Robert, "What Jack McClelland Has Done to Book Publishing in Canada," *Maclean's*, September 7, 1963, supplement; Judith Timson, "Jack McClelland Then and Now," *Toronto Life*, July 1980; Stephen Williams, "Avie Buys the House That Jack Built," *Toronto Life*, May 1986. *Quill & Quire* provides information on all aspects of the book trade in Canada and of course contains much useful information on JGM and M&S; see also

George L. Parker, "The Canadian Author and Publisher in the Twentieth Century," *Editor, Author and Publisher*, ed. William J. Howard (Toronto: University of Toronto Press, 1969), 26–46.

*Interviews:* Margaret Atwood, Margaret Barlow, Avie Bennett, David Berry, Pierre Berton, George Bowering, Phyllis Bruce, June Callwood, Matt Cohen, John Robert Colombo, Patrick Crean, Denis Deneau, Suzanne Drinkwater, Elsa Franklin, Sylvia Fraser, Trent Frayne, William French, Robert Fulford, Graeme Gibson, Peter Gzowski, Tony Hawke, Mel Hurtig, Janet Turnbull Irving, Sean Kane, Dennis Lee, James Lorimer, Carol McCabe, Anne McClelland, Jack and Elizabeth McClelland, Rob McClelland, Sarah McClelland, Linda McKnight, Louis Melzack, John Metcalf, Diane Mew, Lily Miller, Lorraine Monk, Claire and Farley Mowat, Ed Murphy, Frank Newfeld, John Newlove, Peter Newman, Iris Nowell, Anna Porter, Alvin Potter, Mordecai Richler, Peter Scaggs, David Shaw, Sam Solecki, Betty and Henry Stark, Peter Taylor, Ruth Taylor, Jan Walter, Catherine Wilson and Bob Young.

# SHORT TITLES

| | |
|---|---|
| JGM | Jack McClelland. |
| Cameron | Elspeth Cameron, "Adventures in the Book Trade," *Saturday Night*, November 1983. |
| "My Rose Garden" | "My Rose Garden, A Publishing Memoir," 82 pages in length, McMaster. |

"The First Day"                    "The First Day," 38-page memoir,
                                   McMaster.

Knelman                            Martin Knelman, "Business by the
                                   Book," *Financial Post Magazine*,
                                   October 1, 1983.

"The Publishing Scene"             "The Publishing Scene: An Interview,"
                                   *Canadian Author and Bookman* 40,
                                   No. 1 (Summer 1965).

Robert                             Marika Robert, "What Jack
                                   McClelland Has Done to Book
                                   Publishing in Canada," *Maclean's*,
                                   September 7, 1963, supplement.

Spadoni                            Carl Spadoni and Judy Donnelly, *A
                                   Bibliography of McClelland and
                                   Stewart Imprints, 1909–1985: A
                                   Publisher's Legacy* (Toronto: ECW
                                   Press, 1994).

Timson                             Judith Timson, "Jack McClelland
                                   Then and Now," *Toronto Life*, July
                                   1980.

# ENDNOTES

## 1. TO THE MANOR BORN

1 "Senior Bookman," *Saturday Night*, May 12, 1956: 43.
2 "St. Michael's Hospital," JGM manuscript.
3 Cameron, 30.
4 Spadoni, 25.
5 Cameron, 30.
6 Ian Wilkie was the informant. Cameron, 30.
7 Cameron, 30.
8 *The Star Weekly*, January 15, 1921.
9 Cameron, 30.
10 "Senior Bookman," *Saturday Night*, May 12, 1956.
11 Cameron, 30.
12 JGM to Matt Maychak, January 6, 1984.
13 John McClelland, June 1958.
14 Cameron, 29.
15 "My Rose Garden," 18.
16 IBID., 19.
17 IBID.
18 IBID., 20.
19 John Hodgson dinner speech, [1991].
20 Cameron, 30.
21 "Muskoka Memoirs," *Cottage Life* (June/July 1988), 100.
22 Cameron, 30.

23  IBID., 31.
24  IBID., 31.
25  IBID.
26  Deryck Thomson to Peter Gzowski, January 1987, copy in M&S archive.
27  Cameron, 31.
28  IBID., 31.
29  John McClelland to JGM, October 2, 1939.
30  Elizabeth McClelland Stark, "The Family and Its Members," circa 1938, 68 folio pages.
31  Cameron, 32.
32  IBID., 32.
33  JGM to Lily Miller, May 4, 1992.
34  JGM: Address to Alpha Delta Phi, November 12, 1982.
35  IBID.
36  JGM to Clare Shaver, April 14, 1992.
37  Cameron, 27.
38  IBID., 28. Norn Garriock provided this information.
39  JGM: Address to Alpha Delta Phi, November 12, 1982.
40  Cameron, 28.
41  Timson, 54.
42  JGM to Margaret McClelland, March 16, 1944.
43  JGM to Ethel McClelland, April 29, 1944.
44  DND statement of War Service Gratuity, December 5, 1945.
45  Cameron, 33.
46  IBID.

## 2. THE BOSS'S SON

1  JGM to John McClelland, May 6, 1944.
2  IBID.
3  "My Rose Garden," No 2, 3.
4  Timson, 53.
5  "The First Day," 3.
6  Cameron, 34.
7  "My Rose Garden," 28.
8  IBID., 24.
9  September 19, 1946 and September 22, 1955.
10  Speech, "Some of My Best Friends. . .", January 19, 1970, 12.
11  Louis Melzack, interview, May 1998.
12  Cameron, 33.

13  IBID., 34.

14  JGM to W. G. Taylor, December 21, 1956. In 1935, M&S agreed to direct the Dent subsidiary in Canada. As part of this arrangement, M&S stayed out of the lucrative textbook market. When JGM cancelled the arrangement with Dent, he did so in part because he wanted to enter that forbidden area.

15  JGM told John Robert Colombo of the book's influence on him. Interview, May 1998.

16  JGM to John McClelland, June 15, [1947].

17  IBID.

18  Elizabeth McClelland to John and Ethel McClelland, July 4, 1947.

19  JGM to John McClelland, June 15, [1947].

20  "My Rose Garden," 36.

21  IBID., 36.

22  IBID., 37.

23  Gabrielle Roy, *The Fragile Lights of Earth: Articles and Memories 1942–1970*, trans. Alan Brown (Toronto: McClelland & Stewart, 1982), 153.

24  Myrna Delson-Karan, "The Last Interview: Gabrielle Roy," *Quebec Studies* 4 (1986): 196.

25  Earle Birney to JGM, April 28, 1950.

26  As cited by Elspeth Cameron, *Earle Birney: A Life* (Toronto: Penguin, 1984), 17.

27  Earle Birney to Gordon Aldridge, March 26, 1943. Earle Birney Papers, Thomas Fisher Rare Book Library, University of Toronto.

28  Earle Birney to JGM, July 1949.

29  JGM to Earle Birney, August 24, 1949.

30  JGM to Earle Birney, November 17, 1949.

31  IBID.

32  Earle Birney to JGM, November 23, 1949.

33  Timson, 54.

34  Confidential, April 29, 1951. 3.

35  IBID., 4.

36  IBID., 5, 7.

37  M. H. Lipton to George Stewart, October 11, 1951.

38  *Quill & Quire*, March 1953.

39  Speech to the University Women's Club, University of Toronto, October 20, [1958 or 1960].

## 3. JACK OF ALL TRADES

1  As cited in *Quill & Quire*, 60th Anniversary Special, April 1995, 13.
2  Pierre Berton, *My Times* (Toronto: Doubleday, 1995), 8.
3  Speech at Deer Park United Church, December 4, 1956.
4  JGM, "Report on Trip to Western Canada July 15–25, 1956," 5.
5  *The Winnipeg Tribune*, November 24, 1960, 17.
6  Notes for a TV interview, October 20, 1978.
7  JGM memo to Hugh Kane, May 18, 1954.
8  JGM memo to Hugh Kane, undated but 1957.
9  JGM to Angus Mowat, November 26, 1957.
10 JGM memo to Claire Pratt, March 3, 1958.
11 Martin Knelman, "Business by the Book," *The Financial Post Magazine*, October 1, 1983: 41.
12 JGM to Phyllis Webb, September 1, 1961.
13    Hugh Kane to JGM, JGM to Hugh Kane, 1959.
14 Hugh Kane to JGM, October 3, 1961.
15 As cited in *Quill & Quire*, April 1995.
16 John Gray, "Book Publishing," in *Writing in Canada. Proceedings of the Canadian Writers' Conference, Queen's University, July 28–31, 1955* (Toronto, 1956), 58.
17 As cited in *Quill & Quire*, April 1995.
18 Pierre Berton, *Starting Out* (Toronto: McClelland & Stewart, 1987), 11–12.
19 IBID., 26–7.
20 IBID., 18.
21 IBID., 274.
22 IBID., 313.
23 Berton, *My Times*, 105.
24 JGM to Hugh Kane, November 6, 1953.
25 Hugh Kane to JGM, February 24, 1956.
26 Farley Mowat, *Born Naked* (Toronto: Key Porter, 1993), 12.
27 IBID., 13.
28 Farley Mowat, *My Father's Son: Memories of War and Peace* (Toronto: Seal, 1992), 18.
29 Mowat, *My Father's Son*, 222.
30 M&S distributed *People of the Deer.*
31 "My Rose Garden," 46.
32 IBID.
33 JGM to Farley Mowat, April 13, 1955.
34 Farley Mowat to JGM, [April 1955].
35 JGM to Farley Mowat, January 28, 1958.
36 Farley Mowat to JGM, November 25, 1956.

37 JGM to Farley Mowat, May 27, 1958.

38 JGM to Farley Mowat, November 30, 1959.

39 Farley Mowat to JGM, May 8, [1959].

40 Earle Birney to JGM, August 6, 1957.

41 Sylvia Fraser to JGM, *c.* October 1979.

42 "The Business of Books . . . J. G. McClelland," *The Montrealer*, December 1960: 15.

43 IBID.

44 JGM to Ralph Gustafson, January 23, 1962.

45 JGM memo, February 25, 1962.

46 JGM to Alan D. Williams, March 6, 1962.

47 Alan D. Williams to JGM, March 9, 1962.

48 Memorandum from John Robert Colombo, March 7, 1965.

49 Ralph Gustafson to JGM, June 7, 1965.

50 JGM to Ned Bradford, November 29, 1960.

51 JGM to G. Wren Howard, December 21, 1960.

52 JGM to Anna Porter, November 3, 1976.

53 JGM to Earle Birney, November 14, 1950.

54 JGM to Earle Birney, June 30, 1953.

55 JGM to Earle Birney, June 16, 1955.

56 Earle Birney to JGM, May 6, 1956.

57 JGM to Earle Birney, October 18, 1956.

58 JGM to Earle Birney, October 24, 1958.

59 "The Reprinting of Canadian Books," *Ontario Library Review* (August 1957): 188–92.

60 JGM to Ethel McClelland, June 1954.

61 IBID.

62 Timson, 60.

63 JGM to Ernest Buckler, November 15, 1967.

64 Speech at Jarvis Collegiate, Toronto, October 12, 1960.

65 Speech, "Book Publishing in Canada," March 15, 1956.

## 4. THE BOY PUBLISHER

1 JGM to Lorna and Sean Kane, August 28, 1985. The Thomas Fisher Rare Book Room, The University of Toronto. This letter contains a detailed recounting of this transaction and subsequent events concerning the financial arrangement between JGM, Hugh Kane and Mark Savage.

2 Knelman, 44.

3 Bennett Cerf, *At Random* (New York: Random House, 1977), 103.

4 Knelman, 44.

5 IBID., 44.

6 Jack McClelland, *Imagining Canadian Literature: Selected Letters*, ed. Sam Solecki (Toronto: Key Porter, 1998), iii.

7 Cerf, 281.

8 Robert Fulford, *The Toronto Star*, September 25, 1982.

9 *First Statement*, 1 No. 16 (April 2, 1943), 6–7.

10 Irving Layton to George Edelstein, interview, April 11, 1962.

11 Radio Review on CBC's "Critically Speaking": July 15, 1951.

12 *Fornaltutx, Selected Poems, 1928–1990* (Montreal and Kingston: McGill–Queen's University Press, 1992), 118. This poem was first published in *Balls for a One-Armed Juggler*, 1963.

13 John Sutherland. Cited in Elspeth Cameron, *Irving Layton: A Portrait* (Toronto: Stoddart, 1985), 178.

14 Lorne Pierce to Irving Layton, December 15, 1956. MS: Concordia University.

15 JGM to Irving Layton, August 7, 1959.

16 JGM to Irving Layton, May 11, 1962.

17 JGM to Irving Layton, July 6, 1962.

18 Irving Layton to JGM, July 10, 1962.

19 Irving Layton to JGM, July 15, 1962.

20 Robert, 38.

21 JGM to Tony Emery, April 13, 1959.

22 Speech, "Some of My Best Friends . . .", January 19, 1970, 12–13.

23 Gordon Elliott to JGM, March 1, 1959.

24 JGM to Willis Wing, October 10, 1960.

25 JGM to Ian Mackenzie, November 28, 1960.

26 Margaret Laurence to Adele Wiseman, July 21, 1960. MS: York.

27 Margaret Laurence to Adele Wiseman, October 29, 1960. MS: York.

28 Margaret Laurence to Adele Wiseman, January 22, 1961. MS: York.

29 IBID.

30 Blondal also wrote M&S on 30 August 1959 to say she would be in Toronto and wanted to discuss her manuscript.

31 In fact, she had already submitted her manuscript to Simon & Schuster and Macmillan.

32 "My Rose Garden," 52–3.

33 Hugh Kane, Editorial Report, August 5, 1959.

34 Undated memorandum from JGM, 1959.

35 Hugh Kane, Editorial Report, August 5, 1959.

36 "My Rose Garden," 54.

37 Joyce Marshall to Jack McClelland, March 29, 1960.

38 Undated memorandum from JGM to Steve Rankin.

39 *Jack McClelland: The Publisher of Canadian Literature* (Guadalajara: University of Guadalajara, 1996), 54.

40  JGM to Elizabeth McClelland, July 28, 1960.

41  JGM to Farley Mowat, no date but 1961.

42  *The Boat Who Wouldn't Float* (Toronto: McClelland and Stewart, 1969), 40.

43  JGM to Lily Miller, January 21, 1980.

44  Cameron, 36.

45  Iris Nowell, *Hot Breakfast for Sparrows: My Life with Harold Town* (Toronto: Stoddart, 1992), 103.

46  Viola Whitney Pratt, *A Testament of Love*, ed. Mildred Claire Pratt (Toronto: Lugus, 1990), 49.

47  IBID., 52.

48  IBID., 55.

49  Malcolm Ross to JGM, December 9, 1952.

50  Malcolm Ross to JGM, December 30, 1952.

51  JGM and Malcolm Ross apparently discussed the NCL at the 1956 Kingston Conference, at which the status of Canadian literature was discussed; from that seminal meeting came a strong impetus to teach Canadian literature in high schools and universities. See Sandra Djwa, *The Politics of the Imagination: A Life of F. R. Scott* (Toronto: McClelland & Stewart, 1987), 284.

52  In "The New Canadian Library: A Classic Deal," (154-72) and "The Rhetoric of Back Cover Copy: Sinclair Ross's *As for Me and My House*" (173-87) in *Making It Real: The Canonization of Canadian Literature* (Toronto: Anansi, 1995), Robert Lecker examines the motives and strageies of JGM and Malcolm Ross in forming the NCL. In JGM's case, he demonstrates how business acumen and the active manipulation of market forces informed his involvement with this project, i.e., he sought to choose titles (such as *As for Me and My House*) available at low, and thus attractive prices. In so doing, Lecker argues, ease of availability rather than quality was the publisher's main consideration. To a limited extent, Lecker is correct, although he himself recognizes that a publisher is a businessman who should obtain titles at the most advantageous prices. Absent from Lecker's discussion is sufficient recognition of the altruistic aspects of JGM the businessman-planner.

53  *Canadian Business*, March 1958: 69.

54  *Quill & Quire*, January–February 1958: 44.

## 5. THE JUGGLER

1  JGM to Farley Mowat, February 19, 1962.

2  Notes for a TV interview: October 20, 1978.

3   JGM to Farley Mowat, December 27, 1961.
4   Farley Mowat to JGM, January 12, [1962].
5   JGM to Farley Mowat, August 8, 1962.
6   Berton, *My Times,* 175.
7   JGM to Pierre Berton, February 14, 1961.
8   JGM to Hugh Kane, April 11, 1961.
9   JGM to Gabrielle Roy, October 1962.
10  Gabrielle Roy to JGM, October 5, 1962.
11  JGM to Hugh Kane, February 23, 1961.
12  Irving Layton to Desmond Pacey, December 2, 1961.
13  JGM to Irving Layton, July 19, 1962. Apparently, the letter was not sent.
14  JGM to Aviva Layton, November 13, 1962.
15  Finance memorandum by JGM, 4 March 1962.
16  Administrative file labelled "Directors Meeting," undated but almost certainly 1962.
17  "Publishing Policy at M&S," undated but almost certainly 1962.
18  "Introduction to Policy Book," November 23, 1962.
19  A. M. Hunter, "The World of Books," *The Hamilton Spectator,* November 24, 1962, 36.
20  JGM to Hugh Kane, April 3, 1962.
21  JGM to Marika Robert, May 10, 1963.
22  JGM to Robert Weaver, Robert Fulford and William French, April 27, 1961.
23  Ira B. Nadel, *Various Positions: A Life of Leonard Cohen* (Toronto: Random House, 1996), 68.
24  IBID., 45.
25  IBID., 24.
26  Leonard Cohen to JGM, July 26, 1959.
27  "Directors Meeting—Tuesday Sept 3/63."

## 6. A SEAT-OF-THE-PANTS PROFESSION

1   Mel Hurtig, *At Twilight in the Country: Memoirs of a Canadian Nationalist* (Toronto: Stoddart, 1996), 31.
2   JGM to Dave McGill, November 29, 1966.
3   JGM to Marika Robert, May 10, 1963.
4   JGM to William Arthur Deacon, March 21, 1963.
5   Ruth Taylor, interview, June 1998.
6   Beverley Slopen, "25 Years of Minding McClelland's Business," *Quill & Quire,* April 1987, 12.

7   *CBC Times*, December 10–16, 1966: 13.
8   Tim Heald, "A Day in the Life: Jack McClelland," *Weekend Magazine*, April 8, 1978: 12.
9   Operations Manager, CJRN Radio Station to JGM, November 16, 1965.
10  "A Canadian Publisher Goes Canadian," *Monetary Times*, November 1965: 38.
11  JGM to Hugh Kane, November 3, 1964.
12  Memorandum from JGM, December 9, 1963.
13  "My Rose Garden," 31.
14  Robert Fulford, "The Nation's Biggest Bookmaker," *The Toronto Daily Star*, March 5, 1965, 23.
15  Memoranda, Hugh Kane to JGM, JGM to Hugh Kane, [1963].
16  JGM to Marika Robert, May 10, 1963.
17  JGM to Mordecai Richler, December 20, 1963.
18  *The Toronto Daily Star*, March 5, 1965, 24.
19  JGM to Austin Clarke, September 23, 1965.
20  JGM to John Gray, November 8, 1965.
21  Robert, 38.
22  Hugh Hood to JGM, July 24, 1961.
23  JGM to Hugh Hood, August 2, 1961.
24  Cameron, 38.
25  "The Publishing Scene."
26  IBID.
27  Cameron, 38.
28  IBID.
29  Robert, 38.
30  Susan Carson, "Jack McClelland: Valet, Wet Nurse and Publisher," *Globe Weekend Magazine*, March 10, 1973: 8–11.
31  "The Publishing Scene," 3.
32  JGM to Arthur Hailey, January 12, 1965.
33  "Report on Trip to England June 1954."
34  JGM to Mordecai Richler, March 28, 1962.
35  JGM memo to Hugh Kane, October 19, 1962.
36  JGM to Mordecai Richler, March 28, 1963.
37  JGM to Mordecai Richler, October 23, 1960.
38  "My Rose Garden," 56.
39  JGM to Mordecai Richler, January 18, 1972.
40  JGM to Mordecai Richler, December 18, 1968.
41  IBID.
42  JGM to Mordecai Richler, June 10, 1961.
43  Mordecai Richler to JGM, May 22, 1965.
44  JGM to Mordecai Richler, June 2, 1965.
45  JGM to Mordecai Richler, November 22, 1966.
46  Mordecai Richler to JGM, September 10, 1969.

47  JGM to Mordecai Richler, June 25, 1970.

48  Mordecai Richler to JGM, August 31, 1971.

49  JGM to Mordecai Richler, August 29, 1970.

50  Mordecai Richler to JGM, November 21, 1962.

51  Mordecai Richler to JGM, December 22, 1962.

52  JGM to Mordecai Richler, January 22, 1963.

53  Gabrielle Roy to JGM, February 5, 1976.

54  Memorandum of February 15, 1965.

55  Reader's Report, February 6, 1966.

56  John Robert Colombo thinks he saw the manuscript in the slush pile.

57  Margaret Atwood to James King, December 14, 1998.

58  JGM to Marge Hodgeman, July 5, 1967.

59  Memorandum, JGM to Geoff Fielding, August 14, 1967.

60  Margaret Atwood to James King, April 1998.

61  "The Perils of Canadian Publishing," *Time*, March 1, 1971: 8.

62  JGM to Peter Newman, June 19, 1962.

63  JGM to Peter Newman, August 26, 1963.

64  Peter Newman to JGM, January 6, 1964.

65  *Time*, March 1, 1971: 8.

66  Robert, 26.

67  Earlier, in the mid-fifties, JGM had severed M&S's distribution of the Dent imprint because he was forbidden by the terms of M&S's arrangement with that English firm to compete with them in the textbook market.

68  "The Publishing Scene," 4.

69  Robert, 33. However, Jack later acquired a copy, which he donated to McMaster.

70  Cameron, *Irving Layton*, 334.

71  Desmond Pacey to Irving Layton, June 25, 1962. The Desmond Pacey Papers.

72  Mordecai Richler to JGM, February 25, 1963.

73  In October 1970, Elizabeth McClelland was appointed to the board; the other members at that time were JGM, Newfeld, Feheley, Ritchie, Berton, Bob Martin, Elsa Franklin, Totton and R. P. Smith. Christina Newman had resigned by this time and Farley Mowat was appointed in her place.

74  "A Canadian Publisher Goes Canadian," *Monetary Times*, November 1965: 38.

75  JGM to Pierre Berton, March 11, 1964.

76  Berton, *My Times*, 283.

77  I have not been able to locate any document in the M&S archive that provides information on this subject; the copyright pages on 1962 books do not carry the designation whereas those published in 1963 do. However, M&S called itself "The Canadian Publishers" as early as 1952 in advertisements, then dropped the designation throughout the remainder of the fifties and early sixties. It was at Elsa Franklin's instigation that the designation was added to the colophon in 1963.

78  JGM to Pierre Berton, July 22, 1966.
79  JGM to Pierre Berton, October 21, 1966.
80  Berton, op. cit., 320.
81  Robert, 38.
82  JGM to Farley Mowat, October 6, 1964.
83  IBID.
84  Farley Mowat to JGM, October 30, 1964.
85  JGM to Margaret Laurence, March 29, 1965.
86  JGM to Margaret Laurence, July 5, 1963.
87  Margaret Laurence to JGM, July 8, 1963.
88  Margaret Laurence to Adele Wiseman, October 23, 1966. MS: York.
89  *The Toronto Daily Star*, March 5, 1965, 24.
90  JGM to Leonard Cohen, May 10, 1963.
91  JGM to Alfred Knopf, June 12, 1963. Two readers' reports are filed with
    the carbon of JGM's letter.
92  JGM to Leonard Cohen, May 31, 1963.
93  JGM to Leonard Cohen, August 20, 1964.
94  Leonard Cohen to JGM, September 2, 1964.
95  JGM to Leonard Cohen, September 11, 1964.
96  JGM to Leonard Cohen, June 15, 1965.
97  JGM to Claude Bissell and Northrop Frye, 29 December 1965. JGM also
    sought the advice of Kildare Dobbs and Robert Weaver.
98  Hurtig, op. cit., 32.
99  JGM to Leonard Cohen, May 9, 1966.
100 Irving Layton to JGM, May 27, 1967.
101 JGM to Jeann Beattie, September 28, 1965.
102 Cameron, 37.

## 7.  BETWEEN ROCKS AND HARD PLACES

1  JGM: Report of Management Meeting, January 15, 1968, 1.
2  Donald Cameron, "Jack McClelland and the Crisis in Canadian Publishing," *Saturday Night*, June 1971: 11.
3  Report of Management Meeting, January 25, 1968.
4  Donald Cameron, op. cit.
5  Peter Sypnowich, "New Hand at Macmillan's Helm," *The Toronto Daily
   Star*, August 8, 1969, 24.
6  Robert Fulford, "My Dogged Search for a Mystery Man," *The Toronto Daily
   Star*, March 14, 1967, 18.
7  Information supplied by Robert Fulford.

8  There is no evidence in the M&S archive that the list was discarded in this manner; this is probably another example of Jack's "poetic licence" when discussing difficulties in the running of his firm.

9  Robertson Davies to JGM, March 1970.

10  JGM to M. J. McCormick, December 21, 1965.

11  Copy of memorandum is in the McMaster archives.

12  Mordecai Richler to JGM, September 10, 1969.

13  *Time*, March 1, 1971: 8.

14  JGM to Royal Bank (Don Anderson), January 8, 1968.

15  JGM to Alfred Knopf, January 10, 1967.

16  JGM to Alfred Knopf, May 30, 1967.

17  *Time*, July 12, 1963.

18  JGM to Louis Melzack, October 4, 1963.

19  Memorandum, JGM to Hugh Kane, July 8, 1968.

20  Memorandum, JGM to Hugh Kane and Geoff Fielding, May 4, 1967.

21  Memorandum, JGM to Dave McGill, November 6, 1967.

22  Berton, *My Times*, 316.

23  JGM to Peter Newman, November 7, 1967.

24  Memorandum, JGM to Hugh Kane, May 27, 1968.

25  Berton, *My Times*, 318.

26  "Editorial Policy at M&S": undated but filed among 1968–69 documents.

27  Speech on Publishing, October 30, 1969.

28  IBID.

29  IBID.

30  JGM to Peter Newman, May 13, 1971.

31  JGM to Peter Davison, February 6, 1967.

32  JGM to Farley Mowat, February 24, 1967.

33  JGM memorandum to S. J. Totton, February 2, 1966.

34  JGM to Christina Newman, August 14, 1967.

35  Christina Newman to JGM, October 23, 1967.

36  JGM to Christina Newman, November 2, 1967.

37  JGM to Peter Newman, June 10, 1968.

38  JGM to Earle Birney, May 23, 1967.

39  JGM to Irving Layton, March 22, 1968.

40  JGM to Isabel LeBourdais, May 9, 1961.

41  Isabel LeBourdais to JGM, July 5, 1961.

42  JGM to Isabel LeBourdais, July 7, 1961.

43  Isabel LeBourdais to JGM, August 13, 1963.

44  Sheila Hodges, *Gollancz, The Story of a Publishing House, 1928–1978* (London: Victor Gollancz, 1978), 180–81.

45  Stanley Knowles to JGM, March 7, 1966.

46  Scott Symons to JGM, June 1, 1965.

47  Scott Symons to JGM, February 3, 1966.

48  JGM to Claude Hurtubise, February 25, 1966.

49  Charles Taylor, *Six Journeys: A Canadian Pattern* (Toronto: Anansi, 1977), 209.

50  JGM to Scott Symons, September 1, 1966.

51  Scott Symons to JGM, October 9, 1969.

52  This citation is from a twenty-three-page letter dated Oct. 13, 1967, Yorkville, Toronto; June 8, 1968, Oaxaca, Mexico; Jan. 19, 1969, Mackenzie, British Columbia.

53  Scott Symons to JGM, October 30, 1977.

54  JGM to Richard Goldfarb, February 12, 1968.

55  These figures do not always include reprints or reissues of books in paperback series such as the NCL. Such titles can *boost* the numbers significantly. My figures per annum are taken from the Spadoni–Donnelly bibliography, but owing to the inaccuracy of publication records, the actual figures may vary slightly.

## 8. BITING BULLETS

1   *Time*, March 1, 1971: 8a.

2   Agreement of November 1, 1971.

3   JGM to Farley Mowat, February 28, 1969.

4   Cameron, 42.

5   IBID.

6   Information from Peter Taylor.

7   JGM to Charles Fannin, May 7, 1969.

8   George Ramsay to JGM, June 23, 1969.

9   "Some of My Best Friends . . .", speech, January 19, 1970, 7–8.

10  *Time*, March 1, 1971.

11  Terence Robertson to JGM, February 28, 1968.

12  Unexecuted agreement between M&S and Cemp Investments, December 1967.

13  Terence Robertson to JGM, November 6, 1967.

14  "My Rose Garden," 56.

15  Judy LaMarsh, *A Bird in a Gilded Cage* (Toronto: McClelland & Stewart, 1969), 303.

16  JGM to Judy LaMarsh, January 4, 1968.

17  JGM to John Robert Colombo, September 8, 1968.

18  LaMarsh, 151–2.

19  Judy LaMarsh to Robert Martin, November 18, 1969.

20  JGM to M. R. Taylor, March 4, 1969.

21  "My Rose Garden," 55.

22  "Judy: Radio Man's Stories 'Destroyed My Friends,'" *The Ottawa Journal*, January 14, 1970, 8.

23  John Robert Colombo, interview, May 1998.

24  Notes for TV interview, October 20, 1978.

25  Terence Robertson to JGM, November 6, 1967.

26  Terence Robertson to JGM, April 9, 1968.

27  JGM to Terence Robertson, April 15, 1968.

28  JGM to Leo Kolber, May 24, 1968.

29  Terence Robertson to JGM, June 28, 1968.

30  JGM to Leo Kolber, September 12, 1968.

31  Terence Robertson to JGM, October 1, 1968.

32  JGM to Leo Kolber, October 9, 1968.

33  Terence Robertson to JGM, October 30, 1968.

34  Terence Robertson to JGM, December 30, 1968.

35  JGM memorandum to Bob Wilkinson, April 3, 1969.

36  Terence Robertson to JGM, April 30, 1969.

37  Peter Gzowski to JGM, May 19, 1969.

38  JGM to Leo Kolber, June 24, 1969.

39  JGM to Leo Kolber, September 9, 1969.

40  JGM to Leo Kolber, October 10, 1969.

41  Transcript of sworn evidence is in Jack McClelland's archive.

42  Peter C. Newman, *Bronfman Dynasty: The Rothschilds of the New World* (Toronto: Seal, 1979), xiii.

43  Newman, *Bronfman Dynasty*, xi.

44  Berton, *My Times*, 330–31.

45  JGM to Pierre Berton, February 11, 1970.

46  Information from Pierre Berton.

47  Pierre Berton to JGM, September 10, 1970.

48  JGM to Pierre Berton, September 10, 1970.

49  Jack did finally publish this book under the Seal imprint in 1985.

50  Earle Birney to JGM, January 13, 1969.

51  JGM to Earle Birney, January 30, 1969.

52  Sypnowich, *The Toronto Daily Star*, August 8, 1969, 24.

53  JGM to Hugh Kane, August 8, 1969.

54  JGM to Hugh Kane, August 21, 1969. On August 28, 1985, Jack told Lorna and Sean Kane: "When Hugh left we terminated our agreement re shares in M&S for two reasons. First, because of a conflict of interest in his new position. Second, because the company at that time was worth zilch."

55  Peter Taylor, interview, May 1998.

56  Timson, 60.

57  Donald Cameron, *Saturday Night*, June 1971: 14.

58  IBID.

59  These figures were compiled by Dennis Lee and are quoted in Donald Cameron, 15.

60  JGM to Norman Levine, July 29, 1969.

61  Doug Best to JGM, March 17, 1971.

62  As quoted by Donald Cameron, op. cit., June 1971, 12.

63  IBID.

64  JGM to Mordecai Richler, January 17, 1968.

65  Quoted by Peter Sypnowich, "Politician, Publisher Debate American Takeovers," *The Toronto Daily Star*, December 17, 1970, 40.

66  Manuscript, McMaster.

67  Peter Sypnowich, "Only McClelland's Wife Backs Sale of His Book Firm," *The Toronto Daily Star*, February 19, 1971, A22.

## 9. THE PERILS OF NATIONALISM

1   *Time*, March 1, 1971: 8b.

2   "McClelland Wants Out," *Quill & Quire*, February 26, 1971, 1.

3   *The London Free Press*, February 19, 1971.

4   Sypnowich, *The Toronto Daily Star*, February 19, 1971, 22.

5   Mordecai Richler to JGM, February 21, 1971.

6   Sypnowich, *The Toronto Daily Star*, February 19, 1971.

7   *The Edmonton Journal*, February 1971.

8   Berton, *My Times*, 344–5.

9   JGM to Max Saltzman, October 29, 1979.

10  "Pepin Would Consider Using Government Cash to Save Publishing Firm," *Toronto Daily Star*, February 19, 1971.

11  *The Vancouver Province*, March 4, 1971.

12  IBID.

13  Donald Cameron, *Saturday Night*, June 1971: 11.

14  Letter from M.P. Sinclair, Simon Fraser University, *Time*, March 29, 1971, 2.

15  William French, "Will Another Publisher Give Up or Rally Nationalists to Rescue?" *The Globe and Mail*, February 19, 1971, B3.

16  JGM to William Wilder, March 18, 1971.

17  Marsh Jeanneret, *God and Mammon: Universities as Publishers* (Toronto: Macmillan of Canada, 1989), 306–7.

18  Submission to the Royal Commission on Book Publishing, 35.

19  "Randall Accuses McClelland of Incompetence," *The Toronto Telegram*, April 7, 1971, 5.

20  Speech, "The Threat from Within," February 3, 1972.

21  JGM to Farley Mowat, April 5, 1971.

22  Memorandum to Larry Ritchie, June 7, 1971.

23  Cameron, 42.

24  IBID.

25  Memorandum, JGM to Anna Porter, March 1, 1974.

26  Memorandum, JGM to Anna Porter, March 4, 1974.
27  JGM to Earle Birney, May 6, 1969.
28  Earle Birney to John Newlove, December 31, 1970.
29  Earle Birney to Anna Szigethy, no date but early 1971.
30  JGM to Earle Birney, January 11, 1971.
31  Earle Birney to Jack McClelland, February 27, 1971.
32  Circular letter, June 30, 1971.
33  Cameron, 44.
34  JGM to William Koshland, August 13, 1972.
35  Cameron, 42.
36  Information from John Newlove.
37  Information from David Berry.
38  Information from Patrick Crean.
39  Irving Layton to JGM, July 17, 1971.
40  Irving Layton to JGM, March 16, 1972.
41  JGM to Irving Layton, March 24, 1972.
42  JGM to Irving Layton, May 9, 1972.
43  Irving Layton to JGM, July 21, 1972.
44  JGM to Irving Layton, August 9, 1972.
45  Al Purdy to JGM, November 14, 1970.
46  JGM to Al Purdy, November 19, 1970.
47  Al Purdy to JGM, March 27, 1971.
48  JGM to Al Purdy, April 1972.
49  Al Purdy to JGM, 1 May 1972.
50  Undated note in the Purdy–McClelland correspondence of 1971.
51  JGM to Al Purdy, June 16, 1972. Unsent.
52  JGM to Al Purdy, June 22, 1972.
53  Farley Mowat to JGM, February 24, 1972.
54  JGM to Farley Mowat, February 28, 1972.
55  Farley Mowat to JGM, March 1, 1972.
56  Pierre Berton to JGM, undated.
57  JGM to Pierre Berton, August 24, 1971.
58  Information from David Shaw.
59  JGM to Catherine Wilson, August 17, 1971.
60  Pierre Berton to Farley Mowat, October 10, 1972.
61  JGM to Pierre Berton, October 13, 1972.
62  Information from Catherine Wilson.
63  Farley Mowat to JGM, November 10, 1972.
64  Pierre Berton, Harbourfront tribute to JGM, October 1998.
65  JGM to Margaret Atwood, October 22, 1971.
66  Margaret Atwood to Anna Porter, October 16, 1972.
67  Margaret Atwood to JGM, October 25, 1971.
68  JGM to Margaret Atwood, October 26, 1972.
69  JGM to Margaret Atwood, November 12, 1974.

70 JGM to Mordecai Richler, January 18, 1972.
71 JGM to Farley Mowat, August 22, 1972.
72 Marge Hodgeman to Farley Mowat, August 26, 1972.
73 Donald Cameron, *Saturday Night*, June 1971: 15.
74 IBID., 13.
75 IBID.
76 Memorandum from JGM, December 18, 1972.

## 10. GEMSTONE

1 JGM to Roloff Beny, May 8, 1973.
2 Memorandum, June 11, 1973.
3 Cameron, 45.
4 IBID., 36.
5 Irving Layton to JGM, September 26, 1964.
6 Simma Holt to JGM, March 11, 1974.
7 JGM to Simma Holt, March 18, 1974.
8 JGM to Simma Holt, July 12, 1974.
9 Farley Mowat to JGM, December 20, [1973].
10 Pierre Berton to Farley Mowat, February 25, 1974. Copy in M&S archive, McMaster.
11 Peter Newman to JGM, October 25, 1973.
12 JGM to Peter Newman, October 29, 1973.
13 JGM to Larry Ritchie and Anna Porter, June 12, 1973.
14 JGM to Anna Porter, November 29, 1974.
15 Christina Newman to JGM, undated but December 1974.
16 JGM, undated notes.
17 Knowlton Nash to JGM, July 15, 1974.
18 Margaret Laurence to JGM, February 23, 1976.
19 JGM to Mordecai Richler, April 16, 1973.
20 GM to Thomas H. Raddall, May 31, 1973.
21 IBID.
22 Margaret Laurence to JGM, October 7, 1973.
23 JGM to Claire Mowat, November 18, 1974.
24 Roloff Beny, *Visual Journeys* (Vancouver: Douglas & McIntyre, 1994), 22.
25 IBID.
26 IBID., 26.
27 IBID., 35.
28 "My Rose Garden," 68.
29 JGM to Roloff Beny, January 9, 1968.

30  JGM as cited in *Visual Journeys*, 127.
31  JGM to Roloff Beny, April 24, 1969.
32  Roloff Beny to JGM, November 5, 1970.
33  Roloff Beny to JGM, May 19, 1970.
34  Roloff Beny to JGM, July 16, 1970.
35  Beny, *Visual Journeys*, 158.
36  IBID., 160.
37  "My Rose Garden," 69.
38  JGM to Roloff Beny, June 21, 1973.
39  NCL No. 109, ix.
40  JGM to Gabrielle Roy, August 8, 1974.
41  JGM to Gabrielle Roy, September 19, 1974.
42  JGM to Gabrielle Roy, December 24, 1974.
43  IBID.
44  William French, "Jack's Gamble," *The Globe and Mail*, February 12, 1974, 15.
45  Letter printed in the University of Toronto student newspaper, *The Varsity*, in response to Jack's speech of January 15, 1974.
46  JGM to *The Toronto Star*, March 27, 1973.


## II. A MODERN CANADIAN FOLK FIGURE


1  Robert Stewart, "Eye on Books," *Book-of-the-Month Club News*, September 1975.
2  Jack Cole, as quoted by Roy MacSkimming, "Authors Tempted to Get Arrested inside Bookstore," *The Toronto Star*, January 23, 1975, D11.
3  IBID.
4  "Publisher Offers Firm to Students," *The Toronto Star*, February 27, 1975, A18.
5  Memorandum, Anna Porter to JGM, December 1, 1975 and Anna Porter to Marian Engel, July 19, 1976.
6  JGM to Farley Mowat, March 12, 1975.
7  Adele Wiseman to JGM, November 15, 1975.
8  Marian Engel to JGM, November 15, [1975].
9  JGM to Anna Porter, November 18, 1975.
10  Robertson Davies to JGM, January 6, 1976.
11  JGM to Anna Porter, November 29, 1975.
12  Marian Engel to JGM, February 9, [1976].
13  Sandra Martin, "How did Marian's discreet novel get that brazen cover?" *Saturday Night*, November 1977: 29. In her article, Martin also points out that the reviewers' proof copies had drab grey covers.
14  IBID., 30.

15 Margaret Laurence to John Newlove, August 30, 1977. *A Very Large Soul: Selected Letters from Margaret Laurence to Canadian Writers* (Dunvegan: Cormorant Books, 1995), 137.
16 JGM to Al Purdy, July 7, 1975.
17 Larry Ritchie to JGM, February 21, 1975.
18 Information from Graeme Gibson.
19 Roy MacSkimming, "Salesman McClelland off to Saskatoon," *The Toronto Star*, February 10, 1976, E8.
20 JGM Memorandum, October 6, 1980.
21 Undated holograph, collection of Lorraine Monk.
22 Roy MacSkimming, "Publisher McClelland Won't Sell His Business," *The Toronto Star*, July 5, 1976, D10.
23 Much of this fable was reworked into Fraser's novel *A Casual Affair* (1978).
24 Sylvia Fraser to JGM, undated.
25 Pierre Berton to Larry Ritchie, June 12, 1975.
26 Memorandum, JGM to Pat Bowles, August 21, 1975.
27 Pierre Berton to JGM, August 26, 1976.
28 Christina Newman to JGM, June 6, 1975.
29 Peter Newman to JGM, June 9, 1975.
30 IBID.
31 Peter Newman to JGM, July 16, 1976.
32 JGM to Peter Newman, July 16, 1976.
33 Peter Newman to JGM, July 19, 1976.
34 JGM to Cass Canfield, January 23, 1976.
35 Louis Rasminsky to JGM, November 21, 1975.
36 JGM to Louis Rasminsky, November 25, 1975.
37 Peter Newman to JGM, March 2, 1976.
38 JGM to Peter Newman, March 14, 1976.
39 JGM to Anna Porter, August 19, 1975.
40 JGM to Margaret Laurence, April 6, 1978.
41 "Around the World in Twenty-Eight Days," June 22, 1976.
42 Hugh MacLennan to JGM, March 26, 1976.
43 Lily Miller, interview, April 1998.
44 JGM to Hugh MacLennan, March 26, 1976.
45 Gabrielle Roy to JGM, December 31, 1975.

## 12. SURVIVING COMMERCIALLY

1 JGM to Christina Newman, November 28, 1977.
2 JGM to Farley Mowat, February 10, 1977.

3  JGM to Farley Mowat, January 17, 1978.
4  JGM to Glenda Ray, May 2, 1978.
5  JGM to Pierre Berton, March 4, 1977.
6  JGM to Pierre Berton, May 2, 1977.
7  JGM to Bob Young, February 15, 1978.
8  JGM to Pierre Berton, March 29, 1978.
9  Ken Adachi, "Lévesque 'Traitor' to Canada Publisher McClelland Says," *Toronto Star*, March 2, 1977, B3.
10  JGM to Farley Mowat, September 9, 1977.
11  JGM to Peter Davison, December 7, 1977.
12  Farley Mowat to JGM, August 1, [1978].
13  JGM to Sylvia Fraser, July 26, 1977.
14  Sylvia Fraser to JGM, October 17, 1977.
15  JGM to Sylvia Fraser, November 17, 1977.
16  JGM to Douglas Creighton, March 3, 1978.
17  JGM to Al Purdy, April 1, 1977.
18  Al Purdy to JGM, October 4, 1978.
19  JGM to Al Purdy, October 16, 1978.
20  Sandra Martin, "Don't be impatient: Leonard Cohen will let you see his new poems eventually," *Saturday Night*, November 1977: 30, 35.
21  JGM to Anna Porter, April 7, 1977.
22  JGM to Earle Birney, April 26, 1977.
23  JGM to Jennifer Glossop, September 18, 1978.
24  JGM to Linda McKnight, August 10, 1977.
25  JGM to Adele Wiseman, October 11, 1977.
26  Adele Wiseman to JGM, May 17, 1978.
27  JGM to Adele Wiseman, May 29, 1978.
28  Adele Wiseman to JGM, May 31, 1978.
29  JGM to Anna Porter and Jennifer Glossop, October 14, 1976.
30  JGM to Anna Porter, June 15, 1978.
31  Margaret Atwood to Anna Porter, June 14, 1978.
32  Undated memorandum, Anna Porter to JGM.
33  JGM to Margaret Trudeau, December 7, 1976.
34  JGM to Anna Porter, October 16, 1978.
35  William French, "A marriage of paperback convenience," *The Globe and Mail*, January 20, 1977, 13.
36  Ten years earlier, Jack had taken some real steps to enter the mass-market paperback area—referring to the Canadian Best-Seller Library Series—and had been "badly burned"—he said he lost about $250,000. In April 1977, in a parallel movement to the establishment of Seal, Jack briefly considered closing off additions to the NCL and releasing titles originally destined for that series in a new line of quality paperbacks in a larger format.
37  "Seal Books Makes Splash," *Publishers Weekly*, January 31, 1977: 28.
38  Martin Dewey, "It is no mystery that it pays to be serious about more commercial fiction," *The Globe and Mail*, April 16, 1979, B12.

39 There are a wide assortment of documents labelled "Project Tartan" in the M&S archive; although most are undated, they are from 1977 and 1978 and concern M&S's financial future.

40 Peter Newman to Leo Kolber, May 12, 1978. Carbon copy.

41 Peter Newman to JGM, April 25, 1978.

42 Memorandum, JGM to Peter Newman, March 6, 1978.

43 IBID.

44 Peter Newman to JGM, March 23, 1978.

45 Peter Newman to JGM, May 25, 1978.

46 Jack's handwritten account of his meeting with Leo Kolber.

47 Peter Newman, Harbourfront tribute to JGM, October 1998.

48 Peter Newman to JGM, August 30, 1978.

49 Memorandum, JGM to Peter Taylor, September 8, 1978.

50 Michael McCormick to Peter Newman, August 10, 1976.

51 Michael McCormick to Peter Newman, September 15, 1978.

52 JGM to Dear Bookseller, no date but late October 1978.

53 JGM to Peter Newman, July 6, 1978.

54 Peter Newman to JGM, September 5, 1978.

55 Peter Newman to JGM, October 6, 1978.

56 Peter Newman to JGM, November 27, 1978.

57 Handwritten notes, January 28, 1977.

58 Memorandum, JGM to Peter Scaggs and Lily Miller, September 22, 1977.

59 Beny, *Visual Journeys*, 190.

60 JGM to Peter Scaggs, October 31, 1987.

61 Information from Lorraine Monk.

62 *The Toronto Sun*, March 21, 1978, 6.

63 JGM to Peter Worthington, March 28, 1978.

64 Margaret Laurence to Al Purdy, September 28, 1977. Queen's University.

65 JGM to Margaret Laurence, April 6, 1978.

66 JGM to Gabrielle Roy, February 27, 1978.

67 JGM to Maurits Naessens, Mercatorfonds, December 2, 1977.

68 Memorandum, JGM to Anna Porter and Diane Mew, January 11, 1978.

69 JGM to William Kilbourn, January 23, 1978.

70 Rudy Wiebe to JGM, February 3, 1978.

71 JGM to Rudy Wiebe, February 7, 1978.

72 JGM to Gabrielle Roy, October 11, 1977.


13. TREMORS


1 Clyde Gilmour, "The tough-talking godfather of Canadian letters," *The Toronto Star*, September 18, 1982.

2  Ken Adachi, "A house that Jack built cuts back…with a tremor," *The Toronto Star*, December 2, 1979, B6.

3  *The Globe and Mail*, January 22, 1980, A15; JGM to *The Globe and Mail*, January 23, 1980.

4  William French, interview, May 1998.

5  Adachi, *The Toronto Star*, December 2, 1979, B6.

6  IBID.

7  I am grateful to Matt Cohen for providing me with information on his book's advance and sales in hardback.

8  JGM to Matt Cohen, June 13, 1977.

9  Matt Cohen, *Jack McClelland*, 51.

10 IBID.

11 Timothy Findley to JGM, November 23, 1979.

12 JGM to Timothy Findley, November 29, 1979.

13 William French, "Committed McClelland is a sign of good times," *The Globe and Mail*, October 27, 1981.

14 JGM to Dennis Lee, August 25, 1981.

15 JGM to Irving Layton, October 6, 1981.

16 Cameron, 38.

17 JGM to Aritha van Herk, May 20, 1980.

18 Martin Knelman, "Business By the Book," *Financial Post Magazine*, October 1, 1983: 48.

19 Peter Newman to JGM, November 24, 1981.

20 JGM to Peter Newman, November 30, 1981.

21 JGM to Farley Mowat, July 22, 1980.

22 JGM to Farley Mowat, December 9, 1980.

23 JGM to Pierre Berton, August 17, 1979.

24 JGM to Valerie Thompson, September 11, 1979.

25 Elsa Franklin to JGM, [June 1980].

26 JGM to Elsa Franklin, June 4, 1980.

27 JGM to Elsa Franklin, March 17, 1981.

28 JGM to *Books in Canada*, September 3, 1980.

29 Pierre Berton to JGM, October 14, 1981.

30 Pierre Berton to JGM, November 20, 1981.

31 JGM to Pierre Berton, February 4, 1981.

32 Berton, *My Times*, 386–7.

33 JGM to Linda McKnight, January 15, 1979.

34 JGM to Linda McKnight, January 9, 1979.

35 Information from David Shaw.

36 Peter Newman to JGM, February 8, 1980.

37 JGM to Peter Newman, February 15, 1980.

38 JGM to Len Cummings, October 20, 1980.

39 JGM to Linda McKnight, May 25, 1981.

40 JGM to Margaret Atwood, March 16, 1979.

41  Al Purdy to JGM, May 15, 1981.
42  Irving Layton to JGM, November 25, 1981.
43  Timson, 60.
44  Sylvia Fraser, "Beware recurrent Ides of March," *The Toronto Star*, September 21, 1996, G13.
45  JGM to Sylvia Fraser, January 4, 1979.
46  JGM to Peter Pocklington, February 10, 1981.
47  Draft Report, "McClelland and Stewart—A Summary, January 27th 1981."
48  JGM to Michaela Krissman, August 20, 1981.
49  JGM to Michaela Krissman, September 23, 1981.
50  JGM to James Clavell, August 20, 1981.
51  Cameron, 44.
52  Draft Report, op. cit.
53  Hugh Kane to JGM, August 24, 19[80].
54  Hugh Kane to JGM, September 30, 1980.
55  JGM to Hugh Kane, October 2, 1980.
56  JGM to Hugh Kane, October 7, 1980.
57  Timson, 23.
58  Timson, 50.
59  IBID.
60  The comparison is Farley Mowat's.
61  JGM to Farley Mowat, November 18, 1981.
62  JGM to Leo Heaps, April 12, 1982.
63  Mordecai Richler to JGM, November 23, 1979.

## 14. EMERITUS

1   Information from Linda McKnight.
2   JGM to Linda McKnight, January 26, 1982.
3   Cameron, 45.
4   Information from Jan Walter.
5   Memorandum, JGM to Len Cummings, July 3, 1981.
6   IBID.
7   Timson, 60.
8   Margaret Laurence to JGM, March 16, 1982.
9   Michael Ondaatje to JGM, April 6, 1982.
10  Mordecai Richler to JGM, December 22, 1982.
11  JGM to Mordecai Richler, January 4, 1983.
12  JGM to Conrad Black, August 19, 1982.
13  JGM to Peter Newman, January 28, 1982.

14  JGM to Peter Newman, September 9, 1982.

15  JGM to Michael Levine, November 30, 1982.

16  JGM to Linda McKnight, April 3, 1983.

17  Memorandum, JGM to Linda McKnight, March 20, 1984.

18  Memorandum, JGM to senior staff, December 10, 1984.

19  Michael Hanlon, "Weekend book sale…", *The Toronto Star*, April 19, 1983, F5.

20  Alvin Potter to James King, June 19, 1998.

21  Memorandum, JGM to Linda McKnight, [1984].

22  Memorandum, JGM to Linda McKnight and Norm Gervais, December 13, 1984.

23  Memorandum to Len Cummings, undated.

24  Memorandum, JGM to Lily Miller, May 13, 1983.

25  JGM to Peter Gzowski, January 6, 1984.

26  JGM to Margaret Laurence, June 17, 1982.

27  Margaret Laurence to John Cushman, October 2, 1982. MS: McMaster.

28  Mordecai Richler to JGM, August 8, 1982.

29  JGM to Mordecai Richler, September 2, 1982.

30  Memorandum, JGM to Linda McKnight, June 13, 1984.

31  Memorandum, JGM to Board of Directors, February 20, 1985.

32  Memorandum, Valerie Thompson to Ian Ardill, April 1, 1985.

33  Linda McKnight to JGM, April 14, 1985.

34  JGM's note is inscribed on a memorandum to him from Linda McKnight of April 24, 1985.

35  Linda McKnight to JGM, May 8, 1985.

36  Statement issued by JGM at a press conference held on May 16, 1985.

37  Ken Adachi, "McClelland brouhaha stranger than fiction," *The Toronto Star*, May 20, 1985, D23.

38  JGM to Janet and John Foster, October 25, 1985.

39  Ken Adachi, "Publishing firm's sale a good thing for our literature," *The Toronto Star*, December 31, 1985, B1.

40  Ken Adachi, "McClelland quits publishing with characteristic class," *The Toronto Star*, February 21, 1987.

41  JGM to Brian H. L. Mockler, July 5, 1993.

42  Information from Trent Frayne.

43  JGM to Nora Keeling, September 1, 1992. There are at least ten surviving attempts—varying in length from a few pages to eighty-one pages—to write a memoir. I provide citations from three of these manuscripts in this book.

44  Written in honour of JGM on the occasion of the "Jack Award," July 13, 1993. MS: Farley Mowat Papers, McMaster.

# INDEX